Modern Greece

Modern Greece

A Cultural Poetics

Vangelis Calotychos

BERG

Oxford • New York

First published in 2003 by
Berg
Editorial offices:
1st Floor, Angel Court, 81 St Clements Street, Oxford, OX4 1AW, UK
838 Broadway, Third Floor, New York, NY 10003-4812, USA

© Vangelis Calotychos 2003

Berg is an imprint of Oxford International Publishers Ltd.

Library of Congress Cataloging-in-Publication Data
A catalogue record for this book is available from the Library of Congress.

British Library Cataloguing-in-Publication Data
A catalogue record for this book is available from the British Library.

ISBN 1 85973 711 0 (Cloth)
         1 85973 716 1 (Paper)

Typeset by JS Typesetting Ltd, Wellingborough, Northants.
Printed in the United Kingdom by Biddles Ltd, Guildford and King's Lynn.

www.bergpublishers.com

Contents

Contents

Illustrations

Acknowledgments

'All those who love eat dirty bread,' sings Dionyssis Savvopoulos. This book is dedicated to the memory of my parents, Christos and Panayiota (Lola) Calotychos. They set out from Eftagonia, Limassol and Piraeus respectively, met up, and together ate their share of dirty bread (and drank some nectar) as youngsters in cosmopolitan Alexandria, penniless refugees in Australia, and hard-working immigrants in London. Statues never pursued them – these were in the museum. *Their* brand of love found a stylistic inflection in the passionate neohellenism that informs this book. And while this experience may have deserved a more affective medium, a song with lyrics worthy of Savvopoulos or a tumultuous novel like Taktsis's *Third WeddingWreath*, it has taken the form of an academic monograph.

This book was made largely possible by an interview I had with Margaret B. Alexiou over twenty years ago now. Meg showed understanding at a turbulent time in my life and encouraged me to go to university. Once there, at Birmingham, she was the perfect mentor. There, too, in my senior year, a seminar in modern Greek poetry with Dimitris Dimiroulis and a second, on the novel, with Dimitris Tziovas acquainted me with literature that has kept me company ever since. In 1982, a guest lecture by Vassilis Lambropoulos on Solomos's aesthetics drew critical theory and Greek culture together in provocative ways for me. Its potential would later prompt me to come to America and study in Ohio, in 1985, where I shared my curiosity with Vassili and colleagues whose own work has since benefited the field of Hellenic Studies: Panos Bosnakis, Kostas Demelis, Stathis Gourgouris, Martha Klironomos, and Artemis Leontis.

This project began as a dissertation in the Department of Comparative Literature, at Harvard University. It ended its first life as a dissertation while I was a lecturer in the Department of The Classics at Harvard. Meg Alexiou, then George Seferis Professor of Modern Greek at Harvard University, supervised the work. Like many before me, I benefited from her intellectual range and versatility as well as her unparalleled knowledge of the Greek tradition. I drew also from her humanity. And while, true to our first meeting in 1980, our perspectives on texts and contexts remained different, I like to think that we share some fundamental intuitions. Judith Ryan and Jan Ziolkowski offered administrative support and advice at various times during those years. I am grateful to James Engell for leading me into the eighteenth-century during my first term at Harvard, and for his friendship since; and to Gregory Nagy for guidance on issues of orality and performance in Chapter 2.

Acknowledgments

Barbara Johnson, Seamus Heaney, and Jess Banks (in Birmingham) provided inspiration. Charles Stewart was a trusted friend with constructive advice and ideas, conveyed always in comforting tones. I express my gratitude to fellow teaching assistants and co-students (in order of appearance): Anna Stavrakopoulou, Louisa Veletza, Spyros Maragos, George Syrimis, Panagiotis Roilos, Haris Stavrides, Panayiota Batsaki, Alexandra Halkias. Over coffee, I learnt from all of them. Thanks also to my research assistant Marios Veletzas Broustas. I found a kindred spirit in Matthew Gumpert, whose insight and wit were truly rejuvenating; as was Eva Konstantellou's profound generosity of spirit. I thank Sarah Gore, Karl-Heinz Finken, Nikiphoros Papadakis for years of co-habitation; as I do Paul Simmons for his wisdom, found beyond the academy though always, happily, just around the corner.

From 1996 to the present, I have been fortunate to work in the Department of Comparative Literature and the A.S. Onassis Program in Hellenic Studies at New York University. At NYU, I was fortunate to have the resilient friendship, the animated discussions, and more importantly, the irreverent humor of Phillip Mitsis, John Chioles and Liana Theodoratou (often amidst more turbulence). I thank every last one of my colleagues in the Department of Comparative Literature at NYU. I inflicted this book's good and bad ideas on a talented group of graduate students: Susan Matthias, Artemis Loi, Zamira Skalkottas, Klara O'Neill, Mona Zissimopoulos, and Jessie Labov. Of course, my ongoing engagement with things Greek would not have been possible – contrary to some of this book's musings – without my frequent trips to Greece and Cyprus. Close friends have offered me their hearts, their minds, and their home (their couch, their floor, their bed): Arsinoi Lainiotis and Stavros Stavridis, Yiannis Marinakis, the whole Karayiannis clan (especially the dearly departed Manolis), Nik Pournaras, and Voula Barbeito. In Cyprus, my exchanges with Yiannis Papadakis, Caesar Mavratsas, Mehmet Yashin, and Marios Constantinou have been profoundly stimulating. In London, Evagoras (with a K) Calotychos and the Comdromous provide warm familiarity in a city I feel much for still, despite – I fear – having no feel for it any more.

I am indebted to Effie Flessas and Flora Kondylis, the staff at the Modern Greek Section at Widener Library, at Harvard University. Further material was gleaned from the King's College Library, London; the Gennadeion Library and National Library, in Athens; and the Municipal Library in Zakynthos. Kathryn Earle at Berg embraced the project and was open to all my requests. Thanks, too, to the ever resourceful and patient Ian Critchley, my production editor at Berg. Richard Sieburth, Nancy Ruttenburg, Yiorgos Kalogeras read the book with care as did Timothy J. Reiss, who supported it with true generosity in its latter stages. I am thankful for the support of Michael Herzfeld: his indefatigable scholarly curiosity and intelligence are matched only by his inclination to go out of his way to stand by a good cause. Karen van Dyck remained a good friend and colleague to the bitter end. While Jaime Armin Mejía remains the most faithful friend and inter-locutor, blessed with a unique perspective on life and letters.

Lastly, like everything else, this book, or its passing, is a loving gift to Patricia Felisa Barbeito. Everything in it, in one way or another, has been part of our everyday life together ever since we met. Indeed, parts of Chapter 3 were written as much by her as by me. More recently, this book's pains of conception were eclipsed by the fruits of our common endeavor, the birth of Manolis Christos and Lola Katerina, whose cultural poetics has only just begun and for whom this book has not yet been written.

Acknowledgments

The book's publication was supported in part by a grant from the New York University Research Challenge Fund Emergency Support Program.

The original cover photograph was supplied along with kind permission of the photographer, Demetris Sofikitis, and the director, Theo Angelopoulos. I express my gratitude to Athena Athanasiou for liaising with them in Athens.

I am grateful to the following individuals for permission to reproduce copyrighted material: Manolis Anagnostakis, Cathérine Drossou, Ioulita Iliopoulou.

Reproduction of a facsimile from Dionysios Solomos's manuscript (p.79) is made with the kind permission of the Cultural Foundation of the Bank of Greece. Thanks, too, to Mary Politis and Dionyssis Kapsalis.

Kimon Friar's translations of Manolis Anagnostakis's poetry are reprinted with kind permission from Pella Publishing Co., New York, NY.

Elytis, Odysseus. *The Collected Poems of Odysseus Elytis*, pp. 5–6. © 1997 [The Johns Hopkins University Press]. Reprinted with permission of The Johns Hopkins University Press.

Seferis, George. *Collected Poems.* © 1995 [Princeton University Press], pp. 175–6. Reprinted with permission of Princeton University Press.

Sections of Chapter 3 have been published previously: with Patricia Felisa Barbeito as 'deMan, The Woman, and Her Story: Transference and/or Defacement in Elisavet Moutzan-Martinengou's *Autobiography*,' in G. Nagy and A. Stavrakopoulou (eds.), *Modern Greek Literature: Critical Essays*. New York: Routledge, 2003, 42–61.

Sections of Chapter 8 have been previously published as "Thorns in the Side of Venice? Galanaki's *Pasha* and Pamuk's *White Castle* in the Global Market," in D. Tziovas (ed.), *Greek Modernism and Beyond*. Lanham, MD: Rowman & Littlefield, 1997, 243–260.

Introduction

No Time like the Present

We are so unwise that we wander about in times that do not belong to us, and do not think of the only one that does; so vain that we dream of times that are not and blindly flee the only one that is. The fact is that the present usually hurts. We thrust it out of sight because it distresses us, and if we find it enjoyable, we are sorry to see it slip away. We try to give it the support of the future, and think how we are going to arrange things over which we have no control for a time we can never be sure of reaching.

Let each of us examine his thoughts; he will find them wholly concerned with the past or the future. We almost never think of the present, and if we do think of it, it is only to see what light it throws on our plans for the future. The present is never our end. The past and the present are our means, the future alone our end. Thus we never actually live, but hope to live, and since we are always planning how to be happy, it is inevitable that we should never be so.

Blaise Pascal, Pensées

Modern Greece was built on the ruins of its modernity. A lead article in the culture section of the Athenian center-right newspaper *Kathimerini* previewing the Greek government's proposed expenditures for culture from the European Union's much-awaited, and much-coveted, Third Community Support Framework underscores the continuing validity of this assertion.[1] For while the plan, which covers the period 2000–6 and earmarks the impressive sum of 210 billion drachma ($617 million) for the support of cultural initiatives, allots two-thirds of this amount, or 135 billion drachma ($397 million) to the 'Conservation and Promotion of Cultural Heritage' – to 'antiquities,' the article elaborates – modern culture is assigned less than a third, or 69 billion drachma ($202 million), of these initiative funds. Of these 69 billion drachma allotted to modern culture, 30 billion go to only two projects – the expansion of the Athens Megaron Music Hall and the creation of a sister institution in Thessaloniki, both works administered by the Lambrakis Cultural Foundation. The patronage of these projects is by no means immaterial for explaining the critical tone of the article, for the corporate interests behind *Kathimerini* are in competition with those of the Lambrakis Foundation, which owns and runs – among many other enterprises – Greece's other paper of record, the center-left *To Vima*. These competing interests may reveal a subtext for the article; however, this does not fully explain the perspective of the piece in this very reputable, generally conservative, newspaper. For the strident criticism of the Greek government's negligence over the development of contemporary culture remains; and it is predicated on the alleged inability to think in other than conventional terms: 'Retrogressive structures and outdated perceptions only occasionally allow for the creation of cultural and artistic products worthy of our times, our heritage and our place in the family of European nations.'

Such stiff words can not be brushed aside by pointing to the paper's political allegiances to the parliamentary opposition or to its own aggrieved corporate interests. The admission that a mechanistic acceptance of a classical agenda for culture is utterly deficient in promoting the nation's cultural politics, from a conservative newspaper, is not without significance. Nor, indeed, is the implication that this antiquities-heavy plan comes up short in legitimizing 'our place in the family of European nations.' Maybe it is indicative of the effects of a decade, the 1990s, when two high-profile political issues in Greece marked a watershed for the currency of classicizing tropes and discourses, at a time when Greece was forced to confront its own processes of European integration and modernization. I refer to Greece's failed attempt to win for itself the centennial Olympics, beaten out in the final round of voting by Atlanta, as well as its entanglement in the naming and recognition of the southernmost republic of the disintegrating former Yugoslavia.

The decision of the International Olympic Committee to award the centennial 1996 summer Olympiad of modern times to Atlanta over Athens was met with the silent consternation of the Greek people. A *New York Times* photograph on 'the morning after the night before' depicting a young Greek man, his head in his hands, slumped over his knees with a Greek flag draped over his hunched shoulders seemed appropriate. Greeks pointed an accusatory finger, often vehemently, at a number of culprits: the assurance of huge American television ratings for a US-based Olympiad; last-minute lobbying by black American civil rights figures for the vote of African countries; and the financial inducements of the large soft-drinks corporation Coca-Cola and CNN, both residents of Atlanta. Big money, capitalism, and 'the American way' had beaten out the rightful candidate and betrayed the Olympic Idea. Foreign journalists, most of them sympathetic to the Greek cause, retrospectively criticized the Greeks for overplaying their historical right to the Games and believing too naively that well-worn symbols would win the day – a more pragmatic campaign, they argued, would have fared better.

Whatever the merits of such advice in the face of such powerful corporate interests, a critique along similar lines was leveled against the Greeks for a second time, at about the same time. It came in the form of Western criticism, if not derision and disbelief, for the Greek government's obstruction of formal recognition for the southernmost Yugoslav republic, the former Yugoslav republic of Macedonia. With the break-up of the former Yugoslavia sanctioned by Western powers, Greece's conservative government toed the line by agreeing to recognize Slovenia and Croatia, but then denied and obstructed recognition to 'Macedonia,' as its people called it, on the grounds that the republic had usurped a historically Greek name, and by extension Greek heritage, and had taken for its flag's symbol the Star of Vergina, a sixteen-pronged star excavated from the tomb of Philip II in the Greek province of Macedonia. As the situation in Yugoslavia worsened, and fears grew that the fighting would spread to this republic too, Western powers grew irritable at Greece's unwillingness to lift its objections to the recognition of the 'statelet.' Eventually, it was recognized as The Former Yugoslav Republic of Macedonia (or FYROM). This is the name by which this republic was eventually admitted into the United Nations in a compromise arrangement with the Greek government of the day. (Since states in the Assembly sit in alphabetical order, the state was asked to assume its seat under 'T', i.e. 'The . . .', between Thailand and Tibet; and it was not allowed to fly its flag at UN headquarters.)[2]

The tussle over symbolism in the early days of the crisis, during late 1991 to mid-1992, many observers now contend worked against Greece's overall wish to play a leading role in the emerging, post-1989 Balkans. Western and Greek analysts felt that these disputes overshadowed other more 'substantive' issues and negotiating cards that should have been prioritized in Greek protestations to the Western Allies: FYROM's territorial claims on Greek territory as expressed in Article 49 of its Constitution and its proclaimed guardianship of a 'Macedonian' minority in northern Greece (that Greek officials insisted did not exist). By 1993, the Greek government, seeing that its priorities were neither meeting the approval of their European partners nor convincing them, began to reorient its policy by couching the issue of the new republic's name and symbols in the broader context of geopolitical developments and more substantive issues of stability in the southern Balkans.

Both these recent landmark issues of the 1990s foreground a Greek propensity for wielding a symbolic narrative over more pragmatic strategies. In the case of the Olympics, the Greeks' penchant for favoring an emotional argument is almost excusable, however foreign such sentiment may be to the prevailing corporate principles of the modern Olympic movement. With Macedonia, too, the deployment of 'classical' paternity by Greeks is not so out of place, if one accepts the logic of national essentialism. By this logic, Greece is as entitled as anyone else – perhaps even more so – to claim the symbols in question. And, clearly, politicians in power at the time deployed a strategic essentialism to whip up support on a unifying 'national issue,' and, in the given instance, turn public opinion away from more weighty domestic troubles. At the time of the Macedonian issue, the government-of-the-day 'enjoyed' a tenuous parliamentary majority of one seat and its foreign policy was guided by an ambitious foreign minister who sought to use the issue to create what, in retrospect, turned out to be a pitiful political party.

Today, we can say that these reactions were the effect of a defensive posture. Devoid of ready answers in a post-Cold War world, with Balkan refugees streaming over borders in search of a better life and with a war raging just over the border raising the spectre of past Balkan conflagrations, the appeal to symbolism was meant to be a safe recourse, a holding wall, in the absence of a more developed strategy. This tendency to prioritize abstract narratives, of which the classicizing variety is a privileged mainstay, over more immanent ones constitutes part of what Greek social scientist Nicos Mouzelis has termed the 'formalism' of Greek society.[3] The minutiae of social discourse are forever deflected to lofty debates on abstractions that hide personal ambitions and interests while the status quo is maintained by the expulsion of class issues or problems of basic reform (Tsoucalas 1991: 1–22). And though such recourse to form and formality over substance may not be exclusive to Greece, the tactic was clearly at work in the early 1990s.

However, the outcome of these two incidents, as it was perceived in the early 1990s, suggested to many Greeks that the old philhellene discourse that contributed to the Greeks winning their independence back in the 1820s was now less well received in European and American centers of power than two hundred years ago. An editorial in the *New York Times* on 5 April 1992 seemed to rub this in mercilessly: 'Early in the last century, friends of freedom everywhere supported Greece's heroic struggle to liberate itself from the Ottoman Turks. Today, Greece thwarts the dreams of another Balkan people seeking freedom and peace.'[4] Perhaps the audience for such arguments, the technocrats now in charge of foreign policy in the United States or Britain, are no longer the aristocratic, classically trained gentlemen of bygone decades and their pedigree less well disposed to such sentiment. But even in this, the Greek response assumed, as most do, that admiration of the classical Greeks was the primary motive of Western powers' support back in the early nineteenth century; a factor to be sure, but by no means certain to be the primary one. The notorious Jakob von Fallmerayer's pronouncements on the *racial* impurity of the modern Greeks were, after all, guided primarily by his anti-Russian and pro-Ottoman *political* choices.[5] It might be more precise to say that the discourse, internalized in Greek and European imaginations, now carries weight in certain spheres, but not others. The philhellenic/cultural advantage that Greeks enjoy may still count in world museums; in academe; in tourism; in the metaphors of tabloid journalism that always signpost any Greek news item with talk of 'burdens', 'tragedies', 'glorious legacies', and 'ancestral voices'; or in the logos of styrofoam cups found at diaspora fast-food emporia.[6] After all, the irony is that the average American in the street would not dispute either the Greekness of Macedonia or of classical sites in much of the Balkans. The waning currency of the discourse caught Greeks by surprise in this period and they were leaden-footed in their initial search to examine alternative narratives.[7] Indicatively, when the initial shock over the failed Olympic bid subsided, the only Greek protest entailed the disavowal of quite another set of old symbols for a new set – a vigorous ad campaign, sponsored by Coca-Cola's competitors Pepsi, persuaded Greeks to boycott Coke and drink only Pepsi.

But this was only a preliminary response and both issues, over the course of the decade, have been advanced, if not quite settled, in more enterprising ways. Greece bid for the Olympics a second time and underplayed its classical card in favor of a 'can-do' package of modernization, savvy public relations, and computer-modeled construction projects. As a result, it will be hosting the Olympic Games of 2004. In the matter of the Macedonian issue, too, an interim agreement signed between Greece and FYROM on 12 September 1995, put off agreement over the thorny name issue and instead addressed the very geopolitical and economic factors which had not, to that point, been ably presented to the diplomatic corps of Western European countries and to public opinion. In exchange for symbolic retractions by the 'Party of the Second Part' to the agreement,[8] the 'Party of the First Part,' the Greeks that is, moved ahead with economic investment in the neighboring state as well as in the Balkans as a whole. In addition, Greece promised support for FYROM's stability and future integration into NATO and the European Union. These incentives since 1995 have led to a decidedly more cooperative climate, the promise of compromise on the name issue, and a more dynamic leadership role for Greece in the region.

Neohellenism and Metrohellenism

In no other country, the anthropologist James D. Faubion (1993: 12) observes, has 'history past and present been so dominant an ethical concern.' The experience of the 1990s began with a politics of crisis of the kind that Faubion, in his study of Greek modernities entitled *Modern Greek Lessons: A Primer in Historical Constructivism* (1993), sees as the effect of the 'significative primacy of the past' and 'the fragmented diversity of the past and present' (1993: xxi). This interplay of cultural classicism and historical constructivism, on which the Greek threshold of modernity derives, unfolds in a game of restoration and reformation of identity and its legitimacy. The terms, at once political and cultural, of the Greek impulse or reflex of the early 1990s bespeaks the discursive force and institutional entrenchment of a model of personal and collective self-constitution built on these very tensions. After all, many individuals could see the ineffectual nature of the terms of Greek engagement on these issues, but few were willing, or able, to resist the inevitability of the discourse in public.

This dynamic calls for a consideration of this interplay from the earliest days of the Greek nation-state right up to the present, to the *Kathimerini* article which began this introduction. The book will examine how the dialectic between these two discourses develops in the unfolding formation of Greek identity from the beginnings of the conception of the Greek nation-state to the present. The starting point for this study is not arbitrary. It focuses on the emergence of the modern Greek state. As such, my point of departure does not amount to affirming that the 'modern' begins here. The 'modern' may have preceded this historical realization, the territorialization of the Greek Idea. Certainly, a whole host of critical articles and studies – many of them written outside Greece – have plotted a history, or genealogy, for the emergence of Neohellenism, each one projecting very different relations to Hellenism's historical antecedents. My study can not enter here into synthesis or evaluation of these or other famous essays, on this subject. And, in some cases, it would not wish to do so in their terms.[9]

For Neohellenism elicits varied definitions. It often refers to a Greek consciousness before nationalism and it is often situated as far back as the tenth century. Reference has been made to the first epic in the vernacular; or the closeness of a vernacular idiom to modern Greek in the Ptohoprodromic poems of late Byzantium. Some may remark on the scholar Marcus Musurus's appeal to Pope Leo X to liberate Greece from the Turks in his *Hymn to Plato* of 1517, which makes arguments that would not be amiss in the Enlightenment. Not surprisingly, however, many of these retroactive readings of the phenomenon have been driven by the nationalist sentiments of their own time. One of the few books to confront the concept head on, John Burke and Stathis Gauntlett's *Neohellenism* (1992), begins by locating it squarely in the establishment of the Greek nation-state of 1832, but then sketches the debate surrounding this definition and declares that this 'fact' of history is perceived by many as an accident or perversion of Neohellenism's course. Quite appropriately, then, the volume of collected essays that follows this preface presents a host of perspectives on Neohellenism, its antecedents and origins. Indicatively, in an essay titled 'The Transition from Hellenism to Neohellenism,' the late C. M. Woodhouse seems not to shy away from the challenge of a definition. His opening sentence is equally encouraging: 'Hellenism and Neohellenism are terms easy enough to understand, and even to define.' Alas, the definition that follows – 'Hellenism means the civilisation of the pre-Christian Greeks, Neohellenism is the civilisation of the modern Greeks' – creates a gaping chasm between the two entities that opens up a bigger problem that the one it claims to solve: 'There was a long interval between the decline of Hellenism as the dominant civilisation in the Mediterranean world *and the emergence of Neohellenism in the last two centuries*' (Woodhouse 1992: 31, original emphasis). Neohellenism signifies a post-Antique phase predicated on a notion of decline but it often refers only to the nineteenth and twentieth centuries, as Woodhouse applies it at the end of this quotation. This identifies it with the term 'modern Greek,' which is more often narrowly applied to the mid-eighteenth to twentieth centuries.

My study begins as a Western notion of modernity – carrying with it emancipation, industrialization, consitutionalism, print capitalism, and national centrism

– is forged by Greeks in the hopes of securing a homeland. Although this development in Greece may have conformed to a wider European conjuncture, it also inflected this into a difference that marked the particularities of a 'modern Greek' period primed on the meeting of a regional past with modernization. This modernity, neither belated nor 'alternative,' pits, in often conflicting ways, several pasts with the present of an everyday, lived experience. A number of binaries have been employed to capture the manifestation of nationalism and modernity in Greece. They have tended to endow cultural memory with a blinding aura that disfigures, and is in tension with, a more differentiated everyday practice. This study avoids the practice of romanticizing the suppressed, second term of the binary by presenting it as an antimodern realm free from Western mediation. Such an approach would only generate a number of alternative authenticities, or exceptionalist modernities, and this would only reify the binary and promote a nativist imagination somehow immune to the cross-fertilizations, or rather contaminations, of interdependence. In trying to endow the present moment, it creates another experience, often conceived of as folkloristic and communitarian, that itself claims an eternality untouched by history in a resilient prenationalist consciousness. The task at hand is to navigate between authenticities and cultural exceptionalism to uncover the modern Greeks' often pained attempts to refigure, and do justice to, their everyday life. The performative present needs to be explored in a sensitive and pliable hermeneutic, within a receptive institutional context, because its dismissal has created an acute lack of self-confidence.

Signs of this lack of self-confidence are identifiable in the most recent monument to Greek modernity and modernization, the Athens Metro. One of the most ambitious of modern construction projects, not only in Greece but also in Europe, the belated extension of the one existent subway line in Athens aimed at the reduction of congestion, pollution, and frustration in one of Europe's least easily traveled cities. The opening in March 2000 of a large section of the new subway system was greeted with pandemonium as Greeks from all walks of life, an estimated 1 million in the first weekend, descended underground to 'experience' the new system firsthand. That it opened at about the time that Greece was about to gain official entry into the European Monetary Union (EMU), after years of economic convergence, added a symbolism to the Metro and its opening. This only compounded the symbolism enjoyed by subways everywhere, for they are often read as signs of a nation's past, present and future: 'the evolution of the subway as a symbol is that it starts by expressing faith in the city's future and, once built, quickly becomes a handy rhetorical tool for expressing discontent with its present' (Brooks 1997: 3).

Understandably, the Metro's newness and its speed (especially when compared to the one existing line, sometimes called the 'Balkan line') met with public approval.[10] Furthermore, the project, which like any Greek project of modernization had literally run into the problem of the classical heritage head-on, in the form of archaeological sites in its path, incorporated some of those artifacts and ruins in the new stations, on platforms and in ticket areas. The Metro had cleared a quint-essentially Greek path to modernity, smoothed out with an aesthetic gesture of elision that repaid classical survivalists and cultural constructivists alike.

Unlike the existing line, the new system boasts fine white marble, spanking new signs, and working ticket-sale machinery. Even the escalators work, a quite remarkable spectacle for many Athenians weaned on the mythical sight of the broken escalators of the old, central Omonia Square station that will go down in infamy. The clean environs of the new station have also become something of an obsession with the public and the authorities alike, and they have been held up as a sign of an aspiring European propriety. However, the 'intentionally spare interior' of the Metro has, in some newspaper articles, been faulted for engendering a solemnity in the passengers' demeanor. 'Although one would agree that being treated to a clean public space is rare in this city,' writes one journalist, 'there is still something sterile and unnaturally lifeless in the unadorned gray surfaces of the Metro.'[11] The stations are clear of any shops, raspy-voiced vendors, and lottery salespeople. In quite stark contrast to many European subway complexes that work on the principle of functioning as a city underground, the Athens Metro is empty. Its dead space is adorned by the occasional photograph of a bygone Athens or, as has been mentioned, by showcases with classical vases or artifacts derived from the areas excavated on the very site of the station. For some, this neatness is an improvement over the mayhem of the old, central Omonia Square underground station, which in its last years of operation had become home to groups of heroin addicts, transvestite prostitutes, and bedraggled economic migrants from the war-torn Balkans. This had now been decisively 'cleaned up,' or cleaned away, but so have the kiosks with their newspapers hung on clothes pegs displaying journals of every ideological persuasion imaginable, the *pigadakia* or huddles of sports enthusiasts in deliberation, the shoe-shines, the hawkers – in short, daily life. Smoking is prohibited, as it is elsewhere in Europe; but food and even soft drinks are not allowed. Citizens went so far as to contest the constitutionality of the curbs on such 'freedoms' with the office of the State Ombudsman.[12] For now, the bustling and carnivalesque have been left at the door and remain in view above in the square, which itself has recently endured a lamentable Olympic face-lift in concrete.

This was the case until very recently. The Metro's authorities have organized the installation of modern art pieces in a number of central stations, many the work of some of Greece's most celebrated artists. The move answers those critics who criticize the Metro's perceived lack of a recognizable aesthetic; a charge, by the way, that has been leveled also at Athens' other monument to modernity, the even newer Eleftherios Venizelos International Airport.[13] The 25 meter-long mec-art photograph entitled *Queue* by Nikos Kessanlis that was installed in the Omonia station depicts shadows of human figures, as if to reproduce the fleeting images of passengers dashing through the station. His panel effects the illusion that the shadows are reflected by people coming down the escalators or by people behind the semi-opaque panel. As if this were not enough of an analogy to the Platonic cave, blinking lights and a partition placed elsewhere in the station reflect actual people walking along the panel. Art and life are theorized in splendid ambiguity; the policing of life, the need for its aestheticization and the animation of social practices would seem to be a striking feature of Greek modernity.

Critical Institutions

This lack of self-confidence is also reflected in the profile of the emergent discipline of modern Greek studies in the United States. The use of ancient Greece, mostly, but to predominant effect, by scholars outside Greece to validate the new nation and state did not so much serve to establish a modern state as undermine the very possibility of its becoming one, or at least, undermine people's confidence that it could be one. This effect is also seen in the actual teaching and research of and on modern Greece. Along with Arabic and Chinese, modern Greece is rare in pre-fixing 'modern' to its post-classical condition. The epithet that distinguishes *modern* Greece from Greece, or more appropriately *classical* Greece, is one that, rather than working adjectivally, often appears as somewhat of an appendage. It marks a sense of belatedness, of afterthought. Even the term for the study of modern Greece, 'neohellenism or *neohellenika*, imposed in Greece itself on many areas of study after 1453, is not entirely its own, "neohellenism" having been appropriated by German classicists from the late eighteenth century to refer to the revival of classical studies in the west' (Alexiou 1986: 5). The word 'Neohell-enism' is not to be found in the Oxford English Dictionary; and modern Greek material is often left out of standard works of European, not to say anything of world culture. Institutionally, academic programs in modern Greek are rarely to be found housed alongside other contemporary languages, literatures, and cultural studies. In contrast, Chinese and Arabic are more commonly housed in programs of East Asian or Middle Eastern studies. The prerequisites for work in cultural studies – archives of popular culture, easy accessibility to films and recorded television programs, databases of music – are barely available, and, despite much good will, remain *terra incognita* for Greek government agencies and wealthy cultural foundations.

Let us propose a deconstructive trick and place the 'modern' under erasure. By visualizing the strikeout, and not extirpating it, we leave the term in debate and so confront its problematic nature. This visible mnemonic asks of us to give the term its due and make reparations to it in light of years of underestimation. For the institutional context in the academy has not helped matters. For a long time, the incorporation of programs for the study of the modern culture in Classics depart-ments has facilitated work in philological paradigms of interpretation that stress diachronic considerations. Quite apart from the obstacles posed to disciplinary integrity, this held back areas, like cultural and media studies, in the field of modern Greek studies. The philological model also replicated the continuous paradigm informing the Germanic pedagogical institutional context in Greece itself where, at the University of Athens for instance, contemporary Greek literature and culture were not included in the course of literary study at the university level until recent decades. For those invested in the diachronic study of Hellenism, the adjective 'modern' is not a source of much concern; perhaps, only as a 'beast of burden.' For these scholars, to put the term *modern* under erasure would be as gimmicky as practicing cultural studies or theory. The exhortation to study Greek *tout court* presents modern Greece as a natural extension, and contributive element, to that which is Greece. In this formulation, the sad relic could aspire to 'its modest place in the sun.'[14] But, as Leontis rightly remarks, 'neohellenism already holds that place, as the swarms of tourists annually prove' (Leontis 1995: 224–5). It needs a place out of the shadows of the pellucid light. While the institutional model of the European university system may have been protectionist toward such approaches till now, the corporate models in education now imminent in the United Kingdom and elsewhere will demand, for better and for worse, a more concerted interdisciplinary practice. For ideological reasons, there's a good chance modern Greek will be taught in the context of other European modern languages, literatures, and cultures (including popular culture).

To study modern Greek culture as an *equal* partner within the larger unit of Classics in the U.S. would be admissible if experience up until now had not demonstrated so clearly that the relationship is rarely built on equality. Sadly, and all too frequently, the cohabitation of modern Greek in departments of Classics has been marked by an air of afterthought consummate with the grammatical standing of the adjective 'modern' described above. Fair-minded classicists admit how 'the study of modern Greek was often grafted onto programs in modern languages, or housed within classics, not happily so' (Morris 2001: 10).[15] A cursory glance at a list of the sponsoring departments that host modern Greek classes at the university level worldwide today demonstrates that the majority are within Classics depart-ments.[16] Since the early 1980s, endowments to support the incorporation of modern Greek into antiquity have been established at a host of institutions in the United States. And, at times unwittingly, the donors of these endowments, wealthy Greek Americans, or Greek cultural foundations, seek a classical leaning to such positions in the hope that the affiliation will endow 'the field' some small measure of respectability. Modern Greek, particularly in the minds of Greek diaspora donors, rarely carries with it the *gravitas* or respect to allow it to stand on its own – better for donors to lean on the crutch of already existent programs in classical Greek. The neoconservative desire of many recent programs in modern Greek studies to celebrate their establishment by snuggling up cosily into the embrace of classical studies is worth rethinking. For, to recast the field once again in relation to Classics, to my mind, not only is anachronistic, but also shows little sensitivity to strategic epistemic priorities. Granted, it does dovetail nicely with the classicists' new reorientation. Coming out of their discipline's own 'crisis, after confronting its roots in orientalism and a western-centered sense of destiny [many classicists] turned to contemporary discourse and the investigation of class, gender and ethnicity in antiquity, to revitalize a discipline' (Morris 2001: 11). Some now see Modern Greek as a new partner with the potential to move classics out of antiquity, into comparative area studies etc. In turn, Classical studies will offer modern Greek multiple, interdisciplinary partners under the same roof in a department wherein neohellenists 'can revisit antiquity not as an historical burden with a conservative cast, but for the sake of a secure academic context and intellectual future' (Morris 11). Despite the good intentions of such arguments, it is not clear that such affiliation will provide great security or would trump a more autonomous existence for modern Greek in a less riven household.

Of course, this is not to say that the phenomenon of continuity in the Greek tradition has not had its moments.[17] Margaret Alexiou, who has provided us with some of its most memorable moments, pleaded in the mid-1980s for the field 'to break out of the straitjacket of "tradition" without ignoring the past' (Alexiou 1986: 3). Though my brand of liberation may not be what she had in mind, the classicists' persistence in experiencing Greece along a diachronic axis, even with a revamped language of genealogy and discontinuity, may still not encourage insights attuned to many aspects of Greek modernity. The eminent classicist and philhellene Bernard Knox exemplifies this point in the final essay of his *The Oldest Dead White European Males and Other Reflections on the Classics* (1993). His experience of the Greek present aids him in rereading and reappreciating the past in a reverse survivalism of sorts; in effect, Knox speaks for the classicists' new engagement. By projecting the modern culture's differentiated present back to the past, Knox breathes new life into that past. Indeed, Knox's book as a whole prescribes a moderate dose of class, gender, and ethnicity for classicists. Yet, Knox does not address how such contexts will extend to the study of the modern Greeks, or the ways in which such continuities will be theorized. As a classicist, this is not his responsibility, after all. But neohellenists in the classicist mould must answer how, in fact, will the multifacetedness that scholars such as Knox search for in their classical predecessors be extended, by this reading operation, to the modern Greeks. Since, for all the genuine inclusiveness of Van Steen's presentation of Hellenic Studies (2002), it still strikes me that this conjoining does a better job of helping classicists reevaluate the past than proving that multidimensional and cross-cultural mediations are best pursued from the Classics. In general, with the neoconservative turn, there lurks the risk that in joining those who seek to bring to life one set of dead white European males, one might be condemning their epigones to the same fate, *again*.

The form of my own study proposes a strategic reconfiguration of the socio-cultural field and interposes it into a broader set of contemporaneous social and critical institutions. Discursive as well as non-discursive practices are given their due. A new historicist inclination to reorient the axis of intertextuality by unsettling the *diachronic* text of an autonomous, primarily literary text with that of the *synchronic* text of a cultural system may best revive those atrophied parts of modern Greek studies. We need now to pursue new texts and contexts in more systematic and sustained engagement with the field of cultural studies. This does not imply philistinism or ahistoricity, as some would have it. Nor does it seek to do away with the dialogue with the Classics, which will always remain one strand of the hermeneutic potential of modern Greek studies. A sensitive reading of class, gender and ethnicity across the Greek tradition will always raise important questions. Yet the field is in need of cross-fertilization along other synchronic and lateral as well as diachronic axes, especially in a discipline whose classicist and philological leanings have not privileged such comparativist work. Affiliations with cultural studies, comparative literature, ethnic and postcolonial studies, gender studies provide contexts, as do the Classics, and they must now be pursued from a site wherein the autonomous physiognomy of modern Greek is assured. Any redefinition of the field must demand a greater working insititutional autonomy for 'modern Greek.'

In presenting my notion of a cultural poetics of Greek modernity, I fully submit, and am conscious of, the status of my reading as an interpretation. My objective in presenting here certain observations about the field and the strategic choices ahead – however reluctantly I do so – has been to show how such strategies shape my own interpretive choices, given the impossibility of adequately reconstructing, and the dangers of totalizing, the culture of modern Greece. I do so reluctantly, too, because of scholars' tendency to issue programmatic comments about directions of the field with a frequency that far outstrips their practical ability to do the cultural work of remaking the tradition and keeping pace with their own metacriticism. This is a factor of a hyperprofessionalization that comes with working in a small and precarious field ever conscious of its own need for reconstruction. For such reconstruction requires a multidimensional approach of the kind pursued by such figures as Henry Louis Gates in African American Studies. Naturally, modern Greek will never be dealt Afro-Am's social and political cards. But a multidimensional approach is crucial. The maddening task of finding a publisher for new Greek literature in English translation has only been exacerbated by the inability to contextualize such work in other than recognizable forms. This creates a vicious circle: no translations of new modern Greek works make it increasingly more difficult for critics to justify the induction of new, untranslated Greek literature in their critical studies. Greek literary studies can not live on mythical and classical allusion, travelers, and Cavafy alone. The attendant issues concerning marketing and audience are many and complex and I and others have discussed them elsewhere (Spiropoulou and Tsimpouki 2002). I would argue though that many of the problems outlined above could be better confronted from a critical perspective and an institutional framework that would better engage the differentiated particularities of a rich, modern experience.

Cultural Poetics

In my own exploration of Greek modernity, I have chosen to consider eight moments of tension in the configuration of the modern Greek subject's *poiesis*. In employing this term *poiesis* (ποίησις), I stress the valency of its classical connotation of a 'making,' a 'forming,' or 'creating', while retaining its meaning of 'poetry' (also ποίησις),[18] in a series of historically genial articulations. These articulations are 'virtuosic,' as Faubion (1993: 153) terms the best tradition of historical constructivism. The book considers in each of its chapters a virtuosic act – a map by the 'protomartyr of the Greek Revolution'; the compositional process of the first National Poet; the first feminist text and the first novel in the new Greek state; the first marxist treatise of Greek society; the topographies of the chief Greek modernists; the last National Poem; the first *modern* philhellenists; and the first Greek/Turkish fiction of a global age; the first Greek euro coin. These are read in their ideological, political, and socially productive dimensions and in their interaction with various discursive formations and institutions of their time. Their virtuosity lies not in their connoisseurship. Nor are these texts to be considered sacred or self-enclosed. Noncanonical texts, even ordinary objects and practices, are placed next to the canonical in ways that can elicit an unexpected aesthetic dimension when the object has no such pretensions. To treat all textual traces as representation and event need not lead to the aestheticization of a whole culture – though the implication is that the aestheticization of Greece through classical Hellenism did just this and left little room for anything else to exist. In new historicist terms, I echo the words of Catherine Gallagher and Stephen Greenblatt (2000):

> it is crucially important to have it both ways: . . . to delve as deeply as possible into the creative matrices of particular historical cultures and at the same time . . . to understand how certain products of these cultures could seem to possess a certain independence. In our scholarship, the relative positions of text and context shift, so that what has been the mere background makes a claim for the attention that has hitherto been given only to the foregrounded and privileged work of art, yet we wish to know how the foregrounding came about. (Gallagher and Greenblatt 2000: 16)

I define my field as a 'poetics' since the texts analyzed – among them maps, critical editions of manuscripts, sociological analyses, theoretical treatises, prose autobiographies, currency notes – can not be categorized as 'poetry,' but admit to a broad definition of Poetry. My use of the term goes beyond the long-established meaning of studying patterns in literary, and especially poetic, texts. Russian Formalists, structuralists, ethnographers, and ethnopoeticians have done so already. The by-now acceptable post-structuralist usage, based on the claim that nothing is beyond the text, has overshadowed the more traditional, though more restricted usage, for designating a systematic theory or doctrine of poetry, the principles that govern it and that distinguish it from other forms.[19]

Despite the assortment of divers texts analyzed here, film and popular culture, two vital areas of future study, are largely absent. In part this is because I hoped that the more established notion of 'poetics' would linger and cohabit my term, since poetry and literature will figure prominently in this study. Andrei Tarkovsky once affirmed that poetry is not a literary kind, but 'a special way of bringing the world to awareness, of linking yourself to reality' (Tarkovsky 1994: 355–6). This is an especially attractive definition, given my wish to engage a modern Greek reality. Yet it will amount to an ironic usage as a primary implication of my search for this ordinary reality will be that prevalent paradigms for configuring modern Greece have, in fact, achieved the exact opposite – the evacuation of this very reality. Poetry, in the traditional sense, has been central to this very process. As the supreme form of aesthetic production, after all, it lacks the physical substance of other arts and its primacy among forms since Antiquity has, in part, been predicated on this very characteristic.[20] The voice's breath, its passing, enforces this disembodiment and distances it from the material world. The lyric has always aimed to produce more than the real it confronts and, by so doing, it elicits that which is true precisely because it goes beyond nature.

Writing may have originated in Egypt. But in European eyes and notwithstanding Plato's singular assault on poets, poetry (or Poesy) was regarded to have originated in Greece. Poetry is, therefore, both the vehicle for Greek identity and a genre that, in its reception by Europeans, reflects the mode by which Greece itself was perceived and aestheticized by Europeans. The modern Greeks paid homage to poetry upon establishment of their state, 'a poor house on Homer's beaches.' They privileged a narrative of logocentric continuity based on the primacy of the spoken word in the transmission of folk tradition and Church liturgy and teaching to build a bridge back, over the shameful silence of Ottoman rule, to their august past. These voices preserved the race and compensated for the perceived dearth of chirographic texts during Ottoman rule. Poetry established itself as the basic, indigenous expression of, and pose for, conveying a formative and synthetic imagination and delivering a unifying vision of the Greek world (Bien 1985: 197–200). (Prose was regarded as a foreign importation for much of the nineteenth century in Greece.) It was *with* and *against* so Romantic a notion that the Greek poetic virtuosity of social constructivism was carried out. *Poietes* of different stripes based self-creation on the transcendence of contingency; or, on its recognition in ways that rehearsed the assumptions of pre- and post-Nietzschean philosophy. It is for irony's sake, then, that a vehicle so well crafted to bear originary essentialism, genius, and authenticity on its shoulders all this time will be used here as the vehicle for an expressive counter-archeology.

The bard and the poet may no longer be able to reflect the 'soul of their nation' around the world. But the Romantic notion of a poet's role is not without its acolytes in Greece even today. The bedrock belief in authenticity that underpins the genre is alive and well. After all, Greeks have a vested interest in authenticity. They believe in singing from the heart; preparing and cooking fish as is, with only lemon and oil; using natural ingredients and shunning genetically modified foods; their way is orthodox. All these are themselves ingredients for a cult of authenticity. Shorn of a claim to any such authenticity, I prefer to work from another notion of the poet that rests largely on the Romantic poet's ability to recognize and celebrate ordinary experience. Stanley Cavell's notion of the philosopher comes close to this notion of the poet. So with some poetic license, I extend this definition to include critics and theorists as this aspiration is set the critic in this study.[21] It is a longtime struggle between literary and theoretical texts. Poetry and philosophy, rhetoric and hermeneutics, cultural studies and deconstruction have at different times contested the best way for representing reality by a poetics that comes with a critical theory to justify its interpretation.

This book perceives itself as the latest in a series of critical studies by scholars primarily living and working outside Greece, whose work, since the early 1980s, has ridden the tiger of critical theory to reimagine the nation.[22] The poetic function, as defined here, resides with the diaspora critic. Not a strange conjuncture really as the modern Greek poets who replenished and revivified the language often lived beyond the borders of the Greek nation-state. Kalvos, Solomos, Cavafy 'did not speak Greek,' as Seferis once famously observed, and it was this distance from 'home' that allowed them to theorize and expose the culture's hidden potentialities.[23] Similarly, but more humbly, the diaspora critic exploited the distance and space of exile to engage a view from afar, a *theoria* of Greekness. They interposed Greek concerns into broader epistemological discussions. Their philologist contemporaries met these positions with opposition (or neglect) and bemoaned the fate of particularisms of nativist knowledge.

In response to this history, I choose to conceive of a theory or cultural system in the terms of a 'cultural poetics' that is at once historicist and formalist and that may break down disciplinary distinctions in ways that will embolden the interdisciplinarity of modern Greek studies. In effect, the until-now small number of diaspora practitioners of modern Greek have applied their theoretical positions to Greek textual tradition only fitfully, partly because an aversion to philology has inhibited them from falling into the text's embrace. While the metropolitan Greek literary establishment was slower than other Greek disciplines in the humanities, like history, to engage with wider critical and cultural debates. The will to theorize had some diaspora pedigree behind it. After all, a unified national consciousness in Greece would not have been possible without the ideological engineering – the textualization and totalization of disparate forms of consciousness – by the diaspora Greeks and European philhellenes from the mid- to late eighteenth century into the nineteenth century. The diaspora elite possessed the means of production, print, and the general means to impose their reading of the origins, codes, and symbols for a newly instituted society.[24] Their adulation of the Classical Greek Ideal, their invocation of the French Revolution, and Romantic nationalism were critical in their search for a narrative that would convince the Powers to support Greek Liberation. They gave Greek society 'the status of Ur-Europa for Greece . . . by weaving its story into the master narrative of the West' (Jusdanis 1991a: 21). This study does not branch out to explore Greek diasporas as a whole. It limits itself to the diaspora of metropolitan European centers at the time before the Revolution. Their vision, and the subject position they occupied, had enormous ramifications for the physiognomy of the state. The structuring gaze they initiated *beyond* and *outside* Greece itself led to the negation and objectification of space and particular social circumstance in favor of its temporalization. The analysis that follows strives to discuss how contending political interests conditioned spectral economies of representation among different groups and interests *within* Greek society (where those counted *within* were often, spatially, *within* but effectively *without* the state). In trying to historicize the agonistic claims of classical Hellenism and social constructivism, the book ceaselessly returns to the problematization of the space that opens up between the place of production of an image – here the image of 'modern Greece' that issues out of European visions of the Classical Hellenic Ideal – and the secondary production of its utilization or the indigenous resistance to its implementation. This book tries to historicize this dialectic in the ideological and cultural frame of individual artistic texts and their contexts.

This book, then, examines the contested terrain of Greek modernity by focusing on pivotal moments in its articulation or *poiesis* (in all the formerly noted senses of the word). It does so primarily by tracing the development and effects of a central concept, what I have chosen to call a discourse of ab-sense, or the imposition of external, idealized narratives onto the recalcitrant body of modern Greece. Chapter 1 examines this dynamic by delving into the tensions in the transition from polyethnic coexistence in the Ottoman Empire to national orders of representation as monumentalized in a 'Map of Greece,' drawn up by the diaspora Greek revolutionary, Rhigas Velestinlis, in 1797. The Hellenic Ideal from the West, which informed aesthetic theories and then foreign travelers' trips to Greece, conflicts with an indigenous lifeworld. An aesthetic prevails that represses *aisthesis*, and the perceptions of the modern Greek are occluded from the discursive standing of the 'real.'

But what became of the European Gaze when those who favored this spectral economy, the diaspora Greeks, came to live in the Greek nation-state after the Revolution? They remain in favor with their foreign patrons in the new state. Their cosmopolitanism, their good offices to the Foreign Powers, and their relations with an imposed Bavarian king ensured them some privileges. The chapter considers the unbalanced relations between diaspora Greeks, the so-called heterochthons – 'those sprung from another land,' a cultural elite – and the autochthons, 'those sprung from the land itself.' Surveillance and socioeconomic dependence mark the Greek political predicament; both groups always position themselves in relation to the Great Powers as they engage the genealogies of self-definition filtered through Eurocentrism. A 'double-consciousness' affects the poetics of modern Greek identity and it is examined at three levels of social life: land, citizenship, and poetry (the case of the first National Poet, Dionysios Solomos, is considered here).

The discourse of ab-sense also implies an ongoing crisis of representation. This is evident in debates about the incompatibility of foreign forms – from constitutionalism to prose fiction – applied to represent 'Greek reality' and the 'Greek subject.' Chapter 3 considers the gap between, as well as the interpenetration of, foreign forms and indigenous voices through analyses of the first feminist text and the first novel of the Greek state. Furthermore, by rejecting the ontologized distinction between origin and derivation, one other symptom of Greek modernity, the perceived derivative nature of Greek forms, is challenged by pointing to these works' self-reflexive engagement with the genres that constitute them. The practices of philological reading that have abetted this discourse of derivation and the persistence of a developmentalist logic applied to Greek prose fiction in the nineteenth-century are shown to be poor conduits for realizing a more complex understanding of these works' potentialities.

The central section of the book (Chapters 4–6) focuses on the evolution of resistance to, and critiques of, the discourse of ab-sense. As the nineteenth century progresses, the distinction between heterochthon and autochthon becomes irrelevant and is remade in terms of class. In keeping with postcolonial analogues, 'the national bourgeoisies and their specialized elites . . . replace the colonial force with a new class-based and ultimately exploitative one' (Said 1993: 223). Chapter 4 delineates the evolution of a class-based, materialist critique that interposes the peasant and an urban working class into the symbolic field by questioning the totalizing claims of nationalist discourse. This critique, in Lacanian terms, finds the totalized object of the Gaze looking back at the perceiver to announce the signifier as the product of a socialized vision and cultural idiom of 'seeing.'[25] This dynamic of 'seeing,' belonging to a resistant Gaze, will become central in later chapters on philhellenism and conceptions of local difference in processes of globalization. In this fourth chapter, the first marxist critique of nationalist discourse in Greece is examined alongside poet-syndicalist Kostas Karyotakis's dismantling of the concept of poetic voice, self, and the notion of poetry in their relation to a discourse of ab-sense. Chapters 5 and 6 examine agonistic claims to reimagine a space for Greekness, literal or otherwise, by juxtaposing two very different movements: the liberal Greek modernists or so-called Generation of the 1930s (Chapter 5) and the communists or dissident leftists of the so-called first post-war generation (Chapter 6). In both cases, the relation of politics to poetics, as well as the relation of the conception of Greekness to its Others, is considered.

The final section of the book returns to the fraught relation between external and internal voices – the power dynamic in the exchange of Gazes – to consider the ways in which the discourse of ab-sense has been reconfigured, rewritten, or erased in the contexts of modern philhellenism, cosmopolitanism, transnationalism, and globalization. Chapter 7 juxtaposes three modern travelogues to Greece to examine different perspectives on Greece's place in Europe and its role as a literary *topos*. It also highlights Greeks' response to that Gaze in a more general discussion of their anxieties over the currency of Hellenism and philhellenism. Finally, Chapter 8 turns to a consideration of conceptions of Greek identity and difference as expressed in relation to Greece's neighbors, in order to meditate on the circulation of identity in a globalized world. It does so by focusing on the most sensitive aspect of difference in Greece, the marked difference that separates Greek from Turk.

The book finishes where it began, held in the thrall of Rhigas Velestinlis. Since the early 1990s, events in the post-1989 Balkans have led Greeks to reconceive their relation to their Balkan neighbors. Concurrently, Rhigas Velestinlis has been feted, commemorated, and eulogized as the symbol of a new Balkan interdependence and equality. In this new climate, Rhigas's image circulates as the guarantor of European, Balkan and Greek internal difference and modernity.

Notes

1. Vassiliki Angelikopoulou, *Kathimerini*, 8 October 2000.
2. See Danforth (1995: Chapter VI) for a fuller account of the controversy over symbols.
3. See Mouzelis (1978: 303–30); at that time, Mouzelis himself criticized the Greek government's position on the Macedonian issue as just such a misguided 'formalism' (Mouzelis 1992).
4. 'The Two Macedonias,' *New York Times*, Editorial, 5 April 1992. Other notable attacks on Greek positions were Noel Malcolm, 'The New Bully of the Balkans,' *The Spectator*, 15 August 1992; Roger Thurow, 'Nouvelle Macedonia Pits

Greeks, Slavs in Moniker Muddle,' *Wall Street Journal*, 19 November 1992; and then Assistant Secretary of State's Strobe Talbott's 'America Abroad: Greece's Defense Seems Just Silly,' *Time*, 12 October 1992, who finds Greece 'not guilty of irredentism . . . but merely of paranoia and myopia. The situation,' Talbott responds in kind, 'has all the makings of tragedy, which Aristotle, another great Macedonian who was Alexander's teacher, defined as the result not of wickedness but of foolish pride.'

5. See Herzfeld (1986: 77–8).

6. Yorgos Chouliaras's collection of poetry *Fast-Food Classics* (Athens: Ipsilon, 1992) plays on the point at about this time.

7. The urgency may have been even more pressing, if we lend credence to the conclusions of a symposium held in Paris in November 1990, in which several radical thinkers (Castoriadis, Veyne, Vernant, Loraux et al.) examined the validity of Greece as the traditional philosophical ancestor of modern European civilization. The discussants concluded that Rome was the historical point of European origin (Gourgouris 1992: 43). Also in 1990, a leak of the contents for a planned European Union-sponsored history of Europe and its peoples by Jean-Baptiste Duroselle caused uproar in Greece when, incredibly, it was revealed that he had omitted mention of the classical Greeks. Elsewhere, a round-table discussion of the 'crisis of Greek diplomatic discourse' among prominent Greek politicians and diplomats (*To Vima*, 7 March 1993: B2–4) addressed deficiencies of Greek diplomacy and political strategy during the Macedonian crisis. The deployment of Alexander the Great in Europe was not once mentioned. Either the discussants were in no way critical of its deployment; or the participants did not want to be seen diminishing it in a public forum; or they all tacitly knew that such arguments are used to whip up emotion at home, but are not worthy of discussion when more important strategy is being evaluated (even though this tactic for internal consumption had spun wildly out of the government's control).

8. In Article 7, No. 2, FYROM agreed 'upon entry into force of [the] Accord . . . [to] cease to use in any way the symbol displayed on its national flag prior to such entry into force.' Article 6 of the Interim Agreement rejects any claim by FYROM to any territory not within its existing borders nor interfere in the internal affairs of a neighboring state to protect the status and rights of any persons who are not citizens of FYROM.

9. Some notable examples are: A. Thumb, 'The Modern Greek and his Ancestry,' *Bulletin of the John Ryland Library* II (1914–15): 22–47; D. M. Nicol, *Greece and Byzantium* (Brookline, MA: Hellenic College Press, 1983); Romilly Jenkins, *Byzantium and Byzantinism* (Cincinnati, OH: University of Cincinnati Press, 1963); G. G. Arnakis, 'Byzantium and Greece,' *Balkan Studies* IV (1963): 379–400; 'C. Mango, Byzantinism and Romantic Hellenism,' *Journal*

of the Warburg and Courtauld Institutes XXVIII (1965): 29–43; R. Browning, *Greece – Ancient and Medieval*. An Inaugural Lecture Delivered at Birkbeck College, 15 June 1966 (London: Birkbeck College, 1967); A. Toynbee, *The Greeks and their Heritages* (Oxford, New York, Toronto and Melbourne: Oxford University Press, 1981); see the latter's use of neohellenic in Chapter VIII on 'The Modern Greeks' Heritage from the Hellenic Greeks.'

10. The existing subway route was once occupied by the Athens–Piraeus and Athens–Kifissia steam commuter railway. Subway construction to reach Omonia Square, in the heart of Athens, began in 1895, and electric operation between Omonia and Piraeus began in 1904. Subway operation to the suburb of Kifissia was achieved in 1957; Athenians have grown up riding this one line.

11. Alexandra Koroxenidis, 'Far Closer: Nikos Kessanlis,' *Kathimerini English Edition*, 15 March 2001.

12. See Andonis Renieris, 'Will We Smoke or Not in the Metro?' *Ta Nea*, 16 December 2000.

13. See, for example, the descriptions in a feature published in the Sunday *Kathimerini* issue of 18 March 2001, ten days before the airport's inauguration.

14. David Ricks, 'Greek *tout court*,' *Arion* 1(3) (1991): 29–44, 31.

15. Morris's comments appear in her foreword to a volume of proceedings from a conference, entitled 'Contours of Hellenism: Classical Antiquity and Modern Greek Culture,' and held at UCLA in May 2000.

16. 'About two thirds of the U.S.-based Modern Greek Studies programs are housed or used to be housed within departments of Classics' (Van Steen 2002: 187). The institutional history of practices within these departments testify that classicists have often been called upon to teach modern Greek on the basis of their Greek heritage; neohellenists, by contrast, were and are – quite rightly – barred from teaching the Classics. Even today, classicists with no formal training in modern Greek, as distinct from neohellenists trained in the Classics, compete for modern Greek appointments. And it is still disconcerting to see a modern Greek appointment advertised as 'only open to classicists.' Advertising positions in modern Italian for Latinists would not help matters.

17. The theorization of Greek cultural continuity has been undertaken in only a handful of texts. The work of George Thomson, in particular his 'The Continuity of Hellenism,' *Greece and Rome* 18 (1971): 18–29; Speros Vryonis, 'Recent Scholarship on Continuity and Discontinuity of Culture: Classical Greeks, Byzantines, Modern Greeks.' In Speros Vryonis (ed.), *The 'Past' in Medieval and Modern Greek Culture* (Malibu, CA: Undena, 1978: 237–56).

18. Indeed, the Greek form *poiesis* came into English as 'poesy' in the fourteenth century and though it was at first used interchangeably with the Latin 'poetria,' or English 'poetrie,' the latter eventually supplanted it.

19. The traditional notion of 'poetics' is, of course, to be found in Aristotle's *Poetics* or Horace's *Ars Poetica*. In the Anglo-American tradition, the transition from this traditional usage to a wedding of Russian Formalism and French structuralism was advanced in the work of Roman Jakobson and Tzvetan Todorov in the 1950s and 1960s. The approach known as 'ethnopoetics' among anthropologists and focusing on structures of performance is exemplified by D. H. Hymes (*'In Vain I Tried to Tell You': Essays in Native American Ethnopoetics*, 1981) and D. Tedlock (*The Spoken Word and the Word of Interpretation*, 1983). J. Clifford and G. E. Marcus's volume *Writing Culture: The Poetics and Politics of Ethnography* (1986) questioned the implicit claims to authority and the political contexts behind the anthropologists' own narrative fictions. The more general employment of the term 'poetics' is evidenced in such works as Gaston Bachelard's *La Poétique de l'espace* (1957); Linda Hutcheon's *Poetics of Post-Modernism* (1988); Nancy K. Miller's *Poetics of Gender* (1986); Tzvetan Todorov's *Poetics of Prose* (1977). In studies of modern Greece, Michael Herzfeld in his *The Poetics of Manhood* explains his own usage of the term as an analysis of a Cretan village man's performance of manhood in a field of social relations or larger recognized categories of identity (1985: 10–19). See also his later *Cultural Intimacy: Social Poetics in the Nation-State* (1997).

20. See G. E. Lessing's *Laocoön: An Essay on the Limits of Painting and Poetry.* Trans. Edward Allen McCormick (Baltimore, MD: Johns Hopkins University Press, 1984).

21. In particular, see Cavell's *In Quest of the Ordinary* (1988).

22. Herzfeld (1982, 1987); Lambropoulos (1988); Alexiou and Lambropoulos and Alexiou (1985); Tziovas (1986b, and 1989a in Greek); Jusdanis (1991a), Faubion (1993); Leontis (1995); Gourgouris (1996); Van Dyck (1998); Peckham (2001).

23. See Seferis's essay of 1937 'The Greek Language' (Seferis 1981: 64–76, especially 64–5).

24. Here, the notion of an Imaginary refers to Benedict Anderson's celebrated formulation of a nation as an 'imagined political community' where 'members of even the smallest nation will never know most of their fellow-members, meet them, or even hear of them, yet in the minds of each lives the image of their communion' (Anderson 1991: 15).

25. Out at sea, Lacan stares at objects in the water and is told by a fisherman that, 'You see that can? Do you see it? Well, it doesn't see you!' Lacan interprets the fisherman's comment as untrue since objects do look back on the perceiver as signifiers are caught in networks of socially accepted forms of meaning, signs that make up a discourse of vision (Lacan 1978: 95).

–1–

Ab-sense

Let us imagine that a portion of the soil of England has been leveled off perfectly and that on it a cartographer traces a map of England. The job is perfect; there is no detail of the soil of England, no matter how minute, that is not registered on the map; everything has there its correspondence. This map, in such a case, should contain a map of the map, which should contain a map of the map of the map, and so on to infinity.

Why does it disturb us that the map be included in the map and the thousand and one nights in the book of the *Thousand and One Nights*? Why does it disturb us that Don Quixote be a reader of the *Quixote* and Hamlet a spectator of *Hamlet*? I believe I have found the reason: these inversions suggest that if the characters of a fictional work can be readers or spectators, we, its readers or spectators, can be fictitious.

Jorge Luis Borges, 'Partial Magic in the Quixote,' in *Labyrinths*.

It is significant that 'culture' is sometimes described as a map; it is the analogy which occurs to an outsider who has to find his way around in a foreign landscape and who compensates for his lack of practical mastery, the prerogative of the native, by the use of a model of all possible routes. The gulf between this potential, abstract space, devoid of landmarks or any privileged centre – like genealogies, in which the ego is as unreal as the starting point in a Cartesian space – and the practical space of journeys actually made, or rather of journeys actually being made, can be seen from the difficulty we have in recognizing familiar routes on a map or town-plan until we are able to bring together the axes of the field of potentialities and 'the system of axes linked unalterably to our bodies, and carried about us wherever we go,' as Poincaré puts it, which structures practical space into right and left, up and down, in front and behind.

Pierre Bourdieu, *Outline of a Theory of Practice*

Rhigas's Architectural Plan (1797)

The cartographers of the empire draw up a map whose exact verisimilitude aspires to a pure representation that leaves nothing to be seen of the territory. Baudrillard has notoriously used Borges's quote to bemoan the fate of the sign and the referent in a world where meaning resides in signs disconnected from historical actuality.

Territory no longer precedes the map as a precession of simulacra engender it.[1] Abstracting the logic of this figure – but relieving it of its postmodern context – I consider its relevance to a 'map of Greece' (Χάρτα της Ελλάδος), printed in Vienna in 1797 and comprised of twelve sheets that can be assembled in a pre-ordained order to complete a large map of 2 meters × 2 meters (Fig. 1.1).[2] The map is the work of Rhigas Velestinlis, a protomartyr of the 1821 Greek Revolution against Ottoman rule (Fig. 1.2). He precedes the nation, just as his map projects and precedes a territory, and seeks its engendering. His arrest and execution at the hands of the Ottoman authorities in 1797, long before the desired Revolution, mark his legacy and martyrdom.

Figure 1.1 Rhigas Velestinlis's *Map of Greece*, 1797

Ab-sense

Figure 1.2 Rhigas Velestinlis

Born in Velestino, Thessaly in 1757, Rhigas lived in Greek-speaking areas of
Thessaly throughout the Orlov incidents and uprisings (1769 and 1774) against
Ottoman rule, though accounts differ as to his age at the time of his departure for
Constantinople. He may have been anywhere between 10 and 17, and he did not
return to his local place of origin.[4] He adopted, as was the custom, a surname

derived from his home village, and he always signed himself 'Rhigas Velestinlis.' Others later conferred upon him the name Pherraios, taken from the ancient name of his home village, Pherrai.[5] He appears in Phanariot circles of Constantinople between 1782 and 1785, where he is personal secretary to Alexander Ipsilantis until he moves to work for a Greek sovereign of Wallachia who, in time, appoints him Eparch of Craiova. His literary and revolutionary work begins in earnest once he moves to Vienna in 1790, where he popularizes Enlightenment ideas and translates Montesquieu's *L'Esprit des lois*. Returning to Wallachia in 1791, and in the employ of the French consulate there as an interpreter, Rhigas realizes that the treaties between the Austrians and Russians with the Turks, ending the Austro-Russo-Turkish war (1787–92), dash any lingering hopes that Orthodox Russia might intervene and grant the fellow Orthodox Greeks their freedom.

By 1793, Rhigas becomes an ardent exponent of a francophile Republicanism. His map's debt to French maps is characteristic of a broader debt to French models – his *School for Dainty Lovers* (Σχολείο των ντελικάτων εραστών) (1792) draws heavily from Rétif de la Bretonne's *Contemporaines* stories of the early 1780s, he produces a revolutionary proclamation, a translation of Abbé Barthélemy's influential *Jeune Anacharsis* (1788), war songs played to the tune of the French caramagnoles of 1792,[6] and a *Democratic Catechism* reminiscent of French revolutionary catechisms of the early 1790s.[7] His best known works, the *Thourios* or *War Song* and a Constitution for the new 'Greek Democracy' modeled on the French Constitution of 1793,[8] urge Balkan Christians to free themselves from the Turk. These works borrow from the very touchstones of the European, particularly the French, Enlightenment. Rhigas's Νέα Πολιτικής Διοίκησις των Κατοίκων της Ρούμελης, της Μικρής Ασίας, των Μεσόγειων Νήσων και της Βλαχομπογδανίας (*Nouveau Statut Politique des Habitants de la Roumélie, de l'Asie Mineure, des Iles Méditerranéennes et la Moldovalachie*) presents under its title an emblem of Hercules warding off beasts with his club,[9] and is then followed by a call 'for the laws/freedom – equality – fraternity/and for the fatherland' (Vranoussis 1957b: 681). The map is further embellished with cartouches depicting ancient Greek mythology.

The entity 'Greece,' as represented in this map, is a palimpsest of what was, loosely defined, as 'Greek,' a 'wider Greece,' if not necessarily Greece at a definite point in time. It is also an architectural plan for what will be Greece. It incorporates a number of outcomes of a projected revolution, for the exact terms of the entity to come out of any struggle for liberation differed greatly in the minds of many Greek patriots of the time.[10] The map, with its inclusion of territories as far north as the Danube and as far east as Asia Minor (but not Cyprus), is primarily an imaginary projection that precedes, and seeks the engendering of, such a territory. So which 'Greece' is represented here? The frontispiece announces that it is 'Greece' with its 'many settlements, to the east by Bithynia . . . to the north by . . .

the Carpathian mountains, and the Danube and the Sava rivers, to the west by . . . the Ionian Sea, and to the south by the Libyan Sea.' Snippets of handwritten text superimposed over the area to which they refer describe historical events (Fig. 1.3). There are sketches of battles at Thermopylae, Salamis, Plataea; ancient sanctuaries at Olympia and Delphi; and plans of the ancient theaters of Constantinople and Katasteno. But this depiction of classical Greece and its colonies, which was current in the projections of geographers and Greek Enlightenment thinkers,[11] blends with a Byzantine/Ottoman imaginary that was current among the Phanariots whom Rhigas encountered, and served, in his travels. So, we discover a plan of Constantinople and Rhigas's own home village of Velestino, Thessaly. The outer frames of four sheets bear genealogies and the dates of classical figures, Roman then Byzantine emperors' reigns, and even Sultans. Also included are Rhigas's drawings of both sides of 161 Greek coins, viewed at the Austrian Emperor's Treasury, and depicting Byzantine emperors and ancient Greek mythical figures at the corners of the maps (Vranoussis 1957b: 580–1). In many ways, here we witness the textualization or encyclopedization of *modern* Greece with an inventory of past cultural and historical totems that authorize this enframed area as a closed and homogeneous field of discourse.

The map itself is characteristic of the interest in cartography and its modes in Enlightenment Europe. As de Certeau argues (1984: 120–1), cartography in Europe had originally been conditioned by the itineraries of travelers and pilgrims, and medieval maps, with their rectilinear markings, indicated stops, distances calculated in days and hours, and actions performed on the route and so logged on the map. With the scientific discourse of the fifteenth to the seventeenth centuries, such narrative figures – for example, drawings of ships marking expeditions – were gradually eliminated as the map erased the very practices that produced it. Geometry transformed narratives into abstract places; de Certeau affirms that the map becomes 'a totalizing stage on which elements of diverse origin are brought together to form the tableau of a "state" of geographical knowledge, [it] pushes away into its prehistory or its posterity, as if into the wings, the operations of which it is the result or necessary condition' (de Certeau 1984: 121). More specifically, Rhigas's geography plots space into a palimpsestic historical dynamic typical of a school of 'comparative geography' of the time.[12]

Rhigas's map is not based on first-hand empirical observation. The Hungarian historiographer J. C. von Engel, an acquaintance of Rhigas, tells us that Rhigas traveled extensively in the urban centers of the Greek diaspora, yet he did not visit many of the places that would, in thirty years, constitute the fledgling modern Greek state. Having left Thessaly in his teens, there is no evidence that he ever returned. While Rhigas's maps of Constantinople and Velestino are original, they are exceptions (Dascalakis 1937b: 54).[13] In some details, like a compass shown in the lower right-hand corner, he appropriates a drawing from another Greek

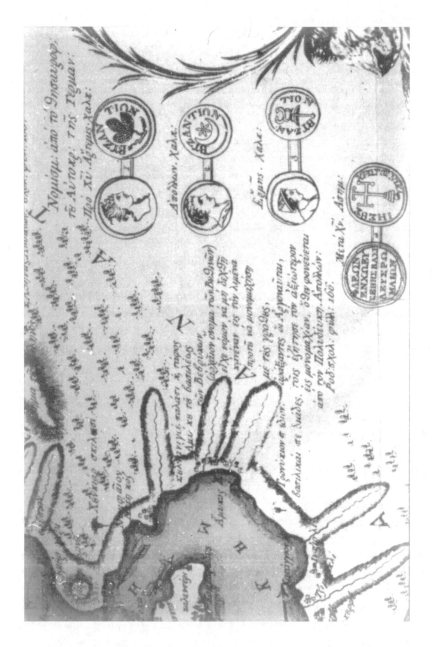

Figure 1.3 Superimposed handwritten text over Map 1

Enlightenment figure, Iosipos Moisiodax and his *Theory of Geography* of 1781 or the work of Meletius the Monk.[14] More frequently, he makes use of and modifies contemporary French maps, which were, at one point in the past, built on the peregrinations of travelers (Dascalakis 1937b: 54).[15] Rhigas's borrowing from French maps marks his broader debt to the narratives of philhellenes and Greeks of the diaspora in the eighteenth century who had been inspired by the Enlight-·enment and the liberal philosophy of the American and French Revolutions. True to its age of production, then, the map erases, or would seem to harbor no oral narratives of, its constitution.

The mapping of national territory in Europe, a veritable 'state' of geographical knowledge, was well underway by this time. The French king had authorized the drawing up of a 182-sheet geometric map of France in 1748; Captain Cook was charting the south Pacific; the Ordinance Survey maps of England were set up in 1791; and only a few years later Napoleon was to declare his wish to map his entire empire in Europe and beyond. Greeks, too, throughout the eighteenth century produced works that mapped out Greek space and its regions, with the most notable example being Daniil Philippides and Gregoris Constantas's *Modern Geography* (1791).[16] Geography was but one of many burgeoning fields in Enlightenment Europe, part of an episteme of 'direct observation.' Like botany and natural history, this 'nomination of the visible,' as Foucault puts it in his *Order of Things*, imposed a Eurocentric structure of knowledge and reason. It went hand in hand with capital and imperialism and, as Mary Louise Pratt and Edward Said have shown in their work, this soon functioned as a justification for the exploitation of colonial peoples and cultures. In colonial contexts, travel writing and enlightenment natural history catalyzed each other to produce a Eurocentered global consciousness. Pratt (1992: 10) has suggested how conventions and writing strategies of such colonial interactions display dynamics of power and appropriation that also characterize northern Europe's claim to the legacy of the Mediterranean at about the same time. In the case of Greece, this appropriation was largely cultural. We have, therefore, the 'rescue' to some and the 'abduction' to Others of marbles and classical symbolic capital. From the pellucid light of Attica, fragments of the past were whisked off to the 'safety,' or 'gloom,' or even 'captivity,' of the museum while, in the opposite direction, the northern tourists sought in the Other disparate social life and a wholeness not perceived 'back home.' The project of modernity implied making the world intelligible as a systematic order through a process of enframing, where the world would be seen as a differentiated and integrated whole. Such wholeness informs the opinion of Rhigas scholar, Apostolos Dascalakis (1937b: 52), when he commends 'the national joy' of Rhigas's appropriations. This estimation, however, dehistoricizes the complex axes of identity that criss-cross both the map and its maker. For, to say as he does that Rhigas's map, true to its age of production, is 'both national and scientific,' understates the implications of its site of production and the complexities inherent in any project of totalization.

If Rhigas's map aspires to a scientific totality which is fleshed out and made tangible, it is also overwhelmed by repeated historical and aesthetic allusions that render it a cultural memorial to the meeting of conflicting discourses. In the European engagement with Greece and the Hellenic Ideal, it was classical philology, aesthetics, the logic of the museum, and travel writing – rather than natural science – that produced the representational strategies that were to condition Greece and Greek self-representation. It is essential that we locate Rhigas's map within these traditions of representation. For the implication of maps in systems of power and knowledge usually carries with it a rhetoric of scientificity which often will suppress the modalities of power embedded in the map. Postcolonial cartographic historiography has undertaken this critique; what follows is a contrapuntal reading of Rhigas's map in the Greek topography of power and knowledge at the end of the eighteenth century.[17]

Winckelmann's Supplements

The emergence of an interest with 'Greece' in Europe arose at the same time as a pre-Romantic shift in sensibility took hold of neoclassical England and Germany. In England, the Dilettanti Society's attack on the Augustan propriety of the Palladian style in architecture by the championing of Doric models began as an oblique attack through aesthetics on the political unassailability of Whig oligarchy (Jenkyns 1980: 4). The society's funding of James Stuart and Nicholas Revett's trip to Greece in 1751, and their subsequent *The Antiquities of Athens, Measured and Delineated* (1762), led to an interest in these erstwhile overlooked Greek forms. Their work galvanized the formation of a body of aesthetic opinion that had already been influenced by David Le Roy's *Les Ruines des plus beaux monuments de la Grèce* (1758), which challenged Adam's elegant eclecticism in architecture. This body of opinion soon organized itself around the Society as artists, historians, and archaeologists united in the cause of Hellenism and to advance their own political aspirations. So successful was this trend, in fact, that Richard Jenkyns notes how, by 1778, the Adam brothers themselves refer to the imitation of the Grecian manner as an ideal standard, adorning the frontispiece of their folio with 'A Student conducted to Minerva, who points to Greece, and Italy as the Countries from whence he must derive the most perfect Knowledge & Taste in elegant Architecture' (Jenkyns 1980: 10–11). Minerva points to Greece, placed directly below Italy, which in turn is below England, tracing the gradual progression of Ideal architectural form northwards to England.

The late-eighteenth-century reaction to Enlightenment progressivism and urbanization led to an exaltation of the 'primitive,' the simple, and the unadorned.

Rousseau's search for a natural humanity had cultivated a malaise with the excesses of civilization, *Europamüde*. In England, urbanization, rural depopulation, and the purchase and consolidation of small landholdings led to a nostalgic yearning for a primal innocence. The redemptive recalling of a state of childhood in such works as Thomas Gray's Horatian or 'lesser' *Ode on a Distant Prospect of Eton College* (1747) or Oliver Goldsmith's evocation of Auburn in his *The Deserted Village* (1770) were all the rage. Anticipating the Romantic mania for childhood, this primitivist strain played into the emergence of a Greek Ideal summed up in Novalis's comment that 'wherever children are there is a Golden Age.' The radical shift from political poetry to this poetry of nostalgia, known as 'the English disease,' led to an interest in landscapes that acted as an objective correlative for melancholy. Certainly, there were enough ruined abbeys in England, many deracinated by the boorish Henry VIII, to go around and a medieval Gothic revival in architecture contributed to this atmosphere. Poets, such as Robert Burns, posed as the 'simple' or 'untutor'd Bard' and a rustic, 'unletter'd Muse' who desires escape society's degradation appears in the most popular elegies of the period – Gray's *Elegy Written in a Country Church-Yard* (1751).

Of course, both activities could be pursued more gloriously in Greece than in England. Nostalgia, loss, a lost childhood, ruins, and the verses of the exemplary 'unletter'd Muse' Homer could all be combined in a trip to Greece. The philologist, archaeologist, and politician Robert Wood was the first to propose that one 'read the *Iliad* and *Odyssey* in the countries where Achilles fought . . . and where Homer sung.' His instantly popular *Essay on Homer* (1767) claimed Homer's ignorance of writing and not only emboldened primitivism and furthered the erosion of Augustan poetics, but also cemented the link between travel and classical poetry: 'the Iliad has new beauties on the banks of the Scamandon plain, with Homer in our hands' (Wood 1827: ii). In short, Greece became the site on which the tensile relationship of discourses at loggerheads in England became negotiated and realigned. In Germany too, philhellenes used Greece to reconfigure aesthetic tenets for sociopedagogic and political purposes. Wood's translated work on Homer fell in the hands of Friedrich August Wolf in Germany. He, in his *Prolegomena ad Homerum* (1795), set about to 'professionalize' Wood's dilettante wanderings in the language of *Altertumswissenschaft*; in time, by way of his working friendship with Wilhelm von Humboldt, the Greeks and Antiquity were placed at the center of *Bildung*, the moral and educational principle behind neohumanist pedagogy of the Prussian Gymnasium and, eventually, the formation of the Prussian state (Vondung 1983).[18] Like Winckelmann's *History of Ancient Art* (1764) before it, Wolf's later scholarship separated Greeks and Romans from other peoples (Wolf 1869). Humboldt and others reflected and built on such exceptionalist thinking:

Our study of Greek history is therefore a matter quite different from our other historical studies. For us the Greeks step out of the circle of history. Even if their destinies belong to the general chain of events, yet in this respect they matter least to us. We fail entirely to recognize our relationship to them if we dare to apply the standards to them which we apply to the rest of world history. Knowledge of the Greeks is not merely pleasant, useful or necessary to us – no, in the Greeks alone we find the ideal of that which we should like to be and produce. If every part of our history enriched us with its human wisdom and human experience, then from the Greeks we take something more than earthly – almost godlike. (Humboldt 1903–36: 188)[19]

As Bernal has argued, the *Bildung* project 'saw in German education and scholarship a third way that broke away from the stagnation of Tory and Whig England while avoiding French radicalism' (Bernal 1987: 317). With the support of the Prussian aristocracy, *Bildung* projected the potential fragmentariness of ethnicity, history, and culture into a totalizing and centralized heterotopia that is the Ideal Greece, one that rewrites the Ancient Ideal, via the disciplines of classics, philology, archaeology and in the terms of German and European modernity.[20] With this in mind, Wolf reworked Wood's peregrinations and commentary on Homer to demonstrate that Homer's voice was not the work of one 'unletter'd muse,' but rather of a group of folk poets who could be configured as the childhood of the Greek, and hence, the European *Volk*.

Stathis Gourgouris has termed the consequences of this classical *Bildung*'s appropriation, and sublimation, of Greek culture as 'no less than an explicit and programmatic *colonization of the ideal*' (1996: 124; original emphasis). For Gourgouris, Greek ideality ensures German historicity; and the colonization of this ideal amounts to an autoscopic project of identity that tends to read a different yet recognizable Other for a definition of the Same. This project expressly excludes and denies the modern Greek any identity. For it is the modern Greek, that 'dirty descendant,' who disturbs this colonization of space for those who read or appropriate Greek landscape as symbolic capital and who then elevate it through the lens of diachrony onto a temporal plane and back to an Ideal Ur-Text.

This would explain a trait shared by the earliest cultivators of the Hellenic Ideal. 'Neither Winckelmann, Lessing, Goethe, Schiller, nor Hölderlin ever saw Greece' (Eisner 1991: 76). Moreover, the majority of Heyne's students on their Grand Tour visited not the sites themselves, but the art galleries and museum collections of Europe. In the late eighteenth century such traveling was made too hazardous by the Napeolonic campaigns. These peregrinations supplemented the work done at the university where catalogues, encyclopedias, paste imitations, and glyptographies, copiously annotated with notes from ancient authors, were key teaching tools: 'engravings, gems, and coins were what those who never left Germany most easily and profitably studied of classical culture' (Constantine 1986: 93). In light of Rhigas's incorporation of numismatics in his maps, he seems a practitioner of just this discipline – one dependent on the logic of the supplement.

Joachim Winckelmann's *Thoughts upon the Imitation of Greek Works in Painting and Sculpture* (1755) was influential in early molding of this Ideal of Greece. His conception of beauty was inextricably linked to the artists of classical Greece and he prioritized Greek art over Etruscan, Egyptian, or Roman art in his *History of Ancient Art* (1764). For many later thinkers, Winckelmann's reading of classical Greek sculpture and art embodied the values of Greek culture as a whole. Herder, Goethe, Schlegel, and Hegel all read his *History*, and it informed their consideration of the debate of Ancients and Moderns. Winckelmann's concern for the statuesque Greek body eventually informed broader sociopolitical issues, such as the theories of racial determinism and, by extension, the expression of national ideals.[21] The universality at the core of Greek culture's appeal informed Winckelmann's reading of an artist's choices: since no human being can be perfectly beautiful, then the artist must pick and choose among subjects and parts in order to approach the Ideal. This Platonist strain makes 'Greek art . . . great because, appealing to the mind rather than merely to the senses, it refers least of any national style to its particular context and is most likely to occasion universal agreement that it is beautiful' (Marchand 1996: 12). He based preference for the Greeks on '[their] innate tendency and desire to rise above matter into the spiritual sphere of conceptions . . . to overcome the hard resistance of matter, and, if possible, to imbue it with life, with soul' (Winckelmann 1873: 320). Like the first founders of religion and poets later exulted by Shelley in his *Defence of Poetry* (1821), Winckelmann adored ideas which excited the imagination to surpass sense. This anti-empiricism has marked the subsequent readings of Winckelmann's theory, even if contemporary scholarship argues that Winckelmann knew that he could not abolish the tensions between art as ideal and art as historical phenomenon. Alex Potts (1994: 2), for instance, has argued that his depiction of the Greek nude as an erotically desirable masculinity is readable as more than a symbolic embodiment of freedom. For the 'stilling of emotion and desire in its perfected marble forms' always mingles with the eruptions of desire and violent conflict. As such, Winckelmann's thought is portrayed as consciously balancing between an ahistorical Enlightenment view of things fixed for all time and a historicizing paradigm attached to modernity. Despite these forceful new readings, spurred on by research in gay studies, the Hellenic Ideal was, in neoclassical times, built on the assertion that Spirit will manifest itself by overcoming and surpassing matter in the 'noble simplicity and calm grandeur' (*eine edle Einfalt und eine stille Grösse*) of a place beyond time and mortality. This was how Winckelmann's theory was received at the time, and it remained for fifty or so years after his death the standard text on the art of antiquity.[22] Winckelmann's vision can thus be said to be marked by an erasure or circumvention, the absence of matter, or an 'ab-sense' (i.e. that which moves away from the sensory). By analogy, this is a fate shared by modern Greeks themselves.

Winckelmann's envisioning of this ideal in his seminal work of 1755 was based on one visit to a collection of statues in Dresden and subsequent studies of Roman plaster-cast copies of the original Hellenistic statues (Constantine 1986: 105). Many of Winckelmann's friends urged him to make the trip to Greece. In a letter by Brandes to Heyne in August 1767, Brandes remarked 'what benefit there would be in it for scholarship and the arts if Winckelmann were to finally go to Greece' (Constantine 1986: 117). However, the nearest he came was a tour to Paestum in Magna Graecia.[23] He did, nonetheless, outdo many of his German counterparts by, at least, venturing outside Germany to live in Rome, which, at that time, could boast much of what might be considered the best in classical art. There, as Papal Antiquary after 1763, he kept a close eye on everything that was collected and discovered. Marchand is right to observe that his momentous project of observation and classification bears the marks of the eighteenth century and rivals similar feats in other fields, as Buffon the naturalist would best exemplify. The taxonomic impulse is built on a Derridean supplementary logic where the object is both a substitute and never quite the same, often indeed more, than the original. In their Grand Tour around Europe, too, young men visited site after site, museum after museum, in search of the taxonomies of this supplementary reality.

Yet since Winckelmann's Ideal is built on the overcoming of matter, it could be argued that his philosophy of the artistic object did not depend on his coming into contact with this reality directly. Such an occurrence, in Winckelmann's terms, would seem improbable in another sense, too. For, the nature of contact is built on a premise of illusion. This is represented quite well in Artemis Leontis's presentation of foreign travelers' reactions to the vision of the Acropolis (Leontis 1995: 40–66). In keeping with the Greek Ideal's character, the Acropolis figures as a space of a quite different realm, a heterotopia, quite outside the normative sociopolitical order. There, the traveler's disbelieving *realization* that this Ideal is real occasions a disbelief and a moment of derealization, in which 'the real from one's relation with the object [is transposed] on the object itself' (Gourgouris 1996: 125).[24] The unreality of the experience in light of the preconception and the evident unreality of the preconception in view of the experience that Gourgouris highlights in his reading of Freud's encounter with the Acropolis in 1936 underscores the paradox. A child of *Bildung* himself, Freud realizes the fantasy of Greece as an object of desire, yet the exposition of the Real as Ideal and the Ideal as Real leads to a necessarily fetishized illusion to be believed in, and placed at the center of one's world. Echoing Leontis's conclusion, we can say, tongue-in-cheek, that the 'current state of Hellas' at the time was, literally, 'of little matter' (Leontis 1995: 53).

Winckelmann's trip to Greece was subsequently made figuratively, in the museum and then by a 'supplement' of sorts, his friend and aristocrat student Baron Johann Hermann von Riedesel, who arrived it Greece in 1768. His *Remarques d'un voyageur moderne au Levant* (1773) was the first such account written by a German. His prior trip to Sicily is covered in correspondence with Winckelmann, yet the Greek trip does not spawn a similar exchange, for Winckelmann is assassinated in Trieste as Riedesel tours the Greek islands. However, Riedesel's observations are clearly influenced by Winckelmann's ideas. Eisner (1991: 76) encapsulates Winck-elmann's influence on Riedesel in Sicily succinctly: 'By the bibliographic act of editing Riedesel's account he toured the island on someone else's feet; just as Riedesel, by following Winckelmann's instructions, saw the place through his friend's learned eyes.' Riedesel was the first of many travelers to put Winckel-mann's theorems to the test of reality. For example, Winckelmann's *Thoughts* had unequivocally located the 'ideal' climate of Greece as the supreme generator of cultural excellence in the ancient Greek world. As a topographical element, the weather may seem an empirical concern; but, for Winckelmann, it is conceived as ideal because its 'moderateness of temperature constituted its superiority, and is regarded as one of the most remote causes of that excellence which art attained among the Greeks' (1873: 286).[25] What happens then when temperate climate undergoes the empirical test of a Riedesel's visit to Greece? Riedesel found the 'happy and creative imagination of the Ancients' incongruent with 'the impetuous north wind that he encountered' there as 'taste, delicacy, and sensibility could not agree with the sudden changes from cold to hot' in the Greek climate (1773: 285– 6). He is at pains to preserve ancient Greek characteristics in the modern Greeks: 'it is true that one comes across original and typical traits that resemble the sketch for a portrait. But they are obscured traits, half-effaced' (1773: 200).[26] Later German nationalists, like Herder and Hölderlin, dealt with this incongruity by claiming that the ancient ideal is legible only in its historic manifestation, and that the reasons for Greek superiority, in terms of individual, local, and national aspects, should be analyzed, so that Germans would not content themselves with a neo-classical *imitatio* of the Greek Ideal, but rather make good taste accessible and reproduce it. The Greek *Geist* would need to be remade, in a unique way. Herder's historicization of Winckelmann's Hellenism located Hellenism's latest glorious manifestation in the German state.[27] Other travelers to Greece, confronted with the same dilemma, incorporated the Ideal into their own modern society.

Romantic Travelers: Reading Greece like an Open Book

The denigration of modern Greece, its material manifestation, is a by-product of attaining the Ideal of Greece. What matters is the subject's imaginative power of suffusing the object of one's gaze with a nobler progeny that could surpass matter and accede to the 'spiritual sphere of conceptions' (Winckelmann 1873: 320). Rhigas's map memorializes mythological and historical events that superimpose themselves on top of the lines of landscape and so elevate her physical matter up into this 'spiritual sphere of conceptions.' Greece, literally, becomes a map to be read, its pieces of land to be read as prose fragments that each in turn memorialize a segment of space. In this, Rhigas's 'landscape-writing' and Riedesel's French travelogue foreshadow the accounts of many subsequent artist visitors to Greece. For many, their trips are bibliophilic. For Lamartine,[28] 'Greece is a book whose beauties have faded because it was read to us before we were able to understand it' (1875: 78). He reads epitaphs and the Laconian mountains in much the same way (Lamartine 1875: 83). For Gautier, the Taygetus mountains, 'rise above the waves as a Georgic verse springs forth from the recesses of memory at the mere sound of the name Taygetus' (Gautier 1881: 35). At his first glimpse of Taygetus, Nerval begins his day like a Homeric song, 'when Young Dawn with her rose-red fingers shone once more!' (Nerval 1964: 92). From every nook and cranny, 'a poem, a temple, a statue, a medal, unequalled in our own civilizations peeks out' (40). This landscape begs for citation. Without it, modern Greece is shadowless, it has no aura. The present only gets in the way. Théophile Gautier's very first impression of Cape Matapa before dusk is conditioned by its 'barbarous name which conceals the ancient name's harmony like a bed of limestone impastes a fine sculpture' (Gautier 1853: 34).[29] Nerval's appreciation of the landscape becomes entangled in orthography: 'I have confused *Syros* with *Scyros*. The fault of a letter *c* means that this pleasing isle has so fallen greatly in my esteem' (Nerval 1964: 117). Sky and sea are still there but the gods have taken flight and, for Lamartine, the denuded landscape brings about a compensatory shift in genre, from poetry to a 'prosaic' state: 'To return to prose, one must confess that Kithyra has retained only its porphyry rocks as saddening to see as simple sandstone rocks' (1875: 93). On the Athenian landscape surrounding the Parthenon's is written only the words: 'C'est fini!' (It is finished!)' (Lamartine 1875: 98).

Though they outdid Winckelmann in reaching Greece, Romantic travelers remained very much in his shadow. Nerval recalls Winckelmann: 'et moi, plus heureux qu'elle [*l'idée* de la Grèce], plus heureux que Winckelmann, qui la rêva toute sa vie' (Nerval 1964: 92, my emphasis). Their gaze on the Other is mediated by an intertextual veil that does not allow for 'faithful' translation and, indeed, even produces white lies. Nerval's claim that he stepped off at Kithyra has been shown to be untrue; his descriptions of archaeological sites and topographical details have been found to be cribs, often word for word, from the guides and travelogues of Demos and Nikolo Stephanopoli, Castellan, and Pausanias (Moullas 1990: 195). According to Riegert, Nerval's guide and the information in his description about Syros is taken straight from Pûckler-Muskau's work of 1836. Chateaubriand, too, claimed that he galloped from Methoni to Athens on horseback, yet his host swears that he came by sea. Gautier's description of the Acropolis in late 1852 is taken in large part from E. Beulé's archeological guide. Eisner (1991: 97) attributes such white lies to 'Chateaubriand's plagiarisms from the travel books he read.' But the foible is more widespread than that.

By the end of the nineteenth century, Gautier reflects on the consequence of a century of Romantic, philhellenic touring: 'In these classical lands, the past is so alive that it leaves hardly any space for the present to survive' (1884: 120). The Greek landscape is so saturated with significance that 'every step' is full of meaning and power (Buzard 1993b:177). Traveling, like viewing an artistic object, allowed the aristocrat, and in time the bourgeois, to escape from the utilitarianism of the everyday at home. As leisure time became more available, travel to places in Europe became an analogy for the emerging bourgeois escape from humdrum reality to the liberating sanctum of Art. The proliferation of museums and libraries in nineteenth-century Europe, packed with the trophies of colonization – 'supplements' of other cultures – brought the activity home to a site where the non-utilitarian and leisurely desires of the bourgeoisie were satisfied. James Buzard (1993a) has shown how nineteenth-century foreign travel readmitted into human life the imaginative and moral energies – the poetry – sacrificed in a Benthamite workaday world. The English traveler's gaze on European otherness produced a touristic 'Europe' that consisted of certain essential features that marked the foreign place from home. Anomic social existence at home was distinguished from the 'cultural' space of wholeness of 'Europe.' The picturesque conventions Buzard describes are adapted by the tourists and sent back in travelogues, diaries, essays, and novels: 'the array of disparate-seeming elements of social life compose a significant whole, each factor of which is in some sense a corrolary of, consubstantial with, implied by, immanent in, all the others' (Herbert 1991: 5). The most incisive comment on the effect of these 'mise en scène' – the price paid – that such image production had in these cultures is to be found in Borges's essay 'The Argentine Writer and Tradition,' wherein 'Gibbon observes that in the Arabian book *par excellence*, in the Koran, there are no camels; I believe if there were any doubt as to the authenticity of the Koran, this absence of camels would be sufficient to prove that it is an Arabian work. Mohammed, as an Arab, was unconcerned; he knew he could be an Arab without camels' (Borges 1969: 181).

It is not long before Greek prose writers of the Greek nineteenth century satirized the distorting effects of Western mediation and the intermediary position of the European as exemplified by the genre of travel narrative. Most savage of all is Iakovos Pitsipios's novel *The Ape Xouth* (1848). It is narrated by a man-turned-ape. But a cast of characters far outdo him in their mimicry and 'aping' of European norms and fashions (which themselves 'ape' Eastern ones). Caught between a Western vision of the Classical Ideal and the impossibility of an unmediated Greek conception of self, the Greek is stranded in no-man's land (O'Neill 2003). What to do but travel himself and relieve, in his turn, his own cultural anxieties on someone else? And so, one of Pitsipios's characters, Ligarides, travels with his uncle eastwards to Smyrna, and then to Alexandria in search of fame. Ligarides consults Western travel accounts of the region in preparation for writing his own travelogue, yet it is not long before he relents and acquiesces to his Armenian hotel manager's offer of 'the edited journal of the tour of Egypt, the one which all the French and English travelers copy from me, each altering just the important names, the dates, and some of the phrases; saying this, he ran and brought the afore-mentioned example of the European Egyptian tourbook' (Pitsipios 1995: 343).

Locating the Gaze

The allusion to classical and mythological personages and events in Rhigas's map claims an immemorial Greek tradition and the recollection of the Byzantine Empire by way of the genealogical tables and assorted coins at a time in Europe when Gibbon was vilifying Byzantium's importance for European civilization. These stories or figures authorize the establishment of this area as a closed and homogeneous field of discourse. This map represents Rhigas's belief in a new polity made up of ethnically and linguistically diverse people, who would be led by the Greeks to rule over an entity supplanting the Ottoman Empire. This central belief appears in Article 34 of his constitution:

> When a single inhabitant of this kingdom suffers injustice, the entire kingdom is injusticed; and again when the kingdom suffers injustice or is under attack, then every citizen suffers injustice and is under attack. It is for this that no-one can say that this country is under attack, yet I don't care because I am at peace in my own country; rather he should say that I am under attack when this country suffers as I am a part of the whole; the Bulgar must stir when the Greek is suffering; and he in return and the both of them for the Albanian and the Vlach. (Vranoussis 1957b: 695)

Due to its predictive nature, Rhigas's map resembles more an architectural plan or drawing than a map. It is a plan for, rather than a map of, what it purports to represent. Marco Frascari's comments on the drawings of fellow architect Carlo Scarpa seem more in keeping with Rhigas's work:

> The lines, the marks on the paper, are the transformation from one system of repres-entation to another. They are a transformation of appropriate signs with a view to the predictive of certain architectural events, that is, on the one hand the phenomena of construction and the transformation by the builders, and on the other hand, the phen-omena of construing and the transformation by the possible users. (Frascari 1984: 30).

Such a plan anticipates social reality even as, in its manner of abstracting space, it imposes an external scientification of 'reality.'

The map's inventory of Classical and Byzantine figures would have been more accessible to foreign philhellenes and Greeks living outside the Ottoman Empire. Foreign support for a Greek Revolution depended on the efforts of just such diaspora merchants and intellectuals, like Rhigas himself, who resided in Vienna, Paris, and Bucharest. It was they who sought to weave the modern Greek story into the master narrative of European identity through allusion to the classical past and its ideals. The map's supposedly universal mode of representation as a set of rhetorical strategies refers back to this European context and locates the map's 'point of presence' *outside* Greece. It is from this vantage point that the Enlightenment scholar Adamantios Koraes, from Paris in his case, expounded his *Memoire sur l'état actuel de la civilization dans la Grèce* (1803), a work which reached primarily fellow members of the Greek diaspora. For, as Iliou points out, only 7 percent of the subscribers to books in Greek resided in areas which were to be initially incorporated in the Greek state.

Yet it is debatable just how much such an image conformed to the self-image of Greeks resident in Ottoman-ruled areas? While the fact that Greek was the language of schooling and culture for large areas of the Balkans may have justified the map's overlay of diachronic Hellenic culture in the present, it is difficult to say whether the classical image as a powerful and integrated ideology held sway with the agrarian populace under Ottoman rule. The historian Paschalis Kitromilides has attempted to recover a history of attitudes from forms of behaviour and symbolic expressions of the 'collective imaginary,' in the late-eighteenth-century Balkans. By close examination of autobiographical sources, Kitromilides (1996) concludes that, prior to the enforcement of mutually exclusive national identities, a common Orthodox, or Balkan, 'mentality' was discernible. Time was defined by an ecclesiastical calendar, space by a geography of faith (shrines), with attendant notions of the supernatural, where notions of sin and repentance were important. This layering of everyday practice is depreciated in the abstracted map. However, it resurfaces in a handful of the map's notations which touch on Rhigas's personal experience. For instance, we note a greater concentration of toponyms in Rhigas's home of Thessaly. And on the bottom left-hand corner of the map a plane representation – the only such representation – of Constantinople (Fig. 1.4).[30] It borrows from Jean Adam Zisla's plan of Constantinople of 1770 and is as a live reconstruction in the present from the perspective 'of one who looks out from *Stavrodromi*, the Crossroads,' in Constantinople. It is, after all, at the Crossroads where, traditionally, acts of transformation take place. An appended quotation laments that:

Looking on the seven-hilled one, the queen of the world,
cry and sigh deeply for her bitter fate.

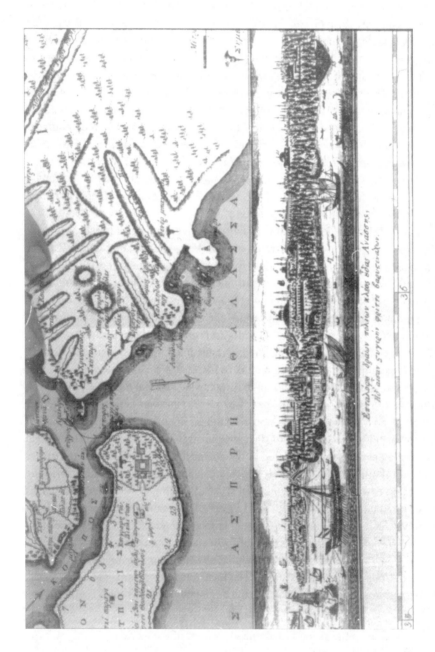

Figure 1.4 Plane representation of Constantinople

This subject position of a viewer's Gaze in present-day Constantinople is immediate and amounts to a conceptualization of space, or chorographic idiom, very different from the external rationalizing Gaze of the Enlightenment perspective found in the rest of the map. The situationist signs of Rhigas's perambulation make malleable the fixity of spaces and bring out the historicity of acts and events, which are to be contrasted to the purer sense of self-identity configured by a viewpoint that locates its gaze outside the map itself. It is precisely this tension in the position of the map's persona(s), or of Rhigas himself, in relation to the different viewpoints and (sub)texts implicit in the map which needs to be further explored. An analysis of this map's chronotopes will show its importance for the future configuration of modern Greek identity construction. For if, as de Certeau asserts (1984: 36), 'to be able to see (far into the distance) is also to be able to predict, to run ahead of time by reading a space,' then in Rhigas's case, this reading is facilitated by ignoring space as it presently is and harking back in time in order to produce the future. By reading Rhigas's map and its intertexts in a manner typical of cultural studies, let us read between the map's lines, to discover its silences and textual repressions in order to explore the workings of power, knowledge, and spatiality at this critical moment in the configuration of Greek identity.

Anarcharsis the Scythian, Rhigas the Vlach, and Alexander the Great

The early part of this chapter sought to locate Rhigas's map in a broader Enlightenment tradition. The map speaks from, and speaks to, this tradition eloquently. But it also betrays one telling 'oral' travel narrative that emerges and speaks out from beneath Rhigas's text. In the major panel of the (fourth) map, Rhigas informs us that his map's panels are conducive to an understanding of the Abbé Barthélemy's work *Travels of Anacharsis the Younger in Greece during the Middle of the Fourth Century before the Christian Era* (1788), the most popular book in France just before the revolution.[31] In fact, Rhigas's map borrows heavily from Barbié de Bocage's maps, which accompanied Barthélemy's work in its third edition. Barthélemy's narrative, a labor of love that took him thirty years, follows a Scythian resident of Athens named Anacharsis as he travels through the provinces of Alexander the Great's time. A travel narrative copiously footnoted from classical authors and divers texts, it presents a readable account of festivals, modes of government, the arts, and details of everyday life. Barthélemy cites two reasons for his fictional choices: first, the age chosen is still linked to the great age of Pericles – the people Anacharsis converses with recall the likes of Sophocles and Socrates; second, 'Anacharsis was a witness to the revolution which changed the face of Greece, and which, some time later, destroyed the empire of the Persians'

(Barthélemy 1825: 122–3). Clearly, Rhigas is making the parallel claim that the modern Greeks still remember the same cast of august characters, and that his chief witness will oversee the destruction of the Ottoman Empire. The time of Alexander's crushing of the Asian horde recurs in the map's frontispiece wherein Rhigas depicts Hercules chasing away an Amazon woman on a horse (Fig. 1.5). In his key for symbols, Hercules's club stands for 'Greek strength' and the Amazon's axe as 'Persian [and, by extension, Ottoman] strength' (Vranoussis 1957a: 574).

In this way, Rhigas displaces his own unembarked-upon trip to another text, one that focuses on the ancient world. Barthélemy's narrator, a distanced observer, reports on practices of a bygone era and footnotes each popularizing description with its classical textual source at the foot of each page. Quite literally, his 'citation' functions precisely as a 'calling forth,' in the classical sense (cf. Gumpert 2001). Rhigas's identification with Barthélemy's text foregrounds the European taste for reading classical texts in Greece, and reading modern Greece as a classical text. Furthermore, by superimposing familiar Lacedemonians and Messenians – read as respectably Greek – over the many distant peoples of his time, the notion of difference is domesticated and rendered more palatable to European taste.

But why does Rhigas select Barthélemy's tale? Why a Scythian and why Anacharsis? The Scythians were a nomadic people of Persian stock, whom Greeks characterized as barbarians. Indeed, Neal Ascherson suggests that 'civilization' and

Figure 1.5 Insert of Hercules chasing off Asiatic horde (from Map 4)

'barbarism' were 'twins gestated and born in the Greek but above all in the Athenian imagination' (1995: 49). This 'ruthless mental dynasty' imposed itself in the Western mind; most notably for our case, in the early modern period, the Scyths' reputed barbarism in the eyes of the classical Greeks led Western European Christians to liken the Ottoman Turks to Scyths. Nowadays, the Ossetians of the central Caucasus trace their heritage back to these peoples. Scythia, land of *eschatia* and *eremia*, a frontier and a deserted one at that, marked a space at the borders of the then known inhabited world. However, its borders were indistinct and the Scythians in their turn were characterized by their nomadism. After all, they left central Asia in the eighth to seventh centuries BC to settle in the Caucasus and then moved ceaselessly: 'For them, the unquestionable division between Asia and Europe does not really exist; they pass from one continent to the other without ever fully realizing what they are doing (in their pursuit of the Cimmerians, they take the wrong route). They fall between two spaces' (Hartog 1987: 32–3).

The Athenian of Antiquity, whose status depended so greatly on his autochthonous birth, found in the Scythian the potent symbol of his opposite, the nomad with no attachment anywhere. Aeschylus and Euripides demonized them, though others, like the much-traveled Herodotus, were less judgmental. Scythian chieftains intermarried with Greeks at the time of Herodotus. And Anacharsis, mentioned by Herodotus as a Scythian of princely rank, traveled widely and was known in Athens. He became acquainted with Solon and it was thought that his travels had brought him much wisdom. Consequently, he was even honored with the Athenian franchise (Hartog 1987: 64). Rhigas was keen to emphasize how both the Scythian race and Anacharsis integrated themselves into a Greek cultural hegemony and civilization at the time of Alexander. In Barthélemy's tale, Anacharsis returns to Scythia from his travels, and it is from there that he sets out his travelogue. However, Anarcharsis's fate, as described in Book IV of Herodotus's *Histories*, casts Anacharsis's assimilation in another light as his cultural wanderings are portrayed as transgressive and bring about his tragic end. Specifically, upon his return home, Anacharsis proceeds to fulfil a vow made to a foreign goddess at a festival at Cyzicus as a mark of gratitude for his return. For his loyalty to her, he is shot dead by Saulius, Anacharsis's brother and the King of Scythia. He is killed by his own for not observing his own Scythian customs and his own gods. Seth Bernadete (1999: 118) points out that both Anacharsis here, and elsewhere Scyles, the second Scythian of the *Histories*, worship foreign deities and meet their death for it: 'both forget their own customs only to practice cults that make them forget themselves; but the Scythians take their revenge by not remembering Anacharsis.' The Scythians, like the Egyptians, after all, 'avoid extremely the adoption of foreign customs.'[32] To forget the existence of barriers would seem a perilous affair.

Clearly, Rhigas's displacement of such assimilative and/or transgressive parables of identity onto submerged narratives makes us wonder about the impulses behind these (sub)texts. Little is known of Rhigas's ethnic background. And quite how 'ethnicity' on the whole constructed itself at this time is a complex affair; especially as other categories of self-ascription, such as a 'local' identity must have been very strong. The author of the best documented work on Rhigas, Leandros Vranoussis, assumes that he was from a Greek family of longtime residents of Velestino. But the accounts that attest to this were written so long after his death and imbued so heavily with national and mythical overtones that a modicum of circumspection is advised. More recently, Exarchos has argued forcefully for Rhigas's Vlach identification over a plain-dweller Greek or Γραικός – Rhigas's predilection for 'Vlach dress' (*vestiario valacco*) is a case in point.[33] His hometown's name, Velestino, points inconclusively to a Slavic past; and, most significantly, Kitromilides (1992: 18), citing Wace and Thompson's *The Nomads of the Balkans* (1914), asserts that the township was a major settlement of Koutsovlachs, to which transhumant shepherds descended during the winter months from their summer pasturages on the Pindus mountains. Indeed, Kitomilides speculates that Rhigas's later relationship with Moisiodax, a key Greek Enlightenment figure mentioned earlier, may have originated from not only ideological but also ethnic affinity, since Moisiodax was from a settlement of Vlach-speaking tribes from the south of the Danube in the area of ancient Moesia. (Incidentally, Rhigas's only reference to a contemporary Greek alive is in Map 12, and this to acknowledge that the town of Cernavoda is the birthplace of Moisiodax.)[34] These Vlachs of the Danube spoke the same language as the nomads known as Koutsovlachs in the southern Balkans who, most likely, lived in Rhigas's village. The ethnographic record certainly shows that Rhigas could have identified as both Vlach and Greek, and even preferred one over another in different circumstances.[35] The Koutsovlach contribution to Greek independence is well attested (Papazisis 1976). But does Rhigas's account of ethnic assimilation of Scythians into a Greek master culture hide his own personal anxiety of a miscegenated background that he believes can be 'overcome' by enlightened scholarship and allegiance to an Hellenic cultural ideal and identity? The irony lies in the fact that Rhigas's attempt to compensate for his ambivalence toward his own difference as a Hellenized Vlach by recourse to Anacharsis is precisely the means by which that difference is inadvertently made manifest and constitutively at issue within the map.[36]

Given this sensitivity to the question of difference, does this reading of Rhigas as the Young Anacharsis give an indication as to how he conceived of Greek identity? To answer this, we must look at some of his other texts, his *Constitution for the Greek Democracy* and his *Rights of Man* (Velestinlis 1994b). For his *Constitution* is drawn up for the successor people to the Greeks (λαός απόγονος), who reside in the areas of the map. Article 4 of the Constitution sets out some very accommodating rules for becoming Greek; Article 7 categorizes 'Greeks, Bulgars, Albanians, Vlachs, Armenians, Turks, and every other race' as potential citizens of this state. Rhigas respects citizens 'beyond race and dialect,' and in the third article of his *Rights of Man*, he states that all men, 'Christian and Turks are equal.' Such stipulations are obscured, though not quite contradicted elsewhere in his work. In his *Thourios*, or *War Song*, Rhigas calls on his people to unite behind the Cross three times; yet, he proposes a unitary state that respects the individual and communal rights of *all* its people(s),[37] and where citizens are free to cast a direct vote. Even if it may not present the federal paradigm that contemporary politicians make of it, it seeks to preserve the integrity of groups while building up the nature of a state.

Culture is called upon to achieving this balance. In matters of language, Rhigas stipulates in Article 22 of his *Rights of Man* that all citizens, male and female, in every last village should benefit from an education. In the towns, French and Italian should be taught while Greek will be mandatory at all levels, for Article 53 of his Constitution states explicitly that 'simple Greek shall be the official language of the state as it is the easiest and best understood language by all the people.' Rhigas's premise by way of Isocrates that 'Greeks will be called all those who partake of Greek culture' in his new state was meant to further the circulation of Enlightenment ideals and classical norms.

But this is also a time of change. The lingering question that arises is how motivated, or innocent, was Rhigas's conception of culture? To what degree, that is, is Rhigas able to balance between maintaining state cohesion and preserving internal difference, especially without discrete borders?[38] Clearly few among the diaspora could then envisage the new state bearing any resemblance to the nation-state of 1830. For they lived with the idea of the orthodox *millet*, or the Byzantine Empire, ideas which were, at their core, polyethnic. But is this a map of Greece as a polyethnic state, a reemergent Byzantine Empire? Or might Rhigas have envisaged, however sketchily, this Greek state in more nation-statist terms? Would it be possible that the map shows a polyethnic entity being framed, controlled, measured, and assimilated into a map of 'Greece'? Does the map offer the first glimpse of an epistemic change? Rhigas may have been as much caught in a transitional moment in history as he was in the interstices of his Greek-Orthodox-Vlach-Ottoman identity. It is even tempting to speculate how certain national sentiments might not have been far from his grasp, consciously or unconsciously. First, his long tenure in Vienna and Bucharest might have made him aware of trends in German thought and the growing discourse about the nation-state and the uniqueness of national character. The *Bildung* project was to channel potential fragmentariness of different ethnicities, histories, and cultures into a totalizing and centralized heterotopia, Ancient Greece. In time, Winckelmann's Hellenism would be historicized by thinkers such as Herder who would pinpoint Hellenism's latest and most glorious manifestation in the German state. Culture, in this form, is transformative, politicized, and has much on its mind. It was only a decade or so earlier that the Phanariot

Dimitrios Katartzis (1730–1807) had proposed Greek as the language of culture and education for the entire peninsula in strident terms. Second, Rhigas's tacit omission of Serbs in any mention of the people of his *Greek Democracy* is a source of some suspicion, especially as the Serbs were at that time the best placed of the other Balkan peoples to seek liberation. Kordatos has made just this point. For, in Rhigas's last work, *The Patriotic Hymn*, published posthumously in Corfu in early 1798, Rhigas solely addresses the Greeks and makes no mention of any other peoples. Is this a hymn for Greek consumption or should we read more into his privileging of the Greeks? Such questions linger, but offer no easy or conclusive answers. It is a source of some dissatisfaction that historians' well-intentioned and productive attempt to deconstruct the nationalist ideologization of Greek and Balkan historiography of the last two centuries has not equally sought to subtly mine the differentiating lines of identity in the region prior to the nineteenth century. The combination of local, guild, and ethnic (for want of a better word) modes of stratification and differentiation have been glossed over in the formulation of a commonwealth of religion-based identity for pre-Enlightenment populations of the Balkans.

Rhigas's revolutionary papers were intercepted by Austrian authorities and he was arrested in Trieste in December 1797. Like Winckelmann, he comes unstuck in Trieste. The map and his translation into Greek of Barthélemy's *Anacharsis* are rudely interrupted. The latter's first three volumes were translated by a Greek Viennese scholar, Georgios Sakellarios, and Rhigas translated Chapters 35–9 of the original that cover Anacharsis's peregrinations in parts of Turkish-occupied Greece, specifically in his native Thessaly and Velestino. In the footnotes to these chapters, Rhigas interposes his own regional knowledge into Barthélemy's original citations as well as provides topographical and anecdotal information. As in the map, Rhigas relates his own experiences *through* another's narrative, at one remove from his own personal identification with place. Only the first and fourth volume were out by the time of his arrest. Sakellarios's volumes were sent to the famous Poulios press and the fourth, by Ventotis and Rhigas, to the Picheler press of Venice.

Many have argued that his martyrdom in failure proved more useful to the Greek cause than if he had made it to Greece, since there was the very real possibility 'the major sources of his work, the Byzantine tradition, the classical Greek ideals and the modern, Western ideas of revolution were difficult to integrate . . . a national uprising would [have] prove[n] incompatible . . . with the hopes of cooperation among the peoples of the Balkans' (Augustinos 1977: 9; Mango 1973: 57). Rhigas's eventual contact with his plan's 'possible users' – the autochthonous Greeks themselves – might have constituted its most serious flaw. Others have predicted a more favorable scenario: Napoleon's generals had by 1797 reached western Greece, and the signing of the Treaty of Campoformio in October gave him a foothold in Greek-speaking lands. The papers intercepted by the Austrian authorities were destined for Preveza, western Greece. An audience with the all-conquering Emperor would have instigated an uprising that would captivate the imagination of the French and European philhellenes and would have drawn them into a conflict that promised the liberation of the Hellenic spirit in its land of origin.[39] But this was not to be. Nevertheless, Rhigas's impulse did make its way to Greece and helped to cultivate Greek revolutionary consciousness, eventually.[40] Rhigas himself did not. Handed over to the Turks in Belgrade, Rhigas attempted suicide, failed, was tortured and killed. He consequently never did travel to Greece to implement the second part of his plan. Like many philhellenes and diaspora figures, Rhigas never did set foot in Greece, which was fitting for one whose image of the place bore many characteristics of a European discourse located and produced *outside* the Greek mainland.

Ab-sense and Self-colonization

Let us name the mode of perceiving Greece and the Greeks described thus far as a 'discourse of ab-sense.' 'Ab-sense' denied presence, immediacy, and specificity to the modern Greeks. In this sense, it is non-sensical too. Its abstraction from materiality meant that the Greeks' customs, beliefs, and actions became despecified and gave up their delimited significance for more portentous semantic status. Such codes of connotation render actions generalized and not instantially meaningful. The discourse of ab-sense works on its object by a cenotaphic logic. The term is adapted from Benedict Anderson's observation that reverence accorded monuments, such as cenotaphs and tombs of Unknown Soldiers, depends on the fact that the former are empty and no one is inside; and, in the latter, no-one cares who, *specifically*, is inside. These quintessentially national forms are 'nonetheless saturated with ghostly national imaginings' (Anderson 1991: 19). Like a cenotaph, modern Greece's cenotaphic signification evacuates its differentiated sign. Neo-hellenic identity undergoes a similar process in the wake of Europe's eulogy of the Ancient Greek Ideal: Greek modernity is crowded out by such imaginings. The diminution of the body within the monument is effected by nationalist discourse's facility to plot the contingent body onto a temporal axis that leads back to an immemorial past or an eternal future, but avoids the present.[41] As in Rhigas's map, horizontal space is reworked by the logic of an ordering, vertical temporal order along whose axis the contours of space and experience are reorganized.

Michael Herzfeld (1991) has focused on a distinction between 'monumental' and 'social' time in his study of the way that the Greek state's Conservation Department has tried to impose the monumental time of the state on the buildings and homes of modern-day Rethimnos, Crete. Such an external interpretation of space, since the 'policy' is laid down by the centralized powers-that-be in Athens, conflicts with the 'social' and familial time of the city's inhabitants. In his exploration of the tensions, ironies, and negotiations at the interface between these two conceptions of time and place, Herzfeld manages to show how the struggle over the two conceptions of time, and the 'future of the past,' amounts unavoidably to a struggle over present identity. Monumental time functions by appropriating familiar space and transforming it into monument by way of a retrospective taxonomic integration into a detemporalized past and desocialized present. This reductive and macroscopic narrative framework functions culturally rather than socially, even though its local imposition effects social consequences. The opposing counter-archaeology of 'social' time wherein events are unpredictable, with distinct, often ephemeral, meanings continually intrudes on 'monumental' time's operation and often appropriates for itself, by creative use, the very controlling forces that 'monumental' time seeks to order it by (Herzfeld 1991: 1–16). The dialectic described here is influenced, as is Anderson, by Walter Benjamin's essay 'Theses on the Philosophy of History.' In it, Benjamin describes two diametrically opposed philosophies of history: the one, an elitist, hegemonic 'historicism' and the second, an historical materialism, analogous to the kernel of Herzfeld's 'social' time, which arrests a specific moment out of the rush of 'empty, homogeneous time' and seeks to brush history 'against the grain.' It so disrupts its continuum and brings forth the depository of true historical knowledge: the oppressed class, the individual, the monad, and 'the time of the now,' for 'History is the subject of a structure whose site is not homogeneous, empty time, but time filled by the presence of the now [*Jetztzeit*]' (Benjamin 1997: 261).

The discourse of 'ab-sense' resembles these models. The monumental time of the diaspora/philhellene discourse suppresses 'social' time, the lifeworld of the autochthonous Greeks. In these terms, Rhigas Velestinlis's map balances between these two modes as it monumentalizes and textualizes even as it socializes and resists. It agon-izes over this fault line in Greek identity even as it seeks to liberate it. The rhetorical situation of surveillance has produced other binaries that have encapsulated this tension throughout Greek history. 'Hellene' and 'Romios' is the most cited. This polarity pits two models of Greek identity that derive from a Classical and Byzantine-Turkish model. It pits a normative and idealized version of Greek identity, with Classical Greece as understood in Western historiography up against a local and practical history of Greek experience. Herzfeld (1987) has associated this 'disemia' with anthropological frameworks of cognition that distinguish between an extroverted collective self-presentation and an introspective collective self-knowledge in a wide range of cultural modes of self-presentation, in language, architecture, culture etc.[42] Treated as a flexible instrument of (self) positioning, critics plot principles of rules/strategies; state/local power and action along this Hellene–Romios axis and valorize one pole or the other in the hope of moving themselves, or Greeks as a whole, in or out of Europe; in or out of the West etc. Herzfeld's own ethnography champions a difference, which he admits resides in the Romios pole (Herzfeld 1987: 94). The political scientist Nikiphoros Diamandouros, by contrast, would far prefer Greek political culture modeled on the other pole in his model of European 'modernizers' and nativist 'underdogs.'[43]

These persistent binaries can not be understood outside a set of power relations, the gazes and interests of insiders and outsiders. 'Disemia is a play of cultural contradictions produced by conditional independence – an independence, cultural or political, that is paradoxically enjoyed only on the sufferance of some powerful entity' (Herzfeld 1987: 123). From the beginning of the period covered in this book this power differential is plotted in geopolitical terms (Chapter 1); in divisions between diaspora Greeks and locals (Chapter 2); in matters of gender (Chapter 3); in class differences that become ideological differences (Chapters 4–6), in the inequalities of global exchange from metropoles to margins in periods of cultural hegemony, colonization (Chapter 7) and in globalization (Chapter 8).

A comparison to other conditional forms of independence, or other forms of subjected consciousness, is illuminating. Colonialism offers a number of suggestive parallels. Of course, Greek society was not colonized in the traditional political sense. But dynamics of power can still be discerned despite differences in the historical specificities. Since the early 1990s, such analogues have informed theorizations of the Balkans and, more particularly, discussions of Western discourse on the Balkans, so-called 'balkanism.' Fleming (2000: 1223) has distinguished between different versions of colonialist analogies: focus on 'metaphoric colon-ialism,' 'surrogate colonialism,' 'colonialism of the mind,' and a 'colonialism of the sort with which Said is concerned.' The colonization of the Greek ideal discussed in this chapter engages the first and third of these schools and, with signs of orient-alism, works to reinforce a form of cultural, intellectual, and political dependence. To ride the analogy a little further, it is worth relating that, politically, nationalism in colonial contexts often created a state patronage that spawned an authoritarian clientelism placed in the hands of Western-educated, urban nationalists.[44] Greece's transition from imperial Ottoman rule to nation-statism differs considerably from the transition of African nations from colonialism to state rule. But the decisive contribution of a Western-educated elite is common to both. In subaltern contexts, at the time of decolonization, this 'class' becomes the 'national bourgeoisie' that fashions 'national identities' 'by methods that [were unable to] break formally with the system of representation that offered them an episteme in the previous dispens-ation: a "national buffer" between the ruler and the ruled' (Spivak 1989: 274).

The power differential at the heart of a state under surveillance offers further parallels. The venerable W. E. B. Du Bois's concept of African American 'double consciousness' in the United States describes the African American's 'sense of always looking at oneself through the eyes of others' (Du Bois 1989: 3). For Du

Bois, the African American self-regard was always conditioned in reference to a reflected image sought in the gaze of white Americans. The refracted *public* image of the African American was always distorted by this 'veil' and remained distinct from the particularity of his or her own self-image. The racialized nature of the analogy to Du Bois and the souls of black folk plays out in an ironic inversion in the Greek example. For the Enlightenment Western concern for resuscitating dead white people through classical Greeks obliged modern Greeks to assume a 'white man's burden' of their own, the racial impurity of not living up to the West's image of them. This double consciousness finds a parallel in Greek culture in a text about contemporary to Du Bois's *The Souls of Black Folk* (1903). Argyris Ephtaliotis's discussion of the nomination Hellene/Romios in his *History of Romiossyni* (1901) prefers *Romios* and *Romiossyni* as terms of self-definition over the classicizing *Hellene* on the grounds that the former is closer to the identity of the people themselves. Ephtaliotis's text embodies the culmination of a century's work of counter-archaeology. The Romeic ensemble constitutes an alternative to Western Hellenism by embracing the populism of the demotic language, by championing the historian Paparrighopoulos's insertion of an Orthodox-Byzantium strand into the narrative continuum of the Greek past, and by encouraging a novelistic encounter with indigenous reality. This contestation of archaeologies provoked a vigorous cultural debate, and it expressed itself at the beginning of the twentieth century partly in class terms (see Chapter 4).[45]

This dialectic has already been engaged by two diaspora colleagues. Artemis Leontis's *Topographies of Hellenism* (1995) and Stathis Gourgouris's *Dream Nation* (1996) have made significant contributions to understanding the effects of the tension between Western Hellenism and Neohellenism. Leontis studies how 'Neohellenism's topographies align the physical expanse of the homeland with the discursive field of a shared heritage or, better, common ground' (Leontis 1995: 11). Like my own book, the physical homeland, the Helladic space, is her point of departure. The establishment of that new state in no way stifled the workings of the cultural and political imaginary. In the irredentist climate of the nineteenth century, Greeks expanded their state and sought the incorporation of all ethnic Greeks within those state boundaries. This goal was expressed in the so-called *Megali Idea*, or Great Idea. And the alignments continue in the Imaginary even when the *Megali Idea* had seen its day (as Chapter 5 will demonstrate). In exploring these *topoi*, Leontis exposes how politics and culture are linked as is 'Neohellenism's contrapuntal relation with Western Hellenism.' *Contrapuntal* is a word that was given a new lease of life by Edward Said in his *Culture and Imperialism* (1993), a couple of years prior to the publication of Leontis's book. In describing the modes of reading the texts that structured the colonial experience, Said promoted the practice of contrapuntal reading. A longtime music critic, Said used this notion derived from a musical counterpoint that refers to the musical technique of combining two or more melodic lines in such a way that they establish a harmonic relationship while retaining their linear individuality. Consequently the reader was to look back into the cultural archive and 'reread it not univocally but contrapuntally, with a simultaneous awareness both of the metropolitan history that is narrated and of those other histories against which (and together with which) the dominating discourse acts' (Said 1993: 51). This reading of imperialism and resistance to it includes 'what was once forcibly excluded.' In so doing, Said's approach took some of the edge from the perceived polarities of his previous, enormously influential *Orientalism* (1978) by striking a tone of reconciliation, by making porous the line that demarcates the colonizer from the colonized. Even so, some, like Eric Hobsbawm, were not convinced of the greater nuance derived.

In examining the analogous line that marks Hellenism from Neohellenism, and the ocean in-between, Leontis is as conciliatory as Said in her negotiation of the line that divides aggressors/victims:

> The most difficult [challenge] has been how to describe the interaction between Western Hellenism and Neohellenism without reducing this to a simple pattern of dominance and resistance, on the one hand, or genesis and imitation, on the other. I have tried to avoid ascribing blame for unequal power relations . . . where an excess of power has led to intervention, the marshals of a new order are not necessarily aggressors, and the recipients of what may be an inspiring blow are not necessarily victims. The most powerful empires and states have their civilizing ideals; they may also have a few good women and men who seek to understand the civility of seemingly 'uncivil subjects.' Conversely the smallest minority or ethnic group may adopt with a vengeance another civilization's ideals, which it then adapts to serve its own interests. (Leontis 1995: 12–13)

Mention of 'uncivil subjects' and the 'ethnic group' reminds us of the colonial context underlying Said's original definition. Of course, the analogous 'ethnic group' in the Greek case, the Greeks themselves, are relearning and (re)adapting their *own* civilization's ideals, after a perceived rupture or break in their tradition. The poet George Seferis's genealogy of a Greek Hellenism, as opposed to a Western Hellenism, marks the anxiety over the distinction. The Hellenic seed, he wrote in a celebrated essay of 1938, had migrated from Antiquity, reappeared in the Renaissance in Europe (where it was kept under the guardianship of the West), and then returned to Greece as 'Western Hellenism'. How was a Greek to extrapolate from this, a *Greek* Hellenism?[46]

Undoubtedly, Western Hellenism contributed greatly to the Greeks winning their independence. It would seem a mark of ingratitude then to insist on preserving the colonial quality of the analogy, and 'the unequal power relations' it elicits, when examining the relation of Western Hellenism and Neohellenism. Yet

Gourgouris does just this in his *Dream Nation*. He applies the dynamics of colonization not to address the relationship of the contemporary Greeks to their longtime ruler, the Ottoman Empire,[47] but rather to appraise the way that Europe invested symbolically in the Hellenic world during the Enlightenment and to consider the effects this had for constituting what was 'forcibly excluded.' By so doing, Gourgouris endows the interface with no less nuance but more tension than does Leontis. Paradigmatically, in analyzing the phenomenon of philhellenism – its repertoire of tropes, symbols, and objectifications – Gourgouris compares it to a similar cultural ensemble constitutive of colonization, i.e. orientalism. The affinities derived from this comparison make the love of 'a few good women and men' from 'the most powerful empires and states' that much more complex, their feelings and motivations in need of untangling (and my own Chapter 7 will seek to do just this as regards modern philhellenism).

Given my description of the institutional profile of modern Greek studies earlier in this book's introduction, it should come as no surprise that my cultural poetics partakes of Gourgouris's approach to colonization and seeks out its effects down to the present. I do so strategically and contrapuntally, as I have just done with Rhigas's map, in order to supply the writer of the *Kathimerini* article that opened this book the basis for a *modern* alternative. As Greeks are, and become, ever more European, we must consider a paradigm beyond the traditional dualities, and their effective and masterful Seferian synthesis, to chart a new order and practice. Working back to the dawn of the nation-state, this study considers how the processes of space and (self) colonization inculcated a poetics of insecurity in the citizens of that new nation-state as well as produced resistances to it. For the Greeks 'self-colonization' is born out of their internalization of the lessons of Hellenism, which they perceive as both foreign and native, both Other and the Same.[48] Roger Just has described the honor and shame of this predicament quite well:

> Lost glory is a common fate; so too is a rueful nostalgia for it or a grandiloquent attempt to reclaim it. The peculiarity of Greece's case is not that everyone else appears to have appropriated it; not that foreign kings and foreign architects should have redesigned her capital but that, as foreigners, they should have kindly done so in an Hellenic style that had securely become 'their' style. Is Greece thus the borrower or lender? the local source of global knowledge or its tardy imitator? (Just 1995: 289)

This may not be Fanonian colonialism. But it produces a double bind. If the Greeks claim Greek civilization as exclusively their own, they are seen as parochial. If they assert Greek culture as global culture, they are arrogant and insensitive to other cultures.

In the pages that follow, we shall consider the experience of the 'possible users' of Rhigas's architectural plan. This genealogy of a 'presence of the now' is neither 'true' nor 'ontological,' and its expression is mediated at the very moment of its textualization. An autonomous self-conception of modern Greek identity devoid of the political and cultural values and categories of Europe is impossible, since the fashioning of neohellenic identity, its textualized determination, occurs at the same time as Western penetration. Moreover, the colonization of a culture that is within Europe and even considered to be Europe's point of origin complicates any totalizing notions of 'Europe' at this time. Parts of the 'West' and 'Europe' are themselves Other and subject to colonizations, as anyone in the Balkans need not be reminded.[49] Within this paradigm, Greeks are not weak agents violated by discourse from without. The implication is that they have wielded their own self-colonization all along – they are both their own 'aggressors' and 'victims.' This cultural poetics hopes to emplot a dialectic between discourses in a historicized manner sensitive to this performative style of modern Greece. For the mass ritual of Neohellenism's cenotaphic figuration has corroded the body that it sought to enable into being. In Anderson's terms, the corpse within the Tomb of the Unknown Soldier retains its anonymity only as long as the ritual's participants accept the formalization of a particular brand of death.[50] Without the aesthetic and abstract coordinates of the nation, or at least against them, the corpse will stand for the excess that resists the representational orders of national formalization. This will leave us with a corpus of Neohellenism's life and death irreducible to the logics of ab-sense.

Notes

1. The episode appears in the very opening of Jean Baudrillard, *Simulations* (New York: Semiotext(e), 1983). For a consideration of map and territory in the postmodern context, see Tennenhouse (1990).
2. Few copies of all twelve sheets exist, though there is one in the Greek Parliament, the Greek Foreign Ministry, the National Historical Museum and the Gennadeion Library in Athens, and in the Romanian Academy of Bucharest.
3. For an accessible intellectual biography of Rhigas Velestinlis, see Woodhouse (1995).
4. In the first tale from the *School for the Dainty Lovers*, the protagonist, Jacquot, arrives in Paris for the first time at the age of 16. Elsewhere in the tale, this is contradicted (Velestinlis 1994a: 27) as Jacquot is said to have arrived at the age of 10. Given that the tales are translations of Rétif de la Bretonne's *Contemporaines*, in which the protagonist had arrived in Paris 'at the age of

ten,' the variation in the very first sentence of the introduction has been interpreted as Rhigas's way of pointing to his own adolescent trip to Constantinople in his sixteenth year, in 1774 (Velestinlis 1994a: 2, fn. 1).

5. By calling him Pherraios, they transformed his name, as he did many of the towns in his map, by using their ancient Greek name and thus privileging the same nationalist discourse of origin and genealogical continuity. Indeed, he employs the name Phera (επιπεδογραφία της Φέρας, λεγομένης τώρα Βελεστίνος) in his small map of his home town. There have been many nationalist biographical descriptions of Rhigas's life and work, e.g. Lambrou (1892); Amantos (1930); Mayiakos (1935); Michalopoulos (1930); Vranoussis (1957a); and others by Kordatos (1931) and Vournas (1956). On the Vlach origins of the name Rhigas, see Exarchos (1998: 18–20, 47–53).

6. In his later trial, Rhigas's examining magistrate was aware that the songs were imitations (*Nachahmung*) of French caramagnoles and the German *Freut euch des Lebens* (Vranoussis 1957b: 740).

7. Upon his arrest, two revolutionary songs and a '*ganz demokratischer Katechismus*' were found. These catechisms were popularizing revolutionary pamphlets that used the accepted Catholic religious format of questions and answers to inform citizens of the Revolution's principles, their own rights and duties. Some well-known French catechisms are: M. Mirabeau, *Catéchisme de la Constitution, à l'usage des habitants de la campagne, par un député de l'Assemblé Nationale* (Paris, 1791) and J. A. Florens, *La Constitution française expliquée pour les habitants de la campagne, ou Entretiens familiers sur les principaux articles de la Constitution française* (Paris, 1791). Just before Rhigas's arrest, a catechism distributed by a Hungarian professor, Ignatius Martinovic, in 1794 as a manifesto for his 'Pest' revolutionary group had caused quite a stir in Vienna.

8. Vranoussis's edition of Rhigas's *Constitution* is presented with an article-by-article facing text of the French Constitution of 1793. Vranoussis (1957b:679) claims that it is only in two articles that Rhigas departs from the 1793 Constitution to use Articles 39 and 62 of the 1795 French Constitution

9. In 1805, Athanassios Parios affirms that Rhigas's manifesto of October or November 1797 was still in circulation and was referred to as 'Hercules's Club' (Vranoussis 1957b:677).

10. Skopetea (1988) begins with a short survey of divergent opinions held by prominent diaspora Greeks of what they imagined would constitute the geographical expanse of the new kingdom.

11. Tolias (2001) relates the geographical expanse of Rhigas's map with Nicolaos Sophianos's map of 1543 (published in Rome, 1552), which depicts 'the Wider Greek World.' This 'wider Greece' appears in the work of Moisiodax and in Gazis's adaptation of Rhigas's map (1800).

12. Barbié de Bocage, a leading light of this school, had produced a map of Greece and was a great influence on Rhigas (Tolias 2001). See Barbié de Bocage (1822) for his works; more on his map for *The Young Anacharsis* later (Barbié de Bocage 1806).

13. There is no evidence that Rhigas visited areas of the Greek state-to-be in preparation for his *Map of Greece*. Camariano makes the undocumented assertion that Rhigas toured Ottoman-controlled Greece for six years in preparation for his maps (Cameriano n.d: 223). While biographies of Rhigas mention accounts of trips he undertook in the 1790s, there is nowhere mention of trips to the Greek mainland or the islands.

14. For an account of Moisiodax's place in Enlightenment thought, see Kitromilides (1992).

15. The map borrows from Guillaume de Lisle's map of 1700, which used travelogues by Wheler and Tournefort (see Tolias 1998).

16. For a readable summary of some of the key works, see Peckham (2001: 9–17).

17. On the theoretical grounding for such critiques, see Derek Gregory, *Geographical Imaginations* (Cambridge, MA and Oxford: Blackwell, 1994); J. Brian Hartley, 'Maps, Knowledge and Power.' In Denis Cosgrove and Stephen Daniels (eds.), *The Iconography of Landscape* (Cambridge: Cambridge University Press, 1988), pp. 277–312; also on geography's Eurocentrism, see David Stoddart, *On Geography and its History* (Cambridge, MA and Oxford: Blackwell, 1986), esp. pp. 28–40. The cartographic metaphor has been taken up in many postcolonial novels: I cite, by way of celebrated examples, Michael Ondaatje's *The English Patient* (1992) and Mahasweta Devi's *Imagined Maps* (1995). Spivak presents the latter's concerns in a preface tailored to current postcolonial theory. For a specific discussion of this postcolonial contrapuntal form of mapping, see Huggan (1989).

18. For a full account of the way that Wolf's critical method fused with Wilhelm von Humboldt's neohumanist ideals to become insitutionalized in the pedagogical practices of the Prussian Gymnasium, see Marchand (1996: Chapter 2); and Wolf (1985) himself. Wolf (1759–1824) was a recalcitrant student of Christian Gottlob Heyne at Göttingen. According to Heyne's son-in-law and biographer, A. H. L. Heeren, Wood's book was in Heyne's estimation the most important book he reviewed among the 7,000 or so reviews he wrote in Göttingen. As Constantine oberves, 'if we may believe Heeren, the way Homer was taught to students at the University of Göttingen was markedly affected by Heyne's reading of Wood's book' (Constantine 1986: 87). An insistence on geography and classical archaeology was passed on to students such as Wolf, and Heyne's view that knowledge of the landscape could enrich a reading of the Classics informed details of the many trips made by scholars in search of the real site of Troy (Constantine 1986: 88–92).

19. The translation here is taken from M. Cowan, *An Anthology of the Writings of Wilhelm von Humboldt: Humanist without Portfolio* (Detroit, MI: Wayne State University Press, 1963), 79.

20. On heterotopia, see Foucault's 'Of Other Spaces,' *Diacritics* 16 (Spring 1986): 22–7.

21. Leoussi (1998) traces the impact of Greek aesthetic ideals, and especially bodily types, as a medium for the expression of aspects of British and French citizenship and national identity in the nineteenth century.

22. For a presentation of scholarly editions for this period, see Potts (1994: 256–7, fn. 4).

23. For details of Winckelmann's hesitation over a trip to Greece, see Constantine (1986: Chapters 4 and 5).

24. Both Gourgouris (1996: 124–8) and Leontis (1995: 48–9) analyze Freud's 'A Disturbance on Memory on the Acropolis.' In *The Standard Edition of the Complete Psychological Works of Sigmund Freud*, Vol. 22 (1932–6). Edited and translated by James Strachey (London: Hogarth Press and Institute of Psycho-Analysis), pp. 239–48.

25. For Winckelmann, the climate encouraged exercise in the nude and this, in turn, allowed artists to study and copy these fine bodies for sculpture and painting.

26. Foreign travelers in earlier centuries had also made such comparisons, see Droullia (1980), especially observations of Pierre Belon du Mans's trip in 1546–49. For overviews of the period covered in this chapter, see also Olga Augustinos, *French Odysseys: Greece in French Travel Literature from the Renaissance to the Romantic Era* (Baltimore, MD and London: Johns Hopkins University Press, 1994); F. M. Tsigakou, *The Rediscovery of Greece: Travelers and Painters of the Romantic Era* (London: Thames and Hudson, 1981); Helen Angelomatis-Tsougarakis, *The Eve of the Greek Revival: British Travelers' Perceptions of Early Nineteenth-Century Greece* (London: Routledge, 1990). For earlier travelers, see Ruth Macrides (ed.), *Travel in the Byzantine World: Papers from the 34th Symposium of Byzantine Studies.* Publication for Society for the Promotion of Byzantine Studies 10 (Aldershot, Hants and Burlington, VT: Ashgate, 2002).

27. For an account of the debate between Winckelmann and his detractors, see Henry Caraway Hatfield, *Winckelmann and his German Critics, 1755–1781* (Morningside Heights, NY: King's Crown Press, 1943).

28. Lamartine leaves Marseilles on 14 March 1832. He arrives in Navarino on 1 August 1832. His trip in Greece takes in Aegina, Salamis, and Athens. He leaves for the east on August 1823. In Greece, Lamartine has a reputation for his Turkish sympathies: he deemed foreign support for Greece at the Battle of Navarino a political faux-pas and his eight volume *Histoire de la Turquie*

(1854–55) led to poetic rebuttals and attacks by Karasoutsas, Soutsos, and others. Lamartine's travelogue was published in four volumes in 1835 under the title *Souvenirs, impressions, pensées et paysages, pendant un voyage en Orient.* It received its present title, *Voyage en Orient*, in 1841.

29. Théophile Gautier leaves for Constantinople, via Syra, in late 1851. He stays in Constantinople for two months and then passes through Athens on his return. He disembarks in Piraeus on 1 September 1852.

30. Rhigas's diagram of the Seraglio is an accurate representation of a 1785 plan by Aubert and Tardieu (Laios 1960: 234).

31. The book was republished frequently after the French Revolution. See Emile Egger, *L'Hellénisme en France*, Vol. 2 (Paris: Didier, 1869); Maurice Badolle, *L'Abbé Jean-Jacques Barthélemy (1716–1795) et l'hellénisme en France dans la seconde moitié du XVIIIe siècle* (Paris: n.d., 227–331).

32. Herodotus IV.76. On the Egyptians, see Herodotus II. 91. In his reading of this event, Hartog (1987: 82) grants more significance to the specific cult that Anacharsis embraces, the cult of Cybele. Considered as Greek, 'Anacharsis is in truth killed not for having introduced foreign *nomoi*, but for having become "effeminate" or, rather, for having lost his virility among the Greeks and for seeking to teach this "effeminate disease": so Cybele is Greek, and the Greeks are women.'

33. See Exarchos (1998: 54–62). Rhigas also favored wearing a helmet and Turkish robe once in a while (Woodhouse 1995: 59–61).

34. These Vlachs were identified with the Dacians of the principalities of Wallachia and Moldavia to the north of the Danube, who were Romanian-speaking, and were known to the Greeks as Moesiodacians.

35. Herzfeld provides examples of the ethnographic contestation over the identity of Koutsovlachs (1986: 72–4).

36. Anecdotally, we might speculate how Vranoussis's own Koutsovlach origins motivated his indefatigable research on Rhigas.

37. See Articles 3, 7, and 34 of Rhigas's *Rights of Man* as well as Articles 2 and 4 of his *Constitution* (Velestinlis 1994b).

38. Botzaris (1962) finds Rhigas's proposal highly questionable because a state without borders would not make the plan viable.

39. Rhigas's later work maintains that revolution will come about only by the efforts of those enslaved and under Ottoman rule (Pantazopoulos n.d.: 46–7)

40. Dascalakis (1937b: 55) refers anecdotally to French travelers who came across the map. Another indication is that though there is only one complete copy at the Romanian Academy in Bucharest, there are many copies all over the Balkans, and particularly in the monastery collections of Greece (Camariano n.d.: 224; Dascalakis 1937b: 55).

41. Anderson is aware that the terms he ascribes to nationalist discourse make it seem a secular version of religious discourse. He is careful to note that he neither claims that nationalism 'supersedes' religion nor that one followed on the talons of the other; rather he proposes that 'nationalism has to be understood by aligning it, not with self-consciously held political ideologies, but with the large cultural systems that preceded it, out of which – as well as against which – it came into being' (Anderson 1991: 19, fn. 4).

42. These are listed in a more playful vein in Patrick Leigh Fermor's table of Hellenic/Romaic traits of Greek life. He also notes the complementarity of the two concepts (Fermor 1966: 96–147).

43. Diamandouros (1993: 1–26; 2000).

44. Davidson (1992) has carried out just such a critique and has devoted two chapters to a survey of comparable post- World War I developments in the Balkans.

45. Leading figures of the time, e.g. Palamas, Xenopoulos, Psycharis, Krumbacher, Hadzidakis and N. G. Politis, partook in the debate. Kyriakidou-Nestoros (1975: 221–38) gives a readable account of it. On Romiossyni, see Mantouvala (1983).

46. See Seferis's seminal essay 'Dialogue on Poetry,' translated by Rex Warner in *On the Greek Style* (Seferis 1967). I have discussed the implications of this essay in an article on the politics of George Seferis's criticism (Calotychos 1990).

47. Peter Mackridge misreads Gourgouris's work in just this manner. See his review in the journal *Nations and Nationalism* 4 (4), (1998): 593–4.

48. The term 'self-colonization' has to my knowledge already been used in a couple of instances. In an interesting discussion about the dualities of Greek culture, Chouliaras (1993: 113) promises a future paper on 'Self-Colonization and Pseudohegemony in (Modern) Greek Culture' in a footnote. It remains forthcoming. The poet Nanos Valorites has used the term to allude to a similar predicament among modern Greek artists in an unpublished article sent to me by the poet and entitled 'Modern Greek Literature after the War.' Valaorites likens Greece's orientalization to that of a postcolonial nation, ever submitting itself in a national condition of inferiority similar to 'subaltern submission.'

49. See Todorova (1995); on the attendant concept of 'nesting orientalisms' within Yugoslavia, as projected by one Balkan ethnic group against another, see the work of Bakić-Hayden (1992). See also Slavoj Žižek (1999) in the *London Review of Books* during the Kosovo conflict on how the Balkans may be more a victim of colonization than Africa.

50. My own consideration of death and its relation to Anderson's crucial metaphor of Tombs of Unknown Soldiers benefited from an evocative essay by Marc Redfield, 'Imagi-Nation: The Imagined Community and the Aesthetics of

Mourning,' in a special issue of *Diacritics* 29 (4), (Winter 1999): 58–83. This issue, dedicated to Anderson's work, was edited by Pheng Cheah and Jonathan Culler and was titled *Grounds of Comparison: Around the Work of Benedict Anderson.*

–2–

Centralization

Land, Citizenship and Poetry in a Nation-state

> De la musique avant toute chose
> et pour cela préfère l'impair
> plus vague et plus soluble dans l'air
> sans rien en lui qui pèse et qui pose.

Verlaine, *Art Poétique*

A Greek scholar, who upon meeting the renowned klepht Nikotsaras around 1800 addressed him by the name Achilles, was met with the reply: 'What rubbish are you talking about? Who is this Achilles? Did he by any chance shoot down a lot of enemies with his gun?' (Kakridis 1963: 252).[1] The 'real community' of the Greeks bore little resemblance to the one envisioned in Rhigas's 'imagined community.' The Greek peasant, or *rayah*,[2] must have seemed strange to the classically trained Greek of the diaspora or philhellene. Regardless, such anecdotes cannot form the basis for a portrait of Greek peasant psychology at the time. Hobsbawm's trenchant comment that 'Herder's thought about the *Volk* cannot be used as evidence for the thoughts of the Westphalian peasantry' forewarns against establishing the thinking of those who rarely formulated thoughts on public matters and who never wrote them down (Hobsbawm 1990: 48). Furthermore, members of a nation are not characterized by a single reciprocal relationship played out in an identical place in society (Hroch 1985: 12). Phanariots, high clergy, low clergy, island ship-owners, *kotsabazides*, *kapetanaioi*, *rayades*, heterochthons, all stood for very different material interests and their respective participation, prevarication, or eventual involvement in the Greek War of Independence reflect these.[3]

For centuries, particularly in the latter stages of *Tourkokratia*, the Greek peasant's material interests had been arbitrated by the intermediary archons. The archons – otherwise primates, *proestoi*, or *kotzabasides* – acted as intermediaries between the local Ottoman officials or pashas and the Greek peasantry. They were Christian and wielded power beyond their local community. They collected taxes, including the capitation tax or *haraç*. Though unlike Western feudalist lords, their power was not based on any real claim to property or title, and there was certainly no guaranteed permanence for them.[4] The precariousness of their position made them skilled at positioning themselves flexibly to the changing whims of their Ottoman superiors and the people they were representing (Tsoucalas 1981: 283–4). After all, Ottoman rule had granted communities a large degree of autonomy in religion and language and did not hold to any uniform means of administration. This economic structure, along with the rugged terrain and non-existent infrastructure, engendered sectionalism and regionalism. The intrapersonal politics that had served these communities, the election of community elders or *demogerontes* and the influence of agrarian oligarchies, had developed a relation to power that distinguishes itself from that prevalent in Western societies. Exploitative to varying degrees and from region to region, the archons were the *rayah*'s only visible means of access to an alien and inaccessible centralized power – the Ottoman authorities. Guild and associational forms of political representation, as well as expressions of social differentiation (among classes of a body politic), were unknown in Greek affairs (Tsoucalas 1981: 295). In the West, these intermediary organs (be they guilds, trade unions, an aristocracy, or a clergy) made power more diffuse and had to be dismantled before the citizen could move to more egalitarian and direct representation; in Greece, representation was much more direct. This structure has largely been invoked to explain Greeks' perennial difficulty, or reticence, in recognizing behavior based on abstract concepts independent of personal relationships (Pollis 1958: 22; Tsoucalas 1991: 12). Consequently, the contemporary anti-authoritarian liberal belief in the self-regulation of production and distribution of values in a free market that works on its own and around depersonalized legal norms and political rights that protect the notion of individual freedom has clashed with traditional Greek moral standards and practices centered not on the individual but on the group. For the Greek, a '"system of rights" and "duties" is not conceived as referring to the relation of the axiomatically isolated and self-centered individual to a fictional global society, but concerns the reciprocal egalitarian or authoritarian relations between members of a group . . . each of which develops its proper form of symbolic exchange' (Tsoucalas 1991: 14).

Whatever the continuing validity of such theories today, the ways of nationalism at the beginning of the nineteenth century certainly did enter into a complex dialogue with the forms of Greek village lifeworld and organization. To a great extent, the one molded the other. For example, the first national assembly held in December 1821 in Epidaurus was a tribute to national unity even as members came 'as delegates of their regional governments, not as representatives of constituent parts of a unified state' (Petropoulos 1968: 20). This chapter examines how this complex dialogue, and the interests it represents, conditions the negotiation of important issues of land, citizenship, and poetry. Very different groups evoke the depersonalized forms of the nation for the furtherance of their particularistic interests and often this manipulation occurs at the interface, and by the interpenetration, of a set of structuring dichotomies, such as autochthon/heterochthon, insider/outsider, regional/national, oral/written. The first two sections are not meant to be exhaustive in scope, but they refer to scholarship on land and citizenship so as to argue the conjuncture, or better, the coincidence,[5] of political and administrative practice with developments in the cultural realm. The third section focuses on notions of the poet and poetry by focusing on the first National Poet, Dionysios Solomos, in order to draw out those practices and traditions that have been repressed by an excessive concern for his national credentials.

Land

Monumental discourse envisions a strategic rationalization of space that distinguishes its own place of power and will in relation to that environment. In Rhigas's map, this place was the diaspora's position outside the area framed, whence the observer views praxis as spectacle. Once the War of Independence had begun, and heterochthons had settled in the new Greek state, their Gaze was internalized. The need to assume a centralized locus of power which, again, might order experience and present it in a readable form back to the Great Powers remained. Indeed, heterochthons and autochthons alike were keenly aware that the Greek revolt, from the moment of its inception in the conservative times of the Concert of Europe, was *under surveillance* and that they needed to differentiate it from revolts that had challenged legitimacy and social hierarchy elsewhere, in Naples and Spain in 1820. When the archons disputed with the heterochthon leader Ypsilantis, Vamvas and fifty other European-schooled Greeks over the role of commissar, the chieftain, Colocotronis, urged his irregulars in Vervena to quell internal squabbling, for: 'if we kill the archons the kings will say that these people have not risen up for freedom, but to kill among themselves, and that they are bad people, Carbonari, and then the Kings will help the Turks . . . Don't let your heads get so swollen!'[6]

Greece was 'marked from the start not merely with the usual production of self-images for internal consumption, but also with the grave task of producing the right set of images for export' (Gourgouris 1996: 138). The heterochthons had the diplomatic pedigree for this kind of communication. By concentrating power in a centralized state they could further their interests, and the interests of the Great Powers, by preserving class stratification while containing, competing local forces. This heterochthon strategy was not lost on the autochthonous Greeks who were also alive to the new rhetorical context and would soon creatively reuse monumental discourse to forward their own interests. The question of the land vacated by those fleeing was a pressing issue and proved to be an early battleground for this rhetorical fight. For any move to satisfy the peasants' one real material demand – the ownership of their own land – would undoubtedly alienate the Great Powers.[7] In an agricultural economy, the land constituted the country's most valuable material asset and had to be used to finance the war, since it was the Greeks' only collateral to back bond issues in Europe. The archons, the Christian landowning class, understood this. In the first regional council meetings of 1821, they issued directives to local committees proclaiming that the Christian cultivators of Ottoman lands should continue paying taxes at the established rates and hand these over to the Greek cause.[8] The Kaltetzi regional meeting in Stemnitsa did not address the question of the ownership of the lands nor did it decree the transfer of these 'national estates' (εθνικές γαίες) to their cultivators. It also left undisturbed the private property rights of Christian landholders as defined by Ottoman law. The archons used the 'national cause' to preserve the status quo in the first tax law of 1822. What the nationalist prohibition of land sale under the Second National Assembly concealed was the archons' willingness to use a 'national cause' to 'freeze' factional claims to the land since no one clan trusted any other to dispose of the land. In the mean time, they retained their local privileges and their lucrative tax-farming practices and reveled in administrative improprieties. A governmental committee's investigation in 1827 that found national accounts completely falsified through illegal sales, forgeries, and illicit seizures testified to the success of this policy (McGrew 1976: 127). But the heterochthons also went along with this 'freeze' for it kept ownership of the lands out of the archons' hands, and so obstructed the creation of a landowning class. The temporary nationalization of the lands in order to increase national revenue would benefit future heterochthon trading activities.

As for the peasants who were working lands vacated by their fleeing Muslim overlords, they initially still 'much preferred to see that arrangement continued for the time being, even with the discriminatory tax obligation, than to risk the loss of their farms to a governing clique of primates and outlanders.'[9] McGrew argues that 'if the Greek peasants had been given the Ottoman lands they cultivated as private holdings free of share-cropping obligations, the cultivators of the large Greek-owned farms would certainly have protested their distinctly less favorable circumstances' (McGrew 1976: 126). This would have provoked great unrest. So, the peasants remained cultivators of land still not their own and were no better off. In fact, Vergopoulos (1975: 104–9) considers them to have been worse off. For, whereas under the Ottomans, the peasants did not own the land, they were at least entitled to its usufruct (*tasarruf*), which could be inherited by a descendant (Vacalopoulos 1976: 1–30). Now, the peasants not only had to pay up their tithe and 30 percent to 45 percent of their gross product for their life-tenancy of the national lands to the state, but they did so while no longer holding any right of possession to the land. The peasants found themselves to be landless not out of any fault of the prior Ottoman status quo, but precisely because of the radical abolishment of that system. In the final analysis, the national lands were not a remnant of the precapitalist Ottoman system, but an invention of the Germano-Romaic law of the new state.

Citizenship

The Greek state established by the Treaty of London in 1830 bore little resemblance to Rhigas's map. 'The cramped body of Hellenism lay uneasily upon the Procrustean bed which diplomacy had cynically constituted for it' (Miller 1978: 28). Concurrently, the Great Powers influenced foreign clienteles that mobilized kin groups in Greece from 1825 onwards. Clan leaders, Phanariots, and military chieftains all sought to win the support of the Great Powers. The drawing up of constitutions; the offer of a crown to a European royal family; the avoidance of class conflict or anything that would bring about the charge of 'Jacobinism' were meant to placate all sides. Foreign protectors, promising benevolent fiscal supervision of Greek loan repayment, exercised direct political intervention in Greek affairs, and Greeks in turn played one power against the other.[10]

This surveillance, the continual exchange with external centers of power for domestic profit, led to a transformation in the ruling factions. Petropoulos has outlined a three-phase process by which the initial class divisions of the groups of 1821–3 (oligarchs/chieftains and peasants) were supplanted by factions realigned along sectional lines (Roumeli/Mani/Peloponnese/Islands) which, finally between 1825 and 1827, became identified according to one of three parties: 'English,' 'French,' and 'Russian.' The establishment of foreign clienteles took shape as the Greek Revolution was running into military and financial trouble (particularly at the time of Ibrahim's intervention with 10,000 Egyptian soldiers on behalf of the Ottomans). All the protagonists, whether autochthon or heterochthon, turned toward Europe. Europe, in turn, sought to buoy up its influence by seeking to cancel out factionalism for the consolidation of a centralized power, in the hands of an individual, who could focus the centrifugal elements of power. Capitalizing on Codrington's naval victory over the Ottomans at Navarino, the British under Canning sought for a 'foreigner' to take charge. Ioannis Capodistrias, a Corfiot with a Russian diplomatic career, seemed to fit the bill, but steered a course not between factions but beyond them by establishing a unitary, bureaucratic state on Western models. His low estimation of the existing oligarchic groups, be they archons or Phanariots, led him to circumvent democratic power by suspending the provisions of the Constitution of Troezene of May 1827 that had been passed before his arrival in Greece. He transferred power to his presidency in the name of the People, while empowering a consultative body of twenty-seven members (the *panhellenion*), made up primarily of heterochthons (Skopetea 1988: 49; Jelavich 1976: 159). Capodistrias's creation of a state polity ran concurrently with the development of an heterochthon-led bureaucracy that sought to establish a centralized tax system, a civil code, a court system, orphanages, a national mint, a national bank, and a reorganized army.[11] Capodistrias's underestimation of local power was fatal. The ill-feeling that centralization provoked among the oligarchical interests peaked and he was shot by the recalcitrant Mavromichalis clan of Mani in 1831. As Tsoucalas has pointed out, no charismatic leader, even though they existed (the chieftain Colocotronis, for instance), could draw in the dispersed nodes of power within the state. Two heterochthons had tried – Ipsilantis had been quickly weakened and Capodistrias was murdered.

The 'foreigner' Capodistrias was replaced by a foreigner one further step removed – King Otto of Bavaria.[12] The new independent Greek monarchical state, under guarantee of the three powers and backed by a Bavarian force of 3,500 men and foreign loans of 60 million francs, became 'a Bavarian protectorate under the suzerain control implicit in the ambiguous "guarantee" of the three powers' (Kaltchas in Petropoulos 1968: 145). This unpopular absolute monarchy intensified processes of centralization and conscripted the services of more heterochthon diplomats and secretaries, thus further alienating the autochthons. Indicatively, there were only three autochthon ministers (and fourteen heterochthons) in Otto's first council. The archons resented centralized power and characterized it as Bavarian and heterochthon. An enraged notable, Zaimis, complained: 'It's easy for us to chase away the bavarian, but will the Phanariots and the rest of the heterochthons follow?' (Tsoucalas 1981: 286). The Bavarians exercised power absolutely and though the predominantly heterochthon ministers exercised little effective power, the autochthon parties managed to direct popular interest 'not on issues that divided specific and well-defined interests within the state, but rather issues on which the bulk of the nation was on the one side and foreigners, heterochthons, Westernized Greeks, or the king on the other' (Petropoulos 1968: 479). The revolt against Otto's abuse of monarchical power in September of 1843 was inevitable.

The borders of the new nation-state in 1830 had not extended far enough to include all Greek-speaking peoples nor, in fact, all those who had fought in the revolution for independence. Full rights to the Greek earth were extended, on paper, to immigrants to the new state fleeing Ottoman recriminations.[13] Yet, analysis of Greek constitutions and oaths from 1823 to 1864 show a gradual change in fundamental terms: 'The race [γένος] is supplanted gradually, rights are replaced by duties, as the fatherland [έθνος] . . . is reified steadily so that from an abstract concept it winds up meaning nothing more, and nothing less, than the Greek state [κράτος]' (Skopetea 1988: 32). Who was Greek, after all? The issue would surface in the National Assembly at the end of January 1844 in a discussion over the requirements to work in the civil service and the definition of a 'Greek citizen.' Autochthons perceived themselves excluded from this body by the heterochthons and they petitioned to deprive heterochthons of citizenship. Seven different amendments were debated, one even required twenty years' residency as a prerequisite for citizenship. The more extreme amendments were struck down in favor of a more moderate version that, after the charismatic intervention of heterochthons Mavrokordatos, Kolettis, and Metaxas, defined 'the citizen' broadly to include natives of the liberated provinces and anyone who had taken up arms in the revolution and had settled in Greece by 1827. All others were to be removed from office, with the exception of those in the navy, army, consular service, or teaching profession. Other favorable additions meant that only a handful of heterochthons were to be removed from office,[14] and all that was accomplished was that a rift between the two groups was solemnized.[15]

It is certainly no coincidence that at an assembly held only a week before this assembly, on 14 January 1844, Prime Minister Kolettis, an heterochthon leader of the French party, proclaimed the *Megali Idea*. Like many a Greek leader before and after him,[16] Kolettis employed the diversionary tactic of positing a foreign policy aspiration to which all could be drawn to allegiance. He used it in a timely fashion. The supranational *Megali Idea*, expounded in splendid indeterminacy, made domestic opponents seem enemies of the national interest. Clientelism and patronage were to be left out of this assembly, since they worked against the greater good. Better that they be deployed on the international scene where the sentiments of the three Great Powers could be gauged than have to deal with an undifferentiated Greek public, access to which was effected by means incommensurate to representational governance. The heterochthons were also personally more comfortable with the international scene and could better influence the King by working through the Great Powers' representatives (Psomiades 1976: 152–3). As a result, Kolettis had revitalized the heterochthon role by articulating an irredentist goal that would fuel the Romantic project of a Hellenism unfinished, measurable only by the assimilation of all Greek populations into an ever-growing Helladic state.

This survival tactic only preserved a political and administrative system that turned its back on internal political practice. 'The *Megali Idea* . . . relegated all other goals to subordinate roles . . . The fulfillment of the *Megali Idea* became the essential prerequisite for the satisfaction of all other needs, for the solution of all other problems' (Pollis 1958: 130). This allowed the autochthons to continue their hold on the clientelistic networks of their respective regions, outside the chamber. However, they went further by appropriating Western constitutional practice to legitimize their own power networks. The autochthons' proposal of universal male suffrage in the Second National Assembly of 1844 'to all those with property in the country . . . engaged in a profession or independent trade,' though not instituted until 1864, secured their power base. Autochthon advancement in the civil service and the nurturing of an indigenous elite from the newly formed University of Athens (which would replace diaspora centers as the intellectual nursery of Hellenism), saw to it that autochthon interests were served. Autochthon advancement in a *katharevousa* bureaucracy at about the same time as autochthons fought for the vote underscores their willingness to wield the exclusory rights to an artificial language of state that excluded the masses' voices from the social and economic order while simultaneously claiming the right of speaking for them. Institutionalization mattered over effective practice. Patronage entailed bestowing favors, not necessarily speaking for clients. Alas, 'there were no subsidiary organizations, apart from that of patronage, capable of conveying the sentiments of the rank and file to the party leaders' (Petropoulos 1968: 504). Indeed, the creation of such subsidiary organizations was further delayed by Greek diaspora entrepreneurship, which originated from outside the Greek state and had little organic connection with native social bodies or activity. The effect was to further bolster the formalist and rootless brand of Greek institutional life. The totalizing rhetoric of nation-statism had reduced praxis to form.

Poetry

Print Culture and National Centralization

Nationalization and modernization went hand in hand with a reorientation in the dissemination of print and knowledge within the borders of the new state. Rhigas's inscription of a Greek national consciousness needs to be viewed in the context of a broader Enlightenment project of textualization: grammarians, lexicographers, folklorists, and publicists formulated the revolutionary and national experience in a growing print market. The brothers Markides-Poulios produced the first Greek newspaper on 31 December 1790 in Vienna.[17] It circulated among 15,000 Habsburg and Ottoman citizens of Greek descent for a period of eight years and was, in fact, produced at the brothers' printing presses, which also served as host to many of Rhigas's revolutionary writings. It was this very collaboration with Rhigas that obliged the Habsburgs to close down the press soon after Rhigas's execution.

However, the start had been made and other newspapers and literary periodicals were to follow: Anthimos Gazis's *Ermis o Logios* in Vienna (1811–21); Demetrios Alexandrides's *Ellinikos Tilegrafos* (1812–36); also *Kalliope* (Vienna, 1819–21), *Museion* (Paris 1819), *Melissa* (Paris 1819–21) etc.[18] The circulation of these papers among the reading classes meant that distribution was centered among families of some power in the diaspora: favored merchants of the Habsburg Empire, scholars, and ecclesiastics. This imagined community drawn together by print-language was a restricted one. But the journals facilitated the production of a consciousness configured and consumed by a group with common interests. In England, formation of a bourgeois public space in print culture, in such early-eighteenth-century periodicals as *The Tatler* or *The Spectator*, sought to deal the mercantile class into the modern world by ordaining that Taste was no longer an aristocratic ethos, but an acquirable commodity. Subscribers bought the periodical and then engaged themselves in acquiring Taste lest they be considered vulgar. The financial trope used to present this goal – the increase of one's 'stock of sense' – betrays the mercantile constituency served by the development of 'public opinion.'

Greece did not see its first newspaper published on Greek soil until the beginning of the armed revolutionary struggle. The first paper, Σάλπιγξ Ελληνική, or *Greek Bugle*, published by Theoklitos Farmakides, in Kalamata in August 1821, paved the way for three more such hand-written papers at Galaxeidi, Vrachori (Agrinio), and Messolonghi. But only in 1824, and with the technical know-how of Swiss philhellene I. Mayer, did a printed paper appear in Messolonghi. Others in Athens and Hydra heralded the Revolution, and two of them – *Telegrafo Greco* and *Abeille Grecque* – were published in foreign languages and shipped to Europe (Koumarianou 1971, 1991). Beyond their revolutionary goals, their intent was also pedagogical and cultural, supportive of democratic ideals and institutions for the new state. A number of editors clashed with Capodistrias when he suspended the state's constitution in 1828. Despite their opposition and even the formation of the first newspaper of the Opposition in Greece in March of 1831, a vote taken on 26 April 1831 and implemented, with Otto's signature, two years later, severely curbed the freedoms of the press (Koumarianou 1991). Tsoucalas argues that this censorship may have seemed strict, but it was not really enforced during Otto's reign since the newspapers continued to systematically publish attacks against cabinet ministers and the King himself. This early resistance to the 'letter of the law' and the law of the letter in Greece continues right down to our day.

The introduction of writing changes the psychological, economic, and institutional order of a society (Kittay and Godzich 1987). The availability of print among the social elite led to the hierarchization of the written language and a valorization of its code as well as the gradual assimilation of the oral into the ideology of the written (e.g. anthologies of folksongs). As in most Western societies, statehood in Greece engendered a tension between a centralized, hegemonic culture and segmented subcultures, which tried to further 'a dream of disalienation, of reconciling person to person, and person to the world' (Zumthor 1990: 14). The press, for instance, remained exclusive and published in purist Greek. Vernacularization was a long way off and this meant that the heterochthon '*grapho-kratia*' that constituted the Greek bureaucratic class remained both producers and consumers of much of this capitalization of print. Greeks may not have had to overcome a sacral language (e.g. the change from Latin to a vernacular elsewhere in Europe), but the learned language, wielded by a privileged constituency, was exclusionary in its own way.

At the time of the revolution, Greek society appears to have been at a stage between 'mixed orality' and 'secondary orality,' where the former marks an 'orality coexisting with writing where the influence of the written is still external to it, as well as partial and retarded,' and the latter where 'orality is recomposed based on writing where writing determines the values of voice both in usage and in the imaginary sphere' (Zumthor 1990: 25). The importance attached to literacy was a familiar part of experience even for the illiterate. Mackridge has termed this the quality of a 'para-literate' society (quoted in Holton 1990: 188). A 'written' culture had survived in Turkish-occupied Greece. A small readership is testified to in the small Orthodox schools as well as educational centers of Athos and Ioannina or the neo-Aristotelian school of Thessaloniki that Iosipos Moisiodax studied at in 1752 (Kitromilides 1992: 21–2). A complex interaction of 'literary' texts and 'popular' culture is also attested to in the passage of texts of the Cretan Renaissance dramas into the folk tradition of Turkish-occupied Greece as well as in chapbooks.[19] The illiterate peasantry during *Tourkokratia* recognized a certain authority in the written by way of their reception of Gospel readings in church and in church schools. The Gospel represented the seat of this Truth, and it was transmitted in popularizing sermons and parables. The famous Kosmas the Aetolian (1714–79) preached his sermons in the countryside extemporaneously, and his ministries were not read from a written text but by way of parables and the reworking of accepted myths and biblical narratives.[20] A versatility to move between forms and genres must have been the norm.[21] The reading of texts in public to large audiences of the illiterate during *Tourkokratia* was also prevalent (A. Politis 1982: 275; Iliou 1975: 117). As a result, ethnographers have frequently come across popularized oral renditions of written texts, which often themselves are written down and so return the process of transmission back to writing in another form.[22] It is likely that most were composed in performance, using and reusing familiar themes and oral formulae.[23] Experiences such as reading from the Gospels as well as the peasants' interaction with tax collectors during Ottoman rule must have instilled in the illiterate a relation to the written that, after the revolution, would reproduce itself in their stance toward the alien, statist *katharevousa* – the new 'marker' of external authority. For 'written knowledge never opposed the oral; conversely, books – particularly the religious works which represented the "divine" in society – always transmitted the affirmations of a stronger social body that continually codified and "regulated" behavior, and such texts granted them authority. "Where did you find that written?" is the question posed by oral culture to any innovation' (A. Politis 1982: 280).

Oral poetry in a comparative context often serves to mark local identity by constituting a 'common good' among the group that fosters its production (Zumthor 1990: 27). The peasants continue to recount folktales and sing folksongs well into the modern period as these served a critical function.[24] The community bestows authority on the voice of its oral performer to exteriorize a discourse about itself and perpetuate the ever-changing image of that very community by this speech act. The innovative performer's interaction with his or her fellow villagers (re)structures in performance an expression of regional and differential identity often in direct opposition to the centralized state's projected identity. Like the *rhapsode, jongleur,* or *griot* in comparative contexts, Greek singers or storytellers evoke a shared communal mythic and historical past with their audience. In this respect, every song is always posited in advance, before each performance, in the ever-latent subtext of memory (of performances past). Memory for these cultures grants coherence in time and space and it is only as the sphere of writing expands that its significance declines (Ong 1967: 22–60; Finnegan 1977: 73–87; Bowra 1978: 355).

This assertion of local identity in the present moment distinguishes itself from the written's separation of moment of performance and reception, with its disruption of shared communion between addresser and addressee and its elimination of the spatiality of the body. The priority given to the body and the voice over the written rests on the alleged immediacy and authentic reproduction of the Truth without the distortions of a supplement.[25] Oral storytellers or singers constitute a locus of different representative modes. The performers react, adapt, and reconfigure the narrative they initiate to the interpolations of their audience. Physical presence, expertise, and the authority invested in them by the group draw together the dispersed communicative functions of the cocelebrants into one performed narrative that will register the collective unit in its *durée*. Meaning for the group is understood in the context of the socially accorded place and function, a 'common place,' where claims to universality or abstraction are missing and the use of I of little import. As a consequence, the relationship of the auditor-participant to the story-teller is unique:

> Thus the listener contributes to the production of the work in performance. The listener is author, scarcely less than the performer is author . . . Performance *figures* an experience, but at the same time it *is* experience. As long as it plays, performance suspends the activity of judgment. The text that proposes itself, at the point of convergence of the elements of this lived spectacle, does not call for interpretation. The voice that utters it does not project itself there (as speech would do in writing): it is given, in and with the spectacle, all-present; and yet, no more than the performance, the spectacle is not closed. It challenges exegesis, which will intervene only after its inscription in writing – that is, after being put to death. Its meaning is not such that a 'literary' hermeneutics can serve to explain it, for basically in the most widely accepted sense of the term, it is political. It proclaims the existence of the social group, reclaims the right of speech, the right to its life. (Zumthor 1990: 187–8, original emphases)

The oral text claims the fullness of its meaning in its here-and-now and in relation to the performances that have preceded it and will follow it in a tradition of composition-in-performance. Its power lies in what Paul Zumthor (1972: 65–75; 1984: 160; 1990: 203) has called its '*mouvance*,' a principle that describes the 'work' – if so totalizing a term can be used for an oral manifestation – made up abstractly by the play of its variants and ceaseless reworkings in performance.

Literary tradition constructs ways in which readers are called to relate to texts before them, but also the production of identity is configured in and by new sites and practices (Ong 1977: 53–81). Literature and folklore in Greece were slowly put into the service of *nation*-building and consciousness.[26] It is clearly a radical break for a society that, for four hundred or so years of *Tourkokratia*, had seen little textual production on Ottoman Greek territory. Now in a state under surveillance, the Greeks felt obliged to tell a tale that somehow bridged the years of *Tourkokratia*. They achieved this by granting priority to the Voice and, more specifically, to the folksongs of the Greek *Volk* during this period. This oral tradition, and the ethnographic aspects of the culture, were presented as depositories of Ancient traces, which were notoriously contested with charges of racial impurity by figures such as Jakob von Fallmerayer.[27] Folksong editions, compiled by philhellenes and Greeks, organize this performative tradition. True to the discourse of ab-sense, these early collections were often facilitated by foreigners whose informants were Greeks of the diaspora (M. Alexiou 2002: 173–6; A. Politis 1984). Regardless, the 'full Voice [with its] denial of any and all redundancy, explosion of being in the direction of lost origins, a time of voice without speech' was made the repository of Hellenism (Zumthor 1990: 6). Margaret Alexiou has captured the irony of the situation. In criticizing the assumptions behind Stylianos Alexiou's and Emmanuil Kriaras's disparagement of Cretan written texts 'contaminated' by subsequent 'oral' reworkings, Alexiou notes that 'social factors are permitted, on the one hand, to exclude peasantry from a creative role on grounds of oppressed status, while, on the other, to rest the prestige of the texts as literature on the assertion that they reflect the soul of the Greek people' (1991: 246). Regional divergences, or orally induced variations, to a text which may have been gradually accumulated through chapbooks and performance – the very stuff of assimilation and integration between learned and popular traditions – were read as signs of fragmentation and disintegration through the lens of homogenizing nationalism The *embodiment* of this Voice as 'monuments of the word,' in Nikolaos Politis's frequently quoted phrase of 1909, at the heart of the nation, projected a unified culture back to Europe. In effect, this prioritization of diachronic over synchronic studies of Greek folklore meant that many regional variants of a similar song were often conflated in the collections, and this process symbolized the general way by which dispersed sites of community performance were centripetally drawn in to a unitary center and textualized into a declamatory male voice – that of the National Poet. The regulation of the Greek language had the effect of dissociating it from its social and material contexts (Herzfeld 1990: 159).

This transference of oral modes and functions to the literate culture works in other ways, too. Anthologies and canons are regulatory exercises.[28] The anthologized male voice charged with speaking for the nation had to aspire to the highest standards of European Romanticism. The National Poet was to become the literate successor to the oral community's rhapsode. This was emblematic of the shift from the fragmented *tsifliks* of Ottoman times to a coherent National Imaginary and from the local dynamics of power to the centralized national logics of constit-utionalism. However, the oral and written ought not to be viewed as inimical to one another and, certainly, the changes in Greek signifying practices were, just as in matters of land and citizenship, neither clear-cut nor immediate. Tziovas has remarked how Greek orality was far too tenacious to bow out so compliantly and that the continuing oral character of Greek poetry throughout the nineteenth and twentieth centuries is evidenced even by the term for 'literature' itself in Greece, λογοτεχνία, that privileges the *logos* (Tziovas 1989b: 326–7). The oral and written coexist and interpenetrate (Finnegan 1977: 124). The masses may not have entered the print market or become a readership overnight, but the writing down of folksongs did not mean songs composed in performance ceased, or that the general process of (re)composition-in-performance died out. In arguing against the reific-ation of these twin terms and for the continuation of the contingency of context performance, composition-in-performance, and ongoing oral conception of a poet's function and role, I shall contend that Dionysios Solomos (1798–1857), the first National Poet of the modern Greek state, was not simply the exemplary Romantic poet and instigator of the modern Greek written poetic tradition, but also the next in a long line of oral poets from the local, communitarian tradition.

Critical and Editorial Constructions of a National Poet – Dionysios Solomos

At the time of his death in 1857, few of Solomos's poems had appeared in print. He was primarily known for his 'Hymn to Liberty,' published in Messolonghi and Paris in 1825; 'The Ode to Lord Byron'; a fragment from his 'Lambros' which appeared in the *Ionian Anthology* of 1834; and a handful of other poems in man-uscript copy. In addition, certain early poems from his time in Zakynthos were circulated in manuscript form or were sung to the music of Mantzaros or other Heptanesian melodists (i.e. who hailed from Greece's seven Western Ionian isles). Other short poems appeared in the folksong collections of Tommaseo (1841–2) and Zambelios (1852), while installments of 'Lambros' and the 'Ode to Lord Byron' were known. In the first two editions of his work published in Zakynthos and Athens and appearing in the year of his death, none of his later, commonly regarded 'mature works' – 'The Free Beseiged,' 'The Cretan,' or 'Porphyras' – appear.[29]

Solomos wrote all his poetry in the vernacular, the demotic. On his death, he was acclaimed by both the Heptanesian elite that favored use of the demotic, and more impressively, by the purist Athenian elite. Six valedictories read at his funeral in Corfu and at memorial services held in Zakynthos abound in superlatives

(L. Politis 1985: 276–285; Valetas 1959: 5–8). And though expressions of admiration for Solomos's technical virtuosity exist, two factors win over the purists from Athens: the intensity of the Heptanesian elite's devotion to Solomos and the special place accorded to Solomos's 'Hymn to Liberty.' In 1865, it became Greece's National Anthem. Certainly, the special circumstances of its publication – in the midst of the Revolution and in the then besieged town of Messolonghi – accorded it a special place in the history of the nation and, for the purists, excused its lowly demotic.[30] In 1849, the King had conferred on Solomos the Gold Cross of the Knights of the Saviour 'due to the Greek sentiments expressed in so many of your poems which aroused enthusiasm at that time of the struggle for our country in its independence' (Jenkins 1940: 179). Fittingly, it is this poem, one of his few *finished* poems, that wins for Solomos the acknowledgment of the *unfinished* Greek state.

The Heptanesian circle that had always been around the teacher Solomos – Polylas, Typaldos, Zambelios – had stoked anticipation over Solomos's complete oeuvre even before his death. Days prior to his death, on 1 February 1857, Polylas had published Solomos's 'Η Φαρμακωμένη' (The Poisoned Girl) in the Athenian paper *Pandora*. The paper welcomed the poem 'of this most popular, well-loved, and gold-flowing poet,' and enjoined Polylas to 'alert us to other products of Mr. Solomos' genius, since, unfortunately, the deep silence deprives Greece of one of its most splendid garlands.'[31] Upon his death, Panayiotis Soutsos encouraged Athenians to honor this 'resplendent and bright star' from the Heptanese 'because liberated Greece is the common land of all Greeks, and Greeks everywhere strive so that they may be honored in Greece as was Alexander the Great by leading his armies against India . . . he put himself at risk so that he might be admired in Greece.'[32] The paper *Elpis* calls for a collection of the poet's works in the form of 'a truly Hellenic work' (16 February 1857).

That edition was to appear at the Corfiot printing works of Antonios Terzakis in October 1859, edited by Iakovos Polylas and tactfully entitled Τα Ευρισκόμενα, or *Found Works*. The fragmentary nature of these new works – 'The Cretan,' 'The Free Beseiged,' and 'Porphyras' – caused great dismay (L. Politis 1985: 286–288). Some of the very papers that exhorted the publication of Solomos's extant works ignored the publication, and even Corfiot figures, like the poet Aristotelis Valaorites, expressed disappointment that Solomos's personal excesses (καταχρήσεις) had so impaired his productivity.[33]

The title *Found Works* signals Polylas's belief in the existence of more, as yet undiscovered, written manuscripts (Polylas 1948: 43). His attached *Prolegomena*, printed after the main text with separate page numbering, casts Solomos as the National and Romantic Poet. Lambropoulos (1988) has argued ingeniously that Polylas's narration of Solomos's artistic and moral growth in this foreword takes the form of a *Künstlerroman*, marking out the poet's sensitivity to nature, his genius, unique sensibility, and his moral integrity: 'by aestheticizing the author,

Polylas effectively detextualized his work: he saved the country from the unsettling uncertainties over his dispersed writings by offering it its national poetry' (Lambropoulos 1988: 80). Like other *Künstlerroman*, Wieland's *Agathon* or Mann's *Doktor Faustus*, the work becomes a statement of aesthetics. Both Polylas's reading of Solomos and his presentation of the particular aesthetics that he ascribed to, is conditioned by the period of his own interaction with the poet. Polylas knew Solomos in the last ten or so years of his life, though Solomos had been a close friend to Polylas's mother.[34] Polylas was only 3 years old in 1828 when Solomos came to Corfu. It was not until 1847, when Polylas was 22, that he gained admittance into Solomos's close circle. It was not long before 'the young man's searching mind and deep understanding drew the poet to him. His progress in literature and polymathy were truly excellent.'[35]

Their close friendship and collaboration coincides with Solomos's most intense readings in German Romantic philosophy. Solomos encouraged Polylas to study German, and soon Polylas became Solomos's chief translator of the German philosophers into Italian.[36] It is hardly surprising, then, that these philosophers, and Schiller in particular, take pride of place in Polylas's rendering of Solomos's belief in Man's moral education through aesthetics in the *Prolegomena*.[37] Polylas describes Solomos's isolation in the last ten years of his life in Corfu – the ten years that Polylas knew him – in Schillerian terms, as the artist's devoted obeisance to the higher bidding of Art. Indeed, Polylas justifies Solomos's unwillingness 'to cross over to liberated Greece' on the grounds that he did not wish to compromise 'his pure poetic inclination' and his idealized image of the 'true Greece' (Polylas 1948: 29). Veloudis has paralleled this comment to a statement by Schiller himself, found translated in Solomos's papers by Polylas, that states his unwillingness to travel to France after the revolution in 1795: 'The sweep of events cast the spirit of the times in one direction, from which there is the danger that it might distance itself further from the Art of the Ideal. Its law is to abandon reality, and with respectful fortitude raise itself to where Necessity does not rule; because Art is a daughter of Freedom; and it will submit to the necessity of Spirit, and not to the coercive will of matter.'[38] In a moment reminiscent of the discourse of ab-sense identified in Chapter 1, Polylas goes on to explain that this material contact with Greece does not detract from the National Poet's capacity to perceive the mysterious and divine aspects of this Greece. Only a National Poet, a graced sensibility, feels the 'Greek Future' – even if only *incompletely* – for 'despite all this, his imagination does not feel itself able to embrace it all, because, just as for the starry heaven, just so, many of its corners are visible but others remain hidden' (Polylas 1948: 30). The incompleteness of this exceptionally endowed vision so justified is, in other words, paralleled to the incompleteness of the manuscripts.

But how might we explain the incompleteness of the manuscripts? Some have attributed the cause to Solomos's social circumstances – he was ahead of his time, plainly misunderstood by those around him (Palamas 1925: 43–4; Apostolakis 1958: 112). The writer Xenopoulos blamed Solomos's alcoholism (1901: 68) (never mind if such Romantic excess, like opium for Thomas de Quincey, often ushered 'a sabbath of repose' on the recalcitrant spirit). Others pinned blame on the wear and tear of a five-year court case filed against Solomos's estate by his half-brother in 1833 (Tomadakis 1935: LXXXII). Or maybe it was just his temperament.[39] Those who favor an aesthetic explanation are prone to proceed by uncovering his complete corpus or proving its existence by hypothesizing its contours from the known manuscripts (Dimakis 1964: 86–90; Frangopoulos 1978: 58; Zoras 1957: 139–47). The conflation of the words 'unfinished' and 'fragmentary' is common to such discussions. A distinction is in order. For the 'unfinished' work (*nvollendentes Werk*) implies the author's involuntary inability to complete the work; whereas the 'fragmentary' work (*Fragment'*) is a product of the author's conscious will. Frangopoulos's likening of Romantic 'fragmentary' works to classical statues missing an arm is made with a view to legitimize Solomos's stature as a national and truly Hellenic artist, but does not respect the difference between the two types. Rozanis criticizes Polylas for proposing that Solomos's oeuvre was 'unfinished,' since, he argues, it was never in Solomos's plans to complete any of his poems. Rozanis sees Solomos's fragmentariness (αποσπασματικότητα) as an affirmation of a Romantic belief in the fragment's superiority over the less challenging 'independent wholeness' of an ordered neoclassical universe. In this view, poetry can only relate the subject's inability to render the world, the tension between the attraction and repulsion toward the whole, hence its encoding as fragment should not be predicated on wholeness but should stand as aesthetic internal coherence in and of itself. Linos Politis shares this opinion: 'Solomos's fragments can today be taken not for "fragments," but as separate lyric unities, lyric microcosms of their own autonomous organization and internal necessity' (L. Politis 1985: 255). Since the work is always, like Coleridge's *Kubla Khan*, liable to be interrupted by 'a person on business from Porlock,' the 'short and incandescent passage [is] the manifestation of poetry at its highest' (Abrams 1971: 134).

Certainly, Solomos read Schlegel and other Romantics who wrote on the fragment. He once affirmed that his "Lambros" would remain a fragment because the whole poem did not aspire to the elevation of its parts' (Kriaras 1969: 116). But this comment, made in response to Regaldi's questioning in 1851, late in Solomos's career, does not, as Rozanis argues, clinch Solomos's espousal of the aesthetic of the fragment. Nor should his abandonment of a work be read as a definitive declaration of its final, 'complete' fragmentary state (Kriaras 1969: 116–17; Kapsomenos 1992b: 49). As Kapsomenos puts it, Solomos's aesthetic disquisitions in Italian nowhere promote the notion of fragmentariness. But this does not mean that *Polylas* does not apply a notion of fragmentariness to Solomos's work. Solomos may not mention 'fragmentariness' once, but Polylas mentions it seventeen times only in the Contents page of his 1859 edition (Savidis 1989a: 140). Kapsomenos is right to note that Polylas accepts the 'unfinished' nature of Solomos's oeuvre (even in the very title *Found Works*), but he does not credit Polylas in playing both games by also incorporating, very discreetly, the Romantic notion of the fragment into his rereading of Solomos.

It is futile to speculate on Solomos's intention. But Polylas's critical rehabilitation of Solomos's scattered texts for the frustrated audience of his day is clear. The unfinished nature of Solomos's extant works are presented through the prism of Romantic aesthetics not as simply unfinished, but also glorified as the fragmentary trace of the romantic subject's agony for perfection and absolute truth. The transferral of significance from the art work's failure of mimetic function to the thematization of the visionary poet's noble, Icarus-like flight to this Ideal constitutes, as Lambropoulos has eloquently stated, the moment when 'nostalgia, that most emotional aspect of romantic consciousness, transformed the unfinished work into a "rescued fragment" of absent wholeness, transposing aesthetic criteria to the unattainability of perfection and replacing the rewarded neoclassical expectations with the crucified romantic intentions as a measure' (Lambropoulos 1988: 91). Even Solomos's 'excesses' are attributed to the Romantic artist's martyrdom, to the cause of Truth and the fleeting and visionary apperception of that truth. In the last page of his work, Polylas stresses that Solomos has left behind the fruit of his solitary labor, the work of a dutiful individualism given up to the worship of Art. To those doubting Thomases disbelieving of the existence of other unpublished works, Polylas refers them to eyewitness accounts of other works by the poet, albeit as yet unpublished, that were known to his close circle (Polylas 1948: 42).

Ever since, editions of Solomos's dispersed texts by Linos Politis and Stylianos Alexiou (Solomos 1948–69, 1994) have built on Polylas's foundations and tended to assume, or posit, an organic wholeness in the hope of producing a serviceable text. This approach has steered away from the fragmentariness pursued in more so-called 'analytical' editions that trace Solomos's process of composition by close scrutiny of the manuscripts. Without rejecting the notion that some of Solomos's works were fragmentary while others were not, scholars have been wary of the methods used by 'analytic' scholars to establish 'stages' in Solomos's process, especially when these depend on such factors as the color of ink used etc. (S. Alexiou 1997b: 16, 35–7). By the same token, scholars have been critical of the totalizing presumptions of some editors, as was apparent in the reception of Stylianos Alexiou's edition.

One practitioner from the analytical school, Eleni Tsantsanoglou, challenges Polylas's critical interpretation (1982: 167). She painstakingly analyses one of Solomos's extant notebooks – Notebook Z11 – to prove that his plan was to compose a *magnum opus* made up of four lyrical and four satirical poems, all contained in this notebook. She takes Solomos's scribbling of multiplication sums in the margins of the notebook's leaves as evidence of a grand plan of versification (Tsantsanoglou 1982: 33–62). Tsantsanoglou provides insights into Solomos's non-linear mode of composition, his process of composition-in-becoming, εν τω γίγνεσθαι, whereby he begins the notebook on the first page working into it while, at the same time, he also works from the last page backwards in toward the middle. She also highlights Solomos's habit of setting down Italian notes on his proposed poems or aesthetic principles on the left-hand side of the page with scattered, often incomplete, verses in Greek on the right side of the same page (1982: 26–7). Solomos neither adopts a sequential narrative in his poems nor follows the plan itemized in his Italian draft; instead, he works in small thematic units (Tsantsanoglou 1982: 174), all the while jumping from one to the other. Solomos does not rework these units according to the perceived linearity of his poem, or to his Italian draft's narrative sequence, for different thematic units are crafted on the same page, only later to be brought together in greater units that are then again disassembled (1982: 174).

Although Tsantsanoglou is sensitive to Solomos's idiosyncratic mode of composition and she claims to undermine some of Polylas's totalizing readings, she does not allow that Solomos's working units might be destined for another composition in another notebook. She assumes a unified and complete notebook in the same way that Polylas assumes the existence of a complete and unified poem, arguing that the work in this notebook is executed at about the same time and that there is a 'unitary character' to the workings of the seven or eight poems identifiable in the notebook. Surely, it is problematic to assume that a poet whose works are strewn over a number of notebooks should be read within the limits of one notebook: particularly when the synthesis of other commonly accepted 'autotelic poems' has been achieved by piecing together units from different notebooks. One need only examine Politis's facsimile editions of Solomos's manuscripts of stanzas (Fig. 2.1) from Polylas's edition of only the third draft of 'The Free Besieged' to recognize that the material Polylas draws from is taken from more than ten different textbooks and loose leaves (L. Politis 1964b: 441–70, 615).

Furthermore, Solomos's prose is almost exclusively in Italian and he writes in Greek only in verse.[40] The two languages interpenetrate on occasion diasporically. His Greek retains a vibrant orality in its interface with other languages; 'the large proportion of his work which he placed in the mouths of his characters is another indication of his treatment of modern Greek as an oral language' (Mackridge 1992: 63).[41] Might not the disjointed and non-linear workings of the versified Greek thematic units be conditioned by his difficulty in the Greek language, and the fact that his verbal facility in that language is organized by his oral adaptation of the song tradition? That is, since Solomos did not use Greek as his everyday language, and was palpably more comfortable on paper in Italian, a fact borne out by his preference for Italian in his letters and his drafts, might not his Greek be constrained within the boundaries of his conversational Greek. A diasporic trait, after all – to be caught between languages and limited by registers. Or was his Greek learnt through his passion for the canto and folksong tradition? Certainly, there is considerable evidence of Solomos's interest in these traditions. His erratic

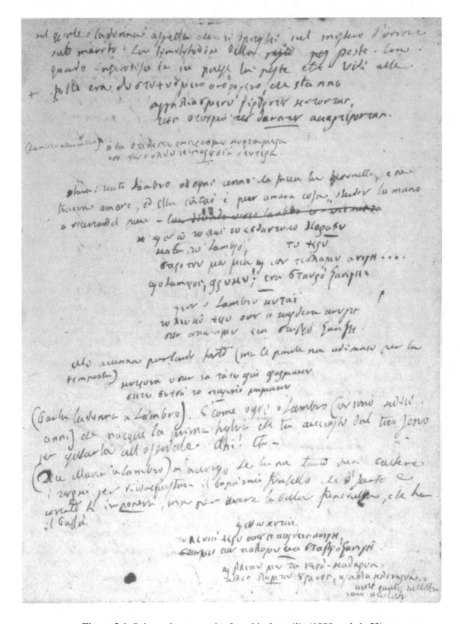

Figure 2.1 Solomos's manuscript from his *Juvenilia* (1999: vol. 1, 53)

composition would not be different from the conception of the composition of an 'oral poet' and, though written on paper, may be the product of this process of situational composition. His handwriting, characterized by Tsantsanoglou (1982: 28) as 'often extremely hurried, thus making it often quite illegible,' may also suggest that Solomos considered his jottings personal and not destined for others' eyes. Let us consider some new approaches to the problem beyond Polylas's or Tsantsanoglou's totalizing, philological ambitions.

Solomos's Performativity

If, as readers, we reject Polylas's Romantic claim to an unachieved totality of oeuvre and consider Solomos's fragments as something other than evidence of an ungrasped whole, what other readings offer themselves? What if we were to dispense with Polylas's 'strong reading' of Solomos's work and its mode of composition and favor an altogether different theory. The lines of such a new perspective appear at the end of Veloudis's study into the German sources of Solomos's work. Though Veloudis ascribes to the view that Solomos willed his work as 'fragmentary,' he maintains that the German Romantic fragmentary work, following Schlegel and Novalis, does not aspire to being, but is a process (*Prozess*) of Becoming, not an είναι but a γίγνεσθαι. The processual theory conforms to the organicism of Romanticism as exemplified in the analogy of the poem to a plant in Solomos's meditations (Στοχασμοί).[42] This train of thought leads to more anti-teleological readings of Solomos's mode of composition and aesthetic theory.

In a short article, Kapsomenos (1992b) notes that Politis's facsimiles of Solomos's manuscripts in his Αυτόγραφα Έργα (1964) display poems, even the mature ones, which do not 'progress' from one draft to the next in any teleological manner. 'By contrast,' Kapsomenos states, 'in many cases, one would characterize the last reworking as more deficient than the previous ones, at least by the criterion of the general plan construable from Solomos' notes and the successive drafts' (1992b: 50). Kapsomenos concludes that we are never left with a final draft, but only a process of composition forever without *telos*, which is, at some moment, set aside or continued in some other form – e.g. in another draft of the 'Free Besieged' or transposed onto another theme. Since Solomos hardly ever publishes any of his texts, this process of recomposition allows him to shift or transfer elements, themes, or variations from one poem to another, thus disrupting any notion of a unified and autotelic work: 'The key aspect of Solomos' principle of creation is not so much its fragmentariness, its half-finishedness or unfinished nature, which are secondary symptoms, but the ceaseless creative process – the continual recreation of the text in new variations and new clusters of thematic and expressive units which never manage to realize their final form (Kapsomenos 1992b: 5). As a result, thematic or lectical 'units' slip from one poem to the next, they entertain various combinations and base themselves less on a syntagmatic but more on a para-digmatic axis. This never-ending and certainly never-published recomposition characterizes all Solomos's work after 1833 and leads Kapsomenos to liken this modern 'signifying practice' as close to Barthes and Kristeva's notion of the ever (re)written text that undoes itself and forever plays at a semiotic level.[43] Kapsomenos's argument certainly cuts loose from Polylas's hold. However, the essay's conclusions, once the parallel to the open text has been made, seem more concerned with legitimizing French post-structuralism than delving further into the implications of the insight. Fortunately, Kapsomenos revisits the issue in a longer article (1992a). There, he plots Solomos's reworking of a specific thematic unit in a number of different contexts in the manuscripts. He also suggests that Solomos's method for reworking these independent units conforms more 'perhaps to the prototype of oral demotic poetry' and, by implication, less to post-structuralism (1992a:178, 199).

The next section builds on this suggestion to advance a theory for Solomos's mode of composition by proposing an 'oral' and performative context rooted in the communitarian tradition. To do this, I counterbalance Polylas's characterization of Solomos's late Romantic quest by looking back to find the repressed traces of an 'earlier' Solomos. The rest of this chapter will seek to uncover a 'Solomos' whose relation to Greek poetry betrays a different conception of the poet's craft, role, and tradition. This reading does not claim exclusive applicability for all of his oeuvre. In fact, it focuses on his early work. However, it does question the assumptions of our approach to Solomos and to the notion of the 'poet' and the 'poem' in Greek 'literature' at this time.

The first National Poet of the modern Greek tradition was not fluent in Greek. Like others in the Heptanesian elite, he spoke Italian in his everyday dealings. Greek was, quite literally, his mother tongue – the tongue of his illiterate mother.[44] Solomos, however, studied from the age of 10 in Italy, had an Italian tutor, and penned all correspondence, save for four letters, in Italian.[45] He was a Greek of the Heptanesian Isles, an area located beyond the borders of the Greek state, under British protectorate rule, and for centuries under Venetian cultural influence. Solomos was a heterochthon, one of those Hellenes who never once stepped on the soil of the Greek state. Appropriately for the discourse of ab-sense, this Greek who spoke little Greek and had never visited the Greek state was to be universally accepted as the first National Poet of modern Greece.

Throughout his life, Solomos's erudition was primarily conducted in Italian. His friends translated German Romantic texts into Italian for him. His own aesthetic jottings and first drafts to poems were made in Italian. When Solomos returned to Zakynthos in 1818 from his tour of Italy, his Greek was confined to conversational Greek. His early compositions in Italian would slowly be supplanted by his work in Greek, but these Italian works provide insight into Solomos's mode of composition and performance. In 1822, some friends published a collection of thirty of his sonnets in Italian entitled *Rime Improvvisate*. Many of these were built on the rhythms of Italian models, and some of his subsequent early Greek stanzas are based on Italian tunes, too (Coutelle 1998: 11). Solomos's friend Ludovico Strani sends these poems to the Zakynthian-born but later celebrated Italian poet Ugo Foscolo. In his letter, he admits that he has stolen them from Solomos, and he describes the circumstances of the poems' composition. They are verses, Strani explains to Foscolo, composed 'before the most educated people of our region and written on the very paper on which Solomos "improvised" (αυτοσχεδίαζε) before those who would propose themes to him, without the alteration of a single word' (Solomos 1979b: 301). I cite at length from Strani's letter:

> Truly, on occasion his verses are so perfect that no-one would believe it except those who saw his pen run across the page with such *speed in the way that someone writes something down that he has had in his mind for a long time*. I leave out the countless comic verses or the other more serious ones he improvised, and I select only those which seem to me the most successful. It is a strange thing to watch him improvise the sonnet in this way; and I would not dare confirm it, had I not been there and had not his Excellency Pavlos Conte Mercatis, at whose house the majority of themes were given, held on to the original manuscript. (Solomos 1979b: 301; emphasis mine)

The circumstances of composition, a parlour game known as *bouts rimés*,[46] required that someone provide the poet with fourteen words, each of which had to appear at the end of a line. The poet would be set a subject on which he would improvise a sonnet.[47] The hand-written manuscript that stands out among many other copies of this presumed original is significant because it seems to be corrected by Solomos himself. Some emendations to the text are in Solomos's own hand.[48] Furthermore, the second page of the manuscript offers us the following additional information about the circumstances of composition: 'Pavlos Mercatis would collect these poems as the poet would compose them, which would not take him more than eight to ten minutes and, sometimes, only four – rarely did he take more than thirteen' (L. Politis 1985: 208). Solomos's expertise in improvisation in an oral setting, and Strani's observation that it seemed he had a facility to draw from a reserve of phrases that had been somehow stored in his memory are reminiscent of the oral performer who draws from a set of formulae.

Let us continue down this path. In a letter to Foscolo, Strani pins hopes on Solomos's potential to 'transform' the Greek language. However, Solomos himself was not at ease in this language, even though his early improvisations in Greek indicate a growing awareness of the language's poetic possibilities. In record time, Solomos studies the works of Christopoulos and the grammar of Vilaras to produce his first short, rhymed poems. 'The Blond Little Girl' (Ξανθούλα), his first poem of eight short four-line stanzas, in its simplicity and crossed rhyme, is reminiscent of Zakynthian musical folksongs (Chatziyakoumis 1968: 148–50). Indeed, many of the rhyming poems of his early Zakynthian period resemble 'party songs' (τραγούδια της παρέας).[49] Solomos drew his models from the folksongs of the demotic tradition and popularized Cretan Renaissance literature as well as the performative canto-singing tradition of the Heptanesian Isles. He may have spoken Italian in everyday circumstances, but he used Greek in company of song. Later folksong collections from Zakynthos point to a strong musical tradition.[50] In fact, the earliest composers of the modern Greek tradition – Nikos Mantzaros, Pavlos Karrer, Spyros Samaras, Spyros Xyndas – came from the Western Isles (Chamoudopoulos 1964: 83–94). Mantzaros, the most famous of these composers and later lifetime honorary president of the Philharmonic Society of Corfu, founded in 1840, put to music a number of Solomos's early compositions, including the first two stanzas of 'Hymn to Liberty' that later became the Greek National Anthem. The hymn was composed to the music of regional demotic dances, to the accompaniment of four voices, and was considered the National Anthem in the Heptanesian Islands long before it was adopted in Athens. In addition, Mantzaros also put a number of the shorter lyrical pieces to music.[51] In his short *Sketch* on Solomos (1848), which was published only seven years after his death in 1880, Mantzaros offers insights into Solomos's intertwining of literary composition and music:

> And so, by instinct, he creates most of his verses with song, improvising melodies that echo consummately with the true expression of a musical spirit's poetic conception of a musical spirit. I, who have heard him many times compose in this manner, have understood that he formed poetic harmony by way of consecutive notes which he articulated by employing a wonderful and most harmonious variety . . . On many an occasion, he himself would tell me that he composed poetry with his musical intuition. (Konomos 1950: 31)

Veloudis argues that this marriage of literature and music in Solomos's mode of composition issues out of his reading of Romantic philosophers and aestheticians' prioritization of the expressive voice over the mimetic image. Like Polylas's reading of Solomos, Veloudis's reading bases itself on the latter part of Solomos's life and so may not be so applicable to his earlier work. The Heptanesian canto tradition intersects with notions of poetry of that time. When Polylas describes Solomos's meeting with the Athenian litterateur Trikoupis at the end of 1822, he describes Solomos 'reading out' (εξεφώνησε) his verses (Polylas 1948: 18–19); Solomos's platonic female friend would often cheer him by 'singing' his verses (Polylas 1948: 21) – recitation was an integral part of the poetic act. Even Solomos's appropriation of the folksong tradition was not undertaken in the hypostasized manner by which others had appropriated it. In a letter to Tertsetis in 1833, Solomos demands that the appropriation of folk poetry be more than sterile imitation. Solomos rejects the *idealization* of the folk and seeks a new *practice* of poetry able to rework the essence of folk material:

> Greece's teachers are turning way back; this is not a return to origins. I am gratified when folksongs are taken as a starting-point. I would hope, however, that whoever uses the klephtic tongue should use it in its essence, and not just in its form. Do you understand me? And as for poetry, be careful, dear George, for it is a fine thing for one to put down one's roots on these tracks, but it is not enough to stop there; one must elevate oneself to the heights . . . Klephtic poetry is beautiful and full of interest as it is through this poetry that the klephts lived their lives, their ideas, and their feelings without affectation. It does not have the same interest in our own mouth; the nation asks from us to produce the treasure of our own distinct intelligence, clothed in national terms. (Solomos in L. Politis 1959: 32)

In matters of form, too, Solomos's use of the decapentasyllable verse favored in folk tradition and regarded as the national meter has led critics to present him as the uniting figure between the folk and national literary tradition. Solomos would again probably have rejected any approval on the basis of his adoption of this verse alone.

All Solomos's companions attest to his preference for reading, reciting, or composing his poems *extempore*. Many attest to longer, more complete versions of Solomos's dispersed written oeuvre. However, this information has always aimed to prove that there were other manuscripts and notebooks of Solomos's works. Though it is generally accepted that Solomos did not care to publish his works – by the end he even scrawled 'shit' over some of them – it is usually argued that he was careless and would misplace many of his compositions (Zoras 1957: 141). True, some, like Melissinos, have affirmed that Mantzaros had not only heard Solomos recite poems or parts of celebrated poems that have never seen the light of day, but even remembered the color of the notebooks in which they were written, but never found (Zoras 1957: 145–6). And even the *Rime Improvvisate* would not have been available to posterity if it were left to Solomos. Mercatis and company had clandestinely taken the sonnets to the printer unbeknownst, at first, to Solomos himself. But the assumption that all allegedly missing material was once written down is presumptuous.

No-one has yet hypothesized that some of these recitations may have been performed without any written aids, in a manner reminiscent of oral performers. Of all the tomes written about Solomos, there is to my knowledge only one study that even touches on such a hypothesis. Nikolaos Tomadakis (1935) analyses a number of possible processes of composition to account for the disordered manuscripts and settles on improvisations of mouth and the ear: 'The poet of this style composes with divine ease, recycles verses, stanzas, poems, he commits them to memory and he revels in them when he so wishes, not a single word escapes him. He reminds us of the poets of demotic songs who, though illiterate, worked in the same manner' (1935: LXXXIV). This scholar's conclusion may well be his way of fitting Solomos into a national genealogy. But Tomadakis's concern for technical detail and his contention that the improvised rhymes are evidence of Solomos's skill in such composition, may well go beyond such a purpose.

For Tomadakis, Solomos's unwillingness to publish is evidenced by his erratic phonetic transcription or spelling of Greek words, a further sign of his preference for committing whole poems to memory (LXXXV). This, and other comments on orthography, are misguided. Linos Politis has since shown that, far from being idiosyncratic phonetic transcriptions, Solomos's spelling is comparable to other texts from Venetian-held parts of Greece-to-be. Indeed, Politis not only juxtaposes the orthography of different texts from this period, but also compares styles of calligraphy that show how Solomos's rarely joined letters in Greek betray malaise in Greek, and a prior Italian education in Latin characters (L. Politis 1985: 49). Politis traces spelling from Venetian-occupied Crete to the Heptanesian Isles and concludes by comparing stanzas from Solomos and Martelaos of about the same time. Their spelling is not simply phonetic for they share some regional, Heptanesian grammatical ground-rules (Tsantsanoglou 1982: 29). There are significant parallels to be drawn between Solomos's orthography and grammatical usage proposed by Vilaras in his demotic study of the Greek language, Ρομεηκη γλοσα of 1814 (L. Politis 1985: 48; Mackridge 1989: 3). Polylas regulates Solomos's spelling in the *Found Works* and streamlines it into the centralized Athenian or Peloponnesian dialect that was gradually establishing itself as a standard demotic by erasing heteroglot dialects in the service of national unitariness. This is another effect of cultural/national centralization. A standard demoticism, just as much as the statist *katharevousa*, works by the same principles of standardization and stratification. Internal differentiation or heteroglossia in dialect and orthography is sacrificed on the altar of the conscious linguistic paradigm of demoticism. Browning's description of the linguistic topography of nineteenth-century Greece whereby 'the majority of Greeks in the nineteenth century spoke their local dialect rather than the common demotic in most situations . . . better described [with purism] as triglossy' (Browning 1989: 106–7) reflects the situation in the Heptanese, where the linguistic situation among Solomos's cohorts could even be termed a 'tetraglossy' due to the prevalence of Italian, too.

Even a cursory glance at Linos Politis's (1964a, 1964b) two-volume publication of facsimiles of Solomos's manuscripts helps us realize just how significantly Polylas edited Solomos's original text. The first volume displays photocopies of Solomos's handwritten textbook pages; the second treats us to a typewritten transcription of the often illegible print.[52] In the latter, it is striking just how extensively Polylas transformed Solomos's orthography. A closer viewing of the multiple fragmented stanzas also impresses the significant editorialization and yoking together of dispersed fragments, mostly from different notebooks into the totalizing poem-texts of Polylas's 1859 edition.

If one were then to develop Tomadakis's 'oral and aural' theory, the appearance of similar verses in different textbooks and poems would further substantiate the possibility that Solomos continually worked and reworked phrasal units which crop up in different sections. In this way, the stanzas or verses appearing in Polylas's footnotes as variations to the version of a line favored in the main text of a specific poem, become not a variation to the line in the specific poem, but the same unit reworked and dispersed in another poem or theme. Furthermore, similar themes, particularly in the more fragmentary mature poems, allow for the reworking of familiar material in other contexts.

Solomos the traditional singer/poet is able to compose in performance. He produces 'complete' poems around familiar themes in the company of his audience and these may never be set down by him or anyone else on paper. This facility might explain the multitude of existing eyewitness accounts of Solomos's complete oral recitation of poems that have been handed down to us in an 'incomplete' form. His process of composition's blending of 'written' and 'oral' characteristics conforms to the late Albert Lord's description of a 'transitional text.' By drawing heavily from the folksong tradition, Solomos uses traditional phraseology and diction, but also occasionally works on paper and creates through the 'written' tradition. It matters not that the poet composes on paper. For the system of perf-ormativity is projected through literary devices on paper by the reworking of formulae, themes, and techniques of anaphora, epiphora, parallelisms, and para-taxis that transpose non-verbal factors or mnemonic devices into written deictic features:

> As long as the systems continue, it does not matter whether the singer composes with or without writing. In fact, the 'oral residue' expressed in the systems, themselves formed in orality, would persist in the world of literacy, in the usage of the literate traditional singer until such time as the nontraditional-minded writer with a pen in his hand should rearrange the words and traditional patterns in the basic systems. (Lord 1991: 25)

Solomos's conception of the poetic act shares this transitional nature. Each new performance, in writing or in oral performance, is for the poet a 'context-sensitive' process of multiplicity and resists a law of terminal realization (Hymes 1973: 35). This resistance accounts for its *mouvance*, and it is this principle that the Romantic tradition of reading Solomos's work and oeuvre, begun by Polylas, tries to repress with the call for 'zero *mouvance*.' 'The Romantic tradition since Schlegel,' affirms

Zumthor, 'has treated the literary work in its *unity*, as the end of an evolving genesis' (1990: 203). Writing, the letter of the law, as the quintessential instrument of state consciousness legislates the 'work' and interrupts the series of nuances and mutations of the performative tradition: 'Writing engenders the law, establishes restrictions along with order, in speech no less than in the state. At the heart of a society saturated with writing, oral poetry (resisting ambient pressure better than our everyday discourses) tends – because it is oral – to escape the law and to submit only to the most flexible formulas: this accounts for its *mouvance*' (Zumthor 1990: 203).

The Unfinished Works of Greek Nationalism

In the famous *Megali Idea* speech of 1844, Ioannis Kolettis proposed for Hellenism a quintessentially Romantic project for the nineteenth century. The process of Greekness was declared 'unfinished,' and the missing segments of Greek earth had to be discovered and integrated into the logic of the centralized nation-state to complete an organic, self-regulated Greece as 'incarnated artwork, art made life' (Lambropoulos 1993: 82). The contours of a perfected Greece would remain fairly indeterminate for the time being, and this suited a wider set of political objectives. It was only later in the century, with the emergence of neighboring Balkan nationalisms and the setting down of distinct borders, that Greeks considered the exact contours of the new state. For now, in a Romantic age, centralization within the state projects wholeness back to the Western Powers, homogenizes difference, and smooths out heteroglossy. Content is reduced to the all-conquering dictates of form and, in the process, the rights of the peasant are co-opted, the representation of the citizen is compromised, and the voice of the poet and the notion of poetry conforms to written regimes. This letter of the law carries with it a concomitant totalization of dialects into standard language, regional poetry and orthography into national poetry and *ortho-graphia* (or 'correct writing'), folk voices into a monumentalized and hypostasized Folk Voice, and variant voices into the single voice of a National Poet. We see a 'coincidence' of effects in the ideological and aesthetic realms. Solomos's oeuvre, as we have seen, is one more victim of this process: the 'unfinished' work of art, like the 'unfinished' work of state, must be made whole.

The Greeks have fought for their land. The heterochthon has claimed autochthony; the outsiders have become insiders; and the 'oral' has become 'written.' Only that this process is forced: no-one owns their land; the heterochthon continues to view the Greek state and its citizens as other; and the 'literate' poet has not yet quite tucked the shirt-tails of Greek oral communitarianism into the breeches of European Romanticism.

Notes

1. Kakridis's anecdote is recorded originally in the work of Koumas (1830–2).
2. *Rayah*, a Turkish word taken from Arabic, originally meant a flock or herd and came to be applied to non-Muslim subjects of the Ottoman Empire.
3. The Phanariots were a Christian administrative and economic elite resident in, and originating from, the Phanar district of Constantinople. Many worked as *dragomans* to the Sultan. The *kaptenaioi* were military chieftains, formerly in the pay of the Ottoman authorities to patrol and to fight off *klepht* brigandage in areas known as *armatoliks*.
4. Apart from three areas of large *chiflik* holdings in Greece – in Attica, Euboea, and Phthiotyis – the archon holdings greater than 1000 *stremmata* were rare (Tsoucalas 1981: 263–4).
5. Gourgouris (1996) sporadically uses the word 'coincidence' to connect levels of experience and praxis without necessarily claiming their causality.
6. This account by Tertsetis may have been embellished with political circumstances of his day in mind (Colocotronis 1986: 73–4).
7. McGrew (1976) informs us that about 20 percent of 'Old Greece's' 45,000 square kilometer mainland was arable. The Turkish minority, numbering only about 65,000, held over half of the arable land for a *per capita* holding of about 65 *stremmata* – a Turkish *stremma* equalled 0.314 acres; later in 1863, the Greek state adopted the 'royal' *stremma*, based on French metric measure and was equivalent to 247 acres and is still used today (Diamandouros et al. 1976: 18). The *rayah* population of about 635,000 held the remaining 4 million *stremmata*, for a *per capita* holding of six to seven *stremmata*. In the more fertile Peloponnese the landholding ratio of Turk to Greek was 20: 1. These quantitative ratios should not divert us from the qualitative difference between the fertile Turkish bottom lands and Greek inhabitation of more remote areas (McGrew 1976: 113–16).
8. Christian cultivators who had paid the usual 30 percent share of the produce to their Muslim landlords were now to pay 20 percent of that amount to the Greek Treasury, as well as a tithe, which had been paid to the Ottoman government, or a total of 30 percent: they kept a slightly larger portion of their yield than before (70 percent instead of 60 percent). Turkish farms cultivated by Turks themselves or by hired labor found their yield entirely claimed by the treasury. Christian-owned estates, the largest of which were owned by the representatives at Kaltetzi, needed pay only a tithe (McGrew 1976: 118).
9. McGrew (1976: 123) concludes that popular concern over the fate of the 'national estates' did not amount to a questioning of property rights in general. Consequently, there was little or no organized movement to dispossess the large Christian landholders. Uprisings in Andros (Kordatos 1946: 154–7) and in Hydra (Finlay 1876: 170–6) were the exception.

10. The belief in Orthodox brotherhood of the Czar led much early Greek revolutionary sentiment to be russophile. Most notoriously, Mavrokordatos, determining Russian unwillingness to offer impetus to insurrections in Wallachia, began to curry favor with England and set about to play both powers off against each other.

11. For Capodistrias's reforms, see Petropoulos (1968: 107–24); Kaldis (1963: Chapter 5).

12. Otto's arrival in Athens, the new (symbolic) 'capital,' was celebrated by the erection of the fulcrum of a column from the Parthenon (Skopetea 1988: 197). The Bavarians busied themselves in the consolidation of such national symbolism by creating an Archaeological Service, an Archaeological Society, an archaeological newspaper, ordinances about excavation sites, neoclassical buildings, and the transfer of the capital from Nafplion to Athens.

13. The 1824 assembly at Salona (Amphissa) was marked by a most welcoming address to the non-native Greeks: 'However many Christians from the enslaved regions take shelter in liberated parts of Greece should be received as brothers, enjoying all the rights accorded to all other Greeks, they should be treated on Greek earth as the autochthons . . . the word "foreigner" be not mentioned among Greeks.'

14. 'Non-combatants who migrated to Greece between 1827–32 became eligible for office after two years, those between 1832–37 after three years, and those between 1837–43 after four years' (Petropoulos 1968: 491)

15. Only five or ten heterochthons were fired, but were reinstated after two years (Skopetea 1988: 57).

16. When Capodistrias in 1828 was reproached for not drafting a constitution, he admonished his critics by resorting to the same tactic: 'is this the time to bring it up, the existence of Greece depends entirely on her foreign policy, and it is her relations with the powers to which she must devote her attention' (Driault and Lhéritier 1925–6: II, 9)

17. There is evidence of a newspaper published in 1784, though no copies have survived (Vranoussis 1992: 52–5). Vranoussis (1992) has published the text of the *Ephimeris* of Vienna with a detailed introduction. Originally, the newspaper published along with a Serbian version from the same press (1992: 103–29); see also Koumarianou (1995: 38–67).

18. For a selective three-volume anthology of early Greek press or periodical articles, see Koumarianou (1971). The position that newspapers assume in Greek public culture in the nineteenth century is treated also in Jusdanis (1991a: 129–35); Tsoucalas (1981: 144–53). The latter gives useful figures for the number of periodicals during the nineteenth century.

19. A. Politis (1982) compiles some interesting information about the circulation of books from the sixteenth century in Ottoman-held Greece. He draws on

Philippos Iliou (1975), who presents material from written accounts chronicling such distribution. For information on the types of books distributed, see Liata (1977). Politis cites as major works the popularized versions of Cretan masterpieces such as *Erotokritos* and *Erophile* as well as popularized religious works and hagiographies. The most popular work recounts the exploits of Alexander the Great.

20. Menounos (1979) synthesizes much of the critical work done on Kosmas and, on this particular point, shows that works by Phaltaïts, Michalopoulos, Kalinderis, Kourkoula, and Constas concur that the eight extant manuscripts, the earliest dated 1780, were set down in print by Kosmas's followers. Only Papakyriakou (1953) favors the theory that Kosmas read from a prepared, written text.

21. Much of Kosmas's Christian preaching makes use of folk legends and adaptations of biblical narratives that places Jews in situations with Greeks and Turks. This 'popularization' is evident in his parables (Menounos 1979: 291–300), translated in Vaporis (1977: 135–46). It is noteworthy that Kosmas himself addressed letters to community leaders urging, and often supporting, their efforts to keep schools open or run new ones (Vaporis 1977: 147–58).

22. Puchner's (1983) survey of thirteen versions of *Erophile* found in regional variations from Crete, Roumeli, Thessaly, and Epirus demonstrates the divergences created by different social and cultural tendencies of performance. The exchange phenomena of migration need to be seen not through the logic of an originary text's organicity but the situating of each variation in its string of variations, its *mouvance*. See some variations in T. Papadopoulos (1969: 353–77); G. A. Megas (1960: 370–4); D. B. Economides (1953).

23. Kosmas's 'Κυριακήν ημέραν έγινεν ο Ευαγγελισμός' is often transformed to 'Κυριακήν ημέρα έγινεν η γέννησις,' a transformation typical of oral formulae (Menounos 1979: 79).

24. Zumthor cites the example of Elias Lonnrot's publication of epic Finnish songs in the cyclic form of the Kalevala in 1835. This textualization did not curb the oral tradition, instead it may even have galvanized it as is demonstrated by the fact of this cycle's republication fifteen years later twice the original size. Zumthor (1990: 26–7) cites other examples from England, Russia, Spain, and Africa.

25. Tziovas (1989b: 324–6); see also Jacques Derrida (1981) on supplement/ *hypomnema* in *Plato's Pharmacy*.

26. See Herzfeld (1982); Alexiou (1985); Lambropoulos (1988); Jusdanis (1991a).

27. See Manousos (1850); Zambelios (1852). Herzfeld (1986) outlines the attack against Greek notions of continuity, and the consequent response, in his excellent work, *Ours Once More:Folklore, Ideology and the Making of Modern Greece.*

28. Jusdanis (1991a; Chapters 3 and 4) examines such anthologies and literary histories as sites for the determination of fluctuating and ever-changing literary and aesthetic norms in nineteenth- and twentieth-century Greece.

29. Συλλογή των γνωστών ποιημάτων του Ιππότ. Διονυσίου Κόμ. Σολωμού. Εν Ζακύνθω, Τυπογραφείον ο Ζάκυνθος, Κωνσταντίνου Ρωσσολίμου. (εκδ. Ροσολίμου), 1857. Ποιήματα Σολωμού και Ωδή εις τον θάνατόν του. Εν Αθήναις, εκ του τυπογραφείου Το Αθήναιον, έκδ. Μαντσαβίνου-Δαλλαπόρτα, 1857.

30. Philologists are still disputing over the 'first' edition of the 'Hymn to Liberty.' The poem appeared at about the same time in Messolonghi in 1825, from the printer D. Menestheos and with a translation into Italian by Gaetano Grassetti. The other 'first edition' appeared in Paris in the second volume of Fauriel's *Chants populaires de la Grèce moderne* (1824–5: 435–88), with a translation into French by Stanislas Julien.

31. Cited in L. Politis (1985: 279) and taken from *Pandora* 7 (1856–7): 503–4.

32. Soutsos cited in L. Politis (1985: 282).

33. Valaorites was not alone in this opinion. However, he was also a poet regarded in literary circles as a potential rival National Poet. His opinion comes with not a little self-interest. In a letter to Constantine Asopios, Valaorites conceded that 'this eventuality somehow worked in my favor' (Savidis 1989a: 140; cf. L. Politis 1985: 287)

34. Solomos would pass by Polylas's house when Iakovos was a child (Kalosgouros 1984).

35. Vellianitis in Valetas (1959: ιε–ιστ).

36. Valetas (1959: ιζ).

37. See, in particular, Schiller's *On the Aesthetic Education of Man in a Series of Letters* (1795). See Veloudis (1983; 1989: 152–72); and Varnalis (1925: 134–54) for a full account of Solomos's borrowings from the work of Friedrich Schiller. Polylas himself twice comments on Solomos's use of Schiller's aesthetic theory in his *Prolegomena* (Polylas 1948: 29, 33–4) and Solomos also directly quotes from Schiller's *Über den moralischen Nutzen ästhetischer Sitter* in the draft prose statement of his poem 'Νικηφόρος ο Βρυέννιος' (Solomos 1979a: 257).

38. Cited in Veloudis (1989). Originally in Friedrich Schiller (1966–73), *Sämtliche werke*, vol. 5, 6th edn (Munich: Hanser, 572).

39. Mantzaros (1963: 51–5); Varnalis (1957: 154); Vlachogiannes (1944: 804).

40. This is not entirely true since Solomos's drafts for *The Cretan*, as they appear in L. Politis's facsimile edition of the manuscripts, show some prose jottings in Greek and even some prose notes begun in Greek and continued in Italian (L. Politis 1964b: 363, 366, 372).

41. Mackridge (1992) makes some interesting points about the poet's orality, the interpenetration of languages and the influence of song. See also Dallas (1997).

42. On *Prozess*, cf. Friedrich Schlegel, *Schriften zur Literatur*, ed. von Wolfdietrich Rasch, 2nd edn (Munich, 1985); Novalis, *Werke*, ed. von Gerhard Schulz, 2nd edn (Munich: C. H. Beck, 1981): 228. For the plant metaphor in Solomos's aesthetic jottings, see Beaton (1976: 161–82). The poem originates, like the flower, which at all times establishes an immediate identity with an original flower since the conception of a natural object in terms of origins leads to a transcendental concept of the idea. For a discussion of notions of organicism and theories of poetic creation, see Abrams's (1971) discussion of Coleridge's theories of organic form and use of the plant metaphor. The fullness of the plant's development, like that of the poem, sees the coincidence of its internal development with that of the perfection of its outward form. To this seemingly unconscious paradigm, Coleridge wills the poet to 'make thyself become' in *The Statesman's Manual* (Abrams 1971: Chapter VII). For a critique of these assumptions, see de Man, 'Structure intentionelle de l'image romantique,' *Revue Internationale de Philosophie* 51 (1960): 68–84.

43. Kapsomenos's discussion of Solomos's work as 'modern' or 'open' text was probably triggered as a response to Veloudis's treatment of the Romantic theory of *Prozess* (Veloudis 1989: 392).

44. Solomos's father, Nicolo, was an aristocrat originally from Crete. At the age of 61, he had an affair with his servant girl, Angelika, then 15. At the time Nicolo was married and only finally married Angelika on his deathbed in 1807, after his first wife had died. The young Dionysios Solomos, or Dionisio Salamon, inherited his father's title, Count of Conte. We know that Angelika was illiterate because of not only her social station but also the fact that her known letters to Dionysios when he was in Italy are written in a different hand and style each time and, thus, point to the likelihood that they were dictated. For more on these letters, see L. Politis (1985: 67–83).

45. The first of four letters that Solomos wrote in Greek first appeared in the Zakynthian journal Επτανησιακά Φύλλα 12 (October 1948): 173. This letter was found by L. H. Zois who later handed the letter to Linos Politis who, by that time, had discovered three other letters, which he published together in an article to be found in Αγγλοελληνική Επιθεώρηση 4 (1949–50): 166. The letters are now in the National Library in Athens.

46. Jenkins (1940: 65) has also referred to them as *rime obbligate*.

47. This game or diversion originated in *précieux* circles of early-seventeenth-century Paris and became popular in England, too. It remained fashionable up to the nineteenth century (see Mackridge 1989: 11). Solomos's brother, Dimitrios, in a letter to his second wife, writes that Dionysios 'would compose

three or four sonnets while improvising on others on the same subject or *in sullo stresso argumento* and *in rima obbligata'* in the privacy of his own home (Pilitsis 1988: 189). The group was comprised of many of the Zakynthian social elite: Antonis Matessis (1794–1875), Pavlos Mercatis (1771–1854), Georgios Tertsetis (1800–74); also Manolis Leontarakis, Dionysios Tayaperas, Nikolaos Lountzis, Andreas Komiotis, Gaetano Grassetti, and others.

48. For more on Solomos's emendations, see L. Politis (1985: 207–12).

49. See, for instance, Chatziyakoumis's juxtaposition of some of Solomos's early verses and Zakynthian or Heptanesian demotic songs and distichs (1968: 148–53).

50. Chatziyakoumis cites later anthologies of Heptanesian folksongs which, though clearly much later than Solomos's time, feature folksongs set to music: De Marcellus (1851); Minotou (1933–4); Karakassis (1965).

51. Polylas (1948: 25) cites some of the poems Mantzaros put to music in his *Prolegomena.*

52. In the first volume, the manuscripts are presented by the *Lichtdruck* photo-copying method and are, for the most part, displayed in their life size. Solomos's manuscripts now exist at three institutions: the Museum of Zakynthos, the Academy of Athens, and a few are at the National Library in Athens. The Zakynthos manuscripts were given to the museum in 1898 by Polylas's sister-in-law, Aspasia Sordina Ringler, who found them in his papers after Polylas had passed away. The great earthquake of 1953 on the island could have ruined the manuscripts but, fortunately, they were saved by the timely inter-vention of N. Varvianis, who carried them to safety. The manuscripts in the Academy of Athens date back to 1934 and are the manuscripts given to Yorgos Kalosgouros by Polylas from the time that the two had decided to work on a new edition (which they never completed together). They were given to the Academy by the executors of Kalosgouros's estate in 1934. Finally, the few documents in the National Library were misappropriated from Zakynthos by K. Kairophyllas and sold to the Library in 1927.

–3–

Derivation

A Greek will never say anything he hasn't already said a thousand times.

Don DeLillo, The Names

'A striking characteristic of political and cultural practices in the Greek social formation,' wrote the sociologist Nikos Mouzelis in the late 1970s, 'is the extent to which conflicts and debates take a formalistic-legalistic character, diverting the attention of the masses away from "substantive" issues (i.e. issues related to fundamental class antagonisms and to conflicting views of the world)' (Mouzelis 1978: 134). Mouzelis's study, in the heady days of post-dictatorship Greece, showed how this formalism – the 'tendency to transform substance into form' – was the outcome of 'a disarticulation between imported and indigenous politico-ideological institutions' (Mouzelis 1978: 147).[1] Institutions not developed endogenously, and often imposed by Western imperialism and with no organic links to native structures, rarely functioned properly and often did so decoratively, 'like parliaments in some African countries,' adds Mouzelis (1978: 138).

The sudden importation of modes and practices, in conditions of political surveillance and economic dependency – be they colonial or otherwise – engender defensive political instincts and prime an inclination for the manipulation of such frameworks. Rather than viewing this as a symptom of Ottoman legacy in Greece, these behaviors should be seen as the results of social conditions and power relations born out of the cross-fertilization of capitalist and precapitalist modes.[2] As we saw in the previous chapter, autochthons and heterochthons alike were adept at learning the language of power and reinscribing the formalisms of the state's totalized structures to further their own ends. Constitutionalism was one such plaything in their hands, as demonstrated in the debate over citizenship in 1844. Such internal maneuvering among contending, newly forming interests is not exclusive to Greece by any means. Voting practices prevalent elsewhere, at the time of the Reform Act in England in 1832 for instance, were clientelistic, too. But formalisms in Greece were particularly risk-free because political systems unfolded in relative autonomy from social and economic structures. Dertilis (1985: 62–85) has outlined the causes for this autonomy: a barely distinguishable rural and urban divide; an urban elite that consolidated their mercantile interests *outside* the Greek state and so did not clash with the agrarian elite; domestic impoverishment under Ottoman rule that did not offer the conditions for an indigenous industry, with the result that no industrial elite existed to compete for resources with the agrarian elite; and, given the smallness of these elites, the predominance of a small group of families that both engendered and sustained an interconnectedness; these are all relevant factors.

Consequently, when universal male suffrage came to Greece, relatively early in 1844, it did so with little of the civil unrest characteristic of the phenomenon elsewhere in Europe. It did not spring out of a realignment of political or social forces or alongside the emergence of a mass party. Instead, it reinstated 'local elites' (to use a term that avoids the frequent ascription of them as 'clans' in the literature, which only feeds notions of precapitalist tribalism). These elites proposed alternatives to the excesses of foreign rule. All the resources of the governing party were channeled unscrupulously toward the goal of securing electoral victory.[3] And though political power remained in the clutches of state officials and elections were contested with some ferocity, democratic exchange of power was peaceful by European standards. The high level of voter participation and relatively limited worker unrest in the second half of the twentieth century points more to the continued potency, adaptability, and autonomy of clientelistic systems than to exemplarity in democratic process, though there was surely some of the latter, too (Tsoucalas 1981: 309–21).

Representation without Representation

All these factors point to a persistent problem of representation in the practices of the Greek social and political system. Forms and mechanisms of representation fell into place early. The assemblies of revolutionary committees in 1821–2, from the very beginning of the Greek Revolution, vouch for a belief in democratic principle, even if that practice left a lot to be desired. The disjuncture of form and praxis played itself out not solely on the macropolitical level, but also in areas of social and cultural life. How it reproduced itself in cultural matters has already been commented upon. The struggle between proponents of purism and demoticism as the language of state, and the debate's ideologization and political exploitation, has been discussed in the context of formalism by both Mouzelis and Herzfeld. The disjunctures of formalism, however, also marked the issue of representation in the literature of the period. And this, too, is a function of uneven (under)development.

It is worth reflecting on the 'coincidental' crisis of representation that seems to mark the depiction of 'Greek experience' or 'reality' in literature. The novel, charged elsewhere in Europe with just this (re)presentation, is a genre that traces its origins back to the late Greek classical tradition.[4] And modern Greeks were aware of this. Indeed, one of the first initiatives taken up by Greek Enlightenment figures in the diaspora, in the last decade of the eighteenth century, was to edit and publish Hellenistic and Byzantine romances.[5] Yet, for much of the nineteenth century, Greeks considered prose fiction a foreign imposition (Voutouris 1995: Chapter 1). Even overlooking the raunchier episodes of their Hellenistic precursors, Korais disapproved of the genre's decadence and he preferred a sanitization in accord with the ideologies implicit in his espousal of *katharevousa*.[6] In a society in which the cultural primacy of poetry was widely acknowledged, the incompatibility of prose for presenting Greek reality meant that it was slow in establishing itself. Just how slow has now become a contentious issue. For, though the prevailing critical wisdom was, until very recently, that the early prose of the modern Greek state entailed chiefly imitative historical novels – and, specifically, ones set in foreign climes and often in bygone times[7] – recent criticism is disputing such characterizations. The recent publication of more texts from the period between 1830 and 1850 has underscored their social and realist ambitions.[8] Early works of prose *were* concerned with contemporary Greek reality, after all. Such assertions severely undermine the prevalent developmentalist narrative of Greek realist prose in the nineteenth century, which described the genre's lugubrious slouch toward a Western-like realist respectability, and found its most representative expression in Mario Vitti's influential essay on the notion of *ethographia* (ηθογραφία).[9]

Today's revisionist trend is welcome, even if it does not quite extricate itself much from the sway of Western developmentalism. That is, it still argues that Greek prose develops in reference to the same Western standards, but it does so only earlier than previously maintained. To identify an indigenous tradition – be it orally transmitted classical archetypes, the Byzantine romance, the lives of saints, or the narrative particularities of the folktale – that such novels draw from would be a useful antidote to such inclinations. As long, that is, as this is accomplished without falling into the isolationism of unreflective continuity (Tonnet 1991). A greater sensitivity to the way these traditions were transmitted, in oral as well as in written forms, would further enrich our appreciation of the heterogeneous resources available to modernity. But, in pursuing these goals, critics need also to place less emphasis on the *derivative* nature of so many early neohellenic prose texts, and focus more on the ways they situate themselves against prototypes to achieve certain ends. In this way, critical analysis would take more seriously the efforts of Greek writers of the time to locate themselves *in*, but also *against*, traditions that they realized, quite consciously, to be incongruent with their artistic needs. If Mouzelis instructs us that Greeks manipulated European forms for their purposes in sociopolitical sites, is it not likely that they did so with cultural forms too? This approach would be in keeping with trends in postcolonial, feminist, and deconstructive theories that emphasize a more heightened awareness of the agency exhibited by the once passive victims of history. Certainly, since Mouzelis's model, anthropologists of Greece have stressed how 'all supposedly recognizable forms, on both sides of each symbolic opposition [that is, along the ideational poles of disemia, formalism and social experience] are demonstrably less stable "on the ground" than official formalism – or than radical critiques, including that of Mouzelis – would suggest' (Herzfeld 1987: 135). Pointing to the negotiability and lability of forms in the keen minds and hearts of the oppressed, or the newly liberated (or both), is a sign of the interpetive times.

The literary crisis of representation discussed in this chapter revolves around the anxiety over the need to capture and represent the differentiated existence of the individual, as he (and to a lesser degree she) exists in the public and private sphere. How was the experience of the individual, both male and female, to be admitted into the field of discourse at the time of the state's founding? And did individuals consider discourse in conformity with that experience? To explore the resistance, rewriting, and exploitation of such 'given' forms of representation will underscore Greek novelists' conscious manipulation of foreign conventions and modes. To argue the case, I take two originary prose narratives of the time. Both works have been deemed incomplete and, in a certain sense, flawed. The first, Elisavet Moutzan-Martinengou's *My Story*, published by her son in 1881 though written in all likelihood in 1831, is one of the earliest prose texts of the modern Greek state. It is also the first to be penned by a woman. It is an autobiography; one that has been read as a stirring testament to this woman's protofeminist credentials – an incomplete yet brave existential cry for recognition from the darker recesses of the home/tomb. The reading that follows argues that Martinengou's autobiography, very self-consciously, comments on its own fictionality and the limits of the genre. Indeed, her narrative is as much a critical appraisal of its relation to the genres that constitute it as it is a presentation of the heroine's life. In this reading, Martinengou reflects on the female subject little served by the written word even as she seeks freedom through writing in the male-dominated public sphere. The circularity and implicit contradiction of this formulation reinforces Paul de Man's theoretical warning against the limits of treating autobiography as a transparent mode.

The second chosen text is often regarded as the first novel of the modern Greek state. Panayiotis Soutsos's epistolary novel *Leandros* (1834) borrows heavily from the genres of the travelogue and the romance. The available criticism has tended to consume itself in a search for foreign antecedents. As a result, the novel's alleged insufficiencies in light of these European antecedents have only served as fodder for claiming its derivativeness. However, such readings do not relate Soutsos's dialogue across genres to the novel's action, its commentary on the very issue of derivation, and Soutsos's position on modernity and the genres that constitute it in Greece.

De Man, the Woman, and her Story: Moutzan-Martinengou's *Autobiography* (1831)

Autobiography deals precisely with the task of authorizing and representing the subject, the individual. It stages the vexed questions concerning the subject, agency, and the referentiality, truth, and sincerity of the reading and writing of experience. To an extent, it is autobiography that has authorized our interest in these questions: 'autobiographical authority may be attributed to human agents but also to genre(s) of self-representation (especially, autobiography itself)' (Gilmore 1994: 67). This aggravating circularity seems to plague the practice and discussion of autobiography – it provokes a blurring of cause and effect, reading and writing, experience and its narrativization. Paul de Man describes this as the intolerable feeling of being caught in autobiography's revolving door (1979: 921).

The power of autobiography stems from its ability to reify the notion of authority and its concomitant claims to truth, power, and the primacy of experience only in order to identify them as illusions. To put it another way, autobiography seems to establish the contours of subjectivity and authority only in order to locate the possibility for their transgression. In fact, autobiography undermines the very generic precepts on which it is founded. As Barbara Johnson writes in her essay 'My Monster/My Self': 'Simultaneously a revelation and a cover-up, autobiography would appear to constitute itself as in some way a repression of autobiography' (Johnson 1987: 146). Furthermore, it does so as a self-writing and self-reading which functions through the substitution and interchangeability of not only the writer, protagonist, and narrator of the autobiography, but also its writer and reader. Autobiography stages the authorizing moment of a particular self-writing (*My* Story) only in order to implicate this authority in a more general authorizing agenda of reading (*My* Story is also necessarily *Your* Story):

> Autobiography, then, is not a genre or a mode, but a figure of reading or of under-standing that occurs, to some degree, in all texts. The autobiographical moment happens as an alignment between the two subjects involved in the process of reading in which they determine each other by mutual reflexive substitution. The structure implies differentiation as well as similarity, since both depend on a substitutive exchange that constitutes the subject. (de Man 1979: 921)

The paradoxes that plague the discussion of autobiography, and the implications of the dialectic between authority and transgression that seem to motivate its writing, are most provocatively exhibited in women's autobiographical writing. After all, 'In a humanistic tradition in which *man* is the measure of all things, how does an appendage go about telling the story of her life?' (Johnson 1987: 147, original emphasis). Leigh Gilmore maintains that autobiography's self-authorizing machinations are complicated by the fact that not all autobiographers write with equal authority from the location of the self-referential *I* (Gilmore 1994: 67). Gilmore focuses on women whose autobiographies are often not categorized as such, and also often appeared under pseudonyms, anonymously, or with authenticating and authorizing prefaces by men.

Given the rather problematic endeavor of writing from the location of a self-referential *I* that defines women's identities as marginal, it is ironic how many recent feminist scholars read women's autobiographies as documents, as a means of direct access to an otherwise silenced female consciousness. In such readings, autobiography appears as an unmediated expression of an authentic and long-hidden experience. The contemporary outpouring of self-writing as a writing strategy of women, minorities, and of 'difference' in general purportedly makes visible what is not adequately represented in society. The historian Joan Scott (1991) has described this trend as the paradoxical endeavor of challenging normative history while remaining comfortably within its disciplinary framework:

> It is precisely this kind of appeal to experience as uncontestable evidence and as an originary point of explanation – as a foundation on which analysis is based – that weakens the critical thrust of histories of difference. By remaining within the epistemological frame of orthodox history, these studies lose the possibility of examining those assumptions and practices that excluded considerations of difference in the first place. They take as self-evident the identities of those whose experience is being documented and thus naturalize their difference. They locate resistance outside its discursive construction and reify agency as an inherent attribute of individuals, thus decontextualizing it . . . The evidence of experience then becomes evidence for the fact of difference, rather than a way of exploring how difference is established, how it operates, how and in what ways it constitutes subjects who see and act in the world. (Scott 1991: 777)

Women's autobiography, therefore, dramatizes the dialectic between authority and transgression in the self-contradictory gesture of writing as a no-body; of calling for a document-like authority based on the 'evidence of experience,' yet at the same time pointing to the limits and paradoxes of that experience.

Women's voices and texts have long been silent and absent from the modern Greek literary tradition. Lately, critics have begun to unearth some early precursors of women's writing as well as to devise paradigms more sensitive to the critical appreciation of later and contemporary women's writing. Elisavet Moutzan-Martinengou's *My Story* is one such text. It has been hailed as initiating and authorizing a tradition of women's autobiographical writing (Dimaras 1978: 216–17). Kitromilides (1983: 56) calls Martinengou 'the progenitor of Greek feminist thought.' Martinengou's text does, indeed, stand apart for the boldness exhibited in writing about herself at a time when women's writing was mainly limited to translation of foreign models. And it is not without significance that a tradition of feminist writing in Greece should be inaugurated by a text that so clearly thematizes the problems of writing as a woman. Tellingly, criticism has so far not considered the text in terms of the narrative strategies it utilizes or its status as an autobiography. Instead, it has been read as a document, a straightforward account by and about a remarkable woman.[10]

Here, I shall read *My Story* in light of its status as an originary woman's text and document in the modern Greek tradition. Focusing on Martinengou's use of autobiography, I shall examine the way the text challenges the grounds of its presentation of self through an insistent interrogation and explicit thematization of the acts of reading and writing in relation to a conceptualization of experience. *My Story* presents the question of authority and experience through the enactment of a meeting between a writing 'I' and a reading 'you,' and, in so doing, exemplifies the paradoxes of the autobiographical gesture.

Women Exemplars?

Martinengou's text is structured around a central irony – it performs the writing of a life that is not a life. Martinengou is held captive in her home, not allowed to walk outside – even to go to church or visit friends – because of what she describes as her family's adherence to 'barbaric, unnatural and inhuman customs.' She describes her need to write as a means of escaping this deadening enclosure. Writing is thus inherently linked to a woman's condition of literal and figurative 'captivity'; and, like many originary women's texts, Martinengou's autobiography is ultimately all about the problems of writing autobiography as a woman. Furthermore, Martinengou repeatedly embeds these problems within larger historical and political narratives; *My Story* thus insistently points to the intrinsic intertextuality (and not derivativeness) of all self-representation.

My Story interrelates the issues of intertextuality, self-representation, and captivity in a manner very similar to other originary texts that inaugurated women's literary traditions. Some have been used to buttress the foundations of national canons and traditions through the reification of the autobiographical voice. In the United States, Mary Rowlandson's famous autobiographical captivity narrative, *A Narrative of the Captivity and Restoration of Mrs. Mary Rowlandson* (1682), is considered to have inaugurated a women's literary tradition. The narrative recounts the eponymous heroine's captivity in February 1676. While her husband was away in Boston, some Narragansetts attacked her New England town, burned down her home, killed most of her extended family, and took her and her three children captive. Rowlandson recounts her experience living with the Narragansetts and her eventual return home, seven years after her release from captivity. It appeared accompanied by a sermon written by her husband and an anonymous preface written by the most influential historian and theologian of the time, Increase Mather. As Tara Fitzpatrick (1991: 2) has written, 'Puritan women's captivity sagas generally relied on two narrators: the redeemed captives themselves and the ministers who propagated the captives' histories for didactic purposes of their own.' The Puritan community was so warned not to stray, either literally or figuratively, from the safety of community and faith. Furthermore, this framing associates Rowlandson's conversion with a larger nationalist agenda; her return and preservation, her escape from Native American taint, point to the community's cultural and spiritual triumph over the Narragansett savages. The exemplarity of this woman's narrative thus rests on its deployment as a nationalist and religiously hegemonic text. Only recently have critics pointed to the way in which the text's silences and contradictions index Rowlandson's particularly problematic use of the autobiographical mode.

Like Rowlandson's account, Martinengou's narrative describes a particularly turbulent time in modern Greek history. *My Story* was written in 1831;[11] she died in 1832 on the island of Zakynthos. From the end of the eighteenth century when Zakynthos had just passed from Venetian to French rule, it found itself in the middle of a power struggle. As part of the Ionian Islands it became part of an autonomous state in 1800, was again taken over by the French in 1807, and became an independent republic under the protection of Great Britain in 1815.[12] These transitions split the island between an established aristocratic faction and a democratic faction aroused by French liberal ideals. Martinengou's father, Franciscus, served as governor (*eparchos*) from February 1818 to February 1823. When the Greek Revolution broke out in 1821, the people of the Ionian Islands were split between supporting the Greeks or following the policy of English neutrality. Martinengou, unlike her father, supported the Greeks. Consequently the allusions to the turbulence of historic events in the narrative are inextricably tied to Martinengou's exploration of self-representation.

The publication history of Martinengou's text, as with Rowlandson's text, contributed to its reading as an exemplary document. It was published in 1881, forty-nine years after her death, in edited form by her son Elisavetios Martinengou (1832–85) as the first part of a volume that included his own poetry.[13] He includes the most 'important excerpts' from his 'late mother's' autobiography, and indicates omitted passages by ellipses.'[14] Martinengou's son rather possessively entitled the account *My Mother: Autobiography of Mrs. Elisavet Moutzan Martinengou* and prefaces the account with a note, which explains that he wants to 'make known such a woman to our society.' Elisavetios, who lost his mother fourteen days after complications from his birth and who came to know his mother through her writing, frames the publication of her narrative as an act of filial duty and emphasizes her maternal qualities.[15] As in Nikolaos Kandounis's portrait of a gaunt and mournful Martinengou that hangs in the Zakynthos Museum which portrays her holding a letter marked 'remember me always, husband and children,' her writing is related to her ability to reach out to her family beyond the grave. The auto-biography is deployed to underscore Martinengou's exemplarity as a mother and woman and to link this exemplarity to her originary position in a women's modern Greek literary tradition.

Both Rowlandson's and Martinengou's narratives are posited as exemplary accounts, meant to exert a normative, even salutary function: 'Reader, if thou gettest no good by such a declaration as this, the fault must needs be thine own' admonishes Rowlandson's anomymous preface writer. Martinengou's life as a self-sacrificing and maternal prototype is an image that her son tries to advance through his framing of the narrative. Despite and yet because of this very framing, both narratives evidence a particularly tense relation to their exemplarity which threatens at every moment to turn into its opposite, a transgressive fragmentation, disfigur-ation, or defacement – to borrow another term from de Man – which undermines the notion of the salutary, cohesive power of reading. 'The restoration of mortality by autobiography . . . deprives and disfigures to the precise extent that it restores. Autobiography veils a defacement for the mind of which it is itself the cause' (de Man 1979: 930).

Lettrée, Piété, Mobilité

Reading and writing are the constitutive tropes of Martinengou's narrative. In fact, *My Story* focuses almost exclusively on the relation of writing to authorizing self-expression. Self-authorization seems to run in the family. Elisavetios Martinengou chose to include his mother's autobiography within a volume of his own poetry, as if this made-to-order literary lineage somehow enhances or adds weight to his own writing. What is most striking in an autobiography in which Martinengou claims 'I decided not to hide anything of the events of my life' (49)[16] is the fact that instead of seeing what we would generally acknowledge as events, we get a progress report on Martinengou's writing that tries almost obsessively to have us appreciate its genius and literariness. In essence, Martinengou conceives of her autobiography as an authorizing supplement to her other fictional texts, which were indeed large in number – Boumboulides (1965) and Kolias (1989) cite twenty-nine different Greek and Italian tragedies, comedies, and moral stories authored by Martinengou herself (Boumboulides 1965: 157–8; Kolias 1989: 113–14). There are, above and beyond these, translations and further works referred to in the autobiography, yet no longer extant.[17] Thirty works were burnt in a fire at the home of Dinos Konomos, editor of the journal *Heptanysiaka Phylla*, during the catastrophic Zakynthos earthquake of 1953.[18]

In the new Greek state 'a general premium [was] put on education as the basic means for the revival of the nation,' which in turn led to 'organized initiatives for female instruction' (Kitromilides 1983: 44). These women writers came from the Phanariot aristocracy and the highly mobile class of merchants, professionals, and intellectuals who provided the primary social basis of the Greek Enlightenment. Kitromilides describes their works as lacking both 'originality [and] literary interest' (1983: 44). Their work has been seen as derivative, comprising mostly of translations of popular French guidebooks for female behavior, or plays extolling the transcendent powers of female virtue. While Martinengou's work is also representative of the set of values which had traditionally been considered the foundation of female virtue, her autobiography is, as Kitromilides argues, 'more remarkable and forceful than the timid female moralists of the Enlightenment' (1983: 56). It is 'a captivating work,' in more senses than Kitromilides (1983: 56) has in mind. Yet it is so not so much because it simply expresses radical feminist views, but rather on account of its commitment to liberation through education and the relation it establishes between Martinengou and her texts. Martinengou's autobiography collapses her life into her writing so that they are essentially one and the same in a way that explores the way the two inform each other.

Like Rowlandson's narrative, Martinengou's autobiography takes the form of a type of confession or conversion narrative, which relates control of reading and writing to a transcendent expression of her gendered identity. Unlike Rowlandson, Martinengou explicitly associates her writing with her expression as a woman; she identifies her narrative as a manifesto of sorts, which argues for greater educational opportunities and mobility for women. The protagonist launches into impassioned calls for the better treatment of girls by their fathers. In a 'terrible letter' to her father, Elisavet speaks for all women: 'especially because they are female you owe it to them to love them more. And you in your turn owe it to them to love them more because they are female, because they (I speak for the females of my country) being imprisoned in a house, have greater need of your fatherly care' (49–50). Her father is 'touched by the freedom' of her plea, though, typically, he ignores its message and sets out on a tour of Italy with Elisavet's brother. This act is representative of the several contrasts made between her own lack of education and mobility and her father and brother's educational and physical freedom.

My Story opens with a line that equates illiteracy with a fallen, sinful state: 'Until this time, that is, until my eighth year, I did not yet know the alphabet' (3). The horror of her plight is made apparent in that she cannot even read or have direct access to the Lord's prayer: 'My mother decided, therefore, to teach me herself the little that she knew, and she bought a booklet and started to read to me slowly every evening: "Holy God, holy and mighty, holy and immortal, have mercy on us." She read it to me once, she read it ten times, but in vain; her efforts were wasted' (3). It is only through her grandmother's syllabization of certain prayers, which the older woman has learnt by heart, that Elisavet makes her first readerly steps. It is so intimated that this lesson is effected by an oral communication, one more consonant with a tradition of female transmission of knowledge, and which is therefore highly limited and circumscribed in the terms set up in the narrative.

This equation between the quest for literacy and the religious quest for redemption is made throughout the narrative and is literalized when Martinengou expresses her desire to become a nun, not because she has a special religious calling, but rather so she might be able to pursue her reading and writing. Throughout, her description of how she learns to read and write turns on a close interrelation of literacy and virtue. Describing the teacher who taught her to read, she writes, 'After my lesson he would sit and explain Piety to me and all those virtues that one should have, especially if one was a Christian, and then he would sit and praise education' (4). Similarly, one of the few times when she appears truly happy in her narrative occurs while staying at the family country home at Pegadakia where not only does her father teach her Italian, but also she goes to hear the liturgy and even goes out for a stroll.[19] It is as if this elusive and much-longed-for trio – literacy, piety, mobility – actually go together. As a consequence, much later in the autobiography, when Elisavet imagines a much desired though improbable move to Italy and the creation of a space and not just a room of one's own, she conceives of herself leading a life that not only 'stays away from error but even from the suspicion of error' (59).

Unwittingly perhaps, in echoing the French revolutionary slogan of *liberté, fraternité, égalité*, Martinengou's triptych again collapses her own individual struggle for authority and freedom into a larger narrative of national identity and liberation. Thus, unlike her father who upholds 'barbaric customs' in relation to women, and therefore also appropriately sides with the British in a neutral stance towards the Greek War of Independence, Martinengou writes, 'I wished in my heart that I could take up arms, I wished in my heart that I could run to give help to those people who did not fight for anything else but for their religion and their country, and for that longed-for freedom which, when used well, brings immortality, glory, and happiness to people' (30). In fact, her father's role in events relating to the Greek War of Independence while never explicitly stated – the most she ever says is that her father was upset because there had been 'political disturbances' (40) – appear in a deflected way through his resistance to her, and others', requests for her freedom. Her father is insensitive to Elisavet's teacher Theodosios Dimadis's wish to return to Zakynthos when, having left only days earlier for mainland Greece at the beginning of revolt, Dimadis seeks to return and take refuge – such assistance, from a 'man of politics' as her father, 'would make him suspicious in the eyes of the [British] government' (31).

Her quest for literacy and authority is also associated with the religious imagery of life and death. The home, the locus of her captivity, is described as a tomb, full of darkness. Martinengou laments: 'Forever in the house! Ah! This thought scared me. I could see very well that this house was to bring a swift and terrible death' (53). In contrast, Martinengou associates writing with freedom and immortality, not only in the episodes in the country, but also in the way she urges the reader to treat her writing. Without writing she would be deadened (νεκρωμένη); her mind grows dark (εσκότισεν τον νουν). By contrast, her parents blame Elisavet's voracious reading for darkening her mind and keeping her from the proper feminine roles of her time. Reading keeps her from her chores, makes her forgetful and clumsy, and, in her parents' eyes, turns her into a monstrous woman outside the bounds of proper social roles.

Repeatedly, Martinengou directly addresses the reader and beseeches to be remembered. She stresses that she composes her fictional pieces by nature without having had much training, and hopes that 'translating many useful texts [. . .] and [. . .] publishing them for my benefit and the benefit of readers' will act as 'a memorial' to her. The use of the word μνημόσυνον for memorial, which refers to commemorations of the dead days after their funeral, draws the analogy still further. In fact, writing appears more than anything as a way of warding off her pathological fear of death and oblivion; the darkness of her home is linked to the fate of being forgotten, to being a no-body, 'I imagined myself obscured by those thick and dark clouds which usually darken and obscure the life and the name of ignorant and uneducated people' (6).

Within this schema, it is imagination that carries the heroine outside the house and beyond death. She revels in her imagination which empowers her to realize her desires, drawing together the notions of ξεφάντωσις (revelry) and φαντασίαν (imagination) – εξεφάντωσα με την φαντασίαν (I revel in/with my imagination) (13).[20] This coupling of writing and death occurs throughout the narrative and, in fact, becomes stronger as the narrative progresses. Near the beginning of the narrative Martinengou writes, 'I began to long for learning in the same way I grieved for Chrysoula, a dearest friend of my mother who had recently died' (6).[21] The analogy is, of course, primarily one of intensity of feeling, yet it also points to a somewhat paradoxical bringing together of longing and grief, of desire and loss. Martinengou's obsessive focus on writing is thus paralleled to an equally obsessive chronicling of death which becomes appreciably more detailed and graphic near the end of the narrative in her exposition of a paralyzing fear of thunderbolts and lightning, and the death of her dearest cousin fourteen days after childbirth. Her imagination transports her to the scenes of these misfortunes: her dreams ferry her to her cousin Angelika's bedside and she yearns to be like her, even though she knows that Angelika has, *in reality*, already died. Moreover, Elisavet's will to be Angelika serves as a prolepsis of her own imminent death in childbirth.

Self-restoration and De-facement

Martinengou thus explicitly identifies her autobiography as prosopopeia. Paul de Man describes autobiography as a discourse of 'self-restoration' and 'prosopopeia is the trope of autobiography, by which one's name is made as intelligible and memorable as a face' (1979: 925–6). The autobiography has her figuratively speaking beyond the grave. Not only does this woman, who exists in darkness in her tomb-like house and who has no public existence, envision her autobiography as her projected embodiment in the outside world, but also we cannot help but be somewhat shaken by the fact that her death, right after the writing of the narrative, literally gives it the status of a tombstone. It is this tombstone-like status of the autobiography that suggests the ways that the restorative power of writing portrayed in the autobiography actually starts to break down and turn into its opposite – a disfiguration or defacement. Paul de Man describes the 'latent threat that inhabits prosopopeia' as follows, 'by making death speak, the symmetrical structure of the trope implies, by the same token, that the living are struck dumb, frozen in their own death' (1979: 928). And this is what starts to happen, very literally, to the way Martinengou conceptualizes the writing of her autobiography; her writing becomes intimately woven into, indeed becomes a part and parcel, of her death-like status.

From quite early on, Martinengou expresses a fear that writing will not live up to its promise of transcendence. The very first two pieces of fictional writing she includes in her autobiography are two Aesopian fables – 'The Myth of the Mouse and the Frog' and 'The Myth of the Mice and the Cat' – which dwell on the fact that even though there are written agreements between the two different parties, a destructive natural force renders these agreements null and void. The *epythimion* to the first fable reads, 'The myth shows that he who attempts to deceive becomes the same as those who are deceived.' The second of the fables ends, 'When the agreements were signed, the mice indeed became friends with the cat, and the cat ate all of them,' while the *epythimion* reads: 'The myth shows that it is not possible to make a friend of a former enemy.'[22] In both cases, Martinengou uses the explicitly fictionalized format of the fable to associate writing to deception, and thus to comment on writing as a medium of falsification and illusory myth-making.

The latent potential of not only the powerlessness of writing, but also more importantly its deceptiveness, comes to the fore in Martinengou's interaction with her relatives. While Martinengou seems to believe that her writing will impress her father and uncle enough to actually grant her a measure of freedom, she receives a rude shock when she realizes that her writing holds no sway over her father, her letters go unanswered or are rebuffed, and in one instance, they are not even sent. Conversely, though, she resolves time and again to stand her ground, Elisavet is easily swayed by *their* suggestions.

The overwhelming melancholy that besets the characters, particularly her depressive father, contributes to a fatalistic atmosphere in the work; one that Elisavet also comments upon. In the middle of the narrative, while describing an earthquake on Zakynthos, Martinengou dwells on her fear of death, only to go on to report that she finished yet another piece of writing, this time a tragedy, and then adds, 'I have to make sure that this is published also to show in this way that the only art towards which I leaned naturally was that of Tragedy' (28–9). Martinengou's confession of an affinity for tragedy is not gratuitous here; in fact, it is constitutive of not only her autobiography as tombstone, but also the way she figures her renunciation of the illusion of the transcendent power of writing. After Martinengou's plans to become a nun are written off, and she fears that her 'children' – her writings – are fated to languish dusty and unread and 'fill the bellies of termites' (54), her narrative quickly comes to an end; she capitulates to the pressures of her family and she decides to marry.

This decision to marry and the concomitant rejection of writing's vocation is prefigured in a strange episode right before the end of the narrative. In the only episode in the whole autobiography that can actually be considered an event, in that the protagonist engages in action in time and space beyond the house, Martinengou reports that she plans to escape from home, make her way to Italy, and find a place for herself. She describes her escape, her attempt to find lodging with two Zagorian woman, their initial rebuff, her subsequent attempt to convince them to let her stay with them by recounting some 'fictitious events' (τα πλαστά συμβεβηκότα) about her life calculated to elicit their sympathy, and their persistence in not letting her in. Eventually left without a place to stay, she returns home and tells her parents she has decided to marry. In a narrative so consumed with the details of literary creation, these purportedly real events appear strangely unreal. They beg the question as to whether they really happened. Martinengou presents them as if they did; yet the fact that no-one, except for the unnamed, common 'Zagorian' women, sees her and that she embeds within this little episode an account of how she fictionalized events in order to make herself appear sympathetic, makes one doubtful. Certainly her statement upon her return to the house raises the issue: 'But how grateful I should be, my reader, for the infinite mercy of my God, who, after he freed me from the *delusion* (to which my distress had led me) that I could travel by myself, led me back to my home without anyone else knowing what I had done, anyone other than him and me' (57–8; emphasis mine). Kolias's correct translation of the Greek word πλάνην as 'delusion' here can not help but hide the suggestive connotations of a word that means not only 'delusion', but also 'beguilement,' 'error,' and – significantly – 'a wandering, often physical.' The intertwined notions of psychological, physical, and errant/erring mobility and wandering neatly reinforce the mutually sustaining relations of freedom, writing, and imagination.

Yet whether the event actually happened or not is not as important as the fact that the episode suspends the boundaries between the real and the fictional in such a forceful way. On the one hand, her deployment of 'fictitious events' leads to an energization of more imaginative, fictional scenarios wherein she vividly conjures up a life for herself in Venice. On the other hand, however, her relief at returning home, which is presented as occurring 'with the same longing as Adam and Eve felt when they looked at paradise' (56), marks a fall into consciousness that sees her return to the confining domesticity of her home and her compliance to her family's wishes. Her aborted and 'fictionalized' run for freedom facilitates and figures the end of her account as a tragic renunciation of writing. It is no coincidence that, upon her return to her home, she destroys the handwritten note that, prior to her escape, she had left for her parents. It is Elisavet now that intercepts her own letters and prevents them from reaching her intended addressee. It is a symbolic, at the same time literal, end to her world of letters!

Consequently, she deems that the only way of achieving some measure of a public identity – and perhaps to protect her existing texts – is by getting married. Martinengou agrees to marry and tries very hard to appear pleased to be marrying someone who puts off the wedding for ten months in order to haggle over her dowry. In fact, her description of the marriage negotiations is so forcefully and transparently dutiful, that it underscores her complete powerlessness in the face of the power of sanctioned social roles. Her ambivalence is dissolved in the face of a resigned calm:

> Within a few days the wedding (which was dragged out for ten months) will be over, and I should be the most happy girl in the world because by God's mercy I am the recipient of such good fortune; but, after so many bitter experiences that I have suffered through, including the ones that he caused with his delays in deciding on the marriage and with the greediness he showed with the dowry, my heart can not feel happiness anymore; it is enough for me however to feel peaceful and calm, as I have felt since the wedding was decided upon. (65)

Having come to the sanctioned end of a woman's coming-of-age story – the romance and marriage plot – Martinengou promises a second installment of her autobiography in her old age, a text that, once again, has the potential of unveiling the truths behind the myth of happy female domesticity: 'in it I intend to make known whether this man whom I am marrying is truly as virtuous as people say' (65). But, of course, we never get a second installment because she dies as a consequence of childbirth. With Martinengou's return to the natural order of things – the roles allowed her within the public sphere – the deathliness of her figurative 'children' is collapsed into the literal deadliness of her one and only real child. Martinengou escapes the figurative death represented by her family home, only to confront the literal death of motherhood.

Death in Zakynthos, Life in Venice

It is a little naive to seriously expect a second installment of her autobiography. For the escape episode, by explicitly identifying Martinengou's autobiography as a tragedy, makes the end of the narrative read like the bravado of a character who shortly will die. By encoding her desire for freedom and her eventual capitulation in an episode that plays with the figurality of experience, Martinengou most potently exemplifies the dangers of self-writing; she does die at the end of the narrative and it seems that this fictionalized narrative acquires a degree of referential productivity. Death, as de Man (1979: 930) has written, does seem to be a linguistic predicament. The ironies, therefore, of reading Martinengou's account are manifold. How do we deal with a narrative that, on the one hand, asks to be read as an example of the triumphant power of writing while on the other demonstrates that writing is nothing without a proper public forum in which the writer can operate? Furthermore, the fact that people have tended to read this narrative as an account of an exemplary feminine experience contrasts oddly with the account's insistence on its status as a piece of writing, on its fictionality, and in turn with the way it draws attention to Martinengou's other writings. This irony is heightened when we consider that much of the existing work on Martinengou makes little mention of her other writings.

Martinengou's originary narrative grows out of a historical moment of evolving conceptions of identity and nationhood, and operates, at least on one level, by collapsing the plight of the individual with the plight of her community and nation. This collapse of the individual and the community, a collapse figured by the meeting of the writing 'I' and the reading 'you' of autobiography, underlines the ways that reading and writing are involved in a particularly complicated negotiation of the interaction of the public and the private. Martinengou's account points to the *failure* of such a negotiation; it points to isolated pockets of a recalcitrant private sphere that has no access to the deceptive and transcendent grand narratives of the public sphere.[23] *My Story* portrays Martinengou's fragmentation among a number of equally unviable roles and narratives: the roles of dutiful daughter, wife, and mother – repeatedly associated throughout the narrative to images of death and highly dramatized self-sacrifice – are pitted against her ghost-like, monstrous position as a writer in captivity. It is perhaps one of the final and most telling ironies in the text that it is the son whose birth killed her who finally facilitates the public birthing of her other 'children.' Martinengou's text is indeed an originary feminist text, but one whose feminism dramatizes the deep fissures and contradictions in any concept of identity. The text establishes an equivalence among different roles – the different resonances of motherhood for example – and explores their significance in terms of public and private negotiations of identity. The text does not allow for a comforting notion of an unmediated experience that speaks to us across the ages.[24] In fact, *My Story* is so concerned with exploring the sometimes conflicting discursive practices that formulate conceptions of the self, that, in the words of Joan Scott, it shows that 'experience is at once always already an interpretation and something that needs to be interpreted' (1991: 797). As such, it speaks more through what it leaves unsaid or awkwardly said, through the silences and the uneven and roughly marked transitions between different types of narratives, that identify *My Story* as an autobiography. The conception of self in autobiography is inextricably tied to a series of masks and translations. The relation of the autobiography to her other writings – both within and outside the autobiography – need to be read as a self-conscious negotiation of self-narration in a number of genres and modes. Martinengou's strategic embedding of, allusion to, and dialogic engagement with fables, archetypes of romance and domestic plots, Byzantine saints' lives, and translations are integral to her presentation of self in the narrative.[25] The location of the Greek subject – and here the Greek female subject – in the discourses that construct her is as problematic as the notion of her existence in the public sphere, the society, that she is to be a part. Writing oneself into discourse, into a Greek public sphere, and into the new Greek state is a conventional problem.

From Nafplion to Athens in P. Soutsos's *Leandros* (1834): A Capital Idea(l)

There may be no more conventional representation than woman as the object of desire. The depiction of Koralia, the heroine of the modern Greek state's first novel,[26] *Leandros* (1834) by Panayiotis Soutsos (1806–68), fits into this category rather unproblematically. That the hero Leandros's unrequited love for Koralia in the face of society's prohibitions leads to her death and his suicide is also very much the norm for such a romance. Quite rightly, the novel has been characterized a Romantic novel. Its earliest reviews focused primarily on its debt to European antecedents in a way that reveals a lack of confidence in the indigenous tradition.[27] Much of the meager contemporary criticism has expended its energy situating the work in relation to the same European prototypes.[28] In undertaking such a task, such criticism is living up to a philological tradition, but it is also reacting to the very first sentence of the prologue, in which Soutsos himself situates his work alongside Rousseau, Scott, Goethe, Foscolo, and Cooper (75).[29] Critical scholarship has stressed most how Soutsos's work draws from Goethe's *The Sorrows of Young Werther* (1774) and Ugo Foscolo's *Letters of Ortis* (1798–1802).[30] *Leandros* is located in the traditions of the European epistolary novel, the Romantic sentimental novel, and the travelogue.

Yiorgos Veloudis's introduction to his own reputable edition of the work is typical in its philological concern for derivation. It considers motifs and subplots to determine the ways in which Soutsos manages to adapt borrowed forms in more or less conventional ways. Both *Leandros* and *Werther*, Veloudis notes, embark on a trip to dissipate the effects of their passion (Veloudis 1996: 55). In this philological frame, the best the work can achieve is to ward off 'the disagreeable impression of seeming a heteroclite collage' and aspire – as *Leandros* does in Tonnet's estimation – to a stylish reworking of his precursors' suggestions and themes (Tonnet 1995: 565). This philological evaluation of derivation is very much the legacy – that is, itself derived – from the classical philological pedigree of much modern Greek criticism. And while such historical emplotments for the text are crucial in the preface to an authoritative edition, they provide an unwieldy mechanism for fathoming the ways that authors locate themselves between genres and discourses; or how authors dialogize such conventions and codes in achieving their work's goals. How do such choices speak to the work's treatment of themes? How do genres speak to each other and function synergistically within a text? With *Leandros* in particular, a work that advertises its status as being at the beginning of a tradition, I shall argue that derivation or linear descent is an important theme of the work as a whole. Quite consciously, it seeks to position itself, and the discourses it uses, in a relation to the course of social, political, and cultural events.

Leandros's Romantic plot depends on a synergistic relation to the travelogue; or, to be more precise, the love interest at the center of this work relates functionally to the spatial displacements and the shifts of locale in the story. The dialogism between these two genres can be understood only by sensitizing the reader to the position of the modern Greek subject in relation to these discourses. For these narrative and generic strands meet on the figure of the novel's heroine, Koralia. A reading of how the politics of representation surrounding Koralia makes certain claims about the clash of discourses within the Greek state – discourses both foreign/native and public/private – at a moment of transition and foundation for the Greek state, will elucidate Soutsos's views on the novel and its role in Greece's future. The Great Powers have just appointed King Otto of Bavaria ruler of the new Greek state and the state capital is about to be transferred from Nafplion to Athens in 1834. In this context, the issue of derivation, both for the novel and the Greek polity, is a matter of major significance at this time.

Soutsos's novel, like Martinengou's autobiography, is a foundational text. It is the first novel of the modern Greek state. Like Martinengou's work, it is both exemplary of its kind, a Romantic novel, but consciously questioning over the limits of the forms that constitute it as such. At the moment of a shift to monarchical constitutionalism, and from Nafplion to Athens, Soutsos's self-reflexive work considers the exhaustion of the very discourses that have until now constituted the Greek polity, and that happen also to be the forms for its representation. Panayotis Soutsos's work is full of lovesick heroes traveling through Greek cities and towns. Long passages are reminiscent of the travelogues considered in Chapter 1. After all, the peregrinations of foreign travelers in Greece were often induced by a love interest of sorts, the feminized and idealized landscape. She, the landscape, offered many disappointments and, in many cases, the true face of things led to a shattering of idealizations and delusions. This is not to say that Koralia is simply a person-ification of the Greek landscape. But her ideal nature, along with the joys and disappointments she engenders, is meant to bind these two levels of meaning together. Certainly, this desired woman does set off a journey. Koralia shares, with other famous female characters, the dubious distinction of launching a thousand narrative ships of sorrow and displacement. Soutsos seems to have had a penchant for such a theme. His early *Ode prononcée sur le tombeau de la jeune Rhalou*, written in 1823 and published in March 1828, as well as his Ο Οδοιπόρος (*The Traveler*) of 1831 borrow heavily from Byronic typologies of this kind.[31] Indeed, Athena Georganta (1992) has argued that *The Traveler* introduces a resilient strain of Byronic Romanticism to Greece. She shows how *The Traveler* shares affinities with Byron's *The Giaour: A Fragment of a Turkish Tale* (1813) – the hero's love for a woman is thwarted by the presence of another suitor and, albeit with plots of variable bloodiness, the hero eventually retreats to a monastery to lead an ascetic life, in anonymity. At the finale, he confesses to a priest and then commits suicide. Byron's travelogue *Childe Harold's Pilgrimage* (1812–18), too, sees a melancholic hero embark on a European tour that includes Greece in its itinerary in order to wash away his guilt over an undisclosed action, conventionally assumed to be incestuous in nature. Leandros, a tamer version of this hero figure,[32] had years before walked away from Koralia, his love, to fight in the revolution, and later does so again so as to recover from the news that she is married to someone else. He embarks on a trip around Greece, its ancient sites as well as locales connected to more recent revolution victories and sacrifices. The monastic retreat, while proposed in *Leandros*, is, as we shall see, somewhat submerged in the text and overshadowed by other narrative strands and denouements. Leandros, does, however, confess to a priest before committing suicide.

Leandros is 30 years old. He is resident in Nafplion, the capital of the fledgling modern Greek state. A Byronic youth, he is deeply melancholic and bemoans the futility of his life with consummate self-pity. Though hardly Don Juan-like in temperament, his strivings, both personal and public, are articulated in terms of female figures. His contributions to the recent revolutionary struggle have disap-pointed him as 'the two women at the heart of the world . . . Virtue and Freedom . . . have both, mother and daughter, gradually proved themselves to be figments of the imagination' (80). To put aside such thoughts, on 22 December 1833, Leandros makes his way to Athens, the home of classical civilization and the soon-to-be-established capital of the modern Greek state, only to run into another, no less ideal, woman. As he explains in a letter to his confidant Harilaos, he encounters the beautiful Koralia who had been a childhood sweetheart and whom he last saw in Constantinople in 1824. As he accompanies her on a series of strolls around

Athens, he fancies her perfection as exquisite as it had been back in 1824. The splendor of the classical monuments is constantly likened, or conflated, with her own radiance. Indeed, it is Koralia who points to the splendid Parthenon and speaks nobly of the 'ancient and great earth' which, with her tread and presence, she graces with her own equal perfection (84–5). Her radiance, an analogy to the springtime Greek sky 'recalls more serene past days' experienced both in the 'spring mornings in Constantinople' of their childhood (91) and the dazzling absolute presence of classical Greece. Through the image of Koralia, these two levels of private and public experience are united in the narrative in the eminently Romantic gesture of eliding personal and collective childhood.

Despite Leandros's true love for Koralia and her own measured reciprocity – or perhaps because of it – Leandros does not envisage a happy outcome for his love. He is devastated to discover that Koralia is married to a reputable man; and that she has a 3-year-old child, as old as the modern Greek state. Her marriage vows and responsibilities – and not the parents and family of other 'star cross'd lovers' of the Western prototype – do not allow her to follow her heart. Following her confidante Euphrosyne's advice, she resists impropriety, i.e. 'the European mores and customs that try to infiltrate themselves in Greece' (95). And, after a short retreat to the quiet of Piraeus to meditate, with some regret and a heavy heart, Koralia returns to advise the smitten Leandros to go a-walkabout around Greece in order to forget her. In other words, to walk it off. Leandros does so and leaves Athens in deep dejection. He bids adieus to many of the key classical sites of Athens – by moonlight on this occasion – with just a few pallid beams illuminating his face: 'Farewell earth, I cried, earth covered in mourning and crying as I; I leave you earth! Earth to which my imagination always looked! Oh Earth! That is home to my Koralia, adieu!' (107).

The next morn sees our hero roused from sleep at a monastery with a monk who proposes solitude and the alternative of *repos*. His quintessentially Romantic 'withdrawal into tranquility' recurs in the narrative (108–14), and so reinforces Soutsos's more general deeply held political beliefs in the qualities of an agrarian Saint-Simonian polity.[33] However, unlike his earlier works, Soutsos's hero does not seek refuge here for long. Eventually he makes his way back to the worldly Nafplion, the place from where he had set off. Not surprisingly, once there, his descriptions focus on the corruption of everyday life, which is contrasted explicitly with the pastoral simplicity of the Attic countryside (115). Still further intermittent scenes of withdrawal to the surrounding countryside arise once he arrives in Nafplion. The landscape functions as the objective correlative of his inner state and vice versa; a symbol, too, of his fall now that he has been chased from the garden of childhood, the agrarian ideal, and classical Athenian totality.

The city of Nafplion is home to the small-mindedness and injustice of political life. Its streets are 'labyrinthine,' 'snake-like,' and 'tumultuous' (116–17). Its politicians godless. The citizens of the city are described as 'insects'; deserving of their politicians, the most degenerate of insects and the epitome of falsehood. Ethics without ethos; eros without eros; friendship without friendship (115). The capital of the modern state, its topography and its everyday lifeworld, is described in orientalist terms. This is, of course, a recognizable depiction of the underside or Other side of the discourse of ab-sense – the unruly and unassimilable hetero-geneity of a Greek modernity. Indeed the history of Nafplion is marked by its heterogeneous traces:

> Nafplion! The paradoxical mix of Greek, Venetian, and Ottoman classical ruins. At the opening to the sea, Hera's mythical spring; there the lion of St. Mark; a little further on, epigraphs with verses from the Koran . . . truly this city is an image, a true emblem of the ethics of its residents, with its mixed Greek, Ottoman, and Venetian physiognomy.
>
> At night, when the silvery moon illuminates the labyrinth of narrow and windy streets; when the waves break on the shores and the winds boom, the dumbstruck imagination grows wary lest any one of the Ottoman, Venetian, and Hellenic spirits might shout out to claim exclusive rule of the world. (126)

Years before Cavafy, this depiction of a miscegenated polis of Hellenism bears a different economy of beauty and ethics than the neoclassical one on which the new Greek state had been built. Like the Athens that he departs from – i.e. the moon-lit one of his last night and not the resplendent one of his early daytime wanderings with Koralia – Nafplion is illuminated, and illuminates, in a light of difference. Indeed, the analogy to Cavafy is particularly appropriate here because Soutsos's vision parallels one of Cavafy's most notable statements on Hellenistic civilization, its aesthetics and ethos. In the poem *In a Town of Osroene* (1917), Cavafy's miscegenated exemplar is drawn in opposition to a classical precursor, Charmides, Plato's model of *sophrosyne*. I quote Cavafy's poem in its entirety:

> Yesterday about midnight they brought home
> our friend Rhemon, wounded in a tavern brawl.
> Through the window which we left wide open,
> the moon lighted his handsome body on the bed.
> We are a mixture here; Syrians, Greeks, Armenians, Medes.
> Rhemon is one of these too. But yesterday
> as the moon illuminated his sensual face,
> our minds went back to Plato's Charmides.

In Soutsos's evocation of Nafplion, only God and the young King Otto rise above the town's messy modernity. When the light of dawn finally comes over Nafplion, Soutsos resumes his description by focusing on a crowd of assembled youth, dressed in the gold-embroidered cloaks who are identified as swearing their allegiance to the King. 'Everything is new; a new generation replaces the old; a new world order, of ideas, ethics, customs, dress. It enters through the gates of Greece silently, and silently it sits on the ruins of the old world. Thirsty Greece, a deer of lights and innovation' (127).

The action then shifts back toward Athens with the intervention of Harilaos, Leandros's confidant, who communicates with Euphrosyne to arrange a meeting for his friend with Koralia. Harilaos suggests that his friend go on a journey and, slowly, make his way to Athens and to a reunion with Koralia. In the mean time, Harilaos hopes that Time, the great healer, will work its wonders on his friend. Harilaos's note of false hope reaches Leandros on 26 January 1834, the one-year anniversary of Otto's arrival on Greek soil. (Otto's assumption of the monarchy was meant to have put an end to the fractious situation that had developed since the murder of the previous premier, Capodistrias, in Nafplion in 1831. For his part, Soutsos was a virulent critic of Capodistrias and had approved of this act.) With the King's presence portrayed as the one redeeming feature of life in Nafplion, and Leandros's renewed hope in his love interest, our hero acts on Harilaos's suggestion to travel around Greece and eventually reach Athens.

The descriptive mode that predominates during his trip is elegaic in nature, and it not only focuses on the traces of a former classical glory, but also seeks to integrate into this recognizable narrative the traces of a much more recent commemoration. Time and again, Leandros stops off in places where, only a few years earlier – eight years typically, harking back to his acquaintance with Koralia and to the battles of the Greek Revolution – heroes of the revolution had fought courageously, but were now alas no more. In Hydra, where in 1824 the Greek fleet accomplished wondrous exploits, Leandros muses gloomily on the death of so many heroes (131–2); in Salamis, he goes to the tomb of Karaiskos (133–5); at Psarra, he commemorates Andreas Miaoulis, 'the Greek Nelson' (136). By the time he reaches Athens, Leandros has commemorated hosts of revolutionary heroes and he has, in effect, dialogized the Western philhellene's classicizing tour with his own more contemporary and updated version of it. This section of the narrative ends in the tone of a funerary address (143).

As with his previous entry to Nafplion, Leandros lingers in the countryside to take in the serenity of nature before entering Athens. Quite appropriately, he reads Homer and meets up with an old philosopher friend, versed in Plato, who lives through his books and who is able to conjure up an εἰκων (image) of a Greece of the future. This image contrasts with Leandros's concurrent realization of the 'image' of the once spring-like Koralia (143). However, his entry into Athens, appropriately embarked upon by 'the marketplace's gate where he first saw [Koralia]' (148) will find a Koralia depleted by illness at the very same 'magical spot'(147).

The denouement of the tale holds few surprises – Koralia dies from her illness. She is loved by Leandros yet faithful to her husband to the bitter end. Clinging on to a life-like 'image' of Koralia, Leandros commits suicide and so brings a melodramatic closure to his mourning and melancholy. He hopes he will be reunited with his loved one in the next life. But the ending is not so bleak. For traces of a silver lining appear in the text. The priest who closed Koralia's eyes on her deathbed consoles Leandros's broken heart and offers him some perspective. For Leandros and for the reader, the scene is recognizable to devotees of both Soutsos and Byron:

> Look at the world you first saw when you came to Greece and the one you see today. New faces have taken center stage; new interests have emerged; new ideas; a new world has replaced the old; with us and to us everything passes; others open the door for us and we open the door for others to come; present times host the future, the future in time becomes the past, and the old image of the world ceaselessly renews itself. (163)

The priest's incantatory repetition of the biblical 'It is finished! It is finished' that follows this speech places Leandros's impending act into context. His resolution, like the literary resolution of a Romantic predicament, is posited not as an end but as part of a world ever in flux. We are on the threshold of a resurrection. In its historical specificity, Soutsos's work here clearly speaks to the exhaustion of a particular Ideal that has structured the Greek experience.

What is left beyond this exhausted discourse is the outstanding promise of the philosopher and the ideal of the King. In the former, the bookish reverie of the cloistered philosopher reaffirms the religious *repos* of many of Soutsos's earlier works. Like Socrates, midwife to the philosopher (*Republic* 507a), the philosopher here will be the dispenser of the offspring to truth (*tokos*) that has been deposited with him and that he will pay out to his interlocutors with interest (*tokos* and *egkonos*). With the second ideal, the King is presented as the authorized legatee of the classical imaginary. 'O! King of Greece! Old Greece [that is, Ancient Greece] has granted Germany her lights; through You, Germany has asked to pay up the debt with interest [μετά τόκου]' (130). The μετά τόκου in Greek plays on the meanings of 'interest' and 'son' and figures King Otto as the potential agent for the revitalization of the πρωτότοκος (first-born) people of the world. For, as Derrida reminds us in his 'Plato's Pharmacy': 'as product, *tokos* is the child, the human or animal blood, as well as the fruits of the seed sown in the field, and the interest on a capital investment: it is return or revenue' (Derrida 1981: 82). The slippage between familial and economic signification inherent in the word *tokos* underscores the meanings as progeny of capital lent at interest with the natural progeny of beings, be they animal or human, and as identified by Aristotle and examined by a series of classical writers.[34] And so the foreign German king, himself now a son of Greece, must discharge his filial duty and return what he has borrowed. For the German here is figured as epigone to the Greek, bearer of the seed of Hellenism for the period of Greece's homelessness. The European debt to the Greek is to be repaid. And now the German-turned-Greek must *return on* and *to* the *capital*.

Analogically, in his preface, Soutsos extends this language of debt to the relation of the European novel to his novel and to a homegrown tradition that harks back to the ancient Greek novel. Soutsos regards *Leandros* as the first modern Greek novel, and he locates it at the inception of an indigenous tradition. He derides those who assert his novel's debt to European works, to Foscolo and to Goethe, for, as his prologue insists, the work's Greek typologies and its debt to Greek poets should not be overlooked (77). It is a Romantic work, after all, but one which does not espouse its European precursors' use of the convention of the found manuscript. It wishes, quite self-consciously, to draw attention to its own genealogy in the very same way that Leandros, in his wanderings, rewrites the Greek landscape *beyond* the narrative of Europeans' touring. Leandros's wanderings are unlike the Romantic travelers of Chapter 1. Leandros interposes a more contemporary narrative, and does so in prose. Like the German king, European Romantic forms will lead back to Greek typologies lent out in bygone times and augur their reconception in a novel designed for a new Greek subject. In effect, Soutsos confronted the dilemma of a self-colonization by boldly asserting that the Greeks are lenders, and not borrowers, of the forms of self-representation. It will be for the Greeks themselves to press ahead with the development of these forms again for their own purposes.

At the end of his prologue, Soutsos urges the youth of Greece to shoulder this responsibility and conceive of a genealogy for the revitalization of Greek culture and society. He appeals to the youth because he senses that his own generation is unable to meet the challenge. It has run its course. Like other Byronic heroes who do not see the realization of their revolutionary hopes, *Leandros* only attests to the exhaustion of the discourse that has reproduced him. In his wanderings, Leandros and his generation have grafted the exploits of the revolution onto the narrative of a hallowed past. But now, left with no ideal, but with the promise of a new and dutiful king (however misguided this hope may have turned out in the long run), it is for the next generation to complete the work of statehood and the novel and so begin anew:

> Oh Greek youth, whatever you may have demanded from our generation, has been accomplished; we have created for you a miraculous future, we gave you a homeland, and we liberated the land of your ancestors. But now disgusted, we have laid down our arms, we demand of you the other half of the task which we have brought to fruition – we mean, that is, the enlightenment of Greece. (77)

Notes

1. For a terse exposition of this disjuncture on a number of levels in Greek society, see Tsoucalas (1991: 1–22).
2. For a discussion of Mouzelis's model, see Gourgouris (1996: esp. 64–70).
3. See Diamandouros (1984: 55–71, esp. 62–71).
4. For surveys of ancient prose fiction, see A. Heiserman, *The Novel before the Novel* (Chicago: University of Chicago Press, 1977); T. Hägg, *The Novel in Antiquity* (Oxford: Oxford University Press, 1983); J. Tatum (ed.), *The Search for the Ancient Novel* (Baltimore, MD: Johns Hopkins University Press, 1994); N. Holzberg, *The Ancient Novel: An Introduction* (London and New York: Routledge, 1995); G. Schmeling, *The Novel in the Ancient World* (Leidon and New York: E. J. Brill, 1996). B. Reardon, *Collected Ancient Greek Novels* (Berkeley, CA: University of California Press, 1989) provides English translations of the key texts.
5. Adamantios Korais, with the assistance of Greek publishers, oversaw the publications of the *Aithiopika* in 1790; *Ismene and Ismenias* in 1791; *Ta Poiemenika* 1792 etc.
6. Tziovas describes Korais's puritanical streak and its influence on perceptions of the novel in Vayenas (1997: 7–11).
7. See, characteristically, Sachinis (1980).
8. For an overview of this revision, see Vayenas (1994: 187–98). The proceedings from a conference (Vayenas 1999) organized by the Institute of Mediterranean Studies and the Goulandris-Horn Foundation entitled 'Greek Prose, 1830–1880,' in Athens (24–5 October 1995) made significant inroads into this topic.
9. See Vitti's often cited essay, Ιδεολογική Λειτουργία τη ελληνικής ηθογραφίας (Vitti 1991). A second essay in this developmentalist vein is Mario Vitti, 'The Inadequate Tradition: Prose Narrative during the First Half of the Nineteenth Century,' in Beaton (1991: 3–10).
10. For a punctilious listing of such critical work, see Boumboulides (1965).
11. Despite the heroine's affirmation that the text was written in 1831, Kolias remarks how a date of 1827 for the work could be maintained if a letter to her brother, written seven years after the earthquake of 1820, be taken as accurate.
12. Napoleon enters Venice in 1797 and signs the Treaty of Campo Formio that grants the Ionian Islands to France. This disturbs power relations in the region: Russia and Austria have their own designs on the Mediterranean; the Pasha of Epirus also covets the Ionian Islands. Britain prevents Turkey from closing the route to India and wants to keep the Russians out. The revolutionary activity of Greek Ottoman subjects for independence and Napoleon's conquest of Ottoman Egypt inspire a coalition between Turkey and Russia which takes

over the Ionian Islands in 1799. Notables of the island, who had been brushed aside by the republican French, were reinstated. In March 1800, the Ionian Isles become an autonomous state, but would swear allegiance to the Emperor of Russia and pay tribute to Ottoman forces. From 1807, the islands fall under French rule again, but were soon thereafter, in 1809, run over by British troops. The status of the island only really became clear with the Treaty of Vienna, in 1815, when the islands became a Crown Colony and remained so until 1864.

13. Martinengou (1881). Other Greek editions include: Porphyres (1956); Boumboulides (1965); Athanasopoulos (1997).

14. Her son Elisavetios confesses to the omission of details of his mother's childhood impressions, her likes and dislikes of family members. He argues that these are matters for the Moutza family exclusively; see Martinengou (1881: 117).

15. That filial duty extended to his stated resolution to publish the remainder of her works. For whatever reasons – perhaps his death four years later – he did not accomplish this.

16. Quotations from the text in English are cited throughout this chapter. I use Helen Dendrinou Kolias's translation: *My Story: Elisave: Moutzan-Martinengou* (Athens, GA and London: University of Georgia Press, 1989).

17. See a listing of references to such works in Boumboulides (1965: 158–62).

18. Some of these pieces were published by Konomos prior to the earthquake: e.g. Επτανησιακά Φύλλα 10 (November 1947). The works saved from the archive of Marinos Sigouros, a relative from Martinengou's mother's side, forms the basis of Boumboulides's publication of 1965.

19. No family house or estate exists today at the village of Pegadakia in Zakynthos. The family home in Zakynthos Town was located at Rouga Square, on the edges of St. Pavlos Square.

20. See also Kolias (1989: 45).

21. Martinengou's use of the word φλόγα (flame) for conveying her 'longing' here draws together the two levels of intense experience.

22. See Kolias (1989: 10–11) for these fables.

23. Rowlandson's narrative could be considered a success story of sorts. Its formative power stems from its ability to identify the plight of the Puritan community with the plight of a woman in captivity, so that this community can begin to reimagine itself under the strictures of an inhospitable New England environment as a community of imagined and dispersed readers.

24. Kolias's point that 'in its sincerity, [Martinengou's] story is bound to touch everyone, for it speaks to everyone' (1989: x) reasserts the notion of a universal experience and is true only in the most general sense. Indeed, Kolias goes on to acknowledge just this by remarking that 'often the value of these writings

lies not so much in what is included but in what is left out. What is left out may indicate the limits of female experience' (1989: xxx).

25. One of Martinegou's surviving translations is of Aeschylus's *Prometheus Bound*, Scene II. In it, Prometheus, all alone, laments his self-sacrifice for the good of humanity. The chorus marvels at his strength in the face of so many tortures (Boumboulides 1965: 131–2).

26. The rush to claim the title as the state's first novel was not without its thrills and spills; see Katsiyianni (1999).

27. The earliest reviews from newspapers of the period are collected in the appendix of Veloudis (1996: 169–86). The most scathing is by one L. in the newspaper *Athina* of 8 June 1834. Soutsos's work deserves legal action against it, according to this critic, because it borrows wilfully from Racine, Foscolo, and Madame de Stael (180).

28. Vitti (1987); Tonnet (1995); Samouil (1996); Veloudis (1996).

29. References hereafter cited in the main body of my text use Veloudis's edition of Soutsos's work (Veloudis 1996). Veloudis's edition is based on the one and only original edition of 1834.

30. *L'Ultime lettere d'Jacopo Ortis* appeared in Greek in 1838. *Werther* was translated from the French into Greek in 1843.

31. For a comparison between Soutsos's two early works, as well as a Greek translation of the original French text of *Ode Prononcée* and a descriptive analysis of *The Traveler*, see Lephas (1991: 151–95).

32. Georganta points out that Soutsos's heroes distinguish themselves from their Byronic counterparts on account of their patriotic and religious credentials (Georganta 1992: 60–1).

33. On Soutsos's Saint-Simonian beliefs, see Samouil (1996: 19–22) and Vayenas (1999: 43–58). For Panayiotis Soutsos's and his brother Alexandros's political philosophy and action, see Lephas (1979).

34. See Aristotle's *Poetics* (1257b): I am indebted here to the unpublished work of Yota Batsaki, a Ph.D student in Comparative Literature at Harvard University, on the notion of interest and its derivatives. For other classical writers on *tokos*, see Shell (1978: 95ff).

−4−

Rupture and Crisis

the debate on such questions as the theoretical criteria of nationhood became passionate, because any particular answer was now believed to imply a particular form of political strategy, struggle and programme. This was a matter not only for governments confronted with various kinds of national agitation or demand, but for political parties seeking to mobilize constituencies on the basis of national, non-national or alternative national appeals.

Eric Hobsbawm, *Nations and Nationalism since 1780*

The eminent historian Eric Hobsbawm argues that the era of democratization and mass politics in Europe after 1880 saw a complete redefinition of the terms of the political phenomenon of nationalism. Whereas, in the classical liberal era, the state was largely able to fashion the nation as a matter of course, after 1880, the state apparatus was more beholden to democratic processes and choices. The new intensity that characterized the modern debate over the 'national question' was evident throughout Europe in the mobilization of different strata of society. Socialist groups, for one, were particularly important in this mobilization because of their awareness that national agendas were a matter of immediate concern to potential or actual voters. However, the emerging socialism that Hobsbawm considers intrinsic to this paradigm shift in Europe is, in Greece, a much less potent factor. For in Greece, as in much of the Balkans in the 1880s, while a liberal middle class was developing and organizing against the old conservative powers, such political bodies were not in a position to mobilize effectively. The universal suffrage discussed in Chapter 3 tended not to be mobilized in internal politics, and class movements in the cities neither dislodged accepted clientelistic and family networks nor were able to create a broad base among the agrarian populace. Socialist groups had formed from the very beginnings of the state.[1] Yet whenever assorted St. Simonians, utopian socialists, and Heptanesian agitators were not also involved in the national struggle, these groups had little effect. They either assimilated into existing parties in power or were imprisoned and silenced.[2] The armed 'new sociologists' of the Democratic Society of Patras of 1876 or the Central Socialist Society of Athens in the mid-1890s were harassed, had their literature confiscated, and were thrown in prison. Generally, their publications had a small circulation and their voices were easily drowned out by the mainstream Athenian press. The shock waves of the Commune in 1871 that had reverberated across Europe were met in Greece by a systematic vilification of marxism.[3] In its very first issue of 1876, the newly established conservative periodical *Estia* announced its intention to guard the nation and the masses from heresy. To this end, it published catechisms of national behaviour to counter syndicalist catechisms (Moskov 1979: 158–9).

Beginning in the 1880s, discontentment and growing pressure for wide-ranging policies of domestic reform precipitated a shift in the existing configuration of political and class divisions. The urban population in a still predominantly agrarian society had risen from 8 percent in 1853 to 28 percent in 1879 (Tsoucalas 1969: 23). The formation of the first guilds in the 1880s, the growing distribution of a socialist press with movements and agitation,[4] particularly after the Raisin Riots of 1895 in Achaia and the Peloponnese and the metal workers' uprisings of the Third Lavrion Disturbances of 1896, all impressed the need for reform. The challenge to political oligarchies and parties mounted and, at a propitious moment and with the backing of the military, the liberal Eleftherios Venizelos rose to power in 1910.

This shift was accompanied by a new cultural agenda centered on the importance of the Language Question. The movement to promote the spoken, or demotic, language over the purist language, or *katharevousa*, proved emblematic of the emergent liberal class. While in the pre-revolution era, the purist language symbolically served to cleanse Greece of *Tourkokratia* and brought it closer to Classicism and the West, by 1880, the reforming middle class affirmed that purism had not brought about modernization. Conversely, it had only consolidated the power of a bureaucratic class and a governing oligarchy. Especially after Greece's humbling military defeat at the hands of Turkey in 1897, language became an extremely loaded issue in anxiogenic times. Alexandros Pallis's translation of the Gospels into the demotic in 1901 sparked riots that left eight dead. In 1903, the performance of the *Oresteia* in demotic Greek provoked further unrest. And, as was discussed in Chapter 1, the most heated cultural debate at the turn-of-the-century involved a dispute over the most suitable name for referring to a 'Greek' – 'Hellene' or 'Romios' (Ephtaliotis 1901). Domestically, the new urban class spoke out in the language of the people, the vernacular, to incite a growing bourgeoisie to back the political philosophy of growth and reform and break with the conservative elite's hold of the centralized *grapho-kratia*. In short, they sought to seize ideological control over the political agenda of nationalism by intervening in the institutions of education and public administration. In 1907 the demoticists founded the National Language Society and, in 1910, an Education Society. In external matters, language played a key role in the pursuit of the *Megali Idea*. Regarded as the only aspect of nationality which could be counted and tabulated by international diplomacy, irredentist nationalists appreciated that language was a determinant in the claims for Balkan territories (Hobsbawm 1990: 102–3). The issue was foremost in people's minds as the 1870s and 1880s had seen the fixing of borders for the new states of Serbia, Bulgaria, and Romania. Moreover, the establishment of the Bulgarian Exarchate in 1870 had precipitated Bulgarian, Greek, and Serb attempts to win over diverse communities in Macedonia and claim those lands. Orthodox liturgy, which had heretofore been conducted in Byzantine Greek, was gradually replaced by a standardized national Bulgarian language that was closer to the Slavic vernaculars spoken by inhabitants in some areas. The competing nationalist claims to the region's inhabitants galvanized cultural and educational associations from all sides. From the Greek side, 176 educational and philanthropic associations were established in the decade 1870–80 alone.[5] The drawing of new boundaries around Greece moved the Greeks themselves to delineate more clearly the projected boundaries of their own state and to claim the Greekness of Macedonia by arguing that the Greek language was spoken by the majority of its inhabitants. Books with patriotic content flooded into the region. Quite remarkably, these were often written in *katharveousa* and were impenetrable to the peasants, who were, variably, Greek-speaking Slavs or Slav-speaking Greeks, not to say Greek-speaking Exarchists or Slav-speaking Patriarchists (Karakasidou 1996: 96). It was an absurd way to win the hearts and minds of the people. Understandably, the demoticists contested the purists' image of national consciousness, but this challenge was not, initially, aimed at splintering or rupturing nationalist discourse at a critical moment for realizing the *Megali Idea*. In trying times, both sides agreed on language's national end, but disagreed over the means to be employed. 'The divisions were then about means, and not ends' (Beaton 1994: 316).[6]

The two groups' common nationalist vision would not be broken down until later. But the first marxist analysis of Greek society by Yorgos Skliros (1878–1919), which appeared in the demoticist periodical *Noumas* in 1907, marks, along with its reception, the first signs of this change. This was ten or fifteen years before the real bloom in Greek economic, social, and political critique. It was then that the first social analysis of such 'national' historical moments as the Greek Revolution appeared.[7] This chapter considers the importance of Skliros's treatise for the breakdown of nationalist discourse and the mobilization of strata of Greek polity for effective socioeconomic change. No longer could one dissociate the determination of the people's language from the political demands of a segment of the 'people.' It became harder to speak out *for* the 'people.' Skliros's analysis splintered the demoticist movement into 'nationalists' and 'socialists,' and led the latter to pursue a vigorous policy of change in the social institutions of the Greek state. It will further be argued that the liberal, modernist poets of the next generation, the so-called Generation of the 1930s, will respond to the threat posed by Skliros against national unity and class status quo. Indeed, one of the seminal texts of this group, George Theotokas's *Free Spirit* (1929) will, in Chapter 5, be read as a belated yet highly conclusive response to Skliros's agenda. The second half of this chapter will trace this development in the work of a prominent poet of the interim period between Skliros and Theotokas. The poetry of Costas Karyotakis (1896–1928), a syndicalist and the chief representative of the 1920s 'poets of decay,' embodies the poetic reenactment of Skliros's questioning of traditional frameworks of meaning and the belief in a unified body politic at the national and personal level. Karyotakis will put into question the image of the self-present individual and fragment the poetic voice. In so doing, he play out the crisis of representation at the heart of this modern realignment of political and cultural agendas of the nation.

Hard Marxism and the Fragmentation of the Body Politic (1907)

Yorgos Skliros's schematic marxist reading of Greek society, *Our Social Question* (Το Κοινωνικόν μας Ζήτημα) (1907), calls for social progress and worker rights from the working class and a segment of the middle-class intelligentsia. It urges idealist youth to stand by the working class in 'fanatical struggle between the social classes, based always on economic interests' (Skliros 1976: 89). Right from his prologue, Skliros attacks the metaphysical abstractions of the discourse of absense. His diagnosis of the 'illness of the state or nation' pinpoints consequences and not causes 'exquisitely hidden behind grand words' (82). This metaphysical discourse devoid of 'natural causes' (φυσικάς αιτίας), 'natural sense' (φυσικόν νουν) is incapable of rendering 'a tough and merciless reality' and guide the public to a 'more natural life' (φυσικότερον βίον). True to his name, Skliros (which means 'hard') advocates a hard empiricism, a more 'well-grounded' vocabulary. His emphasis on *physis* underpins his belief in a natural development of progress (88) to be engendered by the social and economic representation of the working class. He rejects the demoticists' nationalist eulogies of an abstract 'people' as a symptom of bourgeois discourse, itself the legacy of a bourgeois revolution.[8] The worker, 'he who is deprived of all property' (99), demands representation – enfranchisement in the symbolic realm – and a dismantling of the kind of parliamentary constitutionalism described in Chapter 2, which works by abstractions that conceal oligarchic vested interests (94, 122–5).

For Skliros, the demoticists' struggle over the means of symbolic production in the Language Question amounts to a salutary manifestation of bourgeois cooperation in the organization of the working class toward the better management of society. However, Skliros also criticizes the demoticists' lack of social awareness and rebukes them for remaining linguists and not social activists:

> The demoticists imagined that they could solve the Language Question without touching on its social substratum. They did not realize that the Language Question is not so much academic in its nature as it is social and political; it is tightly connected to the whole historical and social system, and, consequently, it will only be solved in practice when

this social system is shaken to its foundations. Academic debate between individuals is not what we require – we require the broad social action of whole classes. (Skliros 1976: 129)

Skliros maintains that the demoticists have fallen victim to the retrogressive scholasticism and academism of the Greek race, which had wasted away the minds of the young by indulging them in the stultifying nostalgic regress of pseudoclassicism and 'the pathological mania to believe that words can substitute for reality' (131). Skliros urges demoticists and students to assail the legacy of great historical traditions incompatible with reality' (120). Admittedly, he conceded that some demoticists had taken their crusade to the people. The leading demoticist, Jean Psycharis, had promoted the idea of social clubs for the language and had advocated a movement in pedagogy. But this was far from decisive to Skliros's thinking. Skliros summons forth new demons (νέα δαιμόνια) to the social and intellectual dialogue (133).[9] He pitches progress in other than national terms. However, Skliros's challenge to contextualize the Language Question in its social and material objective relations came at a time – and this was its undoing – when intense national ferment for the Macedonian issue was raging and the government was pledging to support Cretan liberation from Ottoman rule.

Skliros's call to arms provoked a debate among demoticists in the pages of the group's organ, *Noumas*, between 1907 and 1909. *Noumas*'s editors shared the desire for a progressivist and positivist attack on pseudoclassicism. From early on in the periodical's history in 1903, the editor Tangopoulos asserted that 'the country's restoration would only come about by the necessary struggle against constitutionalism, constitutional demagoguery and every vested interest that works against the people' (1903: 1). Once the debate over Skliros's challenge commenced, the demoticists split into two camps, later characterized as the 'nationalists' and the 'socialists.' The nationalists M. Tsirimokos, I. Dragoumis, P. Vlastos, Y. Chatzis, and A. Poulimenos were all, except for Poulimenos, in positions of power and members of the *haute bourgeoisie*. Only Tsirimokos lived outside Greece. The socialists A. Delmouzos, C. Chatzopoulos, N. Yannios, M. Zavitzianos, and Ph. Politis were *petit bourgeois*, and apart from Yannios, who was resident in Constantinople, all were studying in Germany.[10] The debate between the two camps was long and often divided into smaller intrapersonal debates. Let us focus here on four key issues in the discussion: the autochthony or heterochthony of Skliros and its relevance to his epistemological model; his model's potential applicability for Greece; the struggle over the nature of the individual, and its effect on the development of nationalist discourse in Greece.

The debate did not get off to a flying start. Skliros's work was published in July 1907 and received only one review in the newspaper *Akropolis* on 16 June 1907. Only when Delmouzos, under the pen-name 'Delos,' brought it to the attention of demoticists in an article titled 'To Demoticists' in *Noumas*, did the argument begin in earnest. Nor was it a dignified beginning: Delmouzos quipped that Skliros's work had not been reviewed because it was written in *katharevousa*, and for that reason, had led the readership to discard it after the first two pages. Instead, the debate got off to a nationalistic and rather petty beginning – the nationalists label Skliros's dialectical model as foreign to the Greek scene.[11] Skliros should not be inciting the masses and undermining conservative, centralized power, they argued. Methodologically, Tsirimokos questions whether Skliros's belief in class struggle was a proven catalyst for class progress. He advises Skliros to give up the questionable dicta of sociology for the trusted lessons of history. These, he maintains, would instruct him that the masses were not to be trusted with power, for 'when the feet set about to govern, civilization and the state walk with all the surety and stamina that an acrobat musters in a horizontal position, that is with his head pointed down and his feet up' (SP 65–6). In a pointed response, Chatzopoulos turns the tables on Tsirimokos and defends 'sociology' by summoning history and concluding that 'from above, reform had never come. History tells us this" (SP 38). The *kodzabacides*, he argues, preserve power and rule over others with a 'stagnation' rivaled only by the purist idiom (SP 97). By contrast, he describes worker enfranchisement with all the rushing and overpowering metaphors customarily employed by demoticists to tout the spoken language. Chatzopoulos hopes that the workers' vote will no longer be the organ of their exploitation but the means of their emancipation (SP 102).

The nationalists' attack on Skliros's incitement of class struggle eventually draws a subtler response. The shrewd politician Ion Dragoumis (1878–1920), or Idas, acknowledges class warfare, but attacks Skliros for his inability to locate empirically the more significant Hellenic, rather than Helladic, concerns at stake. By this, Dragoumis raises the question of the *Megali Idea* and demands national unity in light of pressing foreign policy threats (SP 54–61). Other nationalists also acknowledge the importance of Skliros's work for serious internal social debate, yet they decry its timing, his sectarianism in troubled times. Chatzis insists that Skliros not draw readers away from the pressing exigencies of the *Megali Idea* (SP 106). (The tactic is reminiscent of the heterocthons' strategy of invoking the *Megali Idea* to divert attention from internal conflict in the National Assembly debate of 1844 in Chapter 2 yet it may have been as heartfelt as it was strategic.)

Skliros's response embeds such criticism in a more general attack on Dragoumis's essentialism and his use of the terms 'nation' and 'state.' He serves notice that these abstractions, the constructions of feudalism and then bourgeois consciousness, must be understood in their objective social relations and in the context of workers' everyday experience: 'to satisfy Mr. Idas and any common man, the nation's life and the state's existence, must, above all, be humane and not just shadows of a nation and a state' (SP 152). The language of abstraction supports false consciousness.

The ruling classes and the mercurial and messianic leader, or *bon prince*, as Skliros scornfully addresses him, disdains the good of the 'people.' Only science and, by implication, the systemic 'objectivity' of his sociological-marxist model, will deny Dragoumis the abstraction and etherealism of his key concepts and ward any suspect belief in messianism (SP 147–61).

Dragoumis's last response to this attack appears in an article entitled '*Social-isme* and *Sociologie*' (Κοινωνισμός και Κοινωνιολογία). In it, Dragoumis defines the former, *socialisme*, as a wholly subjective desire felt by the proletariat; the latter, true *sociologie*, he casts as a science, a wholly objective study of Man practiced by an academician.[12] Dragoumis grants Skliros's contention that he may well be bedeviled by 'abstract psychoses,' but he goes on to charge theoretical socialism with the same shortcoming. Above all, Dragoumis wants to protect the individual from Skliros's collectivist model and preserve a coherent, pure, and unique Greek self at all costs. A healthy body politic can be unified only from the microlevel up, he affirms, for his is an assessment conditioned by *Realpolitik*. Why, then, does Skliros focus on an unformed class – a native industrial urban working class – when he might, more profitably, focus on a much more needy, enslaved Greek diaspora? Only by lending political support to the industrialists and capitalists will the social infrastructure in Greece be able to absorb and generate wealth among the returning diaspora. In short, Dragoumis's political pragmatism assaults Skliros's order of priorities and defends an essential conservatism that he maintains has served Greeks well over generations (SP 172). This conservatism is activated now in the interests of preserving Greek difference from the threat of rapacious Balkan neighbors. Dragoumis insists on developing the central 'substance' or 'foundation' of Greek identity before adopting Skliros's humanist internationalism, which builds on socialist Balkan peace groups existent since 1875 (Lazaris 1996: 117–26). He does not deny the imminence of cosmopolitanism and socialism and its potential to usher a new universal humanism with 'the help of the first of the nation's sons' (SP 172–3). But, for now, Dragoumis considers it premature, in light of historical and political circumstances, to upset the cart of class status quo.

While Dragoumis is by far Skliros's most challenging interlocutor, his core beliefs, particularly his belief in an oligarchic vanguard, are built upon by more zealous nationalists. Petros Vlastos, or 'Ermonas,' takes many of Dragoumis' points to a chillingly racialist conclusion. In the essay 'The Race' (Η Φυλή) Vlastos attacks Skliros's plan on the grounds that it weakens the centralized state – the poorer classes' only hope. He argues for a militarily strong, spartan, and expansionist state ruled by the 'strong'. Echoing Gobineau's racist principles, Vlastos calls for the formation of an elite that will, over time, raise the race's mean purity and rid itself of those miscegenated taints of Semitic, Slavic, Frankish, and Armenian blood (SP 85). For Vlastos, interclass warfare is not objectionable if it implies also a race war that will destroy the 'inferior' people among the race and grant primacy to a pure and strong *Übermensch*. This position is only a more aggressive form of disparaging comments made by other nationalists. Even Dragoumis, so careful in his formulations, obviously could not hold back a derisory characterization of an indolent working class 'who look to better their fate, to work less, that is, and earn more, to revel and kick back as much as is possible – because they are, poor things, a weary bunch' (SP 165). On the home front, Vlastos sees socialism as 'nothing but the petty voice of slaves who want to be freed from the aristocratic class. This, too, comes out of the degradation of our Race's mean point' (SP 92). Racial cleansing at home would lead to racial cleansing abroad and a 'general race war with the Slav' (SP 86–7). Vlastos decries socialism and seeks its eradication because it weakens the prerequisite hatred for the Turks and retards the crusade of racial purification. Taken to these extremes, the nationalists identify with a strong centralized state and a strong and pure individual. The preservation of national difference, and its eradication of the Balkan Other, is perceived as paramount to notions of Greek self-affirmation. All proposals of cosmopolitanism or socialist internationalism are posed as perilous attenuations of the national body along class and racial lines, and augur a miscegenated and weak body politic.

Skliros's attack on the inviolability of nationalist and demoticist discourse was, in the main, quashed by the force of historical and political circumstances – the *Megali Idea* was to reach both its zenith and nadir in the following twelve years (1910–22). Dragoumis, with his astute political understanding of the times, anticipated this and exploited it rhetorically. However, Skliros's intervention did 'politicize' the demoticist debate and push both sides to seek political represent-ation. The nationalists had been convinced that demoticism needed a political wing; Vlastos was to 'realize immediately that the demoticists [would] one day be a party' (SP 89). The nationalists rejected a working-class base; instead, they resorted to the old ploy of speaking in the name of the 'people' (SP 108, 228). The socialists, in their turn, courted the working class, though their notion of class struggle was on occasion revolutionary, on others, more moderate. Ultimately, Skliros would propose that the agonistic dynamic between different interests and parties serving different bases would produce a more representational constit-utional assembly: 'Today's pliable and colorless parliamentary rabble, the supporter of chiefly vested interests will be transformed into fanatical representatives of certain social classes, responsible for a certain segment of the polity' (122).

Skliros's talk of class struggle foreshadowed the fissures that would mark Greek society. The working class, still relatively small in Greece, may not have been at the center of this struggle, but the petit bourgeoisie played an important role in the famous period of the National Schism between conservatives-royalists and liberal-Venizelists, in 1915–17. Though the feud broke out in 1915 over matters of foreign policy, the dispute was engendered by class struggle. The middle class split into two: one part entrepreneurial and the other in the civil service; one side behind

Venizelos, private capital and a belief in the rewards of Westernization; the other behind the King, institutional conservatism, and the intervention of the petty bourgeois state machine. The more down-trodden classes sided with the anti-Venizelists in defence of old loyalties, in opposition to the entrepreneurial ways of the emerging capitalist middle class (Vergopoulos 1978: 122–5).

Noumas itself was transformed by the debate in a number of ways. Skliros's article, written in *katharevousa*, was the first non-demotic article published in the periodical. Though the editorial staff did not comment on the debate, *Noumas* soon advertised and supported socialist pamphlets and movements. The government was so troubled by the growing demoticist activity that it legislated the proclamation of the *katharevousa* as the official state language by constitutional Decree in Article 107 of the Constitution of 1911. But, more importantly for our argument here, the cohesion of a discourse of nationalist self-representation had been fractured irrevocably. The monolithic relation between discourse and national reality had admitted to a rupture that would demand the reworking of both the national and the individual voice. The renegotiation of cultural and social differentiation proposed by Skliros had been put off for now by an appeal for restraint in light of the exigencies of the *Megali Idea*. But what was to happen when the *Megali Idea* was no longer a factor in the equation? How would notions of the *poiesis* of the Greek self after 1922 reflect the dismantling of the unifying project of Hellenism – the *Megali Idea*? The artwork of a fully integrated Hellenism was forever to remain unfinished. These issues will be addressed in Chapter 5. For the time being, let us examine how the crisis of representation that immediately followed 1922 and Skliros's challenge was treated in the work of the period's most representative poet, the post-symbolist Costas Karyotakis.

Karyotakis's Suicidal Postscript to the Greek Lyric Self (1928)

The collapse of the *Megali Idea* in 1922 marked not only the end of an irredentist dream, but also the redundancy of a concept and a process of defining national identity (Pollis 1958: 397). One and half or so million Greek refugees from Asia Minor were ordered by international treaty to seek refuge within the borders of the Helladic state. They swarmed to the easternmost Aegean islands and the urban centers to swell the underclass, catalyze socialist movements, and make even more redundant the grandiose reverie of the elites. The formalist, phantasmic projections of Hellenic wholeness were *seemingly* dashed once and for all. The generalized allegory of meaning in exile and coming home, be it temporal (a nostalgic recollection of a past) or physical (the return of the far-flung diaspora communities or lands), was disrupted by a *nostos* that was both unexpected and unfulfilling. The *Megali Idea* that had projected outwards a Romantic quest for wholeness, unification, and the perfectibility of an idealized Greek entity now displayed its Romantic nature only in its fragmentation and its permanently unfinished nature. Nationalist discourse had fallen from grace and words were shown to no longer mean what they said. Skliros was right. This circumspect view of idealist language and the assimilation of these populations into the Greek body politic led to a correspondent period of deep introspection and realignment. The uncertainty of the collective voice, deprived of the frameworks it had used to express itself for so long, led also to the undermining of its most authoritative vehicle – the voice of the lyric, nationalist poet. He was to be challenged by the voice of a decentered poet, polyphonic and ironic as never before. The post-romantic oeuvre of Costas Karyotakis (1896–1928), an autochthon and a syndic-alist, disrupts the discourse of ab-sense and Romantic constructs of the National Poet.

The Man, the Myth

Costas Karyotakis is the poet of discontinuity. He has been accused as responsible for 'the crisis of Greek poetry, of the poetic *parlar*.'[13] His 'dissolution of metrics,' part of a more general crisis, has ethical roots. He is a poet of urban decay; his language a threat, like Cavafy's, to the ideology of both the national demoticists and their successors, the modernists of the Generation of the 1930s.[14] Karyotakis's work constituted a rupture from the model of the nineteenth-century National Poet. It neither worshipped Greek beauty nor focused on the continuity of Hellenism; it had none of the inflated rhetoric of Palamas: it did not address itself to Greek history (Tziovas 1986b: 180–2). It evoked foreign landscapes, it flaunted foreign words shamelessly, and dared to write about themes reminiscent of the European Aestheticists and the French Decadents. His Cavafian use of *katharevousa* to effect irony and his rejection of the national decapentasyllable verse (except for the purposes of lampoon)[15] smacked of subversion.

Some, like Kleon Paraschos and Tellos Agras, were appreciative of his verse; the majority, and certainly the doyens of Greek criticism – Palamas, Xenopoulos, Vouteridis and Photis Polites — ignored it (*Nea Estia* 1971: 1568). A commem-orative Karyotakis edition of *Nea Estia* exhumed only sixteen critiques of the poet's work between 1916 and 1928. Four of these belong to one critic. Though his *Collected Works* appeared first in 1938, they were not reprinted until 1965.[16] Karyotakis became 'the superlative representative' of a generation marked by post-Catastrophe disillusionment and *ennui* who sought refuge in Art (Agras 1938: LXXXIX). They were lumped together, given a label – the 'ism' Karyotakism – and were much maligned by the modernists of the 1930s.[17] A critic close to the modernists, K. T. Dimaras, did not even consider Karyotakis a poet in the true sense of the word. George Theotokas's correspondence with George Seferis portrays them as 'cautious and distrustful of Cavafy and Karyotakis' (Savidis 1975: 14).[18] Nonetheless, Karyotakis has endured and has even taken his revenge after time spent in Purgatory.[19]

Karyotakis's suicide in 1928 served only to embolden attacks against the (poetic) values of this line of poets. Biographical and psychoanalytic approaches have speculated on the reasons behind his suicide and fed Greek criticism's passion for a Romantic unity of the poet's art and life. By mythologizing the man, critics depreciated his work (Malanos 1938; Zographou 1981). But had his suicide anything to do with 1922 and its aftermath? Or with the *Megali Idea* for that matter? 'Was it a heroic act or the testament of a deserter . . . was it [a] generation that committed suicide because it lacked faith and strength or was it only Karyotakis?' (Panayotopoulos 1983: 106). Vladimir Mayakovsky, a poet who commited suicide just after him, on 14 April 1930, and who I shall return to later, provoked a similar dilemma among Soviet critics and journalists. Was it, as declared in the official Soviet press, 'a strictly personal matter,' or, was it, on the contrary, the poet's response to Soviet political contradictions, his revolt against what Leon Trotsky called 'pseudo-revolutionary officialdom'? 'Was it a sign of a counter-revolutionary, bourgeois, individualist weakness, or of a revolutionary free will?' (Boym 1988: 3–4).

Whatever the irretrievable 'truth,' Karyotakis's suicide became emblematic of its times. Though he never assumed the role of reinvigorating national symbols decimated after 1922, the poet's public reputation, in a culture that reputedly does not have a word for privacy, became fair game. The publication of Karyotakis's *Collected Works*, introduced by his closest friend Charis Sakellariades, did not connect the poet's personal characteristics to his times or his generation.[20] He resists the mythopoeizing accounts that have 'rewritten' 'that diffident and quiet, almost timid, young man, who would sit slightly out of the way [in literary salons and cafés] as if he were chatting to his *ennui,* contemplating his final immersion into himself' (Spatalis 1929: 521).[21] Post-mortem, as it were, Karyotakis's coffee-shop silence was read as a proleptic sign of his impending suicide. Of course, Karyotakis himself was as aware of people's tendency to 'read' him in ways that even in life he seemed to resist. The persona in a poem about a poet's 'career' visits Vassiliou's publishing house and bookshop:

Κι εκεί βρίσκω τους άλλους
Λογίους και δασκάλους
Τα λόγια μου θα 'χουν ουσία,
η σιωπή μου μια σημασία

And there I find the others
scholars and teachers
My words will hold significance
my silence a meaning

(Κ 112, Σταδιοδρομία)[22]

Later reconstitutive narratives harbored more ideological subtexts. Marxists saw in Karyotakis the decay of the petty bourgeoisie. Lambridis saw in Karyotakis's self-reflection the disenchantment of the middle class.[23] Other works, most representatively Vassos Varikas's aptly named *K. G. Karyotakis: The Drama of a Generation* (1939) disapprove of the poet's skepticism and egocentrism (34–6); his misanthropic disinterestedness for the collective (39); and his conception of temporality rooted exclusively in the present moment. Karyotakis's pessimism deprives poetry of its true vocation, as it was then understood. For when poetry dismantles and questions, it does not build and establish. Palamas's evocation of a gypsy in his *Dodecalogue of the Gypsy* (1907) may have been a free spirit, but he was unmistakably a member of his race. Karyotakis's gypsy, responding to Palamas, is impetuous, unbridled, and fearless in the face of all hierarchy:

Μπρούντζινος γύφτος – τράλαλα! –
τρελά πηδάει κει πέρα
χαρούμενος που εδούλευε το μπρούντζον όλημερα
και που 'χει τη γυναίκα του
χτήμα του και βασίλειο.
Μπρούντζινος γύφτος – τράλαλα! –
δίνει κλοτσά στον ήλιο !

A bronzed gypsy – tra la la! –
jumps madly over there
happy working the bronze all day
and he holds his wife
as property and fiefdom.
Bronzed gypsy – tra la la! –
kicks out at the sun!

(Κ 35, Στροφές)

Karyotakis had cut himself off from the desires and longings of the Greek race. His focus on self-contained and unattached moments lacks for Varikas the transcendental and diachronic dimension to be found in the opening of Palamas's *Dodecalogue*. Many subsequent reviews have duplicated Varikas's critique.[24] Karyotakis was no National Poet.

Yet, elsewhere in Europe, the English 1930s generation, and in particular the pre-1940s Auden, were also trying to capture obliquely detained, singular moments that encapsulated the precariousness of the mid-war period and its disenfranchisement from the past. Like the Asia Minor Catastrophe in Greece, World War I had shaken people into reevaluating their relation to the past. Much has been written about Eliot's *Waste Land*; however, the disenfranchisement with the past was felt even more sharply by the young of the first post-war generation in Britain. They felt rootless and belated: 'We young writers of the middle twenties,' wrote Isherwood, 'were all suffering, more or less subconsciously, from a feeling of shame that we hadn't been old enough to take part in the European War' (Isherwood 1938: 74–5). Auden and his friends in the 1920s hid from contemporary history in the hermetic confines of Oxford's ivory tower and 'carried on' as if the war had not taken place. But autobiographies referring to the time, Cockburn's *In Time of Trouble* and Waugh's *A Little Learning*, bear testament to the precarious foundations that lay underneath the feverishly nervous Oxford cocktail parties and *nouveau* cults. After all, a generation was missing:

> the next older generation, which this one should have followed to maturity, was simply missing; there was a break in time, with no human link between the post-war young and the Old Men whom they blamed for the war. This gap where there should have been older brothers for models, together with the post-war feeling about the pre-war generation, isolated the young in a way that was new; they were like the survivors of some primal disaster, cut off from the traditional supports of the past, and so dependent on themselves for such meanings as their lives might acquire. (Hynes 1972: 20)

Auden's generation was somehow dangling in mid-air, contrary to the buffeting winds of history with no outstretched hand offering support or warmth. What faced the young English poet of the 1920s and 1930s in England was the formidable task of carving out a space for himself while bringing the literary tradition into the present and reordering the ironic and disorderly fragments of a waste land into a poetic vision. Auden's pre-America period focuses on the immediately empirical and unfolding, present moment.[25] Karyotakis shared an analogous predicament.

The commonly accepted construct 'Karyotakis' depends on the fabrication of a myth that rests on a particular conception of the poetic self at variance with Karyotakis's own. But was Karyotakis's aware that he was writing against this myth of the poet? The poem 'Επιτάφιο,' a little-known translation by Karyotakis of seventeenth-century French poet Mathurin Régnier's 'Épitaphe à lui-même,' offers some insight:

Épitaphe de Régnier faite par lui-même
J'ay vescu sans nul pensement,
Me laissant aller doucement

A la bonne loi naturelle;
Et je m' estonne fort pourquoy
La mort osa songer à moy,
Qui ne songeay jamais en elle.

Περνούσε η ζωή μου γλέντι αληθινό
Δίχως μετάνοια μήτε χαλινό,
κι επήγαινα παιχνίδι κάθε ανέμου.
Τώρα παραξενεύομαι γιατί
ο θάνατος να με συλλογιστεί,
που δεν τον συλλογίστηκα ποτέ μου.

(K 130)

A prose English translation of the poem might take the statement at face value: 'My life was spent a veritable feast, without regret or bridle, and I would allow myself to be the plaything of each and every passing breeze. Now I am astonished as to why death preoccupies itself with me – I who have never ever given death a thought.' However in its six-line poetic form, the piece's iconicity and rhyme suggests a more ironical reading. Certainly the word 'bridle' (χαλινό) is overly poetic and the verb 'astonished' (παραξενεύομαι) understated. Does the formal dependency between the last two lines stress the reciprocal relationship between death and the persona? Perhaps the persona had always been preoccupied by death and his life has hardly been a 'veritable feast.'

The poem's title leads the reader to reassess this laconic poem as an epitaph – a self-reflective assessment of the persona's life. The 'veritable feast' now resonates with a macabre sarcasm; the carefree air of ll. 2–3 falls flat in the umbrage cast by death's intrusion in ll. 5–6. The name Mathurin Régnier at the top of the poem – epitaph marks the gravestone. The poem is a gravestone (incidentally, it is written at about the same time – 1917–19 – as Cavafy's tomb poems).[26]

Savidis's footnote invites a biographical approach. Régnier was a French satirist (1573–1613), Savidis tells us. Known primarily for a theoretical attack on Malherbe, he was also secretary to a cardinal, though his dissolute ways impeded his advancement in the Church hierarchy. Lifelong melancholia led to his premature death. Régnier wrote this poem in his debauched youth, when his ailing health told him that he was close to death, informs Savidis;[27] and Greek criticism's reconstruction of Karyotakis resembles this sketch of Régnier. While hardly a cleric, Karyotakis was General Secretary of the Athenian Civil Servants' Union; he led a debauched youth and was fined, reassigned, and denied promotion for his anti-Venizelist positions by his bosses in the Civil Service. Such extrapolations might justify this reading of the poem. But what might Karyotakis's perspective on the poem be? Textually, the reference to Régnier as speaking subject reinforces the relation between the translator and this subject. Karyotakis's fictive speaker-cum-translator looks back on Régnier as he knows future readers (like Savidis) will look back on him. Karyotakis knows that he is to Régnier what we will be to Karyotakis. The conceit recalls an anecdote about Cavafy. When a French journalist in 1930 asked Cavafy who he was, Cavafy replied:

In my opinion, Cavafy is an ultra-modern poet, a poet of future generations. Complementary to his historical, psychological, and philosophical worth, the sobriety of his impeccable style, which occasionally touches on laconism; his balanced enthusiasm which smacks of cerebral emotion; his apt phrase which results in an aristocratic nature; his delicate irony, all are elements which generations of the future, spurred on by the progress of discoveries and by the subtlety of their cerebral mechanism, will come to savour all the more.[28]

Such self-reflexivity undermines and parodies both the processes and the discourse of critical assessment. Who produces the writer's myth, the writer's textual life? Is it the writer, the critic, or the readers? As with Cavafy's 'For Ammonis . . .,' there will always be an Alexandrian writing about an Alexandrian, overseen by another Alexandrian reader of sorts. Karyotakis's translation comments on the processes of interpretation that will affect views of his work long after his death opens a space between the biographical, cultural, and textual figure 'Karyotakis' that will emanate from these processes. It also questions the integrity of the creative subject – whose is this poem, Régnier's or Karyotakis's? Unlike the Romantic correlation of a poet's art and a poet's work, Cavafy and Karyotakis problematize and control the myth of the Poet.[29] Among what Panayotopoulos called the 'gawky snobs of our literature,' Karystakis will redefine the place of poetry in Greek society.

Poetry as Pharmakon

In 1920, the young Karyotakis won the second award in the prestigious Philadelphios Poetry Competition for his *Songs of the Fatherland* (Τα Τραγούδια της Πατρίδας) (Tziovas 1986b: 181). Yorgos Drosinis reported on behalf of the committee: 'This lyrical collection is imbued with a love for the land of our birth, for its exiled children, for the pure traditions of the Greek world, whose joys and mourning the poet follows . . . He [the poet] is more Greek and more simple than many others . . . for he is very Greek in his inspiration' (*Nea Estia* 1971: 1570). The judges deemed Karyotakis's poetry as conforming to the superlative standard of ethnicity – a mirror of the nation. Built on the cornerstone of Romantic organicism, the demoticist association of nation and literature totalized social, political, and artistic aspects of society that found justification in his work.

But his second collection, Νηπενθή, which advertises poetry as a *pharmakon nepenthès*, literally a potion that chases off mourning, is an esoteric venture at Baudelairean transcendence through the poetic act.[30] Taken from Baudelaire's *Les Paradis artificiels* (1860), the reference to *nepenthès* marks Karyotakis's conviction that his poetry is introspective and therapeutic, and not a vehicle for the didactic rhetoric typical of traditional verse. This break with the Romantic conception of the self becomes more and more pronounced in Karyotakis's work. To highlight this break, let us consider Karyotakis's poem, 'Είμαστε Κάτι . . .' ('We are a certain . . .') next to an archetypal Romantic poem, Coleridge's 'Eolian Harp' (1796), with which it is in some sense in dialogue.

First, a few words about Coleridge's 'Romantic poetic self' are in order. In trying to overcome the perceived inadequacies of British empirical philosophy, Coleridge embarks on an analysis of his own perception and sets this up as the universal concept of 'self.' The biographical form or sense of self-consciousness, or 'I am,' will lead the poet to an understanding of self-knowledge. Coleridge does not question the existence of self-consciousness, but begins with it as his first metaphysical postulate to argue for its necessity. He introduces the relationship of objective reality and the perceiving subject by reference to Kant. Early in Chapter 13 of his *Biographia Literaria* (1817) he establishes a connection between the formal purposiveness of nature and the creative impulse of the artist. But Coleridge is equally indebted to Schelling for whom the essential element of the universe, an energy or creative impulse, manifests itself in nature when unconscious, and in Art when conscious. The objective world or the unconscious of nature would become conscious in the subjective activity of the ego. Coleridge coined the word 'esemplastic' to denote this 'molding into unity,' which entails not only the bringing together of all the mind's faculties but also the recreation of that creative impulse of the essential element in the universe.

In the three paragraphs that conclude Chapter 13, Coleridge differentiates between two modes of imagination. The first, or primary imagination, is related to the Kantian notion that every subject can recreate the infinite or providential I AM (or First Consciousness). The secondary imagination is 'an echo of the former,' but distinguishes itself by its self-conscious knowledge of the workings of this primary imagination. The extra-sensitive subject, the poet, is granted primacy to fathom the origin of the primary experience, and not only establish the nexus between reality and consciousness but recreate the unity between being and knowing, thus rendering the primary unity conscious.

Coleridge often explores the transformative powers of the Romantic poet in the conventional and recurring metaphor of a lute or harp that transforms the natural elements into absolute form. The scene is played out in the company of a female lover, which underscores the analogy to the sexual desire that lurks beneath the surface of both poem and creative impulse:

> And that simplest Lute,
> Placed length-ways in the clasping casement, hark!
> How by desultory breeze caress'd,
> Like some coy maid half yielding to her lover,
> It pours such sweet upbraiding, as must needs
> Tempt to repeat the wrong! And now its strings
> Boldlier swept, the long sequacious notes
> Over delicious surges sink and rise,
> Such a soft floating witchery of sound
> As twilight elfins make,

This image serves as an analogy for the poet's mind and its encounter with nature in the artistic process:

> And thus, my Love! as on the midway slope
> Of yonder hill I stretch my limbs at noon,
> Whilst through my half-clos'd eye-lids I behold
> The sunbeams dance, like diamonds, on the main,
> And tranquil muse upon tranquility;
> Full many a thought uncall'd and undetain'd,
> And many idle flitting phantasies,
> Traverse my indolent and passive brain,
> As wild and various as the random gales
> That swell and flutter on this subject Lute!
> And what if all of animated nature
> Be but organic Harps diversely fram'd,
> That tremble into thought, as o'er them sweeps
> Plastic and vast, one intellectual breeze,
> At once the Soul of each, and God of all?

Costas Karyotakis's poem 'Είμαστε Κάτι' expropriates this poetic image to parody the transformative powers of the Romantic poetic self:

> **Είμαστε κάτι ...**
> Είμαστε κάτι ξεχαρβαλωμένες
> Κιθάρες. Ο άνεμος, όταν περνάει,
> Στίχους, ήχους παράφωνους ξυπνάει
> Στις χορδές που κρέμονται σαν καδένες.
>
> Είμαστε κάτι απίστευτες αντένες.
> Υψώνονται σα δάχτυλα στα χάη,
> στην κορυφή τους τ᾽ άπειρο αντηχάει,
> μα γρήγορα θα πέσουνε σπασμένες.

Είμαστε κάτι διάχυτες αισθήσεις,
Χωρίς ελπίδα να συγκεντρωθούμε.
Στα νεύρα μας μπερδεύεται όλη η φύσις.

Στο σώμα, στην ενθύμηση πονούμε.
Μας διώχνουνε τα πράγματα, κι η ποίησις
είναι το καταφύγιο που φθονούμε.

We are a sort of. . .
We are a sort of deranged
guitar. The wind, when it passes,
rouses verses and jarring sounds
on strings which droop down like chains.

We are a sort of unbelievable antennae.
They rise up like fingers to the chaoses,
at their pinnacles the boundless resounds
but soon they will tumble to the ground, decimated.

We are a sort of diffuse feelings
with no hope of composing ourselves.
In our nerve endings the whole of nature entangles itself.

In our body, in our memory we are in pain.
We are repulsed by the things around us, and poetry
is the shelter we envy.

(K 87)

The poem's title, followed by an ellipsis, is marked by incompleteness: 'We are something' or 'we are some' or 'we are of a certain kind of'. Many read the 'we' as referring to the generation of 1920s poets or 'poets of decay.' But the plural 'we' refers to the disrupted and disparate selves of an I – a poetic persona decentered and dispersed beyond the compact and unitary borders of its self-presence. The poet is likened to a guitar, a 'deranged' or 'rickety one' at that, and not an Eolian harp. The incongruity of so modern an object is reinforced by the series of uncontracted colloquial verbs (ll. 2–3, 6–7). The wind rushes through it but gives out unharmonious sounds, jarring and forced internal rhymes (l. 3), which, in the Greek, rhyme obtrusively.[31] The chords, no longer taut strings, hang drooping like chains, sexually flaccid, and impotent to produce or regenerate.

The poets are like 'unbelievable antennae' that rise up like fingers into the 'chaoses.' The adjective here can mean disbelieving, unbelievable, or the antithesis of πιστός, and so rendered as 'unfaithful', or 'untrue' to something. The privatival prefix -a indicates a lack. The 'unfaithful' or 'untrue' transformative power of the antennae attributes a failure in rendering the object of perception; there can be little faith in its mimetic truth. Margaret Alexiou's discussion of 'unfaithfulness' (απιστία) in Cavafy's poem by that name explores the relationship of prophecy and truth: Apollo's actions and beliefs, both as poet and prophet, are brought into question as the voices in the poem uncover 'not only Apollo's faithlessness and Thetis' (lack of) disbelief, but also the need for suspension of all rational *pistis* where *logos* is concerned' (Alexiou and Lambropoulos 1985: 160–3). Something of the same sentiment is at work here, too.

The dialogic allusion to the mythological oaks in the groves of Dodoni in Epirus undermines the mythological image of the poet as a prophet or oracle who speaks out through the rustling of the sacred Eolian breezes. Reverberating the ethers of chaos(es) – the plural of chaos is unknown until its use here to emphasize disorder and make it rhyme obtrusively with the verb at the end of the next line – the antennas are sensitized to the eternal at their apex, but are doomed to fall to the ground, shattered in their failure to render life signifyable. Again, the sexual undertone and the promise of instantaneous fulfillment is thwarted conclusively.

The third stanza reiterates the disintegration of this subject 'we,' the disorder of diffuse feelings without hope of agglomeration into a compact and unified subject. Moreover, this subject is deprived of its agency as nature is the prime mover here that becomes entangles around the subject's passively described nerve endings (l. 11). The conventional subject–object relation is overturned in the last couplet of the poem as it is the things around the subject that repulse him/them. This is a key concern of Karyotakis's poetry. And the subject's only agency appears in the last line's assertion that poetry provides the shelter that we 'envy' (φθονούμε). This last verb, carrying in Greek the seemingly paradoxical meanings of 'envy' and 'bearing malice against someone or something' conveys an ambivalence toward the creative process, a tension underscored by the relationship of the poem's articulation of disorder or chaos even while this sonnet's strictly constructed Petrarchan form assures order.[32] Poetry is a *pharmakon*, in the sense that Derrida cites in his critique of Plato's *Phaedrus*: it is poison and remedy, it can bring on mourning and chase it away. On the one hand, it a threat to the living presence of the language and, on the other, it is the only means to encode presence (Derrida 1981: 70–1, 95–134).

Writing about Writing (Waged Work)

Karyotakis estranges the collective tool of human communication at the same time as being estranged by it. By opting for the double logic of the verb φθονώ, Karyotakis rejects the priority of the signified and spurns the written sign's ability to occasion the transfer, or *metaphora*, of meaning. He disturbs the logic of self-identity and institutes the written inscription as a play of semantic approximations that bring the problematical question of writing and mimesis to the fore, since:

> Imitation does not correspond to its essence, is not what it is – imitation – unless it is in some way at fault or rather in default. It is bad by nature. It is only good insofar as it is bad. Since (de)fault is inscribed within it, it has no nature; nothing is properly its own. Ambivalent, playing with itself by hollowing itself out, good and evil at once – undecidably, mimesis, is akin to the *pharmakon*. No 'logic,' no 'dialectic,' can consume its reserve even though each must endlessly draw on it and seek assurance through it. (Derrida 1981: 139)

Karyotakis makes writing the subject of his writing. Peter Mackridge (1990: 59–62) has stated that this concern for the technicism of the written word constitutes an attack against the logocentric Greek Tradition of the Song, most notably espoused by Palamas. In his poem, 'My Verses' (Οι Στίχοι Μου), the poet's verses dislocate themselves from their originator and work a spell of their own in a sequence of active verbs: 'they speak/they go/they define' (μιλούνε/πηγαίνουν/ορίζουνε). The poet's alienation from his own lyrics, from his own 'sons'' autonomy breaks down the Romantic subject's agency and assails the demoticists' promotion of the naturalness and authenticity of the spoken word:

> Τον ουρανόν ορίζουνε, τη γη.
> όμως ρωτιούνται ακόμα σαν τί λείπει
> και πλήττουνε και λιώνουν πάντα οι γιοι
> μητέρα που γνωρίσανε τη Λύπη.
>
> Το γέλιο του απαλότερου σκοπού,
> το πάθος μάταια χύνω του φλαούτου·
> είμαι γι᾽ αυτούς ανίδεος ρήγας που
> έχασε την αγάπη του λαού του

> They rule the world, the earth.
> But still they ask what is missing
> as the sons always grow bored and melt away
> they who got to know Sorrow as their mother.
>
> The laugh of the softest tune,
> I pour the flute's passion in vain
> I am for them an uninformed king who
> has lost the love of his people

> (Κ 19, 'Οι Στίχοι Μου')

Analogously, the subject is alienated from his own, decentered body. The muscular rhymes mark the poem's materiality even as the subject fades into non-existence. In the first poem of his earliest collection of poems entitled 'Θάνατοι' ('Deaths'), the persona has no control over the parts of his body. Karyotakis does not employ the possessive pronoun: 'hands, eyes and mouths' remain strictly neuter, are given in the diminutive, and are contrasted to Death – given in the plural – whom they are unable to repulse. More significantly, writing is prioritized over logos, and language has become objectivized away from the mouth:

ω, που ' χατε, πολλά να ειπείτε, στόματα
κι ο λόγος σας εδιάλεξε για τάφο,
ω, που ' χατε πολλά να ειπείτε, στόματα,
και τον καημό δεν είπατε που γράφω.

oh! mouths, and you had so much to say
and your speech chose the grave
oh! mouths, and you had so much to say
and you never spoke of the sorrow of which I write

(Κ 3, 'Θάνατοι')

The disintegrating subject submits to the environment:

Σα να μην ήρθαμε σ ' αυτή τη γη
σα να μένουμε ακόμη στην ανυπαρξία . . .

Από χαρτί πλασμένα κι από δισταγμό
ανδρείκελα, στης Μοίρας τα δυο τυφλά χέρια,
χορεύουμε, δεχόμαστε τον εμπαιγμό
άτονα κοιτώντας, παθητικά, τ αστέρια.

As if we had not come to this earth
as if we had remained in non-existence . . .

Made of paper and hesitation
mannequins, in Fate's two hands
we dance, we accept the delusion
languidly watching the stars, passively.

(Κ 89, 'Ανδρείκελα')

or:

Δεν ξέρω ποιος είναι τώρα ο τόπος,
δεν ξέρω ποιος χαράζει τους σταυρούς,
κι όλα τα πράγματά μου έμειναν όπως
νά ' χω πεθάνει πριν από καιρούς.

I don't know what place this is,
I don't know who is drawing the crosses,
and all my things have remained
as if I had died ages ago.

    (Κ 66, ''Ολα τα Πράγματά μου 'Εμειναν')

For Karyotakis, the poet's Romantic pose is a by-product of his self-glorification:

Αφήνουμε στο αγέρι τα μαλλιά
και τη γραβάτα μας. Παίρνουμε πόζα.
Ανυπόφορη νομίζουμε πρόζα
των καλών ανθρώπων τη συντροφιά.

We let our hair and tie
ride in the wind. We strike up a pose.
Unbearable we find prose
the companion of good folk.

    (Κ 103, 'Ολοι Μαζί)

The poet's labor is a painful mixture of self-undermining and self-mythologization. In this last, scathing poem, Karyotakis marks out the strained attempts made by poets 'to (en)title themselves poets' in *katharevousa* ('για να τιτλοφορούμεθα ποιητές']. But they're justified in their snobbery, Karyotakis ridicules, for they misguidedly correspond with metaphysical bodies:

Μόνο για μας υπάρχουν του Θεού
τα πλάσματα και, βέβαια όλη η φύσις.
Στη Γη για να στέλνουμε ανταποκρίσεις,
ανεβήκαμε στ ' άστρα τ ' ουρανού.

Only for us do they exist, bodies
of God and, of course, all of nature.
To send reports to Earth,
we have ascended to the stars of the heavens.

    (Κ 103, 'Ολοι Μαζί)

The last-minute interpolation of the ironic 'of course' (βέβαια) affirms the poet's disinterestedness in the affairs of *physsis* (nature). The bureaucratic or journalistic noun 'reports' deflates the Baudelairean correspondences:

Κι αν πειναλέοι γυρνάμε ολημερίς
κι αν ξενυχτούμε κάτου απ ' τα γεφύρια,
επέσαμε θύματα εξιλαστήρια,
του 'περιβάλλοντος' και της 'εποχής'.

And if we wander about starving all day long
and if we stay up all night under bridges
we have fallen the expiatory victims
of the 'environment' and the 'times.'

(K 103, Όλοι Μαζί)

Attributing their woes to abstract concepts – the 'environment' and the 'times' – demarcated from reality as they are by quotation marks, Karyotakis here recalls Skliros's critique and draws attention to the hermeticism of their textual world. As abstract as the Romantic, nationalist evocation of the 'people' is in the preceding section, Karyotakis is ready, rather like Skliros (yet somewhat more playfully), to point to the yawning chasm between sign and referent and to try to break through the circumscription of the quotation mark. That which is within quotation marks, the word and the poem, and its executor, the poet, is doomed to self-referential existence in a delimited aesthetic realm. In February 1924, one month after the French Surrealists' called for Revolution, Karyotakis, along with twenty-one other poets, published a manifesto in a periodical, *Emeis*, that vowed to promote the social importance of art while attacking cliques (Baloumes 1997: 20–1).[33]

Karyotakis's understanding of the self-referential nature of the sign in the institution of Greek poetry emerges at the time when, as a syndicalist and bureaucrat in the state apparatus from 1923, he worked in the administrative processing of refugees for the Office for the Oversight of Refugee Settlement:

Αλλάζουμε με ήχους και συλλαβές
τα αισθήματα στη χάρτινη καρδιά μας,
δημοσιεύουμε τα ποιήματά μας
για να τιτλοφορούμεθα ποιητές.

We change by sounds and syllables
the feeling in our paper hearts
we publish our poems
so that we may bestow on our good selves the title of poets.

(K 103, Όλοι Μαζί)

The exchange of sounds and syllables in a self-regulating system of circulation is distanced from the realities of society. Analogously, Karyotakis was dubious of the relationship of the civil servant, as executor of state *grapho-kratia*, to the effects and consequences of his own bureaucratic writing. Karyotakis was, after all, most active in the syndicalist movement, especially in 1927–8. Time and again he wrote complaining of the government's negligence of both the civil servants and the workers' needs, and yet his socialist writings were overlooked for a full fifty years.[34] During a civil servants' strike in early 1928, he cites specific measures for curbing government spending and rebukes the government for their willingness to grant increases to the military in 1925. He urges politicians to be more accountable to voters (Papakostas 1990: 346). Not only was Karyotakis's article signed, at a time when the government was threatening jail sentences to strikers, but also it accuses a higher bureaucrat with fiscal impropriety. According to many accounts, this led to his transfer to Preveza (Baloumes 1997: 260ff).[35]

Greece was on the threshold of entering into one phase of modernity, where the differentiation of spheres (*Ausdifferenzierung*) would see to it that art seek autonomy by organizing itself by the commodifying logic of a market economy. His recurring references to paper point to a critique of new conditions of a commercialization in the Greek publishing world (Demelis 1990: 147). But it also addresses the effects of a broader commodification, whereby poetry is but one victim, and the poet is just one more worker alienated from his work. To ironize this new urban reality, Karyotakis brings together the spheres of poet and worker, his poetic self with his civil servant self. In his 'Civil Servants' (Δημόσιοι Υπάλληλοι), workers sit in chairs, the executors of this paper culture, pointlessly despoiling 'innocent blank bits of paper without purpose' as they wilt away and expire like their 'light columns' two by two.[36] Their purposeless scribbling at their 'offices' or 'desks' (*graphia* in Greek) is placed in quotation and in *katharevousa*, a demarcated private language. It bestows on them honor (τιμή) and they return home robotically each evening, carrying with them a hollow self-honor as they mull over the 'laws' (νόμους) and 'rates of exchange' (συνάλλαγμα), which hold sway over their lives. Walter Benjamin's recollection of Marx's words on capitalist production in his essay 'On some Motifs in Baudelaire' comes to mind: 'the worker does not make use of the working conditions. The working conditions make use of the worker; but it takes machinery to give this reversal a technically concrete form. In working with machines, workers learn to coordinate 'their own movements with the uniformly constant movements of an automaton' (Benjamin 1997: 175). Their 'waged work' is to be exchanged, as a poem of that title proclaims (K 73). Poetic and bureaucratic labors exude a brooding dissatisfaction:

Οι ώρες με χλώμαιναν, γυρτός που βρέθηκα ξανά
στο αχάριστο τραπέζι.
(Απ ' τ ' ανοιχτό παράθυρο στον τοίχο αντικρινά
ο ήλιος γλιστράει και παίζει.)

. . .

Απόκαμα, θολώσανε τα μάτια μου και ο νους,
όμως ακόμη γράφω.
(Στο βάζο ξέρω δίπλα μου δυο κρίνους φωτεινούς.
Σα να ' χουν βγει σε τάφο.)

The hours made me grow pallid, inclined as I was once more
before the ungiving table.
(From the open window to the wall opposite
the sun slithered and played).

. . .

Exhaustion, my eyes, my mind have blurred,
but still I write.
(In the vase beside me I sense two radiant lilacs
as if they had come out of a tomb).

(Κ 37, Γραφιάς)

Nature is 'bracketed off' from the writer and his world in these stanzas, set off, though still in communion by rhyme and the effects of iconic form. His table is 'ungiving'; despite his labors, it does not yield a result. Like Byron, in the poem of that name, 'he felt/that verses were/a thankless fate (τύχη)' (Κ 97). The poem can not match the way Byron's 'glorious youth' was eternalized as a result of his gallant stand on the homophone 'τείχη,' 'walls' of Messolonghi's siege. Action and power, admired by Karyotakis (and Palamas) in their evocation of the gypsy's life force far outdoes the performativity of writers:

Σύμβολα . . .
Σύμβολα εμείναμε καιρών που απάνω μας βαραίνουν,
άλυτοι γρίφοι που μιλούν μονάχα στον εαυτό τους,
τάφοι που πάντα με ανοιχτή χρονολογία προσμένουν,
γράμματα που δεν έφτασαν ποτέ στον προορισμό τους.

Symbols . . .
We have remained symbols of times that weigh down upon us
unsolved riddles that speak only to themselves,
tombs that await with open date
letters that have never reached their destination.

(Κ 73, 'Σύμβολα . . .')

The symbol, the 'putting together' or the 'mark' or 'sign' of the half-coin that is carried by one party in a pledge, assumes an act of combination or representation in which what is shown (the material sign) means associatively something *more* or something *else* as an idea or concept (immaterial). As a symbol himself, the poet places analogy or image in lieu of a subject that, by virtue of a conventional association, allows for the inference of more than the analogy or image. In this instance, Karyotakis furnishes us with symbols whose combinational transaction is deferred and frustrated. As Elli Philokyprou (1992) has commented on the relationship between syntactical structures of positive and negative semantic value in the Greek post-symbolists, 'poetic language is deprived of its aims; it serves to undermine or negate itself at the same time that the poets are conscious of their captivity within it' (1992: 243). As such, their incompleteness gives them both their *élan* and their nadir. Poets are symbols of this sort, like the title 'Symbols . . .' followed by an ellipsis, they mark an eclipse of closure in the spluttering of the pen as it defers and as language disappears into discontinuity. The economy of the poem is supported on the unexchangeability of signifier and signified as well as on the signifying surplus that transcends this potential exchange, an excess of meaning that grants poetic value. As Barbara Johnson (1987) has noted, the circulation of language as poetry can be viewed in the same terms as the circulation of money as capital – poetry is the surplus value of language. However, Karyotakis's poetic voice denounces the naturalness of auratic poetry by employing a prosaic style that conflates genres and mixes discursive codes in a way that disallows Romantic poetic attainment of a world anterior to social, temporal, and rhetorical differentiation. This proclamation of writing's performativity, its ability to draw attention to itself, forces the creative Romantic subject to shrink away. The subject is shown to be not a subject who speaks, but one spoken by language. Karyotakis's poems are inhabited by individuals like mannequins 'made from paper' (από χαρτί πλασμένα). It is paper, the site of writing, language, and bureaucracy, and work that confines them to their desks, unfulfilled symbols of their 'environment' and their 'times.'

Death in Preveza? A Poetics of the Unpoetic

In so many of his poems, Karyotakis consciously unveils the very mechanism and social apparatus that an individual taps into, and through which, he or she produces meaning and constitutes a self. This matrix has broken down irrevocably. Many of his poems deconstruct the semiotics of social graces, exemplary codes of suicidal praxis, and the making of military recruits.[37] The space between language and reality is most notoriously thematized in his poem 'Preveza', the town where he eventually committed suicide. In it, Karyotakis focuses on 'death the dirty, insignificant streets/with their resplendent grand names' (Θάνατος οι λεροί, ασήμαντοι δρόμοι/με τα λαμπρά, μεγάλα ονόματά τους). The destitute streets of the Greek provinces appear under the heroic, historical names on the street signs above them. By this, Karyotakis creates a *mise en abîme* of sorts emblematic of the relationship between Greek social reality and its poetic textualization. No transcendental Hellenic signified here. Indeed, the capitalized symbols of centralized authority – the Base, the Guard, the Prefecture of Preveza – are part of the wretchedness of the place, and the deferential designation of the Prefect as Mr. Prefect (ο κύριος Νομάρχης) carries with it a scornful critique of the fawning servility that underpins authority.[38] Death, too, is capitalized and repeated at the beginning of all three stanzas. Everywhere 'Preveza' evokes the ordinary, the petty, and the unidealized. Poetically, it is a landmark of the Greek tradition *not* because it offers us the biographical etiology of Karyotakis's suicide, but because it marks the site of the rejection of the discourse of ab-sense, the site of resistance to poetic metaphorization, *a poetics of the unpoetic*.

It may seem contradictory now for me to proceed to incorporate an assessment of Karyotakis's suicide into this interpretation. However, his death provides us with a *text* that deflates the last vestiges of lyric posture. A day *after* he had tried to commit suicide by drowning, Karyotakis leaves his apartment and sits in a café to compose a suicide note. It is not as dramatic and lyrical as the note left behind by the persona in his poem 'Ideal Suicides', but it is as anti-climactic as that of this poem's failed suicide. Having described the suicide's preparations, the sting in the poem's tail reconditions one's whole reading of the protagonist's actions as it undermines the gravity of this finality:

> Βλέπουν τον καθρέφτη, βλέπουν την ώρα,
> ρωτούν αν είναι τρέλα τάχα ή λάθος
> όλα 'τελείωσαν' ψιθυρίζουν 'τώρα',
> πως θ᾽ αναβάλουν βέβαιοι κατά βάθος.

> They look at the mirror, they look at the time,
> they ask if it is madness perhaps or a mistake,
> everything's 'over' they whisper 'now,'
> certain in their heart of hearts that they will postpone it.[39]

(Κ 114, Ιδανικοί Αυτόχειρες)

The protagonist's formulaic posturing, its performativity, depends on the certainty of failure. Karyotakis's real-life suicide note shares aspects of the poem given above. He announces his 'tragedy' in a message to those he will leave behind. But the note winds up by ridiculing itself as circumstances see to it that he will append the unthinkable – a postscript to an irreversible and final suicide note:

And now, just to change the tone. I advise all those who know how to swim to desist from attempting suicide by water. All night tonight, for ten hours, I fought with the waves. I drank an abundance of water, but every so often, without understanding how, my body rose to the surface. When I get the chance at some point, I will write the impressions of a drowning man. (*Nea Estia* 1971: 1566)

In microcosm, the parodic postscript is the last in a series of texts that charts the passage of Karyotakis's work from lyricism to satire to ironic self-mockery (Colyvas 1980; Koropoulis 1996). Like Mayakovsky's suicide note, and many of his poems, it fictionalizes the poet's own death, textualizing and depersonalizing himself, splitting his self between the text and the real, between the agent and victim of his own death. André Breton, commenting on Mayakovsky's suicide, wrote that: 'Suicide is a badly composed word: the one who kills is never identical with the one who is killed.' Karyotakis's bullet to the heart, which follows a few hours after this note's writing, blasts out the unavoidable crisis of the real by breaking down the distinction between text/subject; poetry/life; and language/ action. The final volley in Preveza on 21 July 1928 is an enactment of a total metaphysical crisis, the anguished transgression of the last tenable border of selfhood and the first avant-garde act in Greek literature.[40] When, as J. G. Ballard

Figure 4.1 Preveza Police photograph of K. G. Karyotakis's suicide scene

observes in his cult novel *Crash*, 'the most prudent and effective method of dealing with the world around us is to assume that it is complete fiction . . . the one small node of reality left to us is inside our heads' (Ballard 1985: 8). The affirmation of the self may be realizable only in the transgression of the line between self and world. The hypostatization of the experience of the self as a dead body, as pure matter, as a complete entity again – a corpse, and not a corpus – is a bold testament. The 'corpse' of Karyotakis's *poiesis, his* suicide, ruptures the non-referentiality of art and shatters it with the praxis of life, a corpse. Socrates's suicide paved the way for the institutionalization of consensual democracy; Karyotakis's death proclaimed a new poetry inscribed on the body overlooked by the discourse of ab-sense. Preveza houses the Tomb of the Known Soldier (Fig. 4.1).

Notes

1. For a detailed account of nineteenth-century socialist movements in Greece, see Moskov (1979: Chapters 10–13); Kordatos (1946: 9–170); Dertilis (1977: 103–71); Lazaris (1996: 1–258). Anarchist and atheist ideas found it difficult to take root in the agrarian communities, except in time of excessive economic hardship.
2. E.g. the gradual assimilation of 'The Union of Friends of the People' or 'The Union of Kalavryta' into Tricoupis's liberal party in 1887.
3. Roidis, Eftaxiadis, and Soutsos all attacked the Commune in 1871. Bosses financed catechism-like manuals for workers, such as the Εγκόλπιον του Εργατικού Λαού ή Συμβουλαί προς τους χειρώνακτας (1869), a translation of a French pamphlet undertaken by Nikolaos Dragoumis. For more on the reverberations of the Commune in Greece, see Lazaris (1996: 81–5).
4. The *Socialist*, the organ of the first socialist party in Greece in 1890, boasted a readership of two thousand and had correspondents nationwide. Other workers' literature helped organize the first May marches in Greece.
5. Often described as 'literary associations,' in contradistinction to their more militant counterparts that were dispatching (sometimes armed) national partisans along with teachers and propaganda materials to Macedonia, these organizations provided coordinated channels for communications and action on the Macedonian issue (Karakasidou 1996: 93). Karakasidou singles out the Hellenic Literature Association of Istanbul and the Propagation of Greek Letters in Athens, both established in 1874, as most important to the Hellenic cause. Karakasidou (1996: 279, fn. 27) gives a longer list of such associations.

6. Beaton has the same opinion on this (1994: 315–20). His views appear as part of a broader, readable account of the Language Question in the modern period (1994: 269–368). Diglossia is, however, not a phenomenon restricted to the modern period in Greece. For a diachronic overview, see M. Alexiou (1982).

7. E.g. Papanastasiou's (1921) critique of the Balkans; Kordatos's (1924) social analysis of the Greek Revolution. A nationalist reaction can be seen in Yanno-poulos (1904), Dragoumis's (1926) work in 1911, or S. Sokolis (1916). For commentary on the proliferation of ideological critique at this time, see Vergopoulos (1978: 101–57).

8. In 'Socialists and Nationalists,' Skliros playfully turns the tables on the nationalist rebuffs of critics such as Dragoumis and Tsirimokos. He faults their essentialism and complains that they have neither entered into the *essence* of his argument nor understood it. The fault lies with Dragoumis's 'abstract psychoses, inspired by foreign interests' (Stavridi-Patrikiou 1976: 157).

9. Like Skliros, Theotokas's *Free Spirit* (1929) also talks in terms of 'demons' and 'new demons' for his own liberal solutions for Greece. More on this in Chapter 5.

10. Members of both sides assumed pen-names in their exchanges. Tsirimokos called himself Ramas; Dragoumis – Idas; Vlastos – Ermonas; Delmouzos – Delos; Chatzopoulos – Petros Vassilikos. The entire debate is collected in Stavridi-Patrikiou (1976). References to this text will hereafter be designated by the abbreviation (SP). More information about the participants can be found in her rigorous introduction. See also the activities of 'The Socialist Demoticist Union' of 1909 (Lazaris 1996: 275).

11. Stavridi-Patrikiou (ξδ - ο) notes that Skliros lifts whole passages from G. Plekhanov's *The Development of the Monist View of History* (1895).

12. This refers also to a group known as 'the Sociologists' (Lazaris 1996: 281).

13. The charge is made by the philosopher Zissimos Lorenzatos in his essay 'The Lost Center' (1980), which is discussed in Chapter 6.

14. Greek criticism often refers to the 1930s Generation or the 'Generation of the 1930s.' Seferis, Elytis, Sarandaris, Theotokas, Dimaras, Katsimbalis, and Karandonis are some of the writers associated with the literary branch of the movement.

15. See his attack on Malakassis in 'Μικρή Ασυμφωνία εις Α ' Μείζον.'

16. The commemorative issue of *Nea Estia* (1971) marked a change in Karyotakis's reception. The latter presents a selection of poems, a couple of biographical articles, and some correspondence. There are no contemporary critical contrib-utions and the material on Karyotakis, unlike other commemorative issues of the period, does not fill an issue. For a full account of his reception, see Dounia (2000).

17. See Theotokas (1938: 68); though they shared none of Karyotakis's originality, conception of form, or irony, poets of this group were nonetheless painted with a broad brush. Napoleon Lapathiotis's poetry has not been given its due; his suicide has.
18. Seferis becomes more appreciative of Cavafy later. Perhaps, his stay in Alexandria with the Greek government in exile during World War II was a factor in this change of heart. Chouliaras proposes that

> Cavafy, understood as the poet of the diaspora, is viewed through the lens of Seferis, understood as a poet and cultural critic responding to the greatest destruction of the Hellenic diaspora, the Asia Minor Catastrophe . . . [Seferis's] cultural synthesis involved a re-orientation away from the diaspora and its destruction and toward a national cultural center with a 'primitive' core and a European orientation. It is, in fact, difficult to see where Cavafy might fit into such a scheme. In fact, it became possible to accept Cavafy into the Seferis fold – and even then as an 'anomaly,' as a poet whose Greek was imperfect – only at a time of tragedy and exile, not dissimilar to many diasporic experiences. (Chouliaras 1993: 119)

19. See Papageorgiou (1989: 45–6, 58–9); Ziras (1989). Karyotakis's work, along with that of Nikos Kavvadias, rivals Seferis and Elytis as the work most often set to music in the post-dictatorship period; see Kokkolis (1978).
20. Sakellariades's account appears as the long introduction to this 1938 edition of Karyotakis's *Collected Works*. A friend of Karyotakis since childhood, Sakellariades does not understate Karyotakis's moodiness or cynicism, but he does not present them as symptoms of Karyotakis's reaction to society or his generation's ills. He was unhappy during his early years in Hania, but enjoyed his student years (Sakellariades 1938: xxv). He was a private man, but one who was well liked by his colleagues at work (xxviii). Some considered him 'the *arbiter elegantiae*' on matters dress among his companions (xxx).
21. On Athenian literary salons and cafés, see Papakostas (1991).
22. All quotations from Karyotakis's poetry are taken from G. P. Savidis's edition of Karyotakis poetry and prose (Karyotakis 1997). They will be identified by a K and a page number in my text; all translations are my own and they aim to be more literal than literary.
23. See Papaioannou (1955); Lambridis (1955); Vournas (1955); Avgheris (1956). Papaioannou (1955) asserted that Karyotakis's work criticized the ruling classes from 'within.' Lambridis (1955) disagreed: for him, Karyotakis was not a son of the ruling class and was, consequently, establishing a critique from 'without.' Vournas (1955) tried to arbitrate the dispute and concluded that Karyotakis was criticizing the ruling class from 'within'; however, he added that both Karyotakis and Cavafy were alienated from the collective, and his 'socially responsible' poems were rare. According to Vournas, both poets

failed to aspire to Varnalis's more publicly committed poetry, whose work is portrayed as more paradigmatic for Greek leftists of the 1950s.

24. See, characteristically, Malanos (1938); Vogasaris (1968); and Kairophyllas's (1986) 'narrative mythologization.'

25. See 'Taller, today, we remember similar evenings' (Auden No. 4); 'What's in your mind, my dove, my coney' (No. 14); 'Dear though the night is gone' (No. 29); his political poems, like the celebrated 'Spain' focus on action in the historical moment that is now.

26. Karyotakis makes this analogy in another poem about the Romantic Athenian poet Spyridon Vassileiades's grave (K 91, Τάφοι).

27. The 1853 Jannet edition of Régnier's work includes a citation that reads: 'Le P. Garasse, jésuite, qui rapporte ces six vers dans ses *Recherches des Recherches*, p. 648, dit que Régnier 'se bâtit jadis cette épitaphe à soi-même en sa jeunesse débauchée, ayant désesperé de sa santé, et estant, comme il pensoit, sur le point de rendre l' âme.'

28. Cavafy's poem 'Hidden Things' plays out this same mask poetically: 'From all I did and all I said/let no one try to find out who I was . . .'

29. Cavafy's tactics for disseminating his own mythology of self by an eccentric and strategic distribution of his poems among friends has been documented by Savidis in his Cavafy's *Editions* and in the introduction to Keeley and Savidis's *Passions and Ancient Days*. Jusdanis interprets Cavafy's rejection of a complete edition of his works as long as he was alive and his techniques for eschewing fixed editions as the adoption of an 'open form.' Restlessly in progress always, this policy amounted to Cavafy's effective intervention in his poems' reception and a measure of control / protectionism in his work's reception in the economy of art (Jusdanis 1987b: Chapter 2; esp. 58–63).

30. Originally appearing in Homer's *Odyssey* IV, 221. For the affinity of Cavafy's conception of the imagination in the poetic act to that of Baudelaire, see Jusdanis (1987b: 15–21).

31. Kargiotis (1999: 285–9) reads the poem's many effects in much greater detail.

32. Mackridge (1989: 61) points out that Karyotakis's working of the sonnet's form, his concern for its acoustic patterns, is so precise that he not only observes the end rhymes of a Petrarchan sonnet, but also aligns the pattern of vowel sounds between the three similar opening lines to the first three stanzas.

33. See the Surrealists' Declaration of 27 January 1924 (Nadeau 1989: 240–1).

34. George Savidis first drew attention to this 'socialist aspect' of his writing in a July 1978 newspaper article. In it, Savidis cites a declaration of the Economic Committee of the Greek Civil Servants' Union and claims it is written by Karyotakis. It has been republished in Savidis (1989b: 93–100). Since this work, an essay describing the fine work done in the agrarian orphanages of 1923 has been attributed to him (Vayenas 1990: 375–83). Dalkou (1986) and Papakostas (1993) have uncovered other details of his Civil Service career.

35. 'I envy your courage, Karyotakis!' exclaimed the poet Costas Varnalis in envy of the poet's commitment to the workers' cause in his 'Rage of the People' (Οργή Λαού).
36. Savidis informs us that these στήλες (columns) were electric batteries, hanging in twos, providing light.
37. See, characteristically, the poems Αποστροφή,, Ιδανικοί Αυτόχειρες, Ο Μιχαλιός.
38. The singer Vassilis Papakonstantinou's raspy growl in his rendition of these words in Manos Loizos's composition of 'Preveza' conveys this scorn very well.
39. In the original Greek, Karyotakis holds back the crucial word βέβαιοι (of course) for as near to the end of the poem as possible for effect. They are certain right up to the 'last' moment that it will, of course, not be their last.
40. I do not share Dimitris Tziovas's (1986a) estimation that Karyotakis and Cavafy's poetry was 'avant-garde.' I do not believe Karyotakis engages in a critique of the institution of art, as described in Peter Bürger's *Theory of the Avant-Garde* (1980), for instance. And despite the affinity of some of his strategies to those listed by Bürger for the historical avant-garde, he does not confront the relative dissociation of the work of art from the praxis of life in bourgeois society in quite the same direct ways, except in his last suicidal act.

–5–

The Cultural Geographies of (Un)Greekness

Yes yes I agreed these seas shall take revenge *One day these seas shall take revenge*

Odysseas Elytis, 'The Kore the Northwind Brought,' from
The Light-Tree and The Fourteenth Wind

In her introduction to a collection of essays on modernism in Greece, Mary Layoun (1990) forgoes an aesthetic context for modernism. Instead, she juxtaposes it to imperialism, arguing, with some reservations, not for a direct formative relation between the two, but rather for a coupling that will allow for the problematization of shared notions of global space. Universalizing modernism promoted global imperialism and was not limited by any inscription in the national space, for: 'the national constructs and is constructed by boundaries that are necessarily crossed over. Meaning, value, resides elsewhere . . . yet that larger global space, that elsewhere of meaning, is not representable; it can not be comprehended or apprehended as a whole. It escapes representational control' (Layoun 1990: 13).

Greek modernism inscribed itself resoundingly *within* the national space (Layoun 1990; Tziovas 1995: 2). But what does it mean for Greek modernism to define itself *within* the national space? It thrived as a bitterly ideologized and contested struggle over the contours of a diachronic narrative of 'Greekness.' But did it not also locate meaning elsewhere? Greek modernism repressed an Other beyond itself, an exotic Other, one that clusters around its physical and psychic margins and enables it to map and encompass traumas and ambiguities as well as provoke syntheses in itself. The Turkic, Romeic, Balkan, and Eastern have often in Greek culture been expulsed or suppressed as signs of (un)Greekness. However, national culture is neither unified nor unitary in relation to itself, nor must it be seen simply as 'other' in relation to what is outside or beyond it. The boundary of outside/inside is inculcated in a process of hybridity, one felt most acutely when the incorporation of new people to the body politic generates new sites of meaning. On occasion, as Homi Bhabha (1990: 4) has observed in colonial contexts: 'such incomplete signification is a turning of boundaries and limits into in-between spaces through which the meanings of political and cultural authority are negotiated.' On other occasions, the trauma of expulsion brings only further expulsions, repression, and a violent reassertion of boundaries.

In Greece, the exchange of inside and outside peoples marked the Greek modernist movement. For the transplanted Anatolians (μικρασιάτες), the new people to the body politic post-1922 were now 'caught between homelands'. They were caught between 'positions in the national story; "liberated" subjects of the "great idea," refugees from a country no longer their own, and they are refugees by virtue of the same "great idea," immigrants to a "homeland" not (yet) their own' (Layoun 2001: 53). Other diaspora Greeks, Cavafy for one, had felt discomfiture with the physical *topos* that was 'Greece' – he was Hellenic, he insisted, and not Greek. The refugee Anatolians in Greece in the 1920s conceived of themselves either in reference to a 'home' that was irretrievably somewhere else – a territory elsewhere, Anatolia – or to their current estranging land, the Helladic state. Their once physical home, a Hellenic home not in the jurisdiction of the Helladic space was no longer graspable immanently. They needed to redefine a concept of Hellenism in the terms of the land they were living in, and some of the prose of the period reflects just this.[1] The Anatolians shared with European modernist exiles a 'deracinated fate,' which proved a material condition for the emergence of a newly formalizing, universalizing thought. Armed with these credentials, they set about this most modernist of tasks.

Following Karyotakis, the Generation of the 1930s undertook the definition of a new transcendental ethos of Hellenism no longer defined in terms of territory or politics, but through culture. This chapter will focus specifically on the ways in which the modernists encode that Greek self in a spectral and spatial regime, a cultural geography. The chapter explores how the spatial projections of their cultural imaginary relates to internal and geopolitical circumstances; how it responds to issues of class, gender, and ethnicity as it charts itself in relation to the coordinates of Europe, Turkey or the 'East,' and Cyprus. I focus on three specific aspects of the modernist moment: the aftermath of what Greeks refer to as the Asia Minor Catastrophe (1922) and the realignment brought about in conceptions of self among intellectuals in Greece between 1922 and 1935, from *Megali Idea* to expectations for union with Europe; an 'orientation' in this modernist poetry to move eastwards – not to Turkey – but to the Aegean Islands and, much later, to the island of Cyprus.

I focus on three prominent figures and select from their works. In the name of a liberal Europeanism, George Theotokas's *Free Spirit* (Το Ελεύθερο Πνεύμα) of 1929 responds to the threat posed by the worker's struggle and a rampaging internationalist communist agenda. Twenty years after Dragoumis, but without the *Megali Idea*, Theotokas addresses the same threat, with much of Dragoumis's aristocratic ethos and egocentrism.[2] To go beyond 1922, Theotokas sets out to cleanse Hellenism of its Byzantine and Balkan traditions in a cultural manifesto that conceals political and economic motives. He combats communism by framing it as an Eastern tradition, a malady of 'Asiatic abnormality' and 'lethargy' and he projects it onto the Greek working classes. I have termed this 'self-colonization,' since, in this case, Theotokas duplicates many of the tropes, subject positions, and power relations of a Eurocentric discourse of colonization. In doing this, I follow Pratt and others, in searching out for related dynamics of power and appropriation across cultures and contexts often in non-equivalent historical and sociopolitical sites to highlight the ways that hegemony transposes itself *within* cultures, and *across* classes.

The second section will consider a particularly favored trope in modernist writing – a journeying away from the metropolitan center to the sea, to the Aegean islands. A very early poem by Odysseas Elytis is read as symptomatic of a reorientation in the nation's monumental time and space, to an alternative eastern Hellenic tradition in the Aegean archipelago. The third section will consider George Seferis's aestheticization of Cyprus in the 1950s, a celebrated event, both for the life of this poet and Hellenism (which, according to Gourgouris and Dimiroulis, was one and the same for 'the poet as Ethnos'). Why did Seferis's Greek fugal poetics of Hellenism emplot itself in this *far-flung* field that is always Greece, at a time of the Greek Cypriots' armed struggle to become part of Greece? What personal and collective tensions was Seferis projecting on the body of an unsuspecting Cypriot diasporic difference. Cyprus was always the other Hellenism *nearby* – indeed, Cypriots say they are more Greek than the Greeks (a Seferian perspective, after all). The proposed *contrapuntal* reading of Seferis's *Logbook III* collection reads Cypriot alterity back into the spectral economy of Seferis's Hellenic Gaze.

Theotokas's Eurocentric Great Idea

Theotokas's seminal work *Free Spirit* (1929)[3] came at the end of a decade in which the pervasive need to find another propulsory ideal to supplant the *Megali Idea* with had become paramount. In Chapter 4, we saw how Skliros's *Our Social Question* (1907), and later *Hellenism's Contemporary Problems* (Τα Σύγχρονα Προβλήματα του Ελληνισμού) (1919) had challenged the Greek intelligentsia, especially the demoticists, to resolve social issues – the Language Question was one – by delving into their social causes. Skliros had urged idealist youth to stand alongside the worker in a class struggle that would improve Greek society and overturn the status quo. By the latter part of the 1920s, at a time when Asia Minor refugees had swelled the ranks of a burgeoning trade union movement, poets and educationalists, like Costas Varnalis and Demetris Glynos, were voicing just such positions in marxist journals. Conservatives and liberals rebutted them in the periodical *Nea Estia*. Some, like Alexandros Delmouzos and Philippos Dragoumis, realized that nationalism could no longer motivate the Greek people and was a poor match for communism's internationalist class appeal. Patriotism, claims

Theotokas at the beginning of his *Forward with our Social Problem* (Εμπρός στο Κοινωνικό μας Πρόβλημα) (1932), was all that his generation knew in their war-torn youth. It served the nation then, but it had evolved no system of ethics and was now bankrupt as it did not address the present crisis of values. Liberals needed a vision of the *ethnos* built on broader ethical and spiritual lines than those fostered by Dragoumis and the supporters of the *Megali Idea* of twenty years earlier. However, Theotokas and other liberals – figures such as Yiannis Economides and Spyros Melas – wished to steer away from the communist ideas of writers like Varnalis and Glynos. And they did so from the pages of a liberal monthly journal, *Idea* (Doulis 1975: 30–5).[4] But it was Theotokas's landmark *Free Spirit* that would truly represent this agenda and rally its writers and thinkers to the cause. *Free Spirit* has hitherto been analyzed very much as an aesthetic manifesto for the emerging Generation of the 1930s.[5] But its sociopolitical context needs to be stressed for it comes in the year of repressive legislation against the Communists, the so-called ιδιώνυμο (1929). And it is, I wish to suggest, an indirect answer to the threat init-ially posed by Skliros. This insight has escaped critics. But not George Seferis who, in a letter to Theotokas as early as 16 March 1932, situated Theotokas's small book in just this debate: '*Free Spirit* reminds me of Skliros' little book which, in years past, more or less opened up the socialist movement in our literature. I find yours superior and I hope, with all my heart, that it will inaugurate a principle of order and measure, at least for those who are meant to follow it' (Theotokas 1975a: 87).

George Theotokas's *Free Spirit* opens with a description of the particularity of each nation in a European garden. Difference abounds within each country; each offers up 'infinite antitheses,' each 'musical note' offers itself up to the 'European concert.' The artistic metaphors sprinkled throughout this discourse amount to an aesthetic depiction of a European political ideal. His appreciation of the European garden is carried out as an aesthete would appraise a work of art, judging the relation of its parts to an organicist and unified whole. With Kantian detachment, in 'airborne flight' over Europe, Theotokas delineates 'general contours' and 'broad horizons.' His Romantic vantage point allows this privileged subject to communicate the true landscape to less privileged 'foot-sloggers' (πεζοπόροι), who are, presumably, less able, literally, to distinguish the wood from the trees! Theotokas's transcendant vantage point reminds us of Rhigas and his map, at a remove from his object of study though privileged with the armature of abstraction that distance endows.[6] As such, Theotokas internalizes Rhigas's external gaze within Greek reality. But he views 'social time' as a distinctly separate realm from his own perspective. In this, he is a successor to the discourse of ab-sense: a voice that stands above and beyond everyday social practice.

Consequently, Theotokas goes on in this essay to stack open-minded, 'airborne,' and virile humanists against petty, scholastic, and 'myopic' academic scholars. The latter, comprised of nationalists and marxists weighed down by formulae and schemata, indulge in a 'spiritual militarism' that squeezes all life out of 'the agony of a soul,' of the artist and the individual. In Theotokas's eyes, even the foreign-trained among this group are able to do no better than import to Greece those national prejudices – be they French, German, Russian, or English – that they have acquired overseas. They squabble among themselves to 'amply show the closeness of their horizons.' A consummate formalist, Theotokas criticizes their political maneuverings: 'Those who demand from the poet . . . that he serve national and social needs show themselves unable to make out the poet's true stature. In order to understand him, they drag him down to the level of the multitude' (1988: 32).

Theotokas's apoliticality, his remove beyond the political fray, is very much the mark of the 1930s Generation. Many of them had not been in Greece for part of the 1920s, they looked askance at Karyotakis's pessimism, and the urban claustrophobia of his generation.[7] Instead, they formulated a poetics of escape and 'journeying outwards' to a vibrant Aegean – a subliminal projection of the national imaginary into a metaphysical essentialism beyond the material confines of the bedraggled Helladic state. Hellenism's failure to extend its physical and psychic borders to cover the imagined homogeneous space of the *Megali Idea* led them to displace this yearning into the cultural realm with the adoption of the Bildung-like category of ελληνικότητα, or Greekness.[8] Its unit of currency was individualism, and a difference always subservient to a homogenizing no-place (ou-topia) of monumental Hellenism, a marriage of Hellenism and aestheticism (cf. Chapter 1). In effect, this discourse yearned for a European identity by projecting back a totalized image of Greekness to the very European origins of that discourse. All the poets of this generation negated space and prioritized form over content: 'Hellenism is something more than a geographical region and a sum of mores and customs. Hellenism is primarily a way of "thinking and feeling," a certain stance toward the world and life, an attitude, a spirit, indeed a spirit that is universal, born to conceive of ideas and forms higher than any borders' (Theotokas 1953: 1505; Tziovas in Theotokas 1989: 34–5, fn. 41). Theotokas's vision is echoed by most of the modernists. To locate the character of 'a vivid and creative people which is perpetually active and untouchable like fire'(18), Theotokas advises that Greeks follow the example of Thibaudet's study of the 'real' France.[9] The Greek nation would affirm itself by admitting, even parading, its own contradiction and variety: 'solely the antithesis Dragoumis-Cavafy (or the antithesis Koraes-Solomos) suffices to show how multifaceted, contradictory, and how rich is the modern Greek character' (Theotokas 1988: 19). In other words, Theotokas sought to win for Greek society the trophy of self-differentiation, a quality heretofore reserved for more advanced, Western or European nations.

Theotokas's quest for self-contradictions harbors a number of contradictions of its own. Why is Thibaudet's model, a French model, any less 'militarist' than the nationalist or marxist ones that Theotokas rejected so sharply? Why is his not an example of a petty intellectual importing his Gallic models to the Greek scene? And why is this eulogy of antitheses within his canon of tradition spoken of approvingly when similar disputation among others – the French, English, Russian and Germanophiles – is merely a sign of squabbling and small-mindedness? Answers to such reasonable reservations are telling. For Theotokas's position exemplifies the political and ideological self-effacement claimed by the 1930 generation's liberals. He claims for Greeks the internal diversity or disunity of a European people. If practiced by a European, this difference of contradiction is ordered in a transcendent unity. This operation is reminiscent of the way in which early European imperialist powers, once confronted by grand cultures such as the Chinese, explained and justified their superiority to others when the simple claim of superiority ceased to be a viable enough argument (Hazard 1953; Eade 1983). In his attempt to equate European statist ideology with anthropological exoticism, Michael Herzfeld has stated that these features of Eurocentrism: 'affect the representation of cultural differences internal to European societies, reducing everyday discourse and local variation to epiphenomena of a transcendant sameness. Thus, for example, the divisiveness that at home Europeans regarded as beneficial individualism became, among exotic or peasant others, mere egotism, a definitive sign of depravity' (Herzfeld 1987: 87–8). Theotokas is clearly seeking to turn Greek divisiveness into European 'beneficial individualism' or difference. In trying to achieve this none-too-deplorable anthropological feat, Theotokas divides the Greek people into two along this axis at a moment when the political scene, rent in two by communism, is without a center. The diversity of his own humanist sect is seen through the Eurocentric prism of disunity as a sign of the center's sophistication; whereas the disunity of the 'myopic ones' is read as an intolerable sign of irreducible cultural diversity at the periphery – a difference that amounts to no more than the parochial inanity of an undervalued Other. In short, Theotokas partakes in a process of *national self-colonization*. Greek alterity is desirable and understandable only in the context of a Eurocentric field of signification. Theotokas's worldview is thoroughly Eurocentric and Hellenic. The complexity and inexhaustibility, yet also the 'unity' of Theotokas's privileged image of Greece, exemplify a Romantic aesthetic in which: 'The Beautiful, contemplated in its essentials, that is, in kind and not in degree, is that in which the many, still seen as many, become one.' Greece, like the formalist work of art, presents an internal significatory diversity that surpasses simple ideological delimitations that enclose the work of art from the outside. Greece, like the Romantic artwork, is a closed yet complex unity. It is viewed from a distance, and judges itself by, and aligns itself to, an organic and Western conception of Greek history and culture. Those perceived as serving the wrong ideological forces are left out of the picture – a determination largely based on class, as we shall presently see.

In *Forward with our Social Problem* (1932), Theotokas historicizes this process. There, he argues that Greece needs to graft itself onto a narrative of European civilization that reached its pinnacle in Classical Greece and saw its resurrection in the Renaissance. To achieve this, Greece must sidestep the one affliction emanating out of the Renaissance – namely, scholasticism – for 'out of scholasticism came the asphyxiating machinery of our time' (1932: 19). Modern scholasticism disrupted the Renaissance's ideal equilibrium of 'mind, heart, and body' and ran untrammeled over it to produce: 'capitalism, the proletariat, class struggle, economic crises, communism' (15). He speaks of these forces in one breath and yokes them together. The last in this series (communism) becomes the natural recipient of all its antecedents. The Communist Revolution 'is overflowing with the strength of flood waters, rising, approaching, and becoming ever more menacing' (17). In the wake of the Wall Street Crash of 1929, Theotokas has reservations about the conclusive adoption of any one economic system – capitalism or socialism. And his later writings in the 1940s espouse ideas from both traditions, while being, for the most part, essentially procapitalist, and admitting the need for incorporating elements of socialism as a counterweight to capitalism's inequities.[10] In the *Free Spirit*, however, he believes the danger of a revitalized and all-consuming communism must be beaten off conclusively. So he declares communism 'a materialist mysticism, a strange amalgam of Slavic and Asiatic fanaticism and German scholasticism' (26) and he stigmatizes this strain of 'eastern' Hellenism.[11] Indeed, he goes much further. Early in his *Free Spirit*, Theotokas makes a landmark statement: 'In the Balkans, the one discordant voice is that of Greece, a country which for centuries had a unified civilization, and now suddenly throws all its byzantine and Balkan traditions into the sea as it searches for a new way'(6). It is this listlessness (ανία), a Balkan version of decadent *ennui* and a word often used of Karyotakis, that Theotokas finds despicable. He sees it in Cavafy. He finds it in the intolerable bureaucracy and clientelism attributed to *Tourkokratia*. Theotokas pins his new generation's hopes on a youthful urban Athenian generation. In effect, he competes for Skliros's constituency of 1907 and he even uses Skliros's terms to do so. Theotokas's 'rebellious sons' are like the students enlisted by Skliros; only his youth will have the *free spirit* to throw off the lethargy and pettiness of their eastern heritage. *Free Spirit* depicts Theotokas's youth brigade as iconoclasts broken free of political and ideological strait-jackets, driven by an artistic fire, a demon (Δαιμόνιο), moulded in the image of men such as Ion Dragoumis, who will open new horizons. Theotokas's description opposes itself to the 'New Demons' (Νέα Δαιμόνια) of proletarian class struggle, the very terms used by Skliros (1976: 133).

By 1932, Theotokas was sharply critical of the negativity of the previous decade. Yet his absence from Greece, in London and Paris in the late 1920s, marks his critique, which reads more like musings on the French avant-garde than on the hardship of the Greek 1920s. His talk of 'the multifarious dadaisms and surrealisms . . . the worship of the art of Blacks, the disgusting literary mode of vice and sexual perversity . . . the uproarious pillorying of every ethical norm, the disdain for any kind of logic' is unlike anything lived by the Greeks in that decade (Theotokas 1988: 12). Ironically, the European avant-garde, who themselves had appropriated the concept of the 'rebellious son', are rejected by Theotokas in favor of a refined traditionalism reminiscent of Eliot, one tethered to an Outside Authority and resistant to the vagaries of a 'haphazard of consciousness.' All the while Thetokas's individualism does not dissociate itself from nationalism, for solipsism, at the individual and national level, must be avoided at all costs: 'as a nation, one cannot live on one's own' (Theotokas 1988: 45). So, whereas communism is defined as the blind worship of the 'machine' and the 'collective' (Μηχανή και Ομάδα), nationalism is the spiritual reality that has built up its *esprit de corps* 'unmechanically.' It has preserved the 'invisible' and 'immaterial' collective Good that has accumulated over the ages. The parallels to Eliot's conception of tradition, Arnold's notion of culture, and a Leavisite elitism are telling. Only national essences will differentiate Greek society from a communist 'society of insects' (κοινωνία εντόμων) (39). Once again, Theotokas legitimizes his view of difference by dividing the Greek polity into two: in one half, difference is Europeanized and admissible; in the second, mass representation is absolutist and feudal. His 'rebellious sons' will forsake the allegedly indomitable Δαιμόνιο that separated them from the Eastern and communist mob in *Free Spirit*, and conform instead to Eurocentric national ideals.

Theotokas was quite young at the time of this work. His addressees, the 1930s Generation, were not so young. The poet Yorgos Chouliaras has observed that he was a spokesman 'among the middle-aged, but ideologically "young people"' (Chouliaras 1993: 26).[12] In the last part of *Forward with our Social Problem*, he demands of the youth to place its fate in the hands of an elite, for: 'In solidarity with the other European nations . . . Greece will follow their fate, whether she likes it or not' (Theotokas 1988: 57–8). More specifically, in a call to go beyond liberalism, Theotokas calls for the formation of a European Economic Assembly that will respect the economic interdependency of classes and nations and conduct an '*economie dirigée*.' This body will overrule any diversified national parliament – the moderate version of Skliros's demands – and be led by 'a superior brand of men . . . a natural and fateful oligarchy.' This oligarchy, according to Theotokas, will put aside its short-term interest and overcome capitalism's inequities to glorify again the humanist/Hellenic spirit. In the meantime, he advises the working class to choose self-sacrifice and, with a steadfast belief in interdependency, turn its back on class conflict or else 'it will be left without even bread to eat' (1988: 55).[13] Theotokas's solution to the 'social problem' is a pointed response, twenty-five years on, to Skliros's 1907 call for class struggle. He answers Skliros's call for social and class struggle by diverting it to the cultural realm of a homogenizing national consciousness. Greater emancipation is rejected in favor of elite rule supported from outside the confines of the Greek state. Skliros's call for class struggle is counterbalanced by Theotokas's call for 'συναίνεση' – a word that entails 'acquiescence' and 'assent' – in worker restraint as well as faith in interdependency at the national and the European level.

In later years, Theotokas was to modify his views appreciably. In the forties, he accepts some of the lessons of socialism as counterweights to the excesses of capitalism. He also adopts a more benevolent stance toward the Byzantine and Eastern elements of Hellenic culture. Indeed, his last works before his death in 1966 are meditations on Orthodoxy and he writes a travelogue in Mount Athos (Theotokas 1971, 1975b). This volte-face was not peculiar to Theotokas. It is, we shall see in Chapter 6, typical of other members of this generation, too. Theotokas, so anti-Balkan and anti-Byzantine in 1929, advocates the mixing of native Greeks (European Greece) and Greeks of Asia Minor (Byzantine tradition) from 1922 to 1940 to herald a 'new people' at the end of the World War II.[14] Though he remains firm in his belief that a European Union is the ultimate goal, he sees this blending as a prerequisite for its realization. Greece will claim its European identity not by a geographical claim, but by a cultural one based on its contribution to European identity over two thousand years. Theotokas cites the ancient Greek tradition, the disseminated treasures of Byzantium, the Byzantine adaptation of Roman law, and Greece's adoption of Christianity as examples of Greece's 'European' credentials (Theotokas 1976: 48–9). His writings in the mid-1940s are prophetic: they champion interdependency and foresee a growing federalism that will see Greece pursue European integration and demand 'special treatment' from the more powerful European powers.[15] This was, for Theotokas, the only path available toward a world state advanced by industrialization and better communications. Following the destruction of World War II, Theotokas considered such globalism as far-off, though he urged his contemporaries to facilitate its arrival by broadening the spirit through culture.

The nationalists had shrugged off Skliros's call for class struggle in 1910 by summoning the passions of the *Megali Idea*. In 1930, Theotokas critiqued Skliros's marxist undermining of the notion of the nation through a discussion of *cultural* nationalism, which in fact was called by some a new *Megali Idea*.[16] In 1940, Theotokas made the same kind of argument, promoting national harmony and unity not in the name of the *Megali Idea*, as Dragoumis had, but by promoting culture in the name of the dream of European Union, a new *Megali Idea* :

> our admission into Europe . . . will bring about in Greece new sources of activity and
> creative energy, which exist all around us but which are today invisible, because they
> have never been given the chance, the context, the horizon that they need to express
> themselves – multifarious sources of life, be they economic, social, cultural . . . For the

young, who feel the lack of a contemporary and fruitful ideal which might inspire and activate their creative powers, *this could very well be a new Megali Idea.*[17] (Theotokas 1976: 52; emphases mine)

Elytis's 'Eastern' Home from Home

For Greek modernists, a cosmopolitan Western identity for Greece meant a break with parochialism. Western literary trends dressed in a revitalized yet traditional cultural garb would open new horizons. The Generation of the 1930's universalism was inaugurated on an *initial* disdain for 'specific historical legacies.' At the beginning of his *Free Spirit*, Theotokas exhorts Greeks to 'throw all at once our byzantine and balkan traditions *into the sea and find a new way*' (1988: 6). They decided to 'turn' away from the poetry of confinement prevalent in the 1920s, and identify themselves against the self-imagining of the previous generation – the contours of which to a degree they helped mould. Like Theotokas, George Seferis directs them toward an exuberant adolescence of 'free thinking' and 'broad horizons:

> The Karyotakian poet shut himself up in his room, and on occasion even in his coat, with a grumbling condescension. Karyotakism was a poetry without horizon. However, in about 1930, things change. What characterizes the young is a kind of island temperament. The horizons broaden. The dusty streets are put behind us. The Aegean with its islands, its sea mythology, voyaging in all directions . . . these are the things that move one . . .' My room's wall have fallen and I am left in the garden,' Antoniou will write – and the road that excites us among all the roads of Athens, is Syngrou Avenue, because it was the wide, great avenue which led to the ports, toward the open sea.[18] (Seferis 1981: 167–8)

The path from 'parochialism' to 'open-mindedness,'[19] by way of Athens' most developed avenue (a far cry from the 'dusty streets' of Karyotakis's 'Preveza'), leads to the sea:

> And yet I used to love Syngrou Avenue
> the double rise and fall of the great road
> bringing us out miraculously to the sea
> the eternal sea, to cleanse us of our sins.
>
> (Seferis 1978: 167, 'A Word for Summer')

This sea was to be the focal point of Hellenism, a complex trigger of mythic associations that would pervade and unify George Seferis's questing poetry back to a lost mythic home. Seferis first developed this in his collection *Mythistorema*

(1935). His appropriation of the European mythical method allowed him to foreground the quest, forever deferred and thwarted, to return to the fount of purity and origin in the temporal realm of Greek myth and history. For, here, Greeks, and Asia Minor Greeks like Seferis in particular, could cleanse themselves of the sins of the present and redeem themselves from their fallen state.

European modernists, like Conrad in *The Heart of Darkness*, had sought to map an imperial world system in which London stretched to infinity, far out to a colonized other that was invisible and absent, and which reputedly harbored an originary mystery. This is what Mary Layoun has in mind in relating modernism to imperialism. Fredric Jameson (1990: 50–66) has noted that this missing structural segment of the imperial economic system as a whole creates a lack which, for the imperialist metropolitan, can never be made good and, indeed, becomes the formal dilemma of modernism. Perhaps, it is this aspiration to totality forever lost, for an impossible meaning beyond the contingency of objects that links European modernism's, and Greek modernism's, quest for a transcendental home elsewhere. Only the Greek version was dependent on a space transformed by the diachrony of Hellenism that in its early, post-Catastrophe poetics until World War II engaged a Western, or European, discourse of Hellenism, to the exclusion and repression of Greece's spatial syndromes and disturbing recent historical contingencies. This definition of Hellenism distinguished between Western and Eastern traits of Hellenism and Greek intellectuals positioned themselves on either side of this divide. Theotokas chose a Western orientation. The later Nobel Laureate, and youngest member of this modernist generation, Odysseas Elytis, incorporated a more 'Eastern' identity for Hellenism. A study of his earliest work will point to the conventionalism and ideological mediation of identity along the axis of an East/West polarity and will allow us to examine the meaning Greek modernists ascribed to terms as 'eastern' in varying rhetorical and cultural spaces. For traveling eastwards is, I argue here, a recurrent *topos* in this flight from urban reality, and Greek political reality post-1922.[20]

The redemption of Greek space or Greek territory in the cultural imaginary could not be deferred for long after 1922. Constantinople had not been reclaimed; a new center had to be imagined. Odysseas Elytis, not an Anatolian, but a Greek from one of the easternmost islands, and a member of the 1930s Generation, was to oblige. Ten years younger than Seferis, he published his first poems near the end of the 1930s. Elytis was the youngest member of the 1930s Generation and also the longest surviving. He won the Nobel Prize for Literature in 1979, primarily for the grand architectonic poem of Hellenism that is his *Axion Esti* of 1959. We shall return to this poem and its significance for Greek *poiesis* and identity in Chapter 6.

Despite his ties with the 1930s Generation, Elytis's Hellenism is generally regarded as distinctly more 'eastern,' more 'Byzantine,' and more 'surrealist.' His first collections of poems were published in the generation's journal *Ta Nea*

Grammata. They appeared at about the same time as an influential special issue of the journal devoted to the work of Pericles Yannopoulos. Yannopoulos was resistant to Westernizing trends in Greece at the turn of the century and fought for a more 'authentic' and 'indigenous' cultural and political expression. He stressed native 'eastern' trends, local color, and the particularity of the Greek earth. In this, he was following precursors such as Kairis, Zambelios, Paparrigopoulos, and Dragoumis, who constituted an 'eastern' tradition of neohellenism. In his first collection, Elytis announces this orientation to the east, by conferring upon it the title Προσανατολισμοί or *Orientations,* a word which, once broken down, gives us the words προς and ανατολή (toward the east). Situated within the Aegean archipelago and its islands, Elytis tugged Theotokas's Western ideal eastwards. In space before time, Elytis would claim a *topos* neither truly physical nor spiritual, with elements 'of the Aegean' (as the title of the first poem in the collection betrays) but not the Aegean, an imaginative space not in the exotic East (e.g. of Kavvadias, the rembetika, or of modern Turkey), but certainly east of his own metropolitan center and away from Seferis's historical center, classical Greece. The first poem of the collection is entitled 'Του Αιγαίου' (literally, 'Of the Aegean,' or, if alluding to the convention of folksong titles, a 'Song of the Aegean,' though most often translated simply 'Aegean').

ΤΟΥ ΑΙΓΑΙΟΥ
I
Ο έρωτας
Το αρχιπέλαγος
Κι πρώρα των αφρών του
Κι οι γλάροι των ονείρων του
Στο πιο ψηλό κατάρτι του ο ναύτης ανεμίζει
Ένα τραγούδι

Ο έρωτας
Το τραγούδι του
Κι οι ορίζοντες του ταξιδιού του
Κι η ηχώ της νοσταλγίας
Στον πιο βρεμένο βράχο της η αρραβωνιαστικιά προσμένει
Ένα καράβι

Ο έρωτας
Το καράβι του
Κι η αμεριμνησία των μελτεμιών του
Κι ο φλόκος της ελπίδας του
Στον πιο ελαφρό κυματισμό του ένα νησί λικνίζει
Τον ερχομό.

II
Παιχνίδια τα νερά
Στα σκιερά περάσματα
Λένε με τα φιλιά τους την αυγή
Που αρχίζει
Ορίζοντας- –

Και τ ' αγριοπερίστερα ήχο
Δονούνε στη σπηλιά τους
Ξύπνημα γαλανό μεσ ' στην πηγή
Της μέρας
Ήλιος- –

Δίνει ο μαΐστρος το πανί
Στη θάλασσα
τα χάδια των μαλλιών
Στην ξεγνοιασιά του ονείρου του
Δροσιά- –

Κύμα στο φως
Ξαναγεννάει τα μάτια
Όπου η ζωή αρμενίζει προς
Τ ' αγνάντεμα
Ζωή- –

Φλοίσβος φιλί στην χαιδεμένη του άμμο – Έρωτας
Τη γαλανή του ελευθερία ο γλάρος
Δίνει τον ορίζοντα
Κύματα φεύγουν έρχονται
Αφρισμένη απόκριση στ αυτιά των κοχυλιών

Ποιος πήρε την ολόξανθη και την ηλιοκαμένη
Ο μπάτης με το διάφανό του φύσημα
Γέρνει πανί του ονείρου
Μακριά
Έρωτας την υπόσχεση του μουρμουρίζει – Φλοίσβος.

AEGEAN
I
Love
The archipelago
And the prow of his foam
And the gulls of his dreams
On his highest mast a sailor whistles
a song.

Love
His song
And the horizons of his voyage
And the sound of his longing
On her wettest rock the bride waits for
a ship.

Love
His ship
And the abandon of his *meltemia*
And the jib sail of his hope
On the lightest of his waves an island cradles
the arrival.

II
Playthings, the waters
In their shadowy passing
Speak with their kisses about the dawn
That begins
Horizon –

And the wild pigeons sound
Flap their wings in their cave
Blue awakening in the source
Of day
Sun –

The northwest wind bestows the sail
To the sea
The hair's caress
In the insouciance of his dream
Dew-cool –

Wave in the light
Revives the eyes
Where Life sails towards
The recognition –
Life

III
Surf kiss on his caressed sand – Love
The gull bestows his blue liberty
To the horizon
Waves come and go
Foamy answer in the shells' ears.

Who carried away the blonde and sunburnt girl?
The sea-breeze with his transparent breath
Tilts dream's sail
Far out
Love murmurs his promise – Surf.

Besides the external, towering frame of the title, the first three stanzas are domin-
ated by the single word, Love, which organizes movement in the first part by
sustaining its presence through the recurring use of its possessive pronoun.[21] The
first word, like a Platonic prime mover, activates in each stanza a string of sea
images: 'archipelago,' ' prow of his foam,' gulls of his dreams,' 'ship.' All depend
on it for context, they are Love's reflections: 'his song . . . his ship.' Falling into a
sequence, the 'gulls' are figments of love's dreams, the dreams belong to the poet-
sailor who creates by whistling his song-poem. It is love and the sailor-poet that
activate this sequence of images.

Significantly, 'on her wettest rock the bride waits for/a ship.' Conjuring up images
of Andromeda, chained to her rock and given up to the monster so as to placate
Poseidon, the female figure is defined passively. She is inert and expectant as both
the ship the sailor sails, and the poem the poet writes, are products of a love which
uses the bride (and 'her rock') as the site through which action is defined. Permeated
by sexual connotation, 'on her wettest rock,' the woman's wetness is part of a sea
imagery that will be touched by the transcendental poet's impending mastery:
female desire is subsumed in the notion of abstract, aestheticized love. Similarly,
the line 'On the lightest of his waves an island cradles/the arrival' associates the
female with the island: the motherly island 'cradles' and provides, literally and
metaphorically, the locus for the active arrival of the poet's ship.

The second unit develops the longing *frisson* of the first, punctuated by incid-
ences of physical response to the dawning of the new day. The erstwhile mute
landscape reacts to these stirrings with intimations of speech, movement, and
sensation. Each stanza of fragmentary images flows into a capitalized signifier –
Horizon, Sun, Dew-cool, Life etc. – in a manner that gives order and direction to
the images, only on this occasion, comes at the end of the stanza rather than at the
beginning.

In the third section, the underlying shifting symmetrical pattern is continued,
only this time in the form of a cross-work pattern (Vitti 1998: 24). The ethereal
fondling leads to consummated contact: a kiss and the rhythmic coming and going
of the waves that deposit their suggestive 'foamy answer' into the vaginal 'shells'
ears.' The seed of logos has been planted, and the sea-breeze's 'transparent breath'
gives life to the dream's sail. She, remarkably physical in the midst of so much
romanticized sea imagery, lends a tangibility that evokes the elusive 'who' that
carries her away, while at the same time conjuring up mythical archetypes of such

abductions where the body of the female – say, Helen of Troy or Andromeda – acts as the site for the creation of mythic narrative and the inscription of male abstraction on female physicality. Male poetic endeavour, associated with the moving phallic penetrating of prow and foam, voyage and winds, the highest mast and the jib sail of his hope, gives life to the 'waiting' and 'cradling' female. These descriptions reflect a verticality and hierarchization of the elements described: the male poet swoops down to make away with the essential 'signification' he bestows on the passive, female rock and island below. The final outcome is open: first, the object of desire may have been abducted and fulfillment is deferred; second, the final 'surf' may point to a releasing ejaculation with the Other; third or, more significantly, may be the wish fulfillment through masturbation without the presence of the absented Other. This focus on an incursive male intruder invading and penetrating this feminized and passive paysage shares with colonialist and orientalist fantasies the signs of a 'penetrating' discourse, exhibiting the whole gamut of subordination, gratification for the male-colonizer, all kinds of sensuality and wish fulfilment, objectification and effacement of the Other's subjectivity (Said 1978: 213–20). He has colonized this space, inscribed it in his linguistic orbit, ordered it according to the dictates of the sailor who enters from his home.

Literature has always projected natural paradises or utopias elsewhere and used them to nurture a spirit of self-narcissism whereby exotic cultures and spaces function as primitive versions of European society. Following World War I, when reason and the model of linear progress was under avant-garde assault, the primacy and regenerative impulse of the primitive promised what the post-Enlightenment West had lost. Major European artists after Freud began to question linear models and undermined the notion of formal material accumulation and development in favor of cycles, structural repetitions, primitivism and minimalism. Elytis's affiliation to the French surrealists is often invoked to argue a place for him in this movement. In 'Aegean', we note modernist formal characteristics: the absence of punctuation, the self-reflexive disturbance of conventional rhyme and metre patterns, the increased significance of iconicity, and a violation of the logic of normal syntax.[22] Despite these traits and Elytis's abandonment of conventional schemata for a surrealist adoption of automatic writing, the central agent of his poem, though dispersed over a sequence or axis of images in a seemingly expressionist manner, is, as we have seen, continually and insistently synthesized around a certain abstracted male lyric I. And a paganistic streak that denies any self-consciousness in the construction of his object leads him to espouse a theory of the transparency, 'limpidity' he would say, of reality. Analogous worlds can be seen behind the sentient world. This limpidity is 'irrational . . . my kind of clarity is not that of the *ratio* of the intelligence, not *clarté* as the French and Westerners conceive it' (Ivask 1975: 642). His theory is built on a wholly 'unmodernist' conception of the linguistic medium.[23] Elytis observes: 'On the cheeks of a girl as on the verses of a poem . . . nothing mediates' (Ivask 1975: 29). The analogy between the woman's cheeks and the poem identifies not only the body as the site for the inscription of narrative, but also that poetry is a 'natural' and 'universal' act impervious to the relativization of perception in its interaction with the (feminized) Other. Elytis shows disdain for the distorting effects of the linguistic medium, and he deplores the inability of Western poetics to faithfully capture Greek reality. In part, the West's commitment to Progress and industrialization prevents it from engaging with the truths of such sensuous and naturalistic experience.[24] His first 'excursions into the countryside of Greece' drive this home to him: 'We're talking of Nature, yes. European sensitivity, I knew all along, for I could see it in her poets, had long since done without Nature, it had stored it away on lower floors as one would a pile of stuff that does not find any reverberation in the soul (1974: 260–1). By contrast, Elytis marks his own reaction to this feminized body, 'Greece's material body,' (262) with the following departure: '. . . the way I perceived Nature, . . . it ended up no longer looking like Nature. . . . Were all these things . . . meant to be a landscape? Was it just Nature? Maybe not? Maybe it was the beginning and end of the world, Man's *alpha* and *omega*, God Himself' (261). And, a little further, Elytis concludes: '. . . Greek nature . . . would generate within us justifiably the meaning and weight of a mystical mission' (262).

Elytis concludes that Western modernist models are sensitive only to the ways of logic and surface reality, and thus unreceptive to the mystic voice and metaphysical force that, he claims, passes behind and through things (1974: 348).[25] For Elytis, this was 'the difficulty of fitting together the Western and Eastern spirit; the foreigners' misinterpretation of the Greek spirit impeded our communication, for which we were responsible' (1974: 357). As a result, Elytis attempts to literally 'ground' Hellenism, with its modern loss of center, to an other *topos* where the recovered spirit will manifest itself. In *Orientations*, this apocalyptic and epiphanic moment emerges in an ethereal landscape, suggestive of the Aegean islands yet timeless and tantalizingly on the verge of materiality, within the boundaries of the Greek state yet also strangely atopic and fleeting.

Elytis's *Orientations* mark a fundamental departure from Theotokas's earlier reflex. Buoyed by the drive to establish an explicit differential relation to Western aesthetic standards and tradition, it foreshadows a trend in the 1950s that differentiates itself from the earlier topography of the Greek modernist generation. Elytis's monumental *Axion Esti* (1959) – along with Kontoglou and Tsarouchis's painting, Theodorakis's compositional choices, the movement of the neo-Orthodox, Lorenzatos's 'lost center' (1961), Seferis's appropriation of Cyprus, and Theotokas's late reverence toward Orthodoxy – all move from the west at a time, after the Greek Civil War, when Western and American economic and military penetration in Greece was at its height. But more on this in Chapter 6. Such a nativist impulse had lain dormant from the very beginnings of this generation; or, more correctly, had been repressed. To define autochthony in 'Eastern' ways in the 1930s ran the risk of feeding fear of communist ascendancy. But there had been disputes within the generation even back then. It is clear from his critical writings that Elytis hoped to work with Randos and Embiricos on a Freudian and surrealist journal, tentatively to be called *Thiassos*. His eventual affiliation with this body of conservative and Westernizing modernists was a compromise of sorts. The failure of the journal led him to collaborate with the *Nea Grammata* modernists. It was the only viable option:

> We agreed to insist on our common position, whatever the outcome, not to give way to the *Nea Grammata* group's offers, since we believed that we should not begin with half-measures. I would say these kind of things but deep down a certain worry ate away at me. I understood that the first break had taken place, that Seferis had submitted poems. And though, at that time, Seferis did not figure in the scheme of our revolutionary poetry as we dreamt and wished to impose it, he was, all the same, the poet who, with his second book, had broken the shackles of verse and – not only that – but who sought to define and register a new space to which we would be most fortunate if we could attach ourselves. Before I had fully digested this, there came a second volley to add itself to the first. Yorgos Sarandaris's collaboration with *Nea Grammata*. Karandonis had got poems from him. *Nea Grammata*'s ring was closing in around us and I understood that our time had come. And so, half-courting with their advances and yet also partly on the defensive, I accepted Karandonis's invitation. (Elytis 1974: 283)

All along, Elytis's professed surrealism – which he described as 'a Romanticism in the extreme' – and his heliotropism proposed a metaphysics and linguistic ethos that he hoped would hurl him beyond 'the dim light and penumbra of Western art' (Elytis 1974: 336). As Keeley has remarked, Elytis 'regarded surrealism as the weapon in his struggle to liberate the image of Greece from the strait-jacket of western rationalism' (Elytis 1981: xi). Keeley's comment reproduces faithfully Elytis's adoption of absolute dichotomies between rational and irrational, Western and Eastern, Non-Greek and Greek: a valorized set of dualities that carry with them the assumptions and guiding prejudices of Western rationalism. In this, too, Elytis's definition of national space in *Orientations* in bipolar terms smacks of the Western discourse cited earlier, except that, in his system, Elytis privileges the eastern pole of the Western dichotomy. His belief in a union with a mystical center of life that is quested for, however unfulfilled, only emphasizes the Romantic nature of his predicament. Consequently, he does not surpass the very Western discursive models that he attacks so vigorously. All such easternbound voyages, as Leontis (1987) has pointed out in comments addressed to the work of philosopher Zissimos Lorenzatos, are mired in self-contradiction, for:

All are plagued with the same problem, that in attempting to differentiate their attitude from that of their western predecessors, they nevertheless remain bound to the terms that they denounce. For, at the heart of the Romantic predicament lies the belief that a union with the mystical center of life and expression is desirable . . . and inachievable. The renunciation of western aesthetics in western terms, his claim to identify a national conscience in the rhetorical figure signifying integrity, in their substitution of an eastern over a western solution, all do not make either his concern or his answer more eastern. They simply make it impossibly Romantic. (Leontis 1987: 186)

And so his quest for the transcendent in the terrestrial topography of Greece, most notably presented in Elytis's phrase 'This World The Great The Small' (Αυτός ο Κόσμος ο Μικρός ο Μέγας) rests in a belief in *apocatastasis*, or redemption, of fallen matter. Be this matter cleansed in Hellenism or the Divine, it is to be realized, in the 1950s and 1960s, only in the over-site of a cultural topography further east – be it Elytis's Aegean or Seferis's Cyprus. This flight is compelling for its contradiction: by travelling elsewhere, we locate an *autochthonous* essence in the *heterotopias* of Hellenism. Significantly, Greek claims for a regenerative 'easternness' chart their way by routes that wilfully avoid, sidestep, or repress the present of any Turkish element or borrowing. Elytis's 'Aegean' is predicated on this oversight. It is sought in poetic time, narrative history, and the collective unconscious: it is the displaced trip and wish fulfillment for a Greek Constantinople, the imagined completion of the *Megali Idea*. After 1922, Constantinople still remains, through Orthodoxy and the Byzantine tradition, the *topos* of a Greek loss, and not a Turkish present. Constantinople's cartographic displacement to the Aegean fetishizes this space and fills as well as marks the original scene of trauma in the hope that, eventually, 'the sea which possesses all the values of the Aegean world . . . will take its vengeance' (Ivask 1975: 614). This quotation, reproduced in this chapter's epigraph, appears in Elytis's collection *The Light-Tree* of 1971. The critic Andonis Decavalles (1994: 46–7) is right to draw attention to the 'affectionate and nostalgically doleful references to the Orient' in this collection, written as it is at a time when 'the tragic loss of Asia Minor in 1922 and Turkey's renewed aggressive claims upon the Aegean Greek islands caused the poet's nostalgic references to what had been part of the Greek world' (197–8).[26]

Characteristically, in his essays, Elytis (1986) himself affirms the need to retire to his own 'private way.' He summons forth a logocentric North Wind to breathe 'a strong *meltemi* wind, born in Tinos, which, with the Virgin's blessing, will come and purify the landscape of all kinds of Turkishness and relics of old Europe' (1986: 60). Hellenism's home will be reached in time before space, far from Europe and Turkish barbarism: 'The private way takes a short cut through time. You go home quicker by way of Constantinople' (1986: 30).

George Seferis's Cyprus

In his introduction to a collection of photographs taken by the Greek poet George Seferis in Cyprus, the late Emmanuil Kasdaglis remarks how Seferis was dogged by ill health and beset by the untimely death of his brother in the United States during his diplomatic postings in the Middle East from the mid-1940s to early 1950s. He was also suffering from a nasty case of writer's block. His first trip to Cyprus in 1953 cured him of his ailments and 'the grace of poetry was granted him once more' (Kasdaglis 1990: 12). Upon his return to Beirut from Cyprus, Seferis's journal entries testify to 'a ten-day orgasm of writing' (1986: 119).[27] Cyprus had clearly been good for Seferis. And he had been good for Cyprus. His sojourn there, in particular three personal visits between 1953 and 1955,[28] led him to publish a collection of poems at the end of 1955, which eventually would bear the title *Logbook III*.[29] In time, this collection would constitute an influential mythology of Cyprus, Cyprus as an intense Hellenic heterotopia. It has shaped the imaginations of many Cypriot writers and poets as well as ordinary citizens ever since. It has been vigorously upheld by a phalanx of critics and sung by national bards from 'the mainland.' Back in the 1950s, a coterie of Cypriot intellectuals befriended and chaperoned Seferis in Cyprus. They hoped he would bring his prestige to bear on the Greek Cypriot struggle for *enosis*, the Greek Cypriot struggle to effect political union with Greece, and that he would project this outwards from 'periphery' to the Helladic center, Athens, and beyond to the colonial center, Britain. He would lyricize all he would see and experience there. He would be wined and dined with British Consular agents and litterati; perhaps, he might sway them by sheer force of manner and intellect. By 1963, the artist, Kypros Chryssanthis, admitted as much: Seferis's visit was not a 'fortunate happenstance.' Seferis's vision of Cyprus coincided with the aspirations of Greek Cypriots of that time. Its language and ideology, the transcendent ethos of its Hellenism were engaged in vital ways with the predicament of Greek Cypriots in the Cyprus of the 1950s. And Seferis's writing while in Cyprus was, formally, to establish him not as 'the voice of a poet, but the voice of Greek poetry' (Vayenas 1979: 244–5).

Seferis visited at a critical time. Cyprus has hung precariously between Greece and Turkey throughout much of its recent history, though it has never been a part of the two nation-states. Indeed, the claims of the main Greek and Turkish ethnic communities on the island hark back to periods in time well before the appearance of the Greek or the Turkish nation-state. The Greek Cypriots point to an Hellenic cultural legacy that stretches back to antiquity and privileges the arrival of Achaeans in Cyprus around 1200 BC. The Turkish Cypriots locate their history to the Ottoman Turks' rule of the island from 1571 to 1878. In that year, 1878, the Cyprus Convention rented this island of Orthodox Greeks (73.9 percent) and Muslim Turks (24.4 percent) to the British until, in 1914, the Ottoman Turks' allegiance with the Axis in World War I led the British to annex Cyprus as its colony. Cyprus was declared a Crown Colony in 1925. And so it remained until 1955 when fighting broke out, but the sentiment for *enosis* was stirring at the time of the poet's first visit in 1953

Seferis himself avowed that he was unaware of his visits' politicization or of the politicking taking place between British intellectuals close to the island's Governor and the Greek Cypriot elite. But his personal visits were never just a personal affair. Seferis was, as Dimiroulis cautions, not merely a diplomat in life but in his poetry also. In life as in his work, Seferis took his Hellenism on tour with him: 'Greece paid him and wounded him' (η Ελλάδα τον πλήρωνε και τον πλήγωνε), as an adapted verse of his goes. His personal mythology cultivated by his consistent self-effacement in the name of the transcendental ethos of Hellenism was a diplomat's charge and pose, after all. For Kapsalis, the terms *metaphora* (metaphor) and *paradose* (tradition) that denote a condition of movement in space, are fundamental to Seferis. Like Teucer, a major figure in his Cyprus poems, he wanders about armed with a sling full of metaphors and arrows trained on tradition. Gourgouris builds on Kapsalis's suggestion to describe Seferis as both tradition's executor and its carrier, or *metaphoreus*:

> The self-effacing presence of Seferis consists in rendering himself as the metaphorical device – that is, his ascription to his own self of a metaphorical property . . . Like a modern Hermes, he transposes himself into the various texts and discourses that constitute the (neo)Hellenic tradition and rearranges them as he pleases. The work of the metaphor, as Kapsalis insists, is expansionist in its form, interventional, and Seferis fashions himself in this sense as a modernist *deus ex machina* who will redeem a valiant but mishandled tradition and set it on its proper course. Nothing must stand in his way, not even Greece itself. (Gourgouris 1995: 213)[30]

For what is Greece in the face of Hellenism? Even in Cyprus, where the *enosis* movement sought to use Hellenism to incorporate Cyprus into Greece. To consider the genealogy of Hellenism for Seferis is to blur the lines between the personal and the political realms. Seferis was born in Asia Minor in 1900 and left there before the collapse of the *Megali Idea* in 1922; yet he shared at one remove with Anatolian Greeks the trauma of their deracination. Throughout his life, Seferis, ever in transit, embarked on a journey of *nostos* (return) and *algos* (sorrow), and mythologized it. By excavating a utopian past in his early work, Seferis was ever constituting the topography of his home, only to play out its displacement to *ou-topia* (no-place). In his later work, it is my contention that the same reconstruction and displacement of home takes place in a new *topos*, Cyprus.

On a personal level, this quest eventually led Seferis back to his birthplace of Smyrna or Izmir. There, in July 1950, soon after his brother's death and during an unhappy posting in Turkey, Seferis visited the family home that he had not visited since his childhood. He relates the event in his diary:

After dinner, a few steps toward the location of our house: the *nothingness*. And still a few more steps toward the 'Ke' (quay).

You can spell out faded letters with difficulty. I am somewhere else. As though to return me to my senses, the diplomat accompanying me whispered: 'The Greeks say the Turks burned Smyrna; the Turks say the Greeks burned it. Who can know which is the truth?' I'm not in the mood for talk. (Seferis 1974: 165, Saturday, 1 July 1950)

The return home sends him momentarily 'somewhere else.' And if this were not enough, the next port of call, on past the Sivrihisar (or Seferi Hissar) to his one-time family summer home in Skala, fills him with melancholy: 'I understood how Lot's wife turned into a pillar of salt when she looked back' (Seferis 1974: 170).[31] It would take one more trip to Smyrna, just three months later, for Seferis to turn his back on this home once and for all: 'It is better this way. This stay in Smyrna closes a cycle that started in the last years of childhood. From now on, there's neither starting point nor arrival; the world exists here or there, as the world goes, and one gets nowhere' (Seferis 1974: 178–9, Tuesday, 17 October 1950). In 'Memory,' one of two poems in his Cyprus collection that do not refer explicitly to Cyprus, Seferis refers to this experience when he observes, 'memory hurts wherever you touch it.' It is with this episode in mind, in a world here and there where one gets nowhere, that I propose to follow Seferis on his literary journey to Cyprus.

One of his primary fictional spokespersons on this journey, like Elpenor in his earlier *Mythistorema*, is a minor character – the protagonist Teucer in the central 'Helen' poem of *Logbook III*. Teucer is an important figure in Cyprus and it is through him that Seferis chooses to depict the slings and arrows of outrageous fortune. Like Seferis, he is 'in exile.' Banished by his father, the king of the original Salamis for not having prevented the suicide of his brother Ajax, Teucer acts upon Apollo's decree to settle and found a new Salamis in Cyprus.[32] In so doing, Teucer strives to forget his own guilt, which lingers in response to Odysseus's charge that he had abandoned Ajax (Aristotle's *Rhetoric*, 3–15, p. 1416, b1). The allusion captures some of Seferis's anguish at not being close to his own brother's side at the time of his death in 1950 (Sophocles, *Ajax*, ll. 1099–110). However, the poem does not focus on Teucer's settlement in Cyprus. Teucer's soliloquy is intoned *from* Cyprus, but it reflects on events that have transpired previously, in Egypt. Teucer had been carried by Hermes to the palace of Proteus, King of Egypt, where Teucer met up with Helen of Troy, the instigator or originator of his own and others' wanderings, of the war that he has lived through and which brought about his brother's death. Teucer goes to the source of his troubles, to Helen of Troy. Or so he thinks.

As the poem progresses, Helen shifts from being η Ελένη το μιαν Ελένη, from Helen or *the* Helen to *a* Helen.[33] As Matthew Gumpert (2001) suggests in his wide-ranging study of Helen in the Western tradition, Helen gives herself up, as always, to the interpretative desire of the critic and tells the story he wants to tell. Here, the poem refers to Euripides' play *Helen* and so draws from a long tradition of texts, harking back to Stesichorus, that deliberate over the identity of the 'real' Helen and use her as a metaphor for the inanity of war. For, as Euripides later relates, it was a phantom image of Helen that set sail for Troy, and not Helen herself. It was for 'an empty shirt or tunic' that then, as now, some other Teucer, some Ajax or Priam will go to war. Menelaus's servant in Euripides' *Helen* exclaims his disbelief at the fact that the Trojan War has been fought for Helen's phantom. In the epigraph to Seferis's poem, it is Teucer who exclaims: 'you mean it was for a cloud that we struggled so much?' Teucer is unclear as to what to believe any longer:

Πού είναι η αλήθεια
Είμουν κι ' εγώ στον πόλεμο τοξότης
το ριζικό μου, ενός ανθρώπου που ξαστόχησε

'Truth? Where's the truth?
I too was an archer in the war;
my fate: that of man who missed his target.

Teucer, and by extension Seferis, is the archer who missed the mark – the one who exists here and there, but gets nowhere (Gumpert 2001: 244–50). In Troy, Teucer realized that his arrow did not hit the mark and that he did not fell Hector. He is the son of Salamis obliged to found another Salamis elsewhere as he has been banished from his home. He founds the new Salamis in Cyprus. Seferis, too, banished from Smyrna and his home twice – once in childhood and, for a second time, just three years earlier in 1950 – is ready to found his capital elsewhere, in Cyprus. Yet, he is also suspicious of the metaphor evoked by a name, or by a poem that tries, in vain, to fill the space that can not be filled. The more ethnolyrical brands of Greek philological criticism, buoyed by the testaments of biographical evidence, are less circumspect. They focus on the natural and continuous correspondence between myth and actuality. Admittedly, the material to support a triumphalist view of Seferis's *metaphora* in Cyprus is overwhelming, if the critic bases this view exclusively on Seferis's diaries. Consider the entry for 17 November 1953: 'Cyprus's climate, why does it sit so well with me? Hellenic, but without a Greek policeman or civil servant – a displacement of tradition (μετατόπιση της παράδοσης): more ancient and more native tongue (πιο αρχαία και πιο ντοπιολαλιά). Cyprus and the Cypriots are more Greek than the Greeks, as they often like to say. This phrase is favored today by members of various Greek diasporas around the world to mark their authenticity over their metropolitan brethren. Or so they like to think. The gesture is equally a sign of their anxiety at others' (and their own) questioning of that authenticity. The lingering Homeric survivals found in Cypriot dialect epitomize, for both Seferis and many Greek observers today, a Cypriot hyper-authenticity.[34] However, the ambivalence at the heart of all hyperauthenticities underscores an inherent contradiction between the gesture of proposing and sustaining the illusion of home on the one hand, and foregrounding, very self-consciously, the very artifice that underpins such a formulation on the other. The third and closing stanza of one of Seferis's poems from this collection, 'Details on Cyprus', makes this point most succinctly. The poem's persona wanders in the courtyard of the church of St Mamas:

Είταν ωραία όλ᾽ αυτά, μια περιδιάβαση
᾽Ομως το ξύλινο μαγγανοπήγαδο - τ ᾽ αλακάτιν
κοιμισμένο στον ίσκιο της καρυδιάς
μισό στο χώμα και μισό μέσα στο νερό
γιατί δοκίμασες να το ξυπνήσεις;
Είδες πως βόγγηξες. Κι᾽ εκείνη την κραυγή
βγαλμένη απ᾽ τα παλιά νεύρα του ξύλου
γιατί την είπες φωνή πατρίδας;

All this was fine, a casual stroll.
But the wooden well-wheel – the 'alakatin' –
asleep in the shade of the walnut tree
half in the earth and half in the water,
why did you try to wake it?
You saw how it moaned. And that cry,
brought forth from the wood's ancient nerves,
why did you call it the voice of our country?

(Seferis 1978: 341–4)

This poem was to be titled *Kolokes*, the very demotic Cypriot word for a gourd. Perhaps this word should have been left in its transliterated form in the English translation of the poem's first stanza. But to do this would have detracted from the power of the word *alakátin*, which leaves its stamp on the last stanza and on the poem as a whole. There, in the shade, hidden from view, half in the earth and water and half out presumably, lingers the *alakátin*, or water-wheel, in repose. Its space is filled by its very naming: the ηλακάτη that stood for this object from Homer to Theocritus or the endearing diminuitive ηλεκάτιον or αλακάτιον of a third to fourth century AD papyrus. In its popular form, λακάτην, it would have resonated for Seferis both here in Cyprus and in his native Smyrna.[35] Its activation in speech, as in his motion to 'wake it' from its slumber, energizes it into its metaphoricity.

The poem's ending sets up a scene of recognition typical of *nostos*. With Romantic exemplariness, the speaker addresses the wood only for it to speak back to him, and when the dead speak the living are struck dumb, as de Man (1979) commented. Seferis's poetry accustoms us to such apostrophes to marble columns, the scene marks the return to a recognizable scene of neurosis. But the sentiment is posed in the form of a question. Is it a rhetorical question that affirms this as a scene of recognition? Or does the ending query the very basis of the relation set forth and put into question? In other words, is this a question that stresses the interrogative *why* of the last sentence? Is the watering wheel an activation of a metaphorical usage, attested to in Liddell and Scott's classical dictionary as referring to fate, that elicits a primordial moan and stands for the code of Seferis's highly nostalgic conceptualization of history? Or does the rhetorical nature of the question confer some doubt on the very association summoned? Is it meant to remain suspended between both meanings? The former reading clearly endorses Dimiroulis's (1989) characterization of the fundamental difference in poetic stance between Seferis and his archetypal interlocutor and rival, the diasporic Constantine Cavafy: 'for Cavafy history is a narrative which offers examples . . .; for Seferis, history is a trauma, a wound, which demands the skills of story-telling/solace (*paramythia*). In their very personal attention to poetic form, Cavafy keeps company with history while Seferis suffers with her' (Dimiroulis 1989: 246). The persona's identification with the 'moan of the water wheel' conforms with this description of Seferis. Myth and continuity impose themselves on the Seferian historical con-sciousness. Utterly symbolic, Seferis transforms the specific cultural moment into a personal poetic myth and vice versa.

This reading is evocative of Seferis's early work. Yet, Seferis's *Logbook III*, the collection devoted to 'sea-girt-Cyprus', is also his most Cavafian collection in mood and technique. Indeed, Seferis's poetic experimentation in the 1950s is driven by an ongoing dialogue with Cavafy's work (Mackridge 1997a: 110–13). And this struggle leads him to relinquish mythological contexts in favor of a more historical method reminiscent of Cavafy. Maronitis is right: Seferis's Euripidean journey leads him in Cyprus, 'by the shore of Proteus', to cast doubt on the mythological paradigm and on its very claim to bear any truth. He will focus on minor historical figures and contexts, clothe them in an allegorical and dramatic garb, and even use the chronicle to ground a set of Cavafian examples,[36] the beginning of the 'Cavafian phase of Seferis' mature period' (Maronitis 1987a: 166; Vayenas 1979: 237). The Cavafian 'waters of Cyprus, Syria, and Egypt/the beloved waters of our home countries' with their 'Phoenician ports of calls' where 'we are Greeks also what else are we' and where we have 'Asiatic affections and feelings' had cast their spell on Seferis. Indeed, *Logbook III* lavishes a sensuality repressed in his earlier poetry (Mackridge 1997a:121). But the affinity ends there. As Marios Constantinou has shown, Cavafy's 'heterodox affections literally carnivalize all the biological and cultural predicates of ethnoracial authenticity' (Constantinou 1998: 184). The Afro-Asiatic difference of incommensurable sensibilities in the margins disrupts the claims of a normative or authentic Hellenism. However, if Cavafy taught us that 'We must not be ashamed of the Syrian and Egyptian blood in our veins,' Seferis's historical consciousness of Cyprus hardly lives up to Cavafy's hybrid and differentiated model of identity. For Seferis's historical consciousness in *Logbook III* ranges across Cyprus and its history in its selective manner. He prioritizes certain strands of tradition and the island's history over others. He focuses considerably on the machinations of Lusignan nobles, Crusaders and French noblemen who ruled over Cyprus. It is a land of many conquerors and masters 'in a country where those who lived below the castles/ were forgotten like last year's earth.' His aestheticized populism reaches down deep to write the untold, forgotten story of the common Cypriot, a Hellenized Cypriot, who, in the poem 'Three Mules,' has counted for nothing in comparison to the mules of those who have ruled the island over the centuries. History is built on the back of this forgotten subject. And Seferis's historical poems memorialize this insult in a series of glimpses into transactions that had Cyprus bought and sold and passed from hand to hand. The transactions are posed in sexual terms, often greased with money. The poem 'In the Goddess's Name I Summon You' takes as its reference point an ancient Babylonian ritual recorded by Herodotus, in which all women had to prostitute themselves once in their lives with a stranger (Herodotus I, 131, 199). The women would congregate around the goddess's temple and await some stranger who would summon them in the name of the goddess. Seferis relates the ritual in his diary entry on the very first day of his visit to Cyprus in 1953 and he stresses Herodotus' observation that a similar practice was once observed in Cyprus. In the poem, the persona is in a church courtyard and his imagination's recreation of the ancient scene is evoked in an interplay of present and past by the objective correlative of the smell from an idle nearby oil press. This 'rancid smell' elicits the oil-daubed body of a woman who awaits her stranger wearing a wreath of cords. The cords evoke the rough pores on the unturning stone of the press which, when turned, will release the liquid from the encased olive. The parallel image of the knotted rope amidst the woman's hair evokes a further act of untying or liberation. These synesthetic elements heighten the tension around the woman's faceless confrontation with her stranger:

> Oil in the sun
> the leaves shuddered
> when the stranger stopped
> and the silence weighed between the knees.
> The coins fell:
> 'In the goddess's name I summon you . . .'

The impersonal transaction is foreshadowed first by nature and then by an absent presence between the protagonists' sexual organs. It is a penetration of nothingness, of silence. By the same token, the monetary exchange is similarly connoted in terms of nothingness, as what signifies the completion of the ritual encounter lies only in the power of the words that mark the name of the goddess. The name itself, too, Mylitta – like the father's name, Agamemnon, summoned by Orestes in the epigraph to *Mythistorema III*[37] – does not appear in the text, but is left blank. It is alluded to by its absence. Once again, as in Helen, an empty sign provokes human suffering. The terms of the transaction, marked by lack, are made sacred by ritual performance. However, in the next stanza, Seferis focuses on the woman's 'flexing waist,' which either in rising to join the man or in lowering herself to the grass marks her submission. Seferis passes from an incantatory description of the oil on consecutive parts of her body (in the first line of each stanza) to a shudder or spasm:

> Oil on the shoulders
> and the flexing waist
> legs grass-dappled,
> and that wound in the sun
> as vespers sounded
> as I spoke in the church yard
> with a crippled man.

> (Seferis 1978: 345/7)

Seferis's poem prefigures, and cautions against, the 'sell-off' that is about to take place yet again. For, in an archetypal way, Cyprus is figured as precisely the place which is always about to be sold off and traded. Contemporary artists, most famously by the singer-songwriter Dionyssis Savvopoulos in his song 'For Cyprus' from the album *Rezerva* (1979), depict the island as a 'plot of land' in the hands of foreign business interests.

'In the Goddess's Name' ends by returning to the present and focusing on the figure of a crippled man, who elicits pity and discomfort. The image also reinforces the temporal perspective of ritual repetition in time. History's repetitions are evoked in the collection's allusion to the Greek folksong and the life cycle. And like songs for the fall of cities, formulas, themes, and images are used and reused in different historical contexts, but for the same commemorative process of lamenting a lost set of cultural memoria.[38] Indeed, some more general typologies of folksong are used by Seferis to foreground the interplay of past and present. The poem 'Agianapa II,' prefaced as 'verses for music,' takes place under an old sycamore tree, at the west entrance of the monastery in Agia Napa, a village in the southeastern corner of Cyprus. The poetic persona considers the breeze that passes through the tree. Here, as elsewhere in Seferis's poetry, the natural elements do not bring any comfort or respite. Indeed, as Krikos-Davis (1978: 65) demonstrates, this aspect is conveyed by two negative sentences followed by an affirmative one often found in folksongs and then the rule of three:

> This is no Palm Sunday wind
> no wind of Resurrection
> but a wind of fire, a wind of smoke,
> a wind of joyless life.

That wind of devastation comes from the north. Earlier in the poem, it had risen up and 'gone to the northern castles,' whence it returns in the last stanza to bring with it the smell of an ignominious economic transaction:

> Under the aging sycamore
> the wind returned dry,
> reeking of florins everywhere,
> and bartered us for gold.

(Seferis 1978: 459–61)

Betrayal is in the air of Cyprus! The epigraph's mention of Spring 1156 sets off a series of past transitional and transactional historical moments – 1156, 1191–2, 1878, and 1956. In 1156, Reynald de Châtillon, along with his ally Thoros II, defeated the Cypriot militia and devastated the island. The surviving Cypriots were driven to the coast and obliged to buy back their own livestock and freedom. The Duke of Cyprus, John Comnenus, and his entourage are taken hostage and held by the invaders until the sum was paid in full. Krikos-Davis (1978: 69–70) has argued that the language of parched devastation and terms of monetary exchange link this moment to a second scene of betrayal and sell-out in 1191, known to Seferis from Neophytos's Περί των κατά την χώραν Κύπρον σκιάν (*c*.1196). It was then that a descendant of this hostaged Comnenus, one Isaac Ducas Comnenus, a much-loathed Emperor of Cyprus, was defeated by Richard the Lionheart on his way to Palestine. Richard, an Englishman, was perceived as a welcome alternative to Isaac's calamitous rule by Cypriots, yet their hopes proved misplaced as Richard's reign was short-lived, authoritarian, and marked by his levy of heavy taxes. Furthermore, from Acre where he had encamped later in that year, word came that he sold the island to the Order of the Knights Templar for 100,000 gold dinars, of which he received 40,000 and the rest in installments. The Knights Templar ruled the island ruthlessly for a year. Eventually, they appealed to Richard to cancel the sale and this gave the opportunity for Guy de Lusignan to step in, reimburse the Knights for the 40,000 dinars, and take possession of the island by taking respons-ibility for Richard's debt.

Betrayal, as *Agianapa II* illustrates, has historically been engineered from the north. Richard's intervention of 1191 conjures up British intervention in Cyprus in 1878, with its promise of a more benevolent alternative to Turkish rule.

> The history of western occupation of the island is marked by two cynical acts – in 1192 the English sell Cyprus to the Franks; in 1878 the English 'buy' Cyprus from the Turks, and at the time of poem's writing everything points to something similar about to take place. The Cypriot people's struggle for independence has entered into a critical stage with the English, once again, the arbiters of the situation. Seferis was *smelling* a new 'sell-out.' (Vayenas 1979: 241; italics mine)

Vayenas's choice of verb here, making reference as it does to the olfactory senses, is very much in keeping with Seferis's own terms for describing such betrayal. And it is hard to argue against such a position. Yet it is a rather safe position to take in the context of the Cyprus issue. Small states will always be the playthings of Great Powers, and there are always forks in the road up ahead. The Cyprus issue in the 1950s began as a struggle for union with Greece, but, in time, circumstances compelled the initial goal to be trimmed to the dictates of geopolitical possibility. In the face of overwhelming odds, some Cypriots were unbending; others were pragmatic. Some resolved to fight in 1955 and persevered; others may have wished for the same outcome but pursued less direct strategies. (Others *were* traitors!) The disagreement among Cypriots has been characterized by the positions espoused by Grivas, the leader of the Greek Cypriot fighters on the one hand, and Makarios, the Ethnarch and political leader of the Greek Cypriots on the other. Grivas persevered with *enosis*; Makarios sought a political solution. The debate over the merits of each position rages on to this day.

For his part, Seferis was heavily involved in the debates over Cyprus. When he returned to Greece in 1956, he was appointed Director of the Second Political Bureau of the Ministry of Foreign Affairs (1956–7), with special responsibilities for the Cyprus issue. As Greek Ambassador to Great Britain too, from 1957 to 1962, at the height of negotiations over a new status for Cyprus, he was stationed in the home of the colonial power. Seferis was unswerving in his belief that the Hellenicity of Cyprus could be safeguarded only by its incorporation into the Greek state. A detailed analysis of his positions is, alas, at present impossible since his political memoirs that cover the vital period 1956–60 are as yet unpublished.[39] However, extracts that have seen the light of day point to Seferis's belief that mainland Greek diplomatic efforts were affected adversely by internal bickering and an imprudent willingness to placate the British and NATO,[40] while under-estimating the danger posed by the Turks. For Seferis, 'the Turks are always the danger'; his visceral suspicion of them led him to fall out with the Greek Foreign Ministry.[41] He opposed the proposed solution, and he was sidelined from the vital Zurich talks, which led to Cypriot independence in February 1959. Seferis cautioned: 'An incredible outburst of heroism ends up in Zurich by bringing the Turk back on the island, this Turk who has spent the war without giving anything at all . . . [this Turk] who has not forgotten the Varlikou method or the methods of '55 [the purges against Constantinopitan Greeks]. When he finds the right moment . . . it's obvious, that's the way the Turk is, that's the way he's always been.'

When it came to Greeks and Turks, Seferis was unable to see any room for negotiation. His own traumas, as an Asia Minor Greek and Smyrniot, prevented him from conjuring up any shared historical lifeworld between the Greeks and Turks of Cyprus. The historical incident at the heart of 'The Demon of Fornication' is instructive. The irascible last Crusader king of Cyprus, Pierre I de Lusignan, an incurable vanquisher of Muslims, comforts himself away from home by clutching hold of his wife Eleonora of Aragon's shirt in bed at night. The initiation of action around 'an empty tunic,' seen most poignantly in 'Helen,' is reaffirmed in the poem's scenario. The otherwise dastardly and adulterous king will soon find out that his wife has herself been engaged in an affair for some considerable time with John de Morphou. Seferis here restates a Cypriot epic, Machairas's chronicle as well as Shakespeare's *Othello* (I, 1), where 'an old black ram/Is tupping your white ewe.' Seferis introduces the affair as a diplomatic dilemma faced by the King's counselors. They must advise the king whether to lend credence to this news, which has been supplied him by the letter of one honest and loyal John Visconti. The poem foregrounds the perspective of the counsellors who, with 'responsib-ilities, terrible responsibilities', decide that: 'we aren't sworn to say/where justice lies. Our duty/is to find the lesser of evils. Better for one man to die because he was fated to/than for us to put ourselves and the kingdom in danger.' Their decision to portray Juan Visconti as an 'infamous, perverted liar' serves the purpose of keeping the king from punishing his queen, an act that would incur the wrath of her powerful Catalan family. Clearly, Seferis sympathizes with the honest and scrup-ulous Juan Visconti. But he also casts himself as a counselor unlike those in the poem – he will not find it in him to advise the lesser of evils.

Commentators of the period have tended to commend Seferis for his stead-fastness. The outcome of decisions reached in 1959 to establish independence for Cyprus led to the partition of the island and a Turkish invasion and occupation in 1974. So the argument goes, and deficiencies in the arrangement certainly contrib-uted to this outcome. However, it seems problematic to commend Seferis's positions without placing them in the context of the overwhelming pressures exerted on Greeks and Cypriots alike at this time. Just because Seferis's entrenched view was not the one followed in 1959 does not mean that, if history had been directed by his intransigence in 1959, the Cyprus issue would have seen a better outcome. It may have seen an equally disastrous outcome sooner from a Greek perspective. Habitually, those who spoke up for a negotiated settlement are portrayed as having 'sold out'. Even Makarios, who was moving toward a negotiated settlement and away from *enosis*, is criticized for his 'submission' to outside forces. Still others were painted as traitors. Angelos Vlachos, a Greek diplomat sent to Cyprus in 1956, was one such figure. He has been vilified for his positions by the pro-Seferis and pro-*enosis* camp (cf. Yeoryis 2000). A career diplomat, Vlachos was plunged into the Cyprus crisis as the Greek Consul in 1956. And his autobiography depicts his reluctance at assuming the hot seat in Cyprus in 1956. However, his instinct was to support the Greek Prime Minister and Foreign Minister of the time, Constantine Karamanlis and Evangelos Averoff, in the belief that they were trying to extricate all sides with the least damage done to Greek interests. This belief leads him to make a distinction between a 'nationalist' and a 'patriot': the latter, he argues, is driven by 'reason' as he balances 'existing capabilities with targeted goals' (Vlachos

1985: 225). In drawing such distinctions, Vlachos shows himself to be eminently aware of the risk that patriots like himself, or his superiors, run of earning for themselves the labels of 'cosmopolitans,' 'gravediggers of the national ideal,' or 'traitors.'

The two men had differences: Seferis was a Venizelist and Vlachos was not. It is true that Vlachos shared little of Seferis's emotional attachment to the Cypriots. In his autobiographical writings Vlachos routinely puts Greek interests above those of the Cypriots. Makarios earns his rebuke for being too much of a Cypriot and not enough of a Greek (Vlachos 1985: 205). Yet Vlachos's positions should not too facilely earn him the label of a traitor, for it does not sit so well with one who had fought on the Albanian Front in 1940, in the wartime Resistance, and was imprisoned by the Italians (Vlachos 1985: 248). Like any Greek or Greek Cypriot of the time, Vlachos shared Seferis's vision of Cyprus as a Hellenic island. Vlachos saw Cyprus in almost Greek colonial terms; in this Seferis was, undoubtedly, more sympathetic to a Cypriot perspective. But Vlachos was clearly unnerved by the poetic justice underpinning Seferis's staunch political positions. Though Vlachos's desire to defuse the crisis quickly may be seen by nationalists as a sign of his betrayal, it should also be interpreted in more pragmatic terms. And so should Seferis's positions. In 1958, when the leader of the *enosis* fighters, George Grivas, decided upon resuming the armed struggle, Vlachos sought to dissuade him. Since his own relations with Grivas were tense – Grivas saw Vlachos simply as a messenger for Karamanlis and Averoff – Vlachos tried to convince Seferis to intercede on his government's behalf and advise Makarios, with whom he had a good relationship, to prevail upon Grivas. And it is evident that Seferis, too, at this point, was aware that the armed struggle in Cyprus could no longer be prudently pursued.[42] The gravity of the situation led Vlachos to solicit Seferis's help despite his reservations about Seferis's temperament: 'Seferis used to get carried away by feelings engendered by a Greek liberation struggle. Living with the woe of *Romiossyni* as his companion, he either did not see the factors leading to an impasse clearly enough, or else, he did not have the will to confront them and admit to them' (Vlachos 1985: 419). For Vlachos, Seferis was either infusing poetic precepts to the understanding of a diplomatic problem or else he was hiding behind them. Where others might applaud Seferis for his defense of principle, Vlachos and even Seferis's brother-in-law and later President of the Hellenic Republic, Constantine Tsatsos, rebuked his intransigence on this point.[43] Vlachos concludes that the 'almost clinically cautious Seferis' insisted that he would eventually talk in person to Makarios, rather than write to him, in order to avoid that there be any written evidence in the future that would show Seferis's arguing for the cessaton of EOKA armed activity (Vlachos 1985: 422). As it turned out, Seferis did not meet up with Makarios and his more general opposition to Greek diplomatic tactics led to his marginalization from the international negotiating process.

Seferis was sidelined from the private meetings between Foreign Minister Averoff and his Turkish counterpart, Zourlou, in mid-December 1958. Even in his last journal entry before his death (11 May 1971), Seferis defended himself from colleagues and critics and insisted that he had opposed independence for Cyprus in a note to Averoff back in December 1958. In response, Averoff has claimed that he had discarded the note and that it contained nothing that would change the Greek position.[44] I doubt that publication of Seferis's remaining political diaries will shed any light on this issue. But in the one published letter by Seferis to Averoff from that critical time (25 December 1958), Seferis is deeply suspicious of the Turks and the British. He fears that assenting to independence for the island will only lead to the eventual annexation of the island, and so he opposes it. However, he does not propose a viable plan of action. Averoff, who shares Seferis's concerns, addresses these in a letter of response (1 January 1959), and also explains the political dangers of leaving the issue open at this point in time. Furthermore, he explicitly defends the rationale behind political guarantees formulated to ensure the island's independence, arguing that these safeguards make it hard to imagine a circumstance in which Turkey could compromise that independence, except by open invasion and in flagrant contravention of all international treaties. That occasion, of course, did present itself to Turkey in 1974 – but it did so only at the instigation of the Greek side, albeit by a military junta, which tried to nullify the island's independence and annex Cyprus to Greece. To dwell on the fulfillment of Seferis's prediction should not necessarily justify his position in 1958. Observers should not be distracted from the very real possibility that Seferis's stance might have very well brought on a sorrier outcome sooner, for Cyprus but also for Greece. Perhaps the mutual Greek/Turkish suspicions and hatreds generated among Cypriots, that Seferis shared, were just too intense. Left unchecked during independence (1960–74), they led to inevitable disaster. However more genuine Seferis's concern for the (Greek) Cypriots than his diplomat contemporaries, it can be argued that Seferis's concern for Hellenism would have put Cyprus and Greece at greater risk in 1958. His defensiveness does not amount to a workable plan for Cyprus at that juncture, and, indeed, he underestimates many of the imminent political dangers of the present moment. Though it may be a harsh assessment, the impression is that, typical of his poetry, he grants primacy to the past over the present, and this affects the formulation of his stance to the future.[45]

Clearly, his personal feelings about the Greek experience in Asia Minor, further emboldened by what he perceived as Turkish barbarism in riots against the Greek population in Istanbul in 1955 (triggered by the Cyprus issue, it should be noted), meant that he transferred these lessons of history to Cyprus. The belief in a staunch resistance as opposed to betrayal and 'selling out' informed his political and poetic instincts. This paradigm has, in fact, structured the way Greek Cypriots discuss the Cyprus issue down to our days. It has contributed significantly to a polarization of the political and social terrain among Greek Cypriots in Cyprus, even today. In the post-1974 discussion over the solution of the Cyprus Problem by the creation of a federal state with the Turkish Cypriots, supporters and detractors of such a so-called 'compromise' solution are, sadly, divided into rejectionists and concessionists, patriots and traitors.[46]

Logbook III helps us realize that Seferis's understanding of Cyprus is as much poetic as it is political. Or, otherwise, that his political understanding of the Cyprus issue has a significant poetic dimension to it (certainly in Vlachos's mind). But his poetry is also, in a sense, deeply political and ethnocentric. Many Greek and Greek Cypriot writers and thinkers shared this outlook in Cyprus at that time. And so did the majority of Greeks and Cypriots.

The modernists' cultural fantasies were the Imaginary's response to a political impasse. The repression of Hellenism's modern trauma in 1922 engenders still other repressions. Theotokas represses an eastern cultural ensemble and does so by using it to contain the Greek working class. Like Elytis's turn eastwards to locate an essentialized Hellenism cleansed of a degrading history, Seferis's vision of Cyprus is itself predicated on selective history. And the sense of a Turkish presence, or a Turkish threat, conditions the geography of that new Imaginary. Seferis's historical consciousness is founded on instances of appropriation and an efface-ment of alterity that, in the end, is hardly Cavafian, despite his poem's formal affinities to Cavafy in *Logbook III*. His Cyprus poems do not feature the Turkish Cypriots or a Turkish cultural presence. And such an oversight is the product of a 'political vision' for the island. Seferis ignores all trace of Turkish presence on the island. For one contemporary Turkish Cypriot poet, Mehmet Yashin, this comes as no surprise for 'as a diplomat in Ankara, Seferis remained indifferent to Turkish poetry and literature. Not even in Cyprus did he cast a glance (as his photographs demonstrate) on Turkish or Muslim symbols' (Yashin 1998–9: 314). In discussing his relationship to a Levantine Cavafy and an Ottoman Seferis, Yashin provides an-Other's perspective on the nature and value of difference as it is depicted in the poetry of George Seferis. For, Yashin can relate to the position of the homeless poet: Seferis mourns the loss of his city, Smyrna; Yashin mourns the loss of his city, Lefkosha. Yet did Seferis mourn the loss of Izmir? Did he feel as Yashin did for Lefkosia? Yashin lives in exile, in the process of his own odyssey – a Cypriot citizen, writing in Turkish, living in a cosmopolitan London, a poet of no country. Yashin is clearly at home with Cavafy's conceptualization of identity; but he is less at ease with Seferis's inability to conjure up a historical moment that can be both differentiated and complex in a Cavafian sense. Yashin sees Seferis's blind spot and it is, literally, close to home: '[Seferis] does not want us to see him – a child who froze at the sight of his plundered house in Smyrna, in Klazomenes. He seeks shelter in a history empty of people, he seeks to overshadow the memory of his own life experiences' (Yashin 1998–9: 314). Like his generation, he sought a home away from home in the shelter of poetry.

Notes

1. For an engaging study of an Asia Minor Greek refugee settlement in Piraeus, the port of Athens, see Hirschon (1998). In fiction, the experience is treated in the novels of Elias Venezis and Dido Soteriou.
2. On this, see Tziovas's introduction to his edited volume of Theotokas's diaries (Theotokas 1989: 27).
3. There is one available English translation of *Free Spirit* by Soterios G. Stavrou (Theotokas 1986).
4. The periodical's anti-communist bent is made further clear in letters from the young Theotokas to Seferis in 1930–1 (Theotokas 1975a).
5. Tziovas (1989a), in his introduction to Theotokas's diaries (Theotokas 1989), as well as Klironomos (1992) focus on the intellectual tradition, education, and liberalism in Greece.
6. Theotokas casts Rhigas Pherraios as the epitome of neohellenic liberation (Theotokas 1976: 143). Peponis, editor of Theotokas's political writings, informs us how, in 1946, Theotokas was disturbed by the effect Stalinism was having on the brightest segment of Greek youth. He urged the reinvigoration of another tradition opposed to 'national obedience' – the roots of which he found symbolized in the figure of Rhigas (Theotokas 1976: 13).
7. 'We do not have the right ever to be disillusioned,' wrote Theotokas to Seferis in *Dokimes B* (Seferis 1979: 303).
8. See Theotokas (1976: 23).
9. A short article in *Nouvelle Revue Française* (April 1929) later appears as Thibaudet (1936).
10. See Theotokas (1976) for Theotokas's essays on social issues (73–86), on Greek socialism (136–40), and on distinctions between political Right and Center (113–24).
11. For Skliros, the 'feudal-aristocratic' state of Byzantium is the historical and psychological ancestor of neohellenism (Skliros 1976: 109–10). Not all critics accepted Theotokas's marriage of mysticism and communism. The diaspora art critic Nikolas Calas was unimpressed. In a letter to Theotokas, he writes: 'Why speak of mysticism in relation to Moscow and not Rome, or New York? On what grounds does one judge certain movements mystical?' (Constantoulaki-Hantzou 1989: 22).
12. Theotokas's championing of youth is also a major theme in his important novel, *Argo* (1934).
13. Metaxas's dictatorship of 1936 does institute oligarchical rule. The absolute hypostasization of a new Hellenic spirit, what Seferis termed 'Greek Hellenism,' was promulgated at the time of Metaxas's call for a Third Era of Hellenistic Civilization. A comparison of the main tenets of nationalist demoticism with

the Metaxas regime's driving ideologies would make for an interesting discursive study. How close were these visions rhetorically? Metaxas regime did not consider it necessary to censor the work of the 1930s Generation. That said, the Metaxas regime did not exclude the participation of leftists in Education's Ministry's cultural committees either (Dimadis 1991: 54–6, fn. 33). At the time, Seferis was Metaxas's government spokesman for the foreign press (7 December 1937) in the Sub-Ministry of the Press and Tourism; Terzakis was Director of the Royal Theater; Prevelakis headed the Fine Arts Section of the Ministry of Education (see Dimadis 1991: 53–5).

14. See an essay entitled 'Ο Καινούργιος Λαός', especially Theotokas (1976: 60–2, 67–9).

15. Greece's plea to the EC (now EU) for 'special treatment' during the 1980s because of its Balkan history, geography, and political affiliations comes to mind.

16. Angelos Terzakis (1937: 2), another member of the Generation of the 1930s, had employed the same term to characterize the attempt to define a Greek cultural identity, beginning with the folklorist N. G. Polites's presentation of demotic songs right down to modernists' quest for a neohellenic civilization.

17. This extract is, in fact, taken from a speech entitled 'The European Union and the Future of the Greek Nation,' given at a European Association in Thessaloniki, in 1958.

18. Metropolitan Athens will be the motivating force and center of his new *Free Spirit* since 'in the Athenian air there exists exuberant adolescence, today more so than ever' (Theotokas 1988: 24). It is this youth, contrasted to the sterility of academics such as Photos Polites, which will develop the urban progressivism of European cosmopolitanism (Theotokas 1988: 69).

19. Antoniou, Gatsos, and Kavvadias at this time journey for different ends that we cannot go into here. In oral presentations, Margaret Alexiou has commented on Seferis's constant contrast of himself as 'sea-faring' to his description of Cavafy as 'of the library' and its significance for understanding the difference between a logocentric and grapho-centric narrative of the Greek literary tradition. For a more general discussion of the sea as metaphor in modern Greek literature, see Beaton (1987: 253–72).

20. On this, see the work of political economist Vergopoulos (1978: 203–2). This insightful work is more akin to cultural studies than most of the literary criticism of the time.

21. Carson and Sarris's translation stresses the gender-coding of the possessive pronouns to bring out the sexual 'thrust' of the poem. Other translations downplay this aspect: in line 5 of the second stanza of I, it is 'on her wettest rock [that] the bride waits' (στον πιο βρεμένο βράχο της η αρραβωνιαστικιά

προσμένει) and this bringing together of the 'wet rock' and the 'bride' is crucial for affirming the relation between landscape and passive femininity in Elytis's work.

22. Elytis's disruption of logical syntax, when translated, should not be forced into more conventional grammatical compromises. Vitti is right to point to Elytis's desire to break through the logical presuppositions of likening, for example, 'gulls' and 'dreams.' Elytis abolishes the simile to affirm that 'gulls are dreams' (1998: 24). As late as 1990, his professed goal is to emulate those men who, hundreds of years ago, 'had not locked themselves in the cage of causes and etiology, when chairs would fly and one walked on the sea' (Elytis 1986: 27).

23. See Calotychos (1992: 50). Mackridge (1997b: 119) echoes this reading of Elytis's 'unmodernist' outlook on language and his rejection of cosmopolitan, Karyotakian urbanism.

24.

> In literature, a good half century now, a whole group with Baudelaire at its head, questing solely with an aesthetic instinct, as I judge it, to maintain itself in unexplored areas, has focused now no longer on 'Man' but on the overlooking of Man and has related its worship of the spirit of Evil with all manner of dilettantism. A hedonism for what is forbidden, for guilt, for remorse, for the invocation to pain as a Good, for the juxtaposition of the Artificial next to the Natural, Hell's glory in the place of a redundant Paradise . . . If there does exist a mystical message sent to us from that part of existence that we overlook, then this has never appeared to me in the form of a Bogey Man that stalks the midnight hours. (Elytis 1974: 348)

See Carson (1983) for a sensitive explication of Elytis's perception of how these truths may be apprehended.

25. See also Lorenzatos (1980) and the writings of Yannaras, Metallinos, Ramphos, and other neo-Orthodox thinkers.

26. See the poems 'The Kore the Northwind Brought,' 'Without Yashmak,' 'The Red Horse,' 'Little Green Sea' from this collection. See also extracts from Elytis's late *The Garden with the Self-Deceptions* (1995: esp. 63).

27. The entry is from Tuesday, 19 January 1954, Beirut. Savidis (1961: 305) considers this, along with the Fall of 1946, the most productive time in Seferis's life.

28. Seferis took six trips to Cyprus, if one counts some short stays (Yeoryis 1989: 174–7).

29. A handful of the poems from this collection were first published in the journal *Kypriaka Grammata*, in Nicosia, in 1954. The collection, as it first appeared in Athens in December 1955, was titled 'Cyprus where it was decreed' (Κύπρο ου μ' εθέσπισεν). When Seferis finally gave the collection its current title, this previous title appeared as an epigraph to the collection.

30. On a politics of self-effacement in various aspects of Seferis's work, see Lambropoulos (1988); Calotychos (1990).

31. For miscellany about Seferis's childhood home, see Demetrakopoulos (1992: 68–77). The municipal council of the town of Urla, in the Izmir area, named a street after Seferis in 1999. Turkish artists and media protested the decision: 'It's a shame for Turkey, not Seferis,' wrote the large circulation *Hurriyet*, while singer and composer Zulfi Livaneli expressed his indignation for such lack of respect towards a poet of worldwide stature, in an article in *Sabah*. The story of Seferis Street (tr., *sokak*) began when the then mayor of Urla, Bulent Baratali of the Social Democratic Party, along with the municipal council, voted to ratify the name 'Seferis' for a street in Urla. In 1999, a new mayor, Selcuk Karaosmanoglu of the Motherland (Liberal) Party (ANAP) was elected. In the midst of the Ocalan affair, and notwithstanding the opposition by the mayor, the majority of ANAP members voted to remove Seferis's name from the street. The journalist Suleyman Gencel wrote an article in his newspaper *Yeni Asir* in 19 and 22 June 1999, to denounce this act. The story soon became a topic of national discussion in Turkey and was extensively covered by the Greek media in late June, 1999. In a remarkable turn of events, the leader of ANAP, and one-time Prime Minister of Turkey, Mesut Yilmaz, intervened and called upon the ANAP-dominated council in Urla to restore the name of Seferis Street; and they did. On 1 April, Greeks and Turks commemorated the poet's birth outside his house as part of celebrations and a conference was arranged in Izmir.

32. Aeschylus treats the material in *The Women of Salamis*.

33. Yannis Ritsos also plays upon this distinction and the tradition that accompanies it.

34. Seferis plays with this in a draft of 'Agianapa A': Κάτω από τη συκομουριά (παλληκάρι δέντρο) επούλησάς με, επούλησά σε. ['Under the sycamore tree (young lad tree), you sold me out, I sold you out.']

35. See Savidis's (1961) philological study of Seferis's Cyprus poems for useful intertextual references and literary allusions.

36. Maronitis discusses three chronicle-like poems from *Logbook III*: 'The Demon of Fornication'; 'Three Mules'; 'Neophytos the Monk Speaks' (Maronitis 1987a: 166–9). The tradition engages also with one of Cyprus's most revered texts, *The Chronicle of Leontios Mahairas* (*c*.1555).

37. 'Remember the baths where you were murdered' (Aeschylus, *The Libation Bearers*, 491).

38. For a discussion of typologies for the songs for the fall of cities in the Greek tradition, see M. Alexiou (1974: Chapter V); Beaton (1980: 95–102).

39. Seferis's friend, the diplomat Alexandros Xydis, oversaw the publication of two volumes of his political diaries: 'A' [1935–44], published in 1979, and 'B'

[1945–52], published in 1985 (Seferis 1979–85). The third volume that will cover the period from 1953 to 1960 has been destined to appear for quite some time, under the editorship of Xydis and Demetris Daskalopoulos, but hasn't. The delay has aggravated some (Pavlou 2000: prologue).

40. These extracts appear in *Ta Nea* newspaper (see Yeoryis 2000; 2001).

41. Pieris (1991: 174–5) has combed Seferis's papers and personal books to discover where the poet underlines and comments on specific passages that mention the Turks.

42. 'At the Ministry Averoff and Seferiades had the clear understanding that a new phase of armed struggle would entangle Turkey further, for she had reacted extremely forcefully upon Makarios's liberation from exile' (Vlachos 1985: 361).

43.

> Seferis was wrong over Cyprus because, as Ambassador to Beirut and a regular tourist in Cyprus, he fell in love not just with the beauties of the island but also the patriotic enthusiasms of the Cypriots. He identified so with their feelings and irrational positions. . . . So much so that when he was Ambassador to London and negotiations over the signing of the Zurich and London Accords were underway, he could not understand that these accords were trying to save all that could be saved from Makarios's criminal politics from 1950–58. (Tsatsos 2000: 200)

44. See Pavlou (2000: 227–311) for the fullest account of this controversy; also Pieris (1991: 97–8). For a perspective that is critical of Seferis, see Pitsilides (2000). Though Pitsilides's criticisms often lack a sense of measure and fairness; his chapter on Seferis's stance on the Cyprus issue is balanced and nuanced.

45. The letters appear in Yeoryis (2001) with commentary that is sympathetic to Seferis. For a less sympathetic reading, see Pitsilides (2000: 372–88). See also Averoff's memoirs (1981: II: 166–7).

46. 'Rejectionists' and 'concessionists' are character types at the center of the prevailing nationalist discourse in Cyprus. Their deployment polarizes the public over issues that need flexible and nuanced frameworks of understanding. The lack of political will to solve the Cyprus issue in the last few years has been chiefly due to Turkish intransigence. But the deleterious effects of this thinking among Greek Cypriots has prevented developing the psychology or the political context to facilitate acceptance of a solution in the future. See Calotychos (1998a: 17–20): Papadakis (1998: 69–84).

−6−

Poetry and Politics in the Post-war

Αυτές οι πέτρες που βουλιάζουν μέσα στα χρόνια ώς πού θα με παρασύρουν
These stones sinking into time, how far will they drag me with them?

George Seferis, *Mythistorema*, XX[1]

[Stephen] Spender and [Robert] Lowell discuss what poetry means in the 20th
Century – Stephen naming Joyce and Virginia Woolf as 'poets.' I accuse him of
annexing prose writers out of territorial ambition, and suggest that the existence of
the word 'poetry' is no reason to postulate the existence of poets. I propose that
instead of saying that writers are (or are not) poets, we should simply say that they
use *metaphor*.

Kenneth Tynan, *The Diaries of Kenneth Tynan*

Politics makes strange bedfellows. In modern Greece, the ongoing affair between
politics and national aesthetics has been longstanding. Chapter 1 demonstrated
how aesthetic nationalism was at the core of the early gestation of the neohellenic
ideal. The form and nature of German philhellene interest in Classical Greek
aesthetics over classical Greek history or politics in the eighteenth century was
formative. The aesthetic project assigned King Otto and his Bavarian elite was to
rule Greece and civilise it and see it an 'incarnated artwork, art made life.'[2] Greece
would aspire to the dream of a 'theocracy of the beautiful' that would have made
the likes of Herder and Hölderlin proud. Given this framework, Greeks could
hardly have been expected to avoid conflating of the national and the aesthetic, the
'Greek' and the 'Hellenic.' The slippage between Greek and Hellenic, political and
aesthetic, ethnic (or particularistic) and humanist (or universal) ideals demanded
a diplomatic interpreter to negotiate and differentiate between them. Seferis
considered such distinctions in his critical essays and even played on their differences, urging fellow artists not to ask how 'they can be Greeks, but certain in the
fact that, since they are Greek, the works created out of their souls cannot be anything else but Hellenic' (Seferis 1981: 95). This structural homology implicit in two
ideals of modernity, as Leontis (1995) puts it, brings together the neohellenic as
grounded in the national context and the ideas of the Hellenic artwork as responding directly to the earth and soil. This interdependence of geographic and
discursive *topoi* remain influential all the way down to Greek modernism, which

establishes an indigenous and modern profile, simultaneously of traditional expression and universal value (see Leontis 1995: 119–21).

Seferis's seminal *Mythistorema* (1935) provides the best exposition of how these *topoi* interrelate. The work's epigraph, taken from Rimbaud's *Fêtes de la Faim*, proclaims an interest for the concrete and the specific: 'Si j'ai du goût, ce n'est guères/Que pour la terre et les pierres' (If I have taste, it is only for the earth and the stones). From the very first poem in the collection, Seferis bores into the earth 'one with the plough's blade or keel of the ship' (σμίγοντας την κόψη του αλετριού με του καραβιού την καρένα) in search of the 'first seed' (πρώτο σπέρμα). He quests for a point of origin that would impose a limit on the text and initiate the grand narrative or inner code that will precede all else. This becomes time and again a quest of deferred possession, ever under erasure. 'Hellas is always ours, yet never entirely possessed' (Leontis 1995: 130). As a result, the meaning of Greece is always metaphorical and transpositional, inhabiting the space between the national plaint and the Ideal phantasm, between topos and ou-topia, as Gour-gouris (1996) concludes in his reading of Seferis's critical texts:

> [his] nostalgia for utopia is simultaneously propelled in antithetical temporal directions: on the one hand, it is a nostalgia for Greece as a utopia of the past, a vanished world (Aeschylus, the monastic caves of Cappadocia, Erotokritos, Makriyiannis); on the other, it is a nostalgia for Greece as a utopia of the future (a *topos* that will come out of our Hellenic vision, as our vision gradually realizes itself: Hellene as *anthropos*. (Gourgouris 1996: 223)

All nature, earth and stones, are *potentially* transubstantiated into a unique sub-stance. This code breaks through the exclusiveness of signs and exorcizes the natural substance of a thing in order to unify the multiply marked *topos* (the Helladic state) under the synthetic coherence of a system that universalizes the *topos* under a single Word (the Hellenic). This approach is symptomatic of what has been termed Seferis's 'spatial atopia,' his tentative relationship to the geo-graphical space of Greece, which is always devalued in relation to the 'intellectual landscape' or tradition of Hellenism. Consequently, both Seferis's wish to treat 'only the stones and earth' as well as his later professed desire to do 'no more than to speak simply' should be considered circumspectly.[3]

The previous chapter showed just how the modernist poets renegotiated a cartography of Greek (intellectual) space. In their poetry, they restaged the communion between the signifier and the all-embracing transcendental signified of Greek Hellenism, correlating them so as to produce an associative total that would perform homogenizing social and ideological operations of Greekness (ελληνικότητα). They sought to Hellenize the Helladic and aestheticize the national ideal so as to resolve the antinomies of Greek culture not militarily, but aesthetically, in the utopian space of Greekness (Jusdanis 1991a: 116). In so doing, Jusdanis rightly argues in his work on modernity that the eventual aestheticization of social practices amounts to an ethical ideology that permits them as individuals, or as a class, to exercise power while denying participation, belief, and investment (1991a: 93). As we saw in the first section of Chapter 5, Greekness was to chart a course for liberalism, in-between an exhausted conservatism and a threatening communist internationalism. After 1922, Leontis puts it well, loss is figured as a 'matter of transcending history, finding the eternal seed to replay an ancient drama rather than facing the inelegant drama of the present' (1995: 139). Only after World War II, at the beginning of the Cold War and while Greece was engaged in a brutal civil war, did this modernist vision reach a broader audience (Leontis 1995: 121). However, neither Seferis nor Elytis confronted the Civil War directly in their creative work. Perhaps the readership of the day probably had its fill of the war in newspapers, in their everyday discussions, in the depredations of daily life. But the elite also regarded disinterestedness more appropriate than divisiveness as an aesthetic response to the crisis (Leontis 1995: 140). The modernists' neglect of the civil war is quite remarkable, given the war's status as the preeminent form of struggle over the meaning of Hellenism at this time. Put differently, it is as if Seferis retains the discreet New Critical categories of political and aesthetic domains. He confronts the civil war as he did his own transcendental homelessness in Cyprus, metaphorically.

Jusdanis charts the evoluton of literary and linguistic demoticism to the modern-ists' autonomization of the aesthetic and culture sphere. But while he does consider the disputes within demoticism discussed in Chapter 4, he does not follow the evolution of the counter-position of social demoticism as it developed into an ideological assault on liberalism and the modernists' aestheticization of Enlighten-ment principles. Nor does his study endeavour to trace this formally, in the literary work of writers and artists on either side of the debate. Other poets could not avoid the cleavages of Greek society as did the modernists. A generation of communist poets writing at about this time confronted the events of the civil war head-on, both in their praxis and in their *political* poetry. While this group owed a formal debt to the 1930s Generation in many ways, the modernists' treatment of events during a decade of truly *territorial* battle (occupation, resistance, and civil war) seemed incongruous to them. It was absurd for communists to appreciate Elytis's Aegean poems of the late 1930s when, in these very same Aegean islands, 1000 socialists, trade unionists, and democrats had experienced internal exile and imprisonment during the Metaxas regime of 1936–41 (Kenna 1991: 63–82). Like Karyotakis before them, they did not share the spatial atopia of the diasporic 1930s writers. Karyotakis had seen the effects of the exchange of populations on the Helladic state in the 1920s with his own eyes. Similarly, the leftist poets witnessed the turbulent 1940s on the ground. Unlike Seferis, who spent almost the entire war with the government-in-exile in Egypt or from the Tyrrhenian coast,[4] they participated in the resistance. This struggle was predominantly led by the Communist Party of Greece, or KKE, and numbered nearly 2 million by December 1944. The movement's military wing – the Greek Popular Liberation Army or ELAS – numbered up to 150,000 troops by the end of the war. In the Mountains, in 'Free Greece,' these organizations attracted a great following and even implemented a modernization policy, which introduced services that the pre-war, Athens-dominated, political regimes had not undertaken. By 1943, EAM/ELAS controlled approximately 75 percent of Greek territory.[5] The Greek government-in-exile may have been the legitimate government of Greece in the opinion of the Great Powers, yet it had no representation in 'free Greece.' Conversely, the KKE, through EAM/ELAS, had acquired a power base but no official representation in the legitimate government. The December Incidents of 1944 that pitted ELAS members against British and government troops in Athens was the first armed conflict of the Cold War, as Seferis noted in his diary.[6] Eventually Churchill's resolve to keep Greece in the West's sphere of influence led to open civil war and the Truman Doctrine's financial backing of the restored government's war against the communist insurgency led to the communists' defeat. Their fighters fled into exile, mostly behind the Iron Curtain while others were detained or imprisoned for much of the next two decades, their party was banned, their politics excluded them from the civil service etc.

Conventionally, these post-war poets in Greece have been divided into generations and discreet categories – surrealist, existentialist, and social/political (Menti 1995: 18; Orsina 1997: 13; Vayenas 1994: 125). Though the divisions are hardly airtight, I will use them to focus on a handful of poets customarily listed in the third group: Manolis Anagnostakis (1925–), Aris Alexandrou (1922–78), Titos Patrikios (1928–), and Michalis Katsaros (1921–98).[7] Born within a few years of each other, they all paid a heavy price for their convictions and their poetry suffered the ignominy reserved for social realism. For, typically, communism was deemed incompatible with poetry, even if many of the twentieth century's most innovative poets were fully engaged with the ideology (Mayakovsky, Neruda, Hikmet, Ritsos).[8] The poets under discussion here were all very critical and questioning of party policy. Alexandrou split from the party in 1942, and Anagnostakis by 1946, even though he did not exploit this in his military trial in 1949, at which he was sentenced to death. Judged to be significant more for political rather than aesthetic reasons, their work was dismissed as unpoetic and unmetaphorical, prosaic and metonymic.[9] To be a nationalist was never incompatible with the role of a poet; to be a communist was an altogether different matter. Imprisoned for long periods, these poets had plenty of time to think long and hard about what it is poems *do* (if anything). No wonder that they wrote many poems on poetics. Yet their poetic travails were not especially noted until after the dictatorship (1967–74). This chapter charts the poetics of this generation, from Anagnostakis' early symbolism to Katsaros's transformative anarchism in order to argue that their poetry, far from unpoetic, harbors a radically modernist, self-reflexive alternative to the 1930s Generation. In part, this is due to the relation of politics to poetry in their work. In the second section of the chapter, I will argue that one of the masterpieces of Greek poetry, Elytis's Άξιον Εστί (*Axion Esti*) (1959) is, at one level, a response to the challenge posed by their poetics. Elytis responds to a relativization of the sign advocated by the leftist poets. His highly metaphysical and ritualistic work seeks for the redemption (*apocatastasis*) of Greek reality, and its (re)union with Hellenism's 'lost center.' Finally, the short, third section of the chapter will, cursorily, suggest how, with its concern for the body and everyday objects, the leftist poets' work informs post-nationalist, feminist and micropolitical poetry of the 1960s and beyond.

Resistance Poetry

Despite service to his country in the snow-covered mountains of Albania in World War II, Odysseas Elytis did not divert his poetry from the themes of his earlier collections. Poems like the poem 'Aegean,' discussed in Chapter 5, were his trademark. His rationale for not changing his spots during wartime is famously encapsulated in the following assertion:

> During the years of Buchenwald and Auschwitz, Matisse painted the most juicy and unripe, the most charming flowers or fruits which were ever made, as if the very miracle of life had found a way to coil within them for good. That's why today they still speak more eloquently than the most macabre, cadaverous description of the period . . . A whole literature of our time has made the mistake of competing with the events, of going beyond them in presenting horror instead of counterbalancing it. (Elytis in Ivask 1975: 30)

Elytis's *jouissance* does show signs of relenting in his *Heroic and Tragic Song for a Second Lieutenant Lost in Albania* (1945). In this work, the poet defends individual freedom in the face of the injustices that have momentarily shaken his will:

> Ήλιε δεν ήσουν ο παντοτεινός
> Πουλί δεν ήσουν η στιγμή χαράς που δεν καθίζει;
> . . . γιατί ένας τέτοιος ουρανός εκεί που πρώτα εκατοικούσε ο ήλιος.

> Sun weren't you eternal?
> Bird weren't you the moment of joy that never rests?
> . . . why such a sky there where the sun once rested? (Elytis 1976: 16–17, E')[10]

Yet despite Elytis's treatment of history and the horrors of war, his 'situations are not wholly materialized' (Rotolo 1975: 76). Furthermore, the poem ends hopefully with the resurrection of the fallen second lieutenant: 'Tomorrow, tomorrow, tomorrow: the Easter of God' (Αύριο αύριο αύριο· το Πάσχα του Θεού) (Elytis 1976: 36, ΙΔ ').[11]

Nikos Gatsos's poem *Amorgos* (1940), acclaimed at the time of its publication in 1940, was very much in the tradition of Elytis's journeying to a resplendent Aegean archipelago. It received a mixed review from Anagnostakis in one of his earliest critical essays in 1944: 'When it comes down to it, Gatsos is arguing that art, and especially poetry, has nothing to do with our lives; that "the life of the poem" – I cite this word for word – is completely different and independent in its essence from the rest of life around us' (Anagnostakis 1985: 11).[12] Anagnostakis rebukes Gatsos's view in no uncertain terms: 'Art that has no relation to our lives, which does not come out of our lived experience, is not art. It can never be art' (12). In 'The New Song' (Το Καινούργιο Τραγούδι), perhaps his first of many poems on poetics, Anagnostakis attacks Elytis and Gatsos's ethereal images and concerns:

> Φτάνει πια αυτές οι μέρες που μας κούρασαν τόσο
> (Οδυνηρές παραστάσεις άϋλων οραμάτων)
> Φτάνει πια η γαλάζια αιθρία του Αιγαίου με τα
>   ποιήματα που ταξιδεύουν σ'ασήμαντα νησιά
> για να ξυπνήσουν την ευαισθησία μας
> Τα κορίτσια που ερωτεύονται την ίδια τους μορφή στον καθρέφτη
> και προσμένουν να λικνίσουν τ αβρά όνειρά τους.

> We've had enough now of these days that have wearied us so
> (Painful images of immaterial visions)
> We've had enough of the Aegean's azure serenity with poems that
> voyage toward insignificant islands
> to awaken our sensitivity
> Of girls who fall in love with their own forms in the mirror and
> wait to cradle their tender-hearted dreams.

> (Anagnostakis 1989: 40)[13]

However, Anagnostakis's early poetry is itself partial to Christological themes and he uses apocalyptic metaphors of salvation. The poem 'Haris 1944' (Χάρης 1944) commemorates the deceased leader of a band of resistance fighters:

> Είν' η δική του φωνή που βουίζει στο πλήθος τριγύρω σαν ήλιος
> Π αγκαλιάζει τον κόσμο σαν ήλιος που σπαθίζει τις πίκρες σαν ήλιος
> Που μας δείχνει σαν ήλιος λαμπρός τις χρυσές πολιτείες
> Που ξανοίγονται μπρος μας λουσμένες στην Αλήθεια και στο αίθριο το φως.

It is his voice that hums around us in the crowd like a sun
Or that embraces the world like a sun, that slashes sorrow like the sun
That like a brilliant sun shows us the golden cities
Spreading before us bathed once more in Truth and lucid light.

(Anagnostakis 1989: 38)

The mythologization of the eponymous hero is a feature typical of resistance literature the world over, which narrates daily and historical details as well as mythopoeizes actors of revolutionary struggle. Ernesto Cardenal has described this trait as the *exteriorismo* of Central American poetry and Elias Khouri highlights this 'documentary or realistic poetry,' *shi'r waqi'i*, in Palestinian literature (Harlow 1987: 73). The apocalyptic vision in Anagnostakis's poem is dressed in religious symbols and Christ: 'He yearned that by forgetting his own body he could offer to the others a Spring' (Λαχταρούσε ξεχνώντας το δικό του κορμί να χαρίσει στους άλλους μιαν ΄Ανοιξη) (1989: 37). Yet Anagnostakis's 'Charis' is narrated in a retrospective past tense and its last stanza is bleak and short on triumphalism. This language is duplicated in the works of other young leftist poets who were also members of communist youth movements in the mid- to late 1940s.[14] Consider the title of Aris Alexandrou's first collection of poems in 1946 – *Still Waiting for this Spring* (Ακόμη τούτη η άνοιξη) – or the very metaphorical language of much of the older Yiannis Ritsos's poetry.

By his second collection, *Epochs 2* (Εποχές 2) (1946–48), Anagnostakis was disheartened by the betrayals suffered by the leftists in the civil war. But he perseveres: 'Then laugh again, try your youth for one more Spring; it is not in vain' (Ύστερα γέλασε πάλι, δοκίμασε τη νιότη σου ακόμα μιαν ΄Ανοιξη· δεν είναι μάταιο) (45). The imperative 'try' (δοκίμασε) connotes both trying and suffering (as in an ordeal). Elsewhere, Spring is conclusively undermined:

Τίποτα πια δε θ'αλλάξει δω μέσα.
Είναι μια ήρεμη σιωπή μην περιμένεις απάντηση
Κάποια νύχτα μαρτιάτικη χωρίς επιστροφή
Χωρίς νιότη, χωρίς έρωτα, χωρίς έπαρση περιττή.
Κάθε Μάρτη αρχίζει μιαν ΄Ανοιξη.

Nothing will ever change again in here.
There is a serene silence, do not expect an answer
Some March night with no return
Without youth, without love, without undue conceit.
Every March begins a Spring.

(Anagnostakis 1989: 71)

Here, Spring keeps its appointment with calendrical time, but it is stripped of all metaphorical properties.[15] Autumn is declared violently anti-poetic, and its signification is circumscribed in a more pragmatic language of survival: 'What we named Autumn was a legitimate, fixed necessity' (Αυτό που ονομάσαμε Φθινόπωρο ήτανε μια τιμητική ορισμένη αναγκαιότητα). The inevitability of the communist defeat was now only a matter of time. With Tito's withdrawal of aid to the Greek communists in 1948, their fortunes took a decided downturn – idealism and metaphor had no place in leftist discourse and soon, these leftist poets went by the label of 'poets of defeat.' The poet and critic Vyron Leondaris coined the term in 1963.[16] Though, according to Patrikios, this perception 'was developed primarily by literary critics who had not taken part in the civil war or post-civil war struggles, or who had not even experienced its consequences' (Patrikios in Pappas 1990: 15; cf. Papageorgiou 1989: 49). The poets themselves expressed their disenchantment in defeat in many forms. Anagnostakis did not accept defeat until as late as 1954. Nikiphoros Vrettakos acknowledged an atmosphere of defeat, but found that 'poetry of defeat' did not capture his stance beyond defeat and was, to his mind, particularly inappropriate in the case of Patrikios.[17] Patrikios's poem 'Report' (Απολογισμός) runs through the variations on the leftist experience:

Μεταστροφές, αποστασίες, ξεπεράσματα
επαναστάτες πειθαρχούν, εισχωρούν τη σκέψη τους
στον παραπάνω καθοδηγητή, άλλοι τρελλαίνονται
άλλοι ασειεύονται, απομονώνονται, συντρίβονται
άλλοι γίνονται δήμιοι των ίδιων των συντρόφων τους
άλλοι ανοίγουν μαγαζιά, πάντα ικανοί ανοίγουν μαγαζιά
άλλοι κερδοσκοπούν, άλλοι μοιχεύουν . . .

Changes of opinion, apostasies, recoveries
revolutionaries are bowed, their thought gives way
to the higher party cadre, others go mad
others joke, are isolated, are crushed
others become the executioners of their very own comrades
. . . others, ever canny, start up their own shops
others profiteer, others commit adultery.

(Patrikios 1981: 112)

In 1963, Patrikios summed up the situation: 'We have been defeated. I refuse to admit it with an almost biological reaction. Yet we have been defeated.' The last phrase encapsulates the double-voicedness of the generation. For does it assert resignation to defeat by overriding the defiance of the previous line? Or does it assert more emphatic defiance even after, or in, the very affirmation of defeat?

Patrikios has considered the label 'poets of defeat' and explained the way it has affected readings of his generation's work:

> This characterization was not given to all the poets of the so-called 'first post-war generation' but only to some of them and to some of their work. It first began in 1963 as a result of a review of a book by Thanassis Kostavaras, *The Return*, and one of my own, *Schooling*, and it was extended to Aris Alexandrou, Manolis Anagnostakis, Costas Kouloufakos, to a degree it encompassed Tasos Leivaditis, and a few others. Though it first appeared as a critical tool for the better comprehension and interpretation of a series of poetic works with common characteristics, in essence, it was nothing more than an ideological-political assessment.
>
> . . . [Each poet] expressed, in his own way and without idealizing, the tone, particularism, and the way they lived through the dramatic adventures of the revolutionary movement and the painful outcome of the civil war. They deliberated over every position, weighed events and people and searched for truth over its embellishment. All these things led to the characterization 'poets of defeat.' This label from being an ideological-political assessment later became a polemical expression, and ended up with the taint of a moral stigma.
>
> And so we moved from 'poetry of defeat' to 'poets of defeat,' who were themselves then characterised as 'defeated' or 'defeatist,' and were regarded by others as almost culpable. (Patrikios in Pappas 1990: 15)

As with 'Karyotakism,' the label affected readings of these poets' work. Conservatives read their poems as sociohistorical document at best; the official Left, troubled by these poets' rejection of the party, kept their distance. However, this fate should not send us in search of formalist or depoliticized alternatives on their behalf, of the kind the critic Nasos Vayenas puts forth. His impulse to downplay politicized elements of Anagnostakis's work by making a case for the poet's existentialist and 'universalist' credentials – even if we were to ignore *The Target* collection of 1969 as Vayenas advises – is a flawed proposition. Giddy in his New Critical revisionism, this Seferian poet-critic's attempt to repackage Anagnostakis as an epigone of Seferis ignores the crucial interrelation of politics and poetics. These poets' 'universal' value can be justified without sacrificing the political vision intrinsic to their poetics. Moullas is right: Anagnostakis is political and his politicality enriches the notion of poeticity (Moullas 1997: 34–5).

The generation's reputation did not fare well until a series of newspaper articles, penned by the critic Demetris Maronitis after the fall of the junta in 1974–5, examined their 'political and poetic ethics.' Specifically, Maronitis focuses on the poetry of Anagnostakis, Alexandrou, and Patrikios, on 'mature poems, not mature poets' and 'poems, not poets' (Maronitis 1976: 14).[18] The leftist poets all reacted to the collapse of the communist ideal in Greece by shunning metaphor and allegory. This shift aimed to reject an hypostasized Hellenism for a more reified

Hellenism expressible in the everyday and the contingent.[19] The theological and philosophical meanings of the word 'hypostasis' here only highlight the importance of transubstantiation to the redefinition of the poetic sign. In theology, the word connotes the unique essence or nature of the Godhead and the three persons of the Trinity; in philosophy, it refers to a more secular definition of the underlying principle or essence of a thing. Both connotations underscore the metaphysics that these poets strive to resist. Their 'resistance realism' comes at a time when action escapes the control of words; when words are shown to have little control over action. In the introductory poem of his first collection in 1948, Patrikios expresses the excitement of an immature lad running to a demonstration, at a time when: 'Action would anticipate thought/thought would not fit in song' (Η πράξη προλάβαινε το στοχασμό, ο στοχασμός δε χωρούσε στα τραγούδια) (Patrikios 1990: 9). The relationship of word to action becomes critical. Unlike the withdrawn, surveying gaze of their modernist predecessors, the personae in these poems are full participants in the action (Maronitis 1976: 22–3). They seek to reinvest 'real things' with a potency beyond the distorting, falsifying control of language and ideology. Marxist ideology, nationalist ideology – any ideology – cannot capture desire. Alexandrou's early poem 'Undelivered Letters' (Ανεπίδοτα Γράμματα) highlights this shortcoming:

Σύντροφε, κοιμάσαι
῾Ηθελα να μου πεις, ξέρεις καμιά σελίδα μαρξισμού
που να βουλιάζουνε οι λέξεις στο χαρτί
σαν την σιωπή μου
στις κόρες των ματιών της

Comrade, are you asleep?
I wanted you to tell me, do you know of any page of marxism
where the words on the page sink
like my silence
in the pupils of her eyes?

(Alexandrou 1981: 36)

Their privileging use of nouns of everyday objects, material items of everyday social existence,[20] echoes Karyotakis's concern with a 'poetics of the unpoetic' and the Surrealists' initiative at defamiliarizing poetic language. The gradual induction of the everyday into Greek poetry speaks to their wish to share the same language with the people. As Tziovas (1993: 101) observes, they feel guilty for indulging in an act, poetry, that may be inconsequential in a society primed for action. This guilt is reflected in their tendency to reject metaphoricity, or a transubstantiation of objects. As Leondaris (1983) points out, in language that unearths the theological dimensions of the dispute, their historical materialism incurs the displeasure of literary critics and bars their accession to aesthetics:[21]

> A brand of criticism that, blindly and persistently, held that ideas in this poetry were not transubstantiated poetically but remained 'preaching,' 'slogans,' 'shouts,' etc. has not come in for much criticism of its own. It is true that many elements in resistance realism remain untransubstantiated, but these elements are anything but the ideas themselves. For these ideas had no serious difficulty in finding their transubstantiation, since myriad elements of any redemptive ideology are exemplarily receptive to poetic transub-stantiation. We could even say that redemptive ideologies are themselves 'poetic.' Thus, for instance, in the verse: 'the sky begins from the bread' . . . (Ritsos) – a verse no better or no worse than others accepted by 'poetic' criteria – the historical materialist belief in the priority of materialist terms of existence achieves its own 'transubstantiation.' (Leondaris 1983: 22)

This historical materialist bias in perceiving events, which drives 'social time' and resists the discourse of ab-sense, separates words, and words as things, from the grasp of a hierarchizing and metaphorizing grander narrative. The Greek surrealists had defamiliarized 'unpoetic' words by using purist idiom in incongruous contexts that they hoped would upstage and disorient bourgeois propriety, well-worn expression, and the hierarchies of genre. The leftist poets of the 1950s introduce objects in the demotic, with all the weight that they had accumulated in everyday lived circumstances. Without transubstantiation, metaphors of flight from the Helladic to the Hellenic are grounded. The titles of poems and collections and poems are telling: Patrikios's Επιστροφή στην Ποίηση (*Return to Poetry*), Χρόνια της Ασφάλτου (*Years of Asphalt*) and Χρόνια της Πέτρας (*Years of Stone*); Alexandrou's Μέσα στις Πέτρες (*In the Stones*), Yannis Ritsos' Πέτρινος Χρόνος (*Stone Year*), Dimitris Doukaris's Το γυμνό χώμα (*The Bare Earth*).

These poets see their place among 'the earth and stones' in a very different way to Seferis. The struggle for Hellenism is identified with the Helladic *topos* in all its devastation and ruin, and the ruinous fragment of a tree and not a classical column becomes personified in the proletarian individual poet:

> Κι όμως δεν αυτοκτόνησα.
> Είδατε ποτέ κανέναν έλατο να κατεβαίνει μοναχός του στο
>   πριονιστήριο
> Η θέση μας είναι μέσα δω σ᾽ αυτό το δάσος
> με τα κλαδιά κομμένα μισοκαμένους τους κορμούς
> με τις ρίζες σφηνωμένες μες στις πέτρες

> But I did not commit suicide
> Have you ever seen a pine come down to a saw-mill by itself?

Our place is right here in this forest
with the broken branches and the half-burnt trunks
with the roots wedged in the stones

'Μέσα στις Πέτρες' (In the Stones) (Alexandrou 1981: 84)

This identification between the physical *topos* and the engaged persona is made more immediate by the grammatical form chosen to personify the pine. Alexandrou's use of the masculine gender noun ο έλατος in the Greek over the equally current neuter noun for the same word 'pine,' το έλατο, gives κανέναν έλατο in the text, where *κανέναν* is the masculine accusative singular. This emphasizes the masculine gender of the adjective μοναχός, which refers to the speaker but is, once again, intentionally conflated with the pine.[22] This poetic use of έλατος also conjures up images of the brave young man who is described in such arboreal terms in the folk tradition. The conflation of the poet and material determinants serves to tie the poet to the social and historical context through an identification with the landscape. Even the sun, symbol of the highest moral good, conforms to the daily routine of concentration camp life on the bare islands of Aï Stratis and Makronissos, where many leftist poets served years of exile in the 1950s. Anagnostakis was condemned to death for participating in the guerrilla war in 1948. His sentence was commuted to a three-year term in prison. Patrikios was to be executed at the age of 16 in 1944, but was pardoned and the sentence commuted to prison in Makronissos (1951–2) and Aï Stratis (1952–3). Alexandrou was imprisoned at Moudro (July 1948–September 1949), Makronissos (September 1949–June 1950), Aghios Evstratios (June 1950–October 1951), and then in the prisons of Averof, Aegina, and Yaros. He served a ten-year sentence, later commuted to seven, from November 1952 to August 1958. Patrikios's short poem 'Habits of the Detainees' (Οι Συνήθειες των Κρατουμένων) is typical:

Κάθε πρωί ο ήλιος έβγαινε πίσω απ᾽ τα φυλάκια
Φορώντας μιαν άπλυτη πιτζάμα του νοσοκομείου
και διάσχιζε αργά το προαύλιο τ᾽ ουρανού.
Ύστερα από τόσα χρόνια
είχε κι εκείνος πάρει συνήθειες των κρατουμένων.

Every morning the sun would rise from behind the watchtowers
wearing an unwashed hospital pyjama
and slowly traversing the sky's courtyard.
After so many years
he too had taken up habits of the detainees.

(Patrikios 1990: 179)

The arid and unforgiving topography intrudes into their poetry. Another poet of the time, Miltos Sachtouris, with a psychological surrealism responds to Elytis's conventional images and tropes by plotting their violent mutilation to the beat of folksong meter (Ricks 1998). In a poem dedicated to Elytis, Sachtouris refers to 'butchered doves' that fly not toward a promised Spring, but out of a tombstone:[23]

> Ελάτε βγήτε στον κάμπο περιστέρια μου
> με τις γαλάζιες κορδέλες στο λαιμό σας
> ελάτε βγήτε με το φεγγάρι στην καρδιά
> σα θα σηκώσω την ταφόπετρά μου
>
> Αργοπεθαίνουν γύρω μου τ'άλλα πουλιά
> ελάτε βγήτε στον κάμπο περιστέρια μου
> ελάτε βγήτε σφαγμένα περιστέρια μου

> Come out onto the plain my doves
> with the blue ribbons around your neck
> come out with the moon in your hearts
> as I will raise my tombstone
>
> The other birds around me are slowly dying off
> come out onto the plain my doves
> come out butchered doves of mine.

(Sachtouris 1977: 55)

Sachtouris's doves suffer intolerable pain.'For Spring' (Για την Άνοιξη) is typically stark:

> Ο ήλιος είναι πράσινος
> τα δέντρα καίνε
> περιμένουνε τα χελιδόνια
> οι σιδερένιες χελιδονοφωλιές
> δε μας γελάνε πια με τα λουλούδια
> μας στοίχισαν τα χέρια και τα πόδια μας
> τώρα τα χέρια και τα πόδια μας
> κρέμονται στα δέντρα

> The sun is green
> the trees are on fire
> steel swallow nests
> wait on the swallows
> they don't fool us any more with flowers
> they cost us our arms and legs

now our arms and legs
dangle from the trees.

(Sachtouris 1977: 179)[24]

The last line harks back to Goya's *Great Deeds against the Dead* and the images throughout evoke the modern and postmodern anarchy that, it has been said, begins with Goya.[25]

Even a 'Seferian' poet like Takis Sinopoulos denies the possibility that fragments can be read in associative networks of myth and metaphor. They pile on each other, a clutter of objectness:[26]

Τοπίο θανάτου. Η πετρωμένη θάλασσα τα μαύρα κυπαρίσσια το χαμηλό
ακρογιάλι ρημαγμένο από τ' αλάτι και το φως . . .

Landscape of death. The petrified sea the black cypress trees the low seashore
ruined by salt and light . . .

Πέτρα και φως. Αλάτι και φως. Μια πέτρα ο ήλιος.
Σήμερα κι αύριο περιμένοντας την άνοιξη.
Άνοιξη ελπίζοντας, ποιαν άνοιξη
Το φως τι θα σου φέρει . . . Φως πάνω στο φως.
Τι θα σου φέρει η θάλασσα
και τώρα μεσημέρι με ήλιο – κάτω από
τον ήλιο η θάλασσα –
κατάμαυρο διαμάντι η θάλασσα.

Stone and light. Sea and light. The sun a stone
Today and tomorrow waiting for Spring.
Hoping for Spring, which Spring?
What will the light bring you? Light upon light.
What will the sea bring you
now mid-day in the sun – under
the sun is the sea
the sea a pitch-black diamond

(Sinopoulos 1957b:21)

Whereas 'Elytis resides in a landscape of life and the invigorating sun, Sinopoulos resides in a landscape of death and the corroding sun' (Sinopoulos 1979: 273).

The landscape of the leftist poets refuses to link images to a long-lost mythical or historical substratum. The titles of Anagnostakis' collections Εποχές (*Epochs 1– 2–3*) and Συνέχειες (*Continuations 1–2–3–4*) present him as spokesman for his times: '[his] dialogue with time is not in any way metaphysical . . . his struggle with time becomes specific, in matter and, above all, headlong. There is no attempt in Anagnostakis's poetry for the diachronic consolidation of time-in-its process' (Maronitis 1976: 40). In the tradition of the dialectic materialist, 'he breaks the epoch away from *historical continuity*, and the life from the epoch, and the work from the life's work. But the result of his construction is that *in* the work the life's work, *in* the life's work the epoch, and *in* the epoch the course of history are suspended and preserved' (Eagleton 1992: 121, original emphases). Anagnostakis's 'epochs' freeze his historical moment out of history; the lived moment resists its appropriation by the party, the continuum of Hellenism, or grand metanarratives. More orthodox communist poets intially ordered their own metaphor of the literal by the code or grand narrative of the teleological struggle for the liberation of the proletariat. Their fragments of experience are united by the totality of a marxist philosophy of history, wherein the poeticization of the literal resided in an 'experience,' reputedly, beyond ideology. Their poetry was, in defeat, founded on a metaphor of loss. The totality to be regained is to be found not in the absence of a past (Seferis), but in the projection of a lost future – a kind of reverse nostalgia. Yet this reduction of heterogeneous experience to narrative with a *telos* is rarely a feature of the work of the poets considered here. Even their early work is wary of such schemata. Anagnostakis had rejected the Stalinist line as early as 1946 and had been kicked out of the party for his Trotskyist sympathies.

The space left behind is filled with irony and self-criticism. Soon Alexandrou and Anagnostakis adopt a Cavafian tone to consider contemporary moments of decline, transition, and the anti-heroic.[27] Aris Alexandrou's 'Φρόντισε' (Take care that) harks back to the title of Cavafy's 'Ας Φρόντιζαν' (They Should Have Cared), but more directly to his 'Φιλέλλην' (Philhellene).[28] In this last poem, the barbarian king's affectation, demonstrated in his directions for a 'Hellenic,' aesthetically pleasing, epigraph for a coin is dialogized with Alexandrou's political directions for poetic composition. Cavafy's poem thematizes the aesthetics of coinage to connect artful reproduction with participation in relations of production and exchange. Alexandrou's poem seeks similar access from aesthetics to praxis at a time when, as Nietzsche once famously remarked in his *Genealogy of Morals*, 'metaphors are worn out and without sensuous power; coins which have lost their impressions and now matter only as metal. No longer as coins.' The interior monolgue or address to the reader is directed to an unspecified addressee:

Φρόντισε οι στίχοι σου να σπονδυλωθούν
με τις αρθρώσεις των σκληρών των συγκεκριμένων λέξεων.
Πάσχισε νάναι προεκτάσεις της πραγματικότητας
όπως κάθε δάχτυλο είναι μια προέκταση στο δεξί σου χέρι.
Έτσι μονάχα θα μπορέσουν σαν την παλάμη του γιατρού
να συνεφέρουν με χαστούκια
όσους λιποθύμησαν
                μπροστά στο άδειο πρόσωπό τους.

Take care that your verses have backbone
with the joints of sturdy and concrete words.
Strive so that they be extensions of reality
as every finger is an extension of your right hand.
Only in such a way will they be able, like the doctor's palm
to slap back into consciousness
all those who have fainted
                    before their empty countenance.

                    (Alexandrou 1981: 83)

The title's imperative reflects the unflinching and decisive nature of the proposed writing – the pen as ξιφολόγχη or 'bayonet' where words are natural objects in their own right. Like rap bands whose lyrics slice through the streets, or Mayakovsky's letter omicron which is like the barrel of a gun, this generation of poets strives for the complete identification, or contiguity, of the signifier with its signified, and its reenergization. Aris Alexandrou's 'Ποιητική' (Poetics) seeks just this:

Η κάθε μου λέξη
αν την αγγίξεις με τη γλώσσα
θυμίζει πικρομύγδαλο.

Each one of my words
if you touch it with your tongue
will remind you of a bitter almond.

Immediately, in the second half of this same stanza, Alexandrou focuses on the realities that such poetry does not capture.

Απ᾽ την κάθε μου λέξη λείπει ένα μεσημέρι
με τα χέρια της μητέρας δίπλα στο ψωμί και το φως που στάζει απ᾽ το παιδικό
κουτάλι στην πετσέτα.

From each one of my words
there is missing a mid-day with a mother's hand by the bread
and the light which dripped from the childhood spoon onto the towel.

                    (Alexandrou 1981: 60)

His poetry is unable to capture those now idealized and sentimental parts of everyday experience. Quite self-consciously, Alexandrou evokes that which he says he can not convey and, by deploying the highly metaphorized objects of bread and childhood spoon, stages the falling into an inescapable rhetorical trap.

Poetry and politics in the post-war

To thematize the intertextual nature of poetry, the non-transparency of the sign, and the danger of the word's capacity to refer only to other worlds in self-referential autonomy is an impeccably modernist venture. But it bears a qualitative difference from Seferis's modernism. For all the communist poets' debt to the modernists' use of free verse, idiom, rhythm, their anti-lyrical and unsentimental tone sets them apart and supports a historical consciousness that categorically resists Seferis's historical transcendence and existentialism (Orsina 1997: 63–74). It is precisely their devotion to the present moment that disallows the impulse to evoke an origin or speak of the end-point or *telos* of history. Both entities can not be imagined as long as one is able to talk of them. The material conditions of language predate reality and social conditions precede consciousness, and, consequently, the action of turning back or forward can not be projected beyond the material bounds of discourse. This insistence on spatiality and materiality lays bare the logocentrism and materialism of the symbol and the speaking Seferian voice. In one of his 'Parisian Poems,' Alexandrou sums up the poet's predicament and foregrounds the writerliness of perception:

Έγραψε ένα ποίημα με λέξεις καθημερινές
(δεντροστοιχία πέτρα κέλυφος χαρτόνι)
έχοντας την πρόθεση να το μεταφράσει
στη μητρική του γλώσσα.
Ανασέρνοντας μια-μια τις αντιστοιχίες
Απ' τον βυθό της μνήμης
αλλάζοντας τη διάταξη για να κρατήσει τον ρυθμό
προχώραγε στη νέα παραλλαγή με τόση ευτυχία
που σκέφτηκε να σκίσει την πρώτη γλωσσική μορφή.
Ξάφνου
ο ίσκιος ενός γλάρου πάνω στα νερά
του θύμισε πως όλα τα πουλιά της μακρινής πατρίδας του
είχαν αποδημήσει ή σκοτωθεί.

He wrote a poem with everyday words
(row of trees, stone, rind, cardboard)
with the view to translating it
in his mother tongue.
Drawing out the correspondences one by one
from the depths of memory
changing the order so as to maintain the rhythm
he proceeded to the new variation with such happiness
that he thought of tearing up the first linguistic form.
Suddenly
the shadow of a seagull on the waters
reminded him that all the birds of his far-off fatherland
had all migrated or died.

(Alexandrou 1981: 146)

The persona's self-absorbed process of composition is interrupted by the passing of a flock of segulls overhead. But this event, too, is determined not by direct eye contact with the gulls, but with a trace of the gulls on the water. This inscription shocks the persona into the real and out of his self-absorption, reminding him that the birds of his homeland, which are not those same gulls overhead, have migrated or died. In contrast to Seferis's *Mythistorema*, the trace that signifies absence is filled here more by the activation of a historical specificity than by nostalgia; it is an artifice that becomes a call to realization rather than metahistorical sublimity.

The danger that the poet may succeed in 'calling the wounded wounded,' is of no consequence. For if the poet is not allied to the people, and so alienated from his poetry, then such equivalence runs the risk of aspiring to an empty gesture. It carries no weight beyond the closed system of language.

> Ο ποιητής, ξεκομμένος απ᾽ τους πόθους του λαού
> καταντάει τελικά να μην πασχίζει γι᾽ άλλο
> παρά μονάχα πως να πει την προσωπική του αλήθεια
> καταντάει να λέει τις σφαίρες σφαίρες
> και τους πληγωμένους πληγωμένους
> κι όλο το πρόβλημά του στενεύει μες στα όρια
> μιας αναζήτησης σωστού λεξιλογίου

> The poet, separated from the desires of the people
> ends up toiling for nothing but
> the way that he will express his own personal truth
> he ends up calling bullets bullets
> and the wounded wounded
> and his whole problem constricts itself within the limits
> of a search for the right vocabulary

(Alexandrou 1981: 73–4)

The induction of poetry into life as well as life into poetry leads these poets to engage a number of strategies. Many poems, like the titles of collections cited earlier, use metaphors that point to the terrestrial or the very itinerary of armed struggle. In a Cavafian tone, Alexandrou's 'Νεκρή Ζώνη' (Dead-Man's Zone) discusses the relationship between poetics and ideology by employing a metaphor that hurtles itself *back into* the real. In other words, Alexandrou uses metaphors of literality that turn metaphoricity inside out:

> Με τις λέξεις σου να είσαι πολύ προσεχτικός
> όπως είσαι ακριβώς μ᾽ έναν βαριά τραυματισμένο που κουβαλάς
> στον ώμο.
> Εκεί που προχωράς μέσα στην νύχτα

μπορεί να τύχει να γλυστρήσεις στις κρατήρες των οβίδων
μπορεί να τύχει να μπλεχτείς στα συρματοπλέγματα.

Προς το παρόν, νάσαι πολύ προσεχτικός όπως είσαι ακριβώς μ' έναν μελλοθάνατο
που κουβαλάς στον ώμο.

With your words be very careful
just as you are when you carry a critically injured man
on your shoulder.
As you proceed in the night
you might slip on the shell holders
you might get caught in the barbed wire.

For the time being, be very careful
exactly as you are with a dying man who you carry on your shoulder.

(Alexandrou 1981: 100)

Though Alexandrou's poem does not solve the riddle of language or rhetoricity, it exemplifies a poetics where metaphor is interwoven into praxis; or, if you will, where metaphor and praxis are one and the same. Patrikios (1988) shares this sentiment when he asserts that poetry is both besieged by and besieges reality. It not only expresses a reality but also creates a reality of its own that functions within reality. Poetry may not bring about revolution:

Κανένας στίχος σήμερα δεν ανατρέπει καθεστώτα
Γι' αυτό εγώ δε γράφω πια
για να προσφέρω χάρτινα ντουφέκια

No verse today can overthrow regimes
That is why I no longer write
to offer paper rifles

(Patrikios 1988: 34; 'Οι Στίχοι 2,' 1957)

Yet retrospectively, in 1982, in his 'Οι Στίχοι 3' (*Verses 3*), he claims that poems do something, after all:

Όμως οι στίχοι κάνουν τη δική τους δουλειά
δείχνουν τα καθεστώτα, τα κατονομάζουν

Οι στίχοι δεν ανατρέπουν καθεστώτα
μα σίγουρα ζούνε πιο πολύ
απ' όλες τις καθεστωτικές αφίσες

Yet verses do their own work
they show up regimes, they name them

Verses do not overthrow regimes
but they certainly live longer
than all regime propaganda posters.

(Patrikios 1988: 33–4)

This generation is intensely aware of its predicament. It is suspicious of a language that seeks to tell the truth, yet it is still wants to tell the truth. Truth *is* a function of poetry, and the often noted rhetoricity and explicit moralism of some of Anagnostakis's verse testifies to this. Karen van Dyck (1998) has argued that his poetry was prone to the singular point of view characteristic of much Greek poetry, developed as it was in polarized political circumstances where paradigms survive agonistically. She argues this point by making use of Bakhtin's distinction between monologic and dialogic utterances where 'the important difference between these two types of discourse is that the dialogic, unlike the monologic, is *self-consciously* monologic – it makes us aware that its truth claims are partial. Of course the monologic also exists in relation to the discourses it suppresses, but it tends not to represent these different discourses' (Van Dyck 1998: 29). By referring to Bakhtin, van Dyck pits poetry's monologism against the dialogism of prose. Poetry imposes itself on its readers more forcefully, and its monologic style favors a singular point of view, while prose is more self-consciously dialogic for, like ordinary discourse, it encompasses different sociolinguistic registers' (1998: 28–9).[29] Anagnostakis's univocality and rhetoricity is not so different from Seferis, after all. But this view underestimates the way Anagnostakis undercuts the monologism he deploys. His most famous apology, his 'Poetics' (1969) confronts monologism directly to stage a dialogue between two generations of competing monologies:

– Προδίδετε πάλι την Ποίηση, θα μου πεις,
Την ιερότερη εκδήλωση του Ανθρώπου
Την χρησιμοποιείτε πάλι ως μέσον, υποζύγιον
Των σκοτεινών επιδιώξεών σας
Εν πλήρει γνώσει της ζημιάς που προκαλείτε
Με το παράδειγμά σας στους νεώτερους.

– Το τι **δεν** πρόδωσες **εσύ** να μου πεις
Εσύ κι οι όμοιοί σου, χρόνια και χρόνια
Ένα προς ένα τα υπάρχοντά σας ξεπουλώντας
Στις διεθνείς αγορές και τα λαϊκά παζάρια
Και μείνατε χωρίς μάτια για να βλέπετε, χωρίς αυτιά
Ν' ακούτε, με σφραγισμένα στόματα και δε μιλάτε.

Για ποια ανθρώπινα ιερά μας εγκαλείτε
Ξέρω · κηρύγματα και ρητορείες πάλι, θα πεις.
Ε ναι λοιπόν! Κηρύγματα και ρητορείες.
Σαν **πρόκες** πρέπει να καρφώνονται οι λέξεις
Να μην τις παίρνει ο άνεμος.

You're betraying Poetry once again, you will tell me,
The most sacred manifestation of Mankind
You exploit it again as a means, a pack mule
For your dark aspirations
And in full knowledge of the harm you provoke
As an example to the young.

It's for *you* to tell me what you've *not* betrayed
You and those like you, year after year
As you sold out your possessions one by one
In the international markets and country fairs
Until you were left without eyes to see, without ears
To hear, with sealed lips that do not speak.
In regard to what humane sanctities do you accuse us?

I know: sermons and speeches once more, you'll say.
Well then, yes! Sermons and speeches.
Words must be hammered in like **nails**
That the wind might not take them.

(Anagnostakis 1980: 102–3)

By the end of the second stanza, we are faced with two voices. The second voice reacts with righteous indignation to the essentialist admonishments of the Poetic (capital P) voice of the poem's first stanza. That first voice echoes Seferis's early Eliotic admonishments of ideological or political criticism.[30] Not without reason, then, van Dyck has labeled this voice the 'Seferis position' (1998: 45). It is somewhat parodied by its elevated use of the second person plural formal tone alongside an awkward purist idiom and the essentializing capitalization of the words Poetry and Man. The voice in the second stanza castigates the essentialists for selling themselves to foreign conceptions – ironically, the complaint most commonly made against leftist poets by the Right. For this affiliation has left them 'without eyes to see, without ears to hear, with sealed lips that do not speak.' These last two lines seem to be a direct attack on 'Seferis' himself. Notoriously, for the first two years of military rule in the Greek dictatorship of 1967, Seferis had chosen not to speak out against the dictatorship and only later, in the spring of 1969, released a statement entitled 'Toward a Precipice.' As a result, Anagnostakis sees this essentialism's paralysis and launches a humanist critique of its very humanism, its inability to voice true 'humane sanctities.' The attack is made in a moralising tone – even though its second person singular, familiar form provides a sharp contrast to the weighty self-importance of the first stanza's tone.

The exchange between the two voices is followed by lines set off from the body of the text in a manner typical of Cavafy's poems. Like all such Cavafian 'after-thoughts,' the relation of these lines to what has preceded is ambiguous and paratextual. If anything, the lines step outside the fray and set up a third space which transforms what has preceded from a structure of antagonism or symmetry to a contextualization that reconfigures and puts into question the marked original pair. Moreover, the marked opposition is collapsed by the ascription of both as 'sermons and speeches', pointing, if you will, to their discursivity. The opening 'I know' of the third section incorporates the reader's projected dissension to these positions. By so doing, it would seem to ally the reader with this third space's speaker. Of course, if one reads the second stanza as closer to Anagnostakis's own position, then the opening of the third space is also read as Anagnostakis's knowing response to two decades of criticism leveled at the slogan-like quality of his own work.[31] Regardless, this budding alliance between reader and persona is soon interrupted by the 'well then, yes!', even if its function is again unclear. Is what follows a fatalistic acceptance of the two prior positions' status as sermons and speeches and then, after a formal drop in the line, a separate assertion in altogether different terms? Or is the status of sermon and speeches accepted as unavoid-able – a necessary evil – that then characterizes the strident last two lines? Certainly, the latter explication is reinforced when one considers Ricks's observation of the affinity of these two lines to the biblical pronouncement alluded to near the end of Ecclesiastes (12: 11–12): 'The sayings of the wise are like goads, and like the nails firmly fixed are the collected sayings which are given by one Shepherd. My son, beware of anything beyond these. Of making many books there is no end, and much study is a weariness of the flesh' (Ricks 1995–6: 20).

Anagnostakis's final, firm assertion shakes off vigorously this metacritical pose to launch into an impassioned plea for the power of words. The boldface type reinforces the speaker's vigor even as it underscores the materiality of the words themselves. The 'nails' bore into the page even as Anagnostakis uses a metaphor to underscore the need for direct, lasting words. In just so doing, we have an instance of 'a rhetorical figure to undo a figure, a metaphorical nail to fasten his words' (Van Dyck 1998: 47). We are back to the same rhetorical trap. Even as the poet makes the most categorical of statements, his parabolic utterance takes flight elsewhere. Even as we seem to conclude with monologic certitude, the social and aesthetic foundations of monologic modes or discourses have been questioned and set into a dialogic relation (Bakhtin 1981: 314–15).

In 'Στο Παιδί μου' (To my Child), from the same landmark 1969 collection *The Target* this critique of monologism is taken a step further. Anagnostakis visits another stock idealized scene – a father reading to his son – to reflect on the generational transmission of knowledge or truths:

Στο παιδί μου δεν άρεσαν ποτέ τα παραμύθια
Και τού μιλούσανε για Δράκους και για το πιστό σκυλί
Για τα ταξίδια της Πεντάμορφης και για τον άγριο λύκο

Μα στο παιδί δεν άρεσαν ποτέ τα παραμύθια
Τώρα τα βράδυα, κάθομαι και του μιλώ
Λέω το σκύλο σκύλο, το λύκο λύκο, το σκοτάδι σκοτάδι,
Του δείχνω με το χέρι τους κακούς, του μαθαίνω
Ονόματα σαν προσευχές, του τραγουδώ τους νεκρούς μας.
Α, φτάνει πια! Πρέπει να λέμε την αλήθεια στα παιδιά.

My child never liked fairy tales
And they told him about Dragons and of the faithful dog
Of the travels of the Beautiful Princess and of the wild wolf

But my child never liked fairy tales
Now, in the evening, I sit and talk with him
I call the dog dog, the wolf, wolf, the darkness darkness
I point out evil men with my finger, I teach him
Names like prayers, I sing to him of our dead.
We've had enough! We must tell children the truth.

(Anagnostakis 1980: 104–5)

The task of speaking truthfully is plainly at issue again. The rhetorical repetition of line 1 is typical of how 'his and his generation's sparse, more direct language often relies on the figures it rejects' (Van Dyck 1998: 45). Yet does one equate the cumulative mythology of ll. 5–8 to the competing tradition of ll. 2–3 as the two voices do in the previously analyzed poem? The gradual aspiration to tell the truth leads the speaker, in the second stanza, to go over the ground he has covered with his son. Indeed he goes so far as 'to sing about our dead.' The abrupt exclamation of the final line opens up the third space and the possibility of two retrospective readings: that the speaker has broken off abruptly in recognition that his own idealizations of ll. 5–8 are taking a fairy-tale-like, or self-mythologizing, air that makes them untrue and not unlike the earlier fairy-tales. Or is this to be read as a reaffirmation of the poem's lesson: i.e. that we should, and are in ll. 5–8, telling the truth? The poem ends then with the restatement of the need to tell the truth. But has this truth been conveyed in the poem? Perhaps, it is illogical for a father to seek to avoid fairy-tales in a context – a bedtime reading to his child – that is the traditional site for precisely this kind of activity. Perhaps poetry, clothed in the metaphor of the fairytale, is not the place for such meddling with truth. Or is it the exemplary staging ground for such evocations of the truth?

From the early 1950s on, these poets repeatedly turn monologism on its head. Yet they do so in very different ways. Exasperation, irony, self-parody are conveyed in a number of humors. Alexandrou titles his third and final collection of the 1950s *The Straightness of Roads* (Ευθύτης Οδών), announcing to one and all the very straightforwardness which it seeks to undercut. In its most progressive stage, leftist poetry recognizes itself as a continual transformative practice that undoes the workings of all power. The terms of monologism are undercut and the poetic voice turns in on itself. How else could it be in an environment where so many communists were asked to sign a Note of Repentance – a formal, state-mandated admission of their repudiation of all they had done and all that they had believed, apologizing, in effect, for who they were and – probably – remained! Many had signed this assertion, but how? At what price?

Michalis Katsaros's anarchist 'Η Διαθήκη μου' (My Will) is altogether more upbeat. In this memorable poem, Katsaros's incantatory 'Resist' is directed as much against revolutionary planning committees as it is against the state apparatus. It addresses all authority. Katsaros even undermines the poetic subject as he asserts no less than five times that one should resist 'even to me, even me who tells you / resist.' Katsaros is didactic in telling us to refute everything didactic; monologic in his condemnation of monologism; teleological in his rejection of teleology. I cite from the fourth stanza:

> Αντισταθείτε στις υπηρεσίες των αλλοδαπών
>   και διαβατηρίων
> στις φοβερές σημαίες των κρατών και τη
>   διπλωματία
> στα εργοστάσια πολεμικών υλών
> σ' αυτούς που λένε λυρισμό τα ωραία λόγια
> στα θούρια
> στα γλυκερά τραγούδια με τους θρήνους
> στους θεατές
> στον άνεμο
> σ' όλους τους αδιάφορους και τους σοφούς
> στους άλλους που κάνουνε το φίλο σας
> ώς και σε μένα, σε μένα ακόμα που σας ιστορώ
>   αντισταθείτε.
>
> Τότε μπορεί βέβαιοι να περάσουμε προς την Ελευθερία.

Resist the immigration service
    and passport control bureau
the terrifying flags of states and
    diplomacy
the factories producing military weapons
those who call precious words lyricism
martial songs
treacly songs with laments
spectators
the wind
all the indifferents and the wise
those who pretend they are your friend
even me, even me who tells you
    resist.
Then, we can with certainty pass on to Freedom.

(Katsaros 1986: 233)

The ultimate paradoxes of rhetoricity are flung back in the face of critics as the rhetorics of paradox. Poetry and the poet, in reclaiming a voice, negate their claim to poetry's inalienable right, its special place in the regime of the word. Instead they confront the rhetorical quandary by stripping down the world and the poem to its barest necessities. Ultimately, these poets look to recreate a vital time, described by Anagnostakis as a time when 'poems are written without sounds and words.'[32] 'Bare words, denuded, that show their bones' reveal best 'the anatomy of everyday things' (Anagnostakis 1981: 21). In Anagnostakis's case, the impossibility of this Ideal leads to a gradual withdrawal into silence. His later writings in collections such as *Margins '68–'69* (Περιθώριο 68–9), and then the fragmentary postscripts of *P.S.* (Υ.Γ.), are stepping stones toward the limbo of silence as a political position. Action and silence are equally drastic forms of expression in life's monstrous circumstances, contradictory but able to transcend the bounds of the word, or not even come anywhere near them (1982: 54). 'Silence is itself an expression . . . a form of action' (1997: 22).

The men to whom these voices belonged, spent years in detention camps: appropriated, contained, and interpreted by the state, their individuality homogenized by its objectification and its appropriation by the language of the state. Their actions entered, over a period of time, into the the official narrative of the Greek state. The communist parties were reinstated on the overthrow of the military dictatorship, many of those exiled to the Soviet Union and the Eastern bloc were repatriated and given state pensions by Papandreou's socialist government in the early 1980s. In 1989, the communists even entered into a coalition government with conservatives for a short spell of political 'catharsis' targeting the socialist government's alleged corruption.

Today, many of these poets have been recognized as significant, canonical poets. Some now serve on state literary award committees. Patrikios's proleptic verses forewarned of this day, when the poetry of the post-war generation would be appropriated by the state:

Σκέψου αύριο τους στίχους σου
να τους περιμαζεύουν σε ιδρύματα
να τους αναμορφώνουν, να τους πειθαρχούν
και να τους παρατάσσουν σ' επίσημες εκδόσεις.

Consider your verses tomorrow
gathered together in institutions
constantly being re-formed, disciplined
and then paraded in authorized publications.

(Patrikios 1990: 208)

'It is not enough that we politicize our verses': Elytis's *Axion Esti* – Religion and Metaphysics over Aesthetics and Politics

A period of reconstruction followed the communist defeat in the civil war. In 1949, 10 percent of the population was homeless and about a third of the population was wholly dependent on the state for daily sustenance. A series of rightist governments, backed by American aid, sought monetary stabilization and investment in Greek infrastructure while the economy saw an impressive *per capita* income growth of 5.5 percent and a consistently high rise in GNP. However, Greece's conservative governments ruled with police state tactics, there were frequent purges of leftists, and the King meddled in affairs of state. Rampant emigration further depopulated a countryside that had seen the expulsion of communists behind the Iron Curtain after the civil war. Modernization, represented by the rapid and uncontrolled urbanization of Athens, gripped the country's consciousness.

Many artists wished to affirm cultural independence from this Westernization. The impulse was hardly new. And, as in the previous century, Orthodoxy and Byzantium were called forth to establish a counter-hegemonic narrative of Greek social history. We need only recall that Skliros's opening sentence in *Our Social Question* assigns pride of place to 'Byzantium, to which we have the greatest historical and psychological relation' (Skliros 1976: 109). Leftists have claimed Orthodoxy, albeit begrudgingly at times, as a wedge against assimilation into European or Western models. There was a populism behind this tendency. Indeed, leftist movements were not alone in seeking out a populist crutch on which to prop up their alternative society. The 1930s modernists also incorporated a nativist or autochthonous strain. *Nea Grammata*'s special issue in 1938 devoted to Pericles Yannopoulos is a case in point as is their championing of demotic and folk idioms. By the mid-1940s, the form of their populism was being attacked in the pages of *Nea Estia* by the critic Takis Papatsonis in an article titled 'Our Glorious Byzantinism' (1948). In it, Papatsonis attacked the 'Western' Seferis and Elytis and advised them to seek renewal in the Byzantine soul, its religious typologies, and not in the demotic and folk tradition. By the 1950s, the promotion of Byzantine forms marked the work of many modernists – the architectural patterns of Demetris Pikionis, Yannis Tsarouchis's painting, the Eastern qualities to Mikis Theodorakis's early musical compositions.

Ironically, the most complete expression of this Byzantine and Orthodox vision was Odysseas Elytis's *Axion Esti* (1959), generally regarded as the last *magnum opus* of Greek poetry. When it was set to music by Theodorakis in 1964, it became a national hymn. It eventually brought Elytis worldwide acclaim, reasserted a Romantic and prophetic notion of the poet's voice, and satisfied Greeks' craving for a return to normalcy. Belatedly, 'the Poet's continuity, interrupted by the war, [was] reinstated, enriched with this new element: the consciousness of duration . . . an undefinable long past which he carries with him deep in his entrails' (Zographou 1973: 47). This regained sense of continuity marks work in the late 1950s and early 1960s.[33] Yet, *Axion Esti* is rarely read in relation to other poetry of the 1950s, let alone to the work of the post-war generation. This is curious as *Axion Esti* not only redeemed the occupation and civil war experience for all Hellenism, but it also transubstantiated the leftist poets' experience into the long *durée* of Hellenism. This redemption, or *apocatastasis*, unfolds in a poem whose form is modelled largely on the Greek Orthodox ecclesiastical tradition. And though the poem ranges over the whole Hellenic tradition, Eastern Orthodox and Byzantium assume a prominent place. The title, *Axion Esti*, alludes to a Byzantine hymn glorifying the Virgin Mary as well as a famous icon to be found on Mt. Athos. The poem's formal use of *kontakia*, troparia, and antiphons of the Divine Liturgy of St. John Chrysostom provide a fitting context for the passage through its three 'Genesis,' 'Passion,' and 'Gloria' sections. The reader is led from Christ's 'Passion' through Resurrection and toward the affirmation of the Eternal in every corner of the Greek landscape.

It had been a long time since Elytis himself had fought on the Albanian Front in 1940. He had been silent about that experience from 1945. Now, finally, in 1959, he was to address these memories in the 'Passion' section of his *Axion Esti*. The 'Passion' section consists of psalms in free verse, odes in metrical stanzas, and readings in prose rendered 'with all the realism of an untransubstantiated present' (Lyhnara 1980: 59). Each resonant *anagnosma*, or scriptural 'reading,' is inserted between two Odes and this again by four Psalms. It is within these lyrical forms that Elytis sets about to reunite fallen signifier with transcendent signified. In the poem's most celebrated and most sung stanza, the 'swallow' is set once again to herald the Spring:

Ένα το χελιδόνι   * κι η άνοιξη ακριβή
Για να γυρίσει ο ήλιος   * θέλει δουλειά πολλή
Θέλει νεκροί χιλιάδες   * να 'ναι στους Τροχούς
Θέλει κι οι ζωντανοί   * να δίνουν το αίμα τους.

Θε μου Πρωτομάστορα   * μέσα στις πασχαλιές και Συ
Θε μου Πρωτομάστορα   * μύρισες την Ανάσταση

A solitary swallow   * and Spring's great worth is found
It takes a lot of work   * to make the sun turn round
Their shoulders to the Wheels   * it takes a thousand dead
It also takes the living   * to offer up their blood.
. . .
God my greatest Masterworker   * You are in Easter lilacs too
God my greatest Masterworker   * You smelled the Resurrection's dew!

(Elytis 1980: 39, *Ode* δ ')

Elytis was certainly conscious of criticism his earlier work had received from 'engaged' poets, and this is obliquely referred to in 'Psalm I' from the 'Passion':

Καταπρόσωπό μου εχλεύασαν οι νέοι Αλεξανδρείς ιδέστε, είπαν, ο αφελής περιηγητής του αιώνος!
. . . Που όταν όλοι εμείς πενθούμε
αυτός ηλιοφορεί.
Και όταν όλοι σαρκάζουμε,
ιδεοφορεί.

The young Alexandrians mocked me to my face:
Look, they said, at that naive tourist of the century!
. . . When we all mourn
he wears the sun.
And when we all scoff,
he wears ideas.

(Elytis 1980: 48)

The young Alexandrians, poets who modeled themselves on that infamous Alexandrian Cavafy, had derided the poet. Elytis responds by presenting himself as a poet free from social and ideological constraints. His early surrealism had, after all, been seen as synonymous with a carefree, sunny temperament – 'he wore the sun' (Lyhnara 1980: 75–6). His blithe ethereality met with the sarcasm of his peers. He wore ideas, ιδεοφορεί, a neologism which in Greek sounds remarkably close to αδιαφορεί, 'to be indifferent,' and we scoffed at him, σαρκάζουμε, a word in Greek that contains the root σάρκα or body, flesh. Read as a response to the leftist poets, Elytis is in effect interposing *their* 'Passion' between his Genesis and 'Gloria' sections. To achieve this, Elytis suppresses or collapses the hardships of the resistance and occupation and overlooks the divisive civil war years so that the final resurrection will more easily transubstantiate all Greek people's experiences and sufferings into the continuum of a depoliticized, regenerative Hellenism:

> πάντα πάντα περνάς τη φωτιά για να φτάσεις τη λάμψη
> Πάντα πάντα τη λάμψη περνάς
> για να φτάσεις ψηλά τα βουνά τα χιονόδοξα.[34]

> Always you pass through fire to reach the glow
> Always you pass through the glow
> to reach the high snow-resplendent mountains.

> (Elytis 1980: 40; 'Psalm E ')

In the Gloria section, Elytis glorifies the mystic, spiritual, and quintessentially Hellenic potentiality of all small objects: Αυτός ο Κόσμος ο Μικρός ο Μέγας ('this Small World the Great'). Elytis reasserts a metaphysics of metaphor, one different in its constitution from the classicizing and Westernizing Seferian meta-narrative of the 1930s due to its avowal of a predominently mystical Orthodox and formally Byzantine Hellenism. By the final psalm of the 'Passion' section, the Greek earth and stones have been reinscribed with luminous Text once again:

> Χτυπά η καμπάνα του μεσημεριού κι αργά
> Στις πέτρες τις πυρρές χαράζονται τα γράμματα·
> ΝΥΝ και ΑΕΙ και ΑΞΙΟΝ ΕΣΤΙ.
> Αιέν αιέν και νυν και νυν τα πουλιά κελαηδούν
> ΑΞΙΟΝ ΕΣΤΙ το τίμημα.

> The noon bell strikes and slowly on the sun-red stones these letters are carved:
> NOW and FOREVER and AXION ESTI.
> Forever and ever and now and now the birds sing
> AXION ESTI the price paid.

> (Elytis 1980: 70; '*Psalm* IH ')

The poem is not held back by a modernist anxiety over its own referentiality. It strives for full expression and so privileges metaphysics over aesthetics. In this, *Axion Esti* resembles an essay published at the same time, the philosopher Zissimos Lorenzatos's 'The Lost Center,' which also rejected the compatibility of Western aesthetics for Greek reality. It, too, proclaimed an alternative Eastern, Orthodox metaphysic more sensitive to Hellenic experience and thought. This essay has since been seen as the cornerstone of a movement, the so-called 'Neo-Orthodox Movement.' This movement promoted an Orthodox-inspired philosophy and culture for Greece and emerged at about the same time as Elytis's formulation of Hellenism in his *Axion Esti*.[35] Its influence in Greek intellectual life has continued intermittently down to our days. In retrospect, it was galvanized by the previously cited charismatic blend of leftism and Orthodoxy, a curious marriage that legitimized itself in its wish to repress other more authoritarian Helleno-Christian ideals.

Of course, Elytis was not concerned with the spread of Orthodox religion and thought in the practical way that Lorenzatos was, nor is there any biographical suggestion of his formal affiliation to the Neo-Orthodox Movement, which was anyhow a very loose affiliation of public intellectuals. However, the affinity of the two men's discourses is telling at this time of Western consolidation. Both call for the abandonment of foreign models for understanding Greek reality (Lorenzatos 1980: 110). Both deem that the crisis can not be solved in aesthetic terms (112). Lorenzatos considers Seferis and Cavafy's modernist reformulation of poetics a noble yet misguided response to this impasse, for 'they never for a moment put into question poetry itself' (111). From the work of Karyotakis to the present, Lorenzatos censures a state of 'fallen' modernism. Only the passage from the aesthetic function to the metaphysical function, 'art . . . baptized in the waters of faith,' will help locate 'the "deep-rooted foundations of the race and nation" and the "voice of our country," there to locate and discover, eventually, the "fount of life itself"' (136). The Westernizers' naturalistic and anthropomorphic perspective can not aspire to totality, but only to 'a kind of mystical worship of the visible world' (138). Even Seferis, whom Lorenzatos looks upon with great empathy, was unable to attain the inner light, had failed 'to express this basic thing.' His 'self-projection of European *rationalismus* on ancient Greece' and his presumption that Greece was a land without mystics was flawed. To redress Seferis's misperception, Lorenzatos gives an account of the older Greek-speaking world's (in particular Syria's) tradition of Christian mysticism and describes the exportation of this tradition from the *sketes* to the West, where Western mystics adopted and cultivated it while Greeks lost and have yet to regain and reappropriate it for themselves. Lorenzatos's narrative is reminiscent of Seferis's account of 'Greek Hellenism' in his essays. The specific mention of this mystic power's dormancy in the West parallels Seferis's depiction of the Hellenic seed that had deserted Greece in the period of Ottoman rule and which had found a new home in the Renaissance West. There, it served as a universally applied aesthetic framework for all humanists. Lorenzatos's narrative is founded on the same principle of unbroken genealogical continuity; it differs in taking a detour by way of the Orthodox Church Fathers. Consequently, his hope for the lapsed Seferis is as benevolent as it is revealing: 'My brother, I pray that you may find it, this basic thing, this foundation of life, "the ultimate of aspirations," to quote from a Hesychast text' (139).

This reference to the Hesychasts alludes to an Orthodox mystic belief in 'Light mysticism,' as postulated by the greatest of Byzantine mystics, St. Symeon the New Theologian (949–1022). This belief, further elaborated in Gregory Palamas's (1296–1359) doctrinal defense of the Hesychasts of Byzantium, maintains a materialist basis for seeing God. For him, the apogee of mystical experience was the vision of Divine and Uncreated Light, i.e. pure essence. Barlaam the Calabrian attacked this view by restating God's total 'otherness' and unknowability: for God, he argued, could be known only indirectly. In response, Palamas defended the Hesychasts by establishing a distinction between the essence and energies of God. The Hesychast vision of God did not undermine the apophatic doctrine of God because the body, the physical, was adjudged to be part of the holy, since the whole of man was created in the image of God and Incarnation 'made flesh an inexhaustible source of signification.' Quoting St. Basil and the Cappadocian Fathers, Palamas maintained that God is knowable from his energies, but not His essence. Unknowable in his essence (*ousia*), these energies were conceived of as God himself in his action and revelation to the world – i.e. God's immanence and continual presence in the physical world (Ware 1963: 75–9). The West customarily sought a source; the East and primitivistic religions, as well as Lorenzatos and Elytis, sought manifestations of that source. Certainly, the sight of this divine light prevails as the key theme in many of Elytis's earlier short poems.[36]

Clearly the relation of the senses to matter or the world is central to Elytis's world view. As Bertrand Russell once said, matter in philosophy may have been the name of a problem. And, from his poem 'Aegean' to the 'Gloria' section of his *Axion Esti*, and even as late as his Nobel acceptance speech, Elytis confronts this philosophical problem for deciphering the Divine in the world. Often his notion of the Divine seems synonymous with the Hellenic. And in these cases, the *apocatastasis*, or redemption of matter, a tenet of Orthodox teaching often applied in the theory of icons and the Holy Trinity, governs his outlook. The stones inscribed at the end of the *Axion Esti*'s 'Passion' section, and the doxology of every corner of the Greek earth and its redemption in the 'Gloria' section amounts to a mystical transubstantiation of the Greek earth and experience. In a liturgical poem such as this, the Epiclesis, or the Eucharistic scene, of the Poem signals the change after consecration – the actual change of the Body and Blood of Greece into the Body and Blood of the Divine. The *metousiosis*, or transubstantiation, sometimes also referred to as a *metapoiesis*, leads to the revelation of the very True Body of Hellenism.[37] Furthermore, since Orthodoxy does not define the manner in which the bread and wine are changed into the Body and Blood of the Lord, what is important is the fact of the change. The act of transubstantiation remains a mystical event understandable only to God. All that is signified is the fact of the real and true change in substance by intervention of the Holy Spirit, when the *ens in alio* turns into the *ens per se* and is in and of itself (Ware 1963: 290–2). Following St. John of Damascus, the change in the elements occurs truly, really, and substantially (Fouyas 1972: 188–9). The divine act is unverifiable, a hypostasization beyond interpretation and language, the act that simply *is*! It is the liturgical and eucharistic function of the Poem that bestows an eschatological transcendence of the bio-logical hypostasis, be it the body or the medium of language. The poem functions as a site of eucharistic assembly, a divinely instituted rite wherein a supreme community is summoned to manifest and communicate a sanctifying grace. No modernist quandary here. The fact of transubstantiation answers the leftist poets. In effect, Elytis's ritual response poses religion and metaphysical poetry in place of aesthetics and politics. Indeed, Elytis maintains this position firmly. He reiterates it at the conclusion of his 1979 Nobel acceptance speech:

> Can the senses through continual purification arrive at sanctification? If so, their analogies will be reversed on the world of matter and act upon it. It is not enough that we daydream with our verses. This is too little. It is not enough that we politicize them. This is too much. The material world is nothing more than a heap of matter. Whether the final outcome is a Heaven or Hell will depend on whether we are good or bad architects. If poetry assures us of something, particularly in *dürftig* times, it is precisely this: that despite everything our fate is in our own hands'. (Elytis 1999: 63)

Post-Nationalism and Post-Monologism

In 1969, Manolis Anagnostakis reflected on his generation's failure to impose its will in both political and poetic terms. In the poem 'Αν . . .' (If . . .) Anagnostakis stages an apology for his own brand of poetry. Poems, as written by others, do not coincide with the stuff of his own reality. His experiences and his poems, he apologizes in parentheses – always attacking from the margin and with irony – are unworthy of poetic discourse, as it is widely practiced. With a split voice, in a dialogue with himself, he considers his life, and the life of his cohorts, and its relation to poetry:

Αν – λέω αν . . .
Αν όλα δεν συνέβαιναν τόσο νωρίς
Η αποβολή σου απ' το Γυμνάσιο στην Ε' τάξη,
Μετά Χαιδάρι, Άη Στράτης, Μακρονήσι, Ιτζεδίν,
Αν στα 42 που δεν ήσουν με σπονδυλοαρθρίτιδα

Ύστερα από τα είκοσι χρόνια της φυλακής
Με δύο διαγραφές στην πλάτη σου, μια δήλωση
Αποκηρύξεως, όταν σ' απομονώσαν στο Ψυχιατρείο
'Αν – σήμερα λογιστής σ'ένα κατάστημα εδωδίμων –
άχρηστος πια για όλους, στιμένο λεμόνι,
Ξοφλημένη περίπτωση, όπως σε τόσους και τόσους
Συμμαθητές, φίλους, συντρόφους – δε λέω αβρόχοις ποσί
Αλλά αν . . .

(Φτάνει. Μ'αυτά δε γράφονται τα ποιήματα. Μην επιμένεις.
'Αλλον αέρα θέλουν για ν'αρέσουν, άλλη μετουσίωση.
Το παραρίξαμε στη θεματογραφία.)

If – I say if . . .
If it all hadn't happened so early
Thrown out of high school in your junior year,
Then Haidhari, St. Stratis, Makronisos, Idzedhin,
If at 42 you hadn't suffered from spinal arthritis
After those twenty years in jail
Burdened with two expulsions from the party, a statement
Of repudiation when they isolated you in the Psychiatric Ward,
If – an accountant in a food shop today –
Of no more use to anyone now – a squeezed-out lemon –
A closed case, with ideas long outdated,
If – I say if . . .
With a little good will all had panned out differently
Or out of some chance coincidence – as with so many other
Classmates, friends, comrades – I don't mean without difficulty
But if . . .

(Enough. Poems aren't written with such. Don't insist.
They need another atmosphere to please another 'transubstantiation.'
We've insisted too long on theme writing).

(Anagnostakis 1980: 118–9)

Lacking the right kind of transubstantiation, his poems make a different meta-phorical journey. The directness of his final assertion takes a page out of Katsaros's book as it undercuts its own claim by the very fact of the poem itself: 'poems,' like this one, '*are* written with such,' after all. The fact of the poem *is*.

With the fall of the dictatorship, Anagnostakis's poetry and the poetry of his generation, was received warmly by the young poets of the Generation of the 1970s (Papageorgiou 1989: 46–7, 60).[38] In a bout of revisionism they were hailed as precursors alongside Cavafy, Karyotakis, and minor 'Karyotakist' poets, like

Polydouri and Lapathiotis as well as the surrealists Embricos and Engonopoulos. The 1930s modernists did not go unmentioned, but did not predominate in this reappraisal. Seferis's denunciation of the junta in 1969 in a written statement was esteemed more than his poetry in some ways. Many, especially on the Left, deemed it as too little too late. Once Seferis passed away in 1971, Elytis remained the undisputed Greek National Poet until his death. In retrospect, Seferis and Elytis may well have been the last National Poets since they were the last poets to fight for the continuity and unity of Greek poetic voice. They were, as Tellos Agras once said, 'epigones of twenty centuries of poetry.' Greek poetry after 1970 developed organically as long as Elytis continued to publish poems. The *institution* of the National Poet outlasted national poetry: it hung on to the ailing body of Odysseas Elytis and so put off the theoretical redefinition of a post-nationalist Greek poetry. In practice poetic expression and semiology were steadily being redefined in journals and editions, but the retrogressive philological reflexes and narrowly nationalist aesthetics of much of the literary and critical establishment lagged far behind (Karalis 1992: 57). They marked time with structuralist taxonomies of poetic output, satisfying themselves with the labeling of literary generations by decades: the Generations of the 1960s, 1970s, and 1980s. This 'paternal genera-tional plan,' as one critic has put it, 'based on the fathering of texts and . . . characterized by the manhood metaphor . . . deals with the mode of perceiving literary evolution in terms of the generational pattern – [a] pattern tightly bound up with patriarchal society and kinship thinking' (Prinzinger 1992: 1). Other critics monopolized the dissemination of critical editions and unpublished material from letters and works of many of the doyens of the Generation of the 1930s' 'hismeneutic.' Wittingly or unwittingly, their shadow hovered above the scene, offering coolness for some and looming ominously for others. Concurrently, outside Greece, a small circle of philhellene critics and translators were publishing influential translations of Seferis, Elytis, and the modernists in the 1960s and 1970s. Much of the poetry appearing in post-1960s Greece did not receive much attention in the West nor did it enjoy quite the favor that the modernists had enjoyed.

In the mean time, poetic voice since Elytis's *Axion Esti* had splintered into micropolitical pieces expressive of social resistance in differentiated spheres of everyday life. These voices struggled with the legacy of the very dialectic dis-cussed in this book, only now the national had become transnational and the personal had become otherwise political and gendered. The 1970s poets, in particular, mixed traditions, American and Greek, to a degree unknown in years previous. Their anti-authoritarian, anti-capitalist, anti-conformist vision found a rich vein in the sarcasm and questioning of the first post-war generation. The mythical decadence, the pessimism and marginality of Karyotakis and Cavafy spoke to their 'doubt.' And a more personalized idiom in Greece mined the vagaries of 'social time' and rejected metaphysics. In a short triptych entitled 'Short and Bitter' (Σύντομα και Πικρά), one of the earliest women poets, Katerina Anghelaki-Rooke, epitomizes the use of her body as a source of signifying power.[39] Physicality is no longer a resisting symbol of 'otherness.' From the beginning of contemporary women's poetry, it connotes an empowering and meaningful presence:

Εξαντλούνται όλα τα πειράματα,
δεν υπάρχει τίποτα
ν' αντικαταστήσει το φως
τίποτα ν' αποτρέψει το σκοτάδι.
Ο δρόμος είναι ένας
και φέρνει σε κάτι μεγάλο και υγρό·
μυρίζει ψαρίλα
κι όταν χώσεις τα δάχτυλά σου
βρίσκεις το πηχτό σώμα τ' ουρανού.

All the experiments have been carried out
there is nothing
to replace the light
nothing to overthrow the darkness.
There is one way
and it leads one to something big and wet
it smells of fish
and when you thrust your fingers in
you find the sky's thick body.

(Anghelaki-Rooke 1978: 52)

The first line's sense of loss is expressed through purposefully clinical language, and the overtly muscular and sensual physicality of subsequent lines locate the solution to mental stagnation within the female body. If Elytis was renowned for saying that 'there is nothing to replace the light . . . there is nothing to replace the darkness,' then Rooke's indirect response to such etherealism lies in 'the thick body,' and even more earthily, in 'the smell of fish.' Rooke puts her finger on it in the third stanza – metaphysics is for men; contingency for women:

Οι περισσότεροι άντρες
είναι κακοί εραστές
του συγκεκριμένου.
Ας το σκεφτούμε καλά αυτό
πριν
ξαναερωτευτούμε τ' άστρα.

The majority of men
are bad lovers
of the specific.
Let's consider this well
before
falling in love with the stars.

    (Anghelaki-Rooke 1978: 54)

Women poets were crucial to this post-national departure. They had been left out of poetic discourse and needed to carve a space, create a language, and establish a presence in their own terms. Karen van Dyck's admirable book *Kassandra and the Censors* (1998) shows how women poets writing during the dictatorship exploited their long-term gendered repression and were able to capitalize on, and develop, modes of subversive resistance to the regime's demands for linguistic and ideological clarity. As a consequence, their poetry privileged poetic strategies trained on restoring the body and embodying experience in ways that recall priorities set forth by the male first post-war generation. Women poets, like Kiki Dimoula and Maria Laina criticize the inscription of narrative on the female body. Dimoula's early poem 'Mark of Recognition' (Σημείο Αναγνώρισης) (1971: 42) presents a statue of a woman and juxtaposes 'male' and 'female' definitions of woman and subverts their conventional valuations. The collective social 'they' identifies an observed female as an art object, inscribed by aesthetic values which 'petrify' her literally and metaphorically. This gaze is appropriated by the naming act. The 'they' that names the statue of the woman immediately objectifies her, while the 'I' of the poem sees 'a woman.' This 'I' remains outside the realm of objectifying abstractions and is deprived of words – she does not call but sees the 'other' as a living being, and not a statue. The contrast is sustained throughout the remaining stanzas and 'fleshed out' in relation to its implications for the body. The opposition not only defines the female as statue or as an aestheticized illusion caused by a distance produced by a word, but also indicates that captivity is a condition intrinsic to woman in a world mediated by the *logos*: 'I call you a woman because you always end up/a captive' (Dimoula 1971: 42). The persona identifies with the woman not because the sculptor surrendered her to the marble as woman, an *aesthetic* gesture, but because her hands are tied, a *social* circumstance. The affinity between marble and woman in the poem, both literally and metaphorically cut up, describes Dimoula's restricted expression within the 'male' monumentalizing word. Contemporary women poets' resistance and subversion of the male monumentalizing word provides gendered resolution to the Greek social poets' attempts to restitute Greek difference and spatiality from the abstracting and metaphorizing logos of national, 'monumental' poetry. It is not surprising that this female writing engenders a more *visual*, even cinematographic, text that draws attention to its fragmentation, its punctuation, ellipses etc. This formal concern for the materiality of the linguistic sign coincided with other 'experimental' movements in poetry and film-making, beyond Greece in the 1970s, that foregrounded concerns over the materiality of medium in an attempt to politicize fields historically perceived as aesthetic. I have in mind so-called Language Poetry or the Structural/Materialist film-makers.[40] By exposing the objectness of film or of the linguistic sign, these movements were disrupting the nonchalant claims of truth, exposing structure itself as a process of signification, and the broader political and social fabric of knowledge that underpinned it. The intention draws the women poets close to the concerns of the first post-war generation's male poems in suggestive ways.

The first post-war generation's discourse around everyday objects left its mark on the work of later poets. Poets of the 1970s generation – Poulios, Chronas, Steriadis – write poems about everyday items, obscene items in the context of a critique of commodification. Those living members of the first-post war generation still writing have recognized how their own language has not escaped its own metaphorization as well as its commodification. 'Demanding bread for the people' has reached its limit as the 'consumer' of this bread has become as bloated as the discourse that reproduced him:

Αναγκαστική πάχυνση των ζώων
αναγκαστική σίτιση ευτυχίας
όλοι μας τρώμε κατά κόρον
ακόμα διεκδικώντας ψωμί για το λαό
παχύναμε σε πλήρη ακινησία
κι όμως μετακινούμενοι
σαν επιβάτες προσδεμένοι αεροπλάνου
με προορισμό την επόμενη χιλιετία.

Mandatory fattening of animals
force fed prosperity
we all eat till we burst
still demanding the people's right to bread
we have fattened ourselves up by our slothful immobility
yet, regardless, we move forward
like airline passengers strapped in
on a flight to the next millenium.

(Patrikios 1988: 21)

Notes

1. English translations from Seferis's poetry are cited from Edmund Keeley and Philip Sherrard's two-language edition of Seferis's collected works, (see Seferis 1978). The English text has been reprinted in Seferis 1995.
2. For more on the shared formalist assumptions of the national and the aesthetic (in Greece), see Lambropoulos (1987).
3. From Seferis's 'An Old Man on the River-Bank' (Seferis 1978: 285).
4. Egypt was the home of the Greek king and government-in-exile during those occupation years. The Tyrrhenian coast alludes to Seferis's moving poem 'The Last Stop,' written at Cava dei Tirreni days before his return to Greece at the time of German withdrawal in October 1944. For an interesting appropriation of Seferis's experience by one of these leftist poets, see Patrikios's late poem 'Cava Dei Tirreni' (1988: 63). Pappas (1990: 91–4) offers critical and biographical background to the comparison.
5. The Germans saw Greece as a supply line for Rommel's *Afrika Korps*. They resisted deploying the extra resources needed to occupy and administer the whole country.
6. Seferis himself first makes this observation in his diary entry for 8 December 1944.
7. Other poets associated with this group are Dimitris Papaditsas, Tassos Livaditis, Hector Kaknavatos, Panos Thassitis, and Kostas Kouloufakos.
8. See Gourgouris (2000); also Raftopoulos's intellectual biography of Alexandrou (1996).
9. No better testament to this than a polite letter written by the venerable Gregoris Xenopoulos to Manolis Anagnostakis in his teens.
10. I use Jeffrey Carson and Nikos Sarris's translation, (Elytis 1998).
11. Maronitis (1987b: 68–80) situates this poem in the context of national poetry of the period. Nissiotis (1961: 5–6) sees the poem as an early working through of the *Axion Esti*, the *Axion Esti* 'in miniature.'
12. Originally, 'Η Αμοργός του Νίκου Γκάτσου,' Ξεκίνημα, τευχ. 4. Θεσσαλονίκη, 1944.
13. Unless otherwise noted, translations of Anagnostakis's poems are taken from Kimon Friar's translation *The Target* (1980). Translations of all three other poets are my own. Yorgis Sarandis's poem 'Poetry is Not' (Δεν είναι η ποίηση), in his 1963 collection Οι γειτονιές της οιμωγής, launches a similar attack: 'poetry is not/a closed off space for reverie/a path to the fruitless time of nostalgia . . ./it is the other side of things'.
14. See the poetry of Rotas and Vrettakos; on this point, see Ilinskaya (1986: 33–5).
15. See Patrikios's wariness of a 'mistrustful Spring' in his own 'Spring' poem (1976: 180).

16. The article appeared in Επιθεώρηση Τέχνης, τευχ, 106–7, Οκτώβριος–Νοέμβριος, 1963.
17. Vrettakos's defence is in Επιθεώρηση Τέχνης, τευχ, 118, Οκτώβριος, 1964.
18. Beaton (1994: 201) finds this attitude typical of the post-dictatorship 1970s.
19. These underlying theological assumptions justify the use of transubstantiation in this chapter.
20. Pappas (1990: 16–23) notes Patrikios's everyday vocabulary and naming of common objects. (He even gives a list of such common words in Patrikios's collection *Largo* of 1951.) This raw naturalism, he explains, is a consequence of Patrikios's great love for Karyotakis.
21. Vassos Varikas speaks of his disgruntlement at their inability to rework the ύλη (matter) of their poetry 'aesthetically' (*Vima* newspaper, 22 December 1963).
22. A faint allusion here to the closing scenes of *Macbeth* (V, 5–8) wherein Malcolm, Siward, and MacDuff's armies close in on Macbeth and order their troops to camouflage themselves behind boughs and furtively descend toward Macbeth's castle. In this way, 'Birnham Wood be come to Dunsinane' and one of Macbeth's protections against mortality is swept away. It is an appealing example of a folkloric *adynaton*.
23. Also an indirect response to Sikelianos's Ανάσταση (Resurrection) where swallows of death foretell a new Spring, that of 1821 Revolution.
24. For the relation of Sachtouris's poetry to other work of the period, see Dallas (1997) and Chadzivassiliou (1992).
25. For a related postmodern example, see Jake and Dinos Chapman's artwork by the same name. They replace Goya's three mutilated soldiers with shop-window dummies, the artists' trademark. The piece has been exhibited at the controversial *Sensation: Young British Artists from the Saatchi Collection* at Royal Academy of Arts, London (1997), Hamburger Hanhof, Berlin (1998–9) and the Brooklyn Museum of Art, New York (1999–2000).
26. Sinopoulos was a great admirer of Seferis. See his critical studies on Seferis (Sinopoulos 1983). He insists that Seferis was not a 'metaphysical' poet. He admires him for his 'sensuality' (96) and for his Cavafian 'direct sensual perception of thought' (77). This is, in fact, a term Seferis used to describe Cavafy in his essay 'Cavafy – Eliot: Parallels.' This 'sensuality' plays a fundamental role in Seferis's poetry, according to Sinopoulos, even when it conceals itself behind certain 'phrasal disguises or behind symbols.' For Sinopoulos, Seferis manages to blend the sensual and the cerebral so that the 'somatic becomes spiritual' in an equipose of qualities. It is this that makes Seferis aspire in his estimation to 'a sensuality beyond sensuality' (84), echoing a phrase used by Nikolareizis about Botticelli. I think Sinopoulos underestimates the power of these two elements and the effect of a mythical-historical backdrop in attenuating the sensuality of these images. Friar titles his

translations of Sinopoulos's selected poems *Landscape of Death*. These words open one of Sinopoulos's first poems 'Elpenor' (1951), a marginal Odyssean character who is a protagonist in the poem as he was in Seferis's *Mythistorema*. Sinopoulos's poem handles the mythical underlay in a different way to Seferis. Ritsos and Thassitis have also focused on this character: see Savidis (1981); Ricks (1989: 174–7).

27. See Alexandrou's Ο Μάρκος Φλάβιος εις εαυτόν, Δάμων ο εθνικός,, Εν Σταρτόπεδῷ, Katsaros's Κατά Σαδδουκαίων, Μέρες 1953, Περίπου το 30 π.χ. or, later in 1969, Anagnostakis's 'Νέοι της Σιδώνος, 1970, Θεσσαλονίκη, Μέρες του 1969 μ. Χ. Resisting the early marxist disdain for Cavafy's 'marginality' and 'decadence,' mostly as a reaction to his alleged homosexuality, these poets appropriated his language and tone in their work after their defeat in the civil war (Papageorgiou 1983). This was particularly the case in their criticism of the party. Stratis Tsirkas's (1958) works on Cavafy testify to this change in the party's attitude to him. In 1959, Anagnostakis was highly critical of Tsirkas's too deterministic and 'ideological' reading of Cavafy's work (Anagnostakis 1985: 59–61). Anagnostakis also adopted some Cavafian motifs and techniques much later than Alexandrou, though he was critical of Cavafy's homosexuality and what he considered as his 'didacticism' (1985: 53, 66).

28. The word 'φρόντισε' appears in the first line of 'Philhellene.' The tone is reminiscent of other Cavafy poems, e.g. 'Theodotos,' 'As Much as You Can.'

29. As a result, Van Dyck quotes Bakhtin's assertion that monologism insists on history and social relations as objects of representation, whereas dialogism 'simultaneously representing and represented' keeps history and social relations inside the text (1998: 29).

30. I have undertaken elsewhere a detailed analysis of the relation between the critical work of Eliot and Seferis (see Calotychos 1990).

31. The attack is one commonly made against resistance poetry, and the poet's response is reminiscent of the traditional response outlined elsewhere by a poet of FRELIMO, the Mozambique Liberation Front: 'our poetry is also a slogan. Like a slogan it is born out of the necessity, out of reality. While in colonialism and capitalism, culture and poetry were amusements of the rich, our poetry of today is a necessity, a song which goes out of our heart to raise our spirit, guide our will, reinforce our determination and broaden our perspective' (Searle 1982: 309).

32. Cited from Anagnostakis's poem 'You Came When I . . .' (1989: 103–4). In his 'Barer and Barer,' words and phrases are erradicated and inarticulation leads to the microscopic (1989: 148).

33. Ilinskaya (1986: 137–55) makes just this point by juxtaposing the *Axion Esti* alongside work by Yiannis Ritsos and Tasos Livaditis from just about this time.

34. Elytis returns to the very mountains of his own experience in the 1940s. He chooses the exact phrase he used in his *Sun the First*, III.

35. The writings of Stelios Ramphos and Christos Yannaras promote Byzantium and Orthodoxy with a nationalism and essentialism that resists Western values.

36. Consider the 'Seven Noctural Heptastichs' from Elytis's his collection *Orientations* (1979: 22–8).

37. Orthodox writers use the term transubstantiation. But, they grant equal legitimacy to *metousiosis, metabole, trope, metapoiesis* (Fouyas 1972: 189). Among these, transubstantiation has no unique place (Ware 1963: 289–92). Meyendorff (1974) comments that Byzantine theologians

    > would consider a term like 'transubstantiation' (*metousiosis*) improper to designate the Eucharistic mystery. They favor the concept of *metabole*, found in the canon of John Chrysostom, or such dynamic terms as 'trans-elementation' (*metastoicheiosis*) or 're-ordination' (*metarrhythmisis*). What is important is that the Orthodoxy does not define the manner of the change; but they insist on the fact. (Meyendorff 1974: 203–4)

38. The term 'Generation of the 1970s' is first used by the poet Vassilis Steriadis in the journal *Lotos* and refers to four or five poets in the early 1970s. 'A new generation of doubt' is proclaimed in Bekatoros and Florakis (1971). See also Panayiotou (1979); Meraklis (1987). For a discussion of the generation's poetics, see Van Dyck (1998: Chapter 2).

39. For more on the body as the key locus in female self-definition in Anghelaki-Rooke, see Bohandy (1994); more generally for Greek women poets, see van Dyck (1998).

40. 'Language poetry' was chiefly associated with contributors to the bimonthly journal $L=A=N=G=U=A=G=E$, which was started by Charles Bernstein and Bruce Andrews in New York, in 1978. 'Language poets' included the aforementioned as well as Barrett Watten, Nicole Broissard, Ron Silliman and others. Structural film-makers include Paul Sharits and Hollis Frampton, Malcolm LeGrice, and Joyce Wieland. See P. Gidal, *Materialist Film* (London: Routledge, 1989).

7

Love and Sex

The Influence of Anxiety among Friends (Henry Miller, Patricia Storace, and Lawrence Durrell do Greece . . . and Cyprus)

Για την Ελλάδα, ρε γαμώτο!
For fucking Greece![1]

Voula Patoulidou, gold medallist hurdler,
1992 Olympics

Modern Philhellenism

Hellenism and philhellenism are often confused. The ambiguity arises from the significant role that Hellenism played in the goals of philhellenism in the early nineteenth century. If Hellenism captures the European admiration for Greek antiquity, philhellenism denotes a belief in the rebirth of a liberated Greece achievable in large measure by virtue of its Hellenic heritage. In other words, cultural Hellenism is evoked by philhellenes and called into the service of realizing the national project of Greece in political terms.[2] A philhellene is 'one who admires or loves Greece or/and the Greeks.' Rhigas Pherraios, the hero of our first chapter, used the term 'philhellene' to describe anyone who wished, or was inclined, to contribute constructively to the fate of the Greek race, and not merely lament its enslaved fate.[3] Rhigas included himself and all diaspora Greeks in this category, though Michael Perdikaris clearly thought otherwise by titling a book *Rhigas or Against Pseudohellenes* (1811). More customarily, however, and especially after the revolution, the person 'philhellene' denotes is a non-Greek, who claims an interest in the fate of Greece and the Greeks. This seems straightforward enough, until one considers that historically Greece has functioned as a *topos* through which different European peoples have instituted authorizing narratives of authenticity, origin, and culture for *their own* national aspirations. The French Revolution built itself on Hellenism, as Barthélemy's work demonstrated. And yet while one acknowledges that antiquarian fantasies contributed to the Greeks' liberation from the Ottoman Turks at a time when the insurrections of other Balkan peoples were not successful, a price had to be paid realizing Greek modernity in this way. For the shocking 'Byzantinicized Slavs' whom philhellenes encountered were an irritating speck in the eye. This exacerbated an orientalist strain in philhellenic discourse, especially after the revolution, which only encumbered Greece's path to modernity. To many philhellenes, Greece was home to a contemporary civilization that was, 'defined *de facto* by decline in relation to itself and irrelevance in relation to other modern nations' (Leontis 1997: 126).

Much work still needs to be done on the different types of philhellenist discourse at the time, written from the perspective of different kinds of travelers, from different home countries and different walks of life. Clearly, many philhellenes were moved to support the Greek cause out of their devotion to classical aesthetics or philosophy. But Western political support for Greece was not predicated only on these grounds. British philhellenism, for instance, was even more concerned with the political dimension of a new Greece, its potential conformity to liberalism and the free market, its maritime importance, and its geopolitical significance for containing Russia and the Eastern Question.[4] Philhellene perceptions were, naturally, a symptom of the conditions of cultural exchange *and* political necessity. British travelers journeyed to Greece from a privileged position of surveillance, from a culture rising to the peak of its colonial powers, armed with a repertoire of fantasies that instituted Greece as an object of desire on a cultural scale. Gourgouris under-scores the colonialist nature of the traveler's relationship to Greece, one bound to a 'prescribed hierarchy in an exchange of glances' (1996: 133). Even Byron is no exception. One extract from his meditations considers the Greek fate through this lens: 'The Greeks will never be independent; they will never be sovereigns as here-tofore, and God forbid they ever should! But they may be subjects without being slaves. Our colonies are not independent, but they are free and industrious, and such may be Greece hereafter' (Gourgouris 1996: 138). Lord Byron exhibited many of the prejudices about modern Greece and the Greeks that British intel-lectuals shared during the eighteenth and nineteenth centuries (Keeley 1995: 111).

Yet the ultimate irony lies in the inescapable fact that Byron laid down his life for Greece, or for an idea of Greece. Whatever doubts underlay his relationship with the Greeks, these pale in light of the ultimate sacrifice of his death at Messo-longhi. In that swampy field, Byron aspires to the 'dissolution of boundaries between the gaze and the speculated culture/commodity.' In becoming like the object of his study –'a dead Greek' – Byron privileges an image of Greece, which, 'although phantasmic, is resolutely *modern*' (Gourgouris 1996: 138–9). Byron's exceptionalism, according to Gourgouris, lies in his commitment to a neohellenic modernity, to a conception of Greek culture as a Modern Greek culture that transcends the abstractions of western philhellenism. In this, he is far ahead of his time, as the philhellene tradition did not really value this *modern* Greek reality until the mutually sustaining impulse of Greek and Anglo-American modernism and modernists in the 1930s and 1940s. Edmund Keeley, a noted philhellene himself, translator and biographer of these very modernists, reserves this departure for Lawrence Durrell:

> [Durrell] was a pioneer in establishing what is now the prevalent mode of Anglo-American philhellenism, one that not only views Greece from an enlightened perspective but also finds more sustenance in the climate and culture of modern Greece than its ancient counterpart, or at least insists on bringing the ancient into juxtaposition as equally vital aspects of the Greek tradition – and the most enlightened would add the Greek world of Byzantium to this perspective as well. (Keeley 1995: 114)

This is a curious explication. Keeley's definition of modern philhellenism begins by prioritizing modern Greece over its ancient counterpart. But then, as the sentence unfolds, he takes a half-step back to speak only of juxtaposition and equality. Eventually, late in his meandering sentence, the even more 'enlightened' position described incorporates Byzantium and so, by sentence end, the modern culture is slotted once again in the full sweep of Hellenic culture. The impulse to privilege Greece's modernity is for philhellenes always susceptible, at every turn, to qualifications, equivocations, and outright contradictions.

Keeley singles out Durrell as the prime mover of this modern philhellene tradition for another reason too. With his youthful *Prospero's Cell* (1937) Durrell becomes 'the first important British writer to have approached contemporary Greece not with the idea of bringing to it more wisdom than he supposed he would take away, as appears to have been the case with Byron, but to enter the "dark crystal" of Greece, as Durrell once put it, and drink of what wisdom he found there' (Keeley 1995: 114). Curiously, while Gourgouris argues for Byron's ability to experience Greece in all its modernity, Keeley sees Byron as the epitome of one unable to do so. For Keeley, it is Durrell in Corfu who breaks down the distinctions of gazer and gazed and who identifies with, and draws from, the Greeks' gaze – it is Durrell who is 'reborn' *in* and *through* modern Greece. This disagreement over the identity of the first true modern philhellene raises issues examined in this chapter. Given the problematic exchange of gazes brought on by the ambivalence at the very core of the philhellene view of the Greeks, how can we weigh the significance of Byron's death and Durrell's rebirth in Greece? What kind of dynamics of exchange of authorizing texts and authenticating knowledge underlies the reciprocity or interaction of gazes?

This chapter does not aim to present the divers forms of philhellenism. In keeping with this study as a whole, it strives to contextualize the *reciprocity* of the gaze of outsiders and insiders, to trace the ambivalence, resistance and/or complicity in the *returning* gaze of the modern Greeks. Gourgouris's chapter 'The Punishment of philhellenism' in his *Dream Nation* begins to explore the underside, or the other side, of philhellenism – the effects of its orientalist, colonialist, and philological pedigree. Many travel narratives to this day follow these prescriptions. And while oftentimes stylishly written, inexplicably, they sport the delusion of originality. However, the gradual erosion of Classical education in the West on the one hand, and prevalence of tourism on the other, has led to more contacts between Europeans and Greece in ways that have made modern aspects of Hellenism recognizable to more people. Three examples of a genre intimately related to the philhellene tradition – the travel narrative– will here be examined to ask what kind of *philoi* are we, philhellenes and Greeks? Staging a coming together of foreign traveler and Greek native, Henry Miller's *The Colossus of Maroussi* (1941), Patricia Storace's *Dinner with Persephone* (1996) and Lawrence Durrell's *Bitter Lemons* (1957) will serve as templates for an examination of the complexities underlying the exchange of gazes in the modern philhellene tradition. This analysis comes at a time when Greeks, for all their swift strides toward European convergence and union, continue to concern themselves over their position in the West. Modernity creates fears when (phil)Hellenism is not there to protect Greeks. The ambivalence has led to an 'influence of anxiety' in Greece and the diaspora, a concern that Hellenism, loosely defined, is on the wane in the West. The influence of Martin Bernal's *Black Athena* (1987) on scholarly discussions set off a virulent Greek campaign that championed Mary Lefkowitz's 'philhellenic' rebuttals of his work. More recently, a second campaign sought to apprehend who killed Homer and marginalized Greek wisdom.[5]

I explore this 'influence of anxiety' by reading a text that commented on this very discomfiture and, as a consequence, was roundly criticized in Greece – Patricia Storace's travelogue *Dinner with Persephone* (1996). The maelstrom that greeted its translation into Greek is read alongside a work that could not be further removed from this atmosphere of anxiety and censure – Henry Miller's *The Colossus of Maroussi* (1941), which appeared in halcyon times for Hellenism and which is thought by some to have initiated modern philhellenism (Keeley 1999; Roessel 2002). The Greek modernists were generating intense interest among a Western literary and artistic elite. Miller's vision of Greece contributed much to this success in the days before Zorba danced, or stomped (depending on your perspective), on the popular imagination of the mid-1960s. Miller knew little about Greece. But his work became a touchstone of the neohellenic Ideal, received enthusiastically by Greeks and foreigners alike. It was written – let us not forget – at a time when fustanella-clad Greek soldiers routed Axis forces in Albania and when Londoners enduring the Blitz pinned miniature evzones on their lapels and sang 'Leave Mussel to the Greeks!' The 'garden salad' in American diners was to be renamed the 'Greek salad'! By contrast, Storace's highly acclaimed and beautifully written work appeared at a time when Greece was not at the forefront of European cultural interest and was even seen by some as 'the bully of the Balkans.'

Her by-no-means idealized depiction of Greek reality, and in particular her over-determined reading of a rampaging chauvinism, both masculinist and nationalist in the Macedonia-enraptured Greece of the early 1990s, met with profound Greek displeasure.

In the final section of this chapter, I consider a work by Lawrence Durrell. Not his early *Prospero's Cell*, but his later *Bitter Lemons* (1957), which was written in a strife-torn Cyprus in the mid-1950s. The work is considered an affectionate portrayal of Cyprus and the Cypriots; but an elegaic one all the same as it portrays the end of British rule over Cyprus. Durrell was serving in Her Majesty's Colonial Office in Nicosia, Cyprus. Yet he produces a book that is, according to him, remarkably enough, 'not a political book.' Like many works of modern Anglo-American philhellenes – indeed of the Greek modernists too, as we saw in Chapter 5 – it is a work that professes to avoid politics, a work of personal discovery (Roessel 2002: 273). It is important, then, as with Seferis, to unearth the politics submerged at the heart of its philhellene ethos. The confluence of politics, colonialism, and a love of Hellenism, is unique.

Taken together, Miller's (celebrated) *Colossus of Maroussi* and Storace's (momentarily notorious) *Dinner with Perspehone*, and Durrell's (lulling) *Bitter Lemons*, all try to reconcile Greek modernity to their respective understanding of the prevailing Greek legacy. Despite their different historical contexts, all three dramatize this contact by literally thematizing an exchange of gazes. The confrontation with the Greek assumes a central role in these writers' elaboration of their cross-cultural theorization of Greece and the Greeks. Namely, all three writers stage conspicuous scenes of encounter with a Greek male figure or a series of Greek male types. An analysis of this central *mise en scène* will allow us to examine the ways that philhellenism has molded the dynamics of Greece's place in the West, and philhellenism's place in the heart and minds of Greeks.

Persephone's Dinner with the Colossal Male Ego: Henry Miller and Patricia Storace do Greece (and the Greeks Return the Favor)

Patricia Storace's *Dinner with Persephone* (1996) received more than its fair share of coverage for a travel book on Greece. A pre-publication extract in the *New York Review of Books*, then a review by Jasper Griffin in the following issue, was soon followed by a celebrated literary prize. Storace, who had previously published only one slim book of poetry, was much in demand. Her reputation in Greece was a different story. Just before her book appeared in Greek translation, it was alleged that a long, and somewhat tedious, section of her book detailing the life of a turn-of-the-century Greek writer, Penelope Delta, had been substantially lifted from Delta's memoirs. Unlike Delta's other works, which were published before the then fifty-year copyright benchmark, extracts from two works had only recently been published by the Greek publishing house Ermis, and were subject to copyright law. However, Storace had not sought permission to use extracts either from the Ermis publishing house or from the Zannas family, legal executors of Delta's literary estate and archive. The passages, it was alleged, were at best paraphrases of the original; at worst – in places – word-for-word translations of the original. The executors sought explanations from the new owners of Pantheon Books, Random House. Before receiving a formal response, the imminent publication of the Greek translation by Kastaniotis Publishers prompted Mr. Zannas and Ermis, the holder of Greek language rights to Delta's work, to intensify their inquiries. Though they stopped short of demanding the publication's cancellation, the executors asked the Kastaniotis publishing house to include an acknowledgment of the specific chapter's sources. Kastaniotis, one of Greece's largest publishers and a seemingly unwilling participant in the imbroglio, delayed publication to allow executors and American publishers to work it out among themselves first. After some jockeying on the issue of incorporating an erratum to the second edition of the work in exchange for worldwide distribution rights, papers were filed in New York courts in the summer of 1998. The suit was eventually settled out of court, for a modest sum by all accounts, and the consent to an erratum in forthcoming editions.

This hubbub gratified many Greeks, both in the United States and in Greece, for many had developed strong opinions and objections to the book. A long article in *To Vima* newspaper in Athens (4 January 1998), for one, did not conceal its glee at these developments:

> So much toil and trouble, so many man hours, so much expense for a book? Indeed, for a bad one (*kako*) at that, which has already seen more than its fair share of publicity, albeit negative. It's a matter of moral propriety, say those involved. The truth is that if matters were the other way round, if an American claimant were attacking a Greek book, we would have been made to pay everything down to the very last dime. (Papayiannidou 1998)

The 'we' of the concluding phrase betrays the author's sympathies on the issue. The claim that Storace's book had earned bad reviews is far from the truth, at least for the English-speaking world and particularly in the American world of letters. It is more true of the book's Greek reception: the title of Demetris Mitropoulos's review, 'Coming in Strong from Alabama: The Unbearable Lightness of Travel Writing' (*To Vima*, 5 October 1997), gives a fair indication of the caustic criticisms that follow. The American writer's portrayal of Greeks as highly excitable, dogmatic and entrenched nationalists, wont to convey history as creed and not as history, did not go down well (207–8). In one episode of the book, Storace, like Kostas, the one male who earns her favor – if not her favors – shares the observation that 'Greeks have even less sense of history than Americans, only a kind of imperialism with the stories of the past . . . so blindly possessive of antiquity' (158). For Storace, individuality in Greece always comes second to the communalism of family and political life (38). Naturally, Storace would have probably perceived widespread empathy for her litigants among Greeks as further corroboration of this collect-ivism. Whatever the merits of the copyright case, the Greeks were trying to repossess Delta's story and restitute it back to its rightful owners. It was as if the early 1990s tussle over the Macedonian naming issue, so ubiquitous in Storace's book, were being replayed here in another bout of debate over authorization and rightful ownership.

From the perspective of her Greek detractors, Storace's negligence over Greek copyright reveals an imperialism of her own. In addition, her detractors charged that she spoke with little authority. One letter of protest from a regional Orthodox diocese in the United States to the Modern Greek Studies Association, faulted her understanding, as well as her inclination, toward Orthodoxy and concluded by stressing that 'this is, in the final analysis, the work of one American woman poet, and nothing more.' But who said that it was anything else? And if it isn't, who is endowing it with broader powers? Perhaps the vexed deliberations in Greece at the time between the then US Ambassador and the Greek Minister of Press and Information about the extent of piracy, copyright, and bootlegging of American rights in Greece place Storace's work into a broader cross-cultural battlefield.

Given this backdrop, the criticism was not only that Storace should have known *better*, but also that she should have known *more*. This, even though she does absorb a startling amount of material in her one-year sojourn in Greece and she makes no secret of her amateur status. But it is ironic that this issue of *knowing* should emerge when the genealogy of travel literature in modern Greece is pre-dicated precisely on the premise of knowing very little. Knowing the modern Greeks was built, after all, on ab-sense. The fraught struggle over the represent-ation, or propagation of images, of Greece, and the ownership of such images has always been at stake between philhellenes and Greeks, outsiders and insiders. This specific struggle will be examined by placing Storace *against* or *next* to Miller in terms of their interrelation of authorizing cultural narratives and gender, or their contact with colossal male egos.

The Large Devil and his Colossal Alter Ego

Miller sets foot in Greece in 1939. Norman Mailer, of all people, tells us that he was running away from 'woman troubles.' He was also turning his back on France and on European civilization. He relishes the first opportunity to berate a French woman in Athens: 'I don't like your high gardens with their high walls; the pretty orchards . . . the well-cultivated fields' (Miller 1958: 136). He prefers the alter-native of a sorely laden Greek donkey plodding along dejectedly. This nostalgic rejection of progress and the discontents of civilization comes on the eve of World War II. For Miller, civilization and progress will bring death; even for the Greek, according to Miller, who has not benefited in the least by such progress in his village. For the convenience of the use of spoons at his ripaste, the Greek would be asked to die for a degraded civilization.

Miller's impulse to travel elsewhere to seek out spiritual and moral renewal is predictable enough. All of Europe since World War I had been mining African art, the avant-garde, and the unconscious for a new illogicality that would wipe out the 'logic' that had led to World War I. Like Rebecca West, in her *Black Lamb and Grey Falcon* of the same year, Miller sought elsewhere the regenerative nobility that might erase the Munich compromise and offset the march of fascism and imminent disaster. Personally, 'the fuckabout misogynist' Miller's sojourn in Paris in the 1930s had seen him write through the Inferno of *Tropic of Cancer* (1934), the Purgatorio of *Tropic of Capricorn* (1939), and left him teetering on the brink of his Paradise, *The Colossus* (Jong 1993: 102). He was in search of a new rebirth, even though the thought did not inspire his critics. Robert Ferguson lamented: 'a second rebirth, coming so soon after the first one in Paris with tropic of cancer, might seem like one rebirth too many' (Jong 1993: 180). Miller's evocation of Greece was at odds with his prior work's landscapes, too: it is 'full of sea and sun, not slime and sperm' (Jong 1993: 18). From the copulation of clichés, typical of pornographic writing as Nabokov put it, Miller now populated his writing with spirit. The special relationship with Greece, as Freud noted atop the Acropolis in 1936, rooted deep in the cultural unconscious, leads Miller back to a subliminal threshold of childhood innocence: 'Greece is what everybody knows, even *in absentia*, even as a child or as an idiot or as a not-yet-born . . . It stands, as it stood from birth, naked and fully revealed' (Miller 1958: 153). Miller sees in Greece's light and poverty Lamartine's aura. In its paganism, a cultural denuding to first principles, Greece is 'home,' point Zero, the point of pure Vision, pure presence, and self-identity, where the word 'land' rolls over in the tongue and mouth and, in all vitality, and means 'a simple, eternal thing.' Most notably, Miller realizes this vision in the middle of the ancient theatre at Epidaurus: 'merely a place symbol; the real place is in the heart, in every man's heart, if he will but stop and search it' (Miller 1958: 80). There is a Buddhist concept of Nirvana at work here, a 'correct vision' of that which *is*, attainable through a vanishing of the I-process.[6] The self-centered Miller seeks to center his self in Greece, the center of the universe, his ego. But though such observations indicate that all travel narratives, are, ultimately, as Chateaubriand claimed in 1811, only about *moi-même*, Miller's narrative of self-discovery also depends on a moment when 'man meets man in the presence of God.' Miller strives for this in his relationship with the litterateur, George

Katsimbalis, the Colossus of Maroussi of the book's title. This meeting of men is typical of the new philhellenism, though untypical in that 'no other Western male author, including gay authors, has so submitted in print to the dominance of a Greek man' (Roessel 2002: 257). Miller apologizes for the colossal terms of introduction for Katsimbalis. Mercifully, he realizes that it is cheap to always resort to classical allusion to refer to, or legitimize, any individuated modern Greek. But there is 'something colossal about any human figure when that individual becomes truly and thoroughly human' (Miller 1958: 238).

Miller sees great continuity between land and people over the centuries, though he also very much wants to wrest a human Greek modernity from the diachronic sweep of its insistent genealogy. And so he glorifies the tumbledown shacks next to the Acropolis. Katsimbalis, too, carries with him both strands of tradition: like the country and the Acropolis, 'we had known him all our lives.' But Katsimbalis is also Greek modernity configured in all its fragmentariness and untotalizable effusion. His ungainly gait draws attention to his wounds from the Balkan wars. These represent a body marked by history, his scars an irruption on the surface of the phantasmic Ideal. He signifies not an Athenian order, purity and classical perfection, but rather a glorious anarchy: 'He was a curious mixture of things to me on that first occasion; the general physique of a bull, the tenacity of a vulture, the agility of a leopard, the tenderness of a lamb, and the coyness of a dove. He had a curious overgrown head . . . which, for some reason, I took to be singularly Athenian' (Miller 1958: 28). He is as sympathetic and ruthless as a boor, contradictory and human. Miller is drawn to Katsimbalis as man to man, or as this man to himself: 'He seemed to be talking about himself all the time, but never egotistically. He talked about himself because he himself was the most interesting person he knew. I liked that quality very much – I have a little of it myself' (Miller 1958: 28). Katsimbalis's speech, his free associations on every topic overwhelm the assembled company of men, 'a spread eagle performance about the clear atmosphere' (Miller 1958: 39). On one such occasion, arising from a dreamy, shaman-like state, Katsimbalis takes verbal flight off the Athenian verandah in Rabelaisan monologue. Miller, who has been looking at him admiringly from up above, is transported by Katsimabalis's voice to the scene around:

As he talked I was taking in for the first time with my own eyes the true splendor of the Attic landscape, observing with a growing exhilaration that here and there over the bare brown sward, amidst anomalous and eccentric growths, men and women, single solitary figures, were strolling about in the clear fading light, and for some reason they appeared to me as being very Greek, walking as no other people walk, making clearcut patterns in their ethereal meanings, patterns such as I had seen earlier in the day on the vases in the museum. There are so many ways of walking about and the best, in my opinion is the Greek way, because it is aimless, anarchic, thoroughly and discordantly human. (Miller 1958: 39)

In this passage, the interchange of foreground and background allows Miller to signify the true meaning of Katsimbalis for/as Greece. Just as Katsimbalis's persona engulfs and organizes the landscape around him, so too Miller assimilates modern Greek difference (amidst anomaly and eccentricity) through a cultural narrative that hearkens back to ancient ethereality and purity. In this aspect, the scene oddly recalls for me the scene excised from the original version of the late Stanley Kubrick's *Spartacus*, where a boyish Tony Curtis rubs Laurence Olivier's back in the bath. The homosexual innuendo of their dialogue, conveyed in the power differential between a slave and a Roman general, continues as they walk from the bathroom to a second room. There, in the background, Roman hoplites make their way up the hill on their way to fight for Rome. Olivier's suggestive and leading questions, which try to determine whether the beskirted Curtis likes oysters or clams and whether it is wrong for 'one' to like both oysters and clams, still hang in the air as Olivier begins to comment on the army's march in the background. The effect is to draw the two discussions together and impress the homosocial and homoerotic impulses driving the army, in the *polis*. The analogy I make to Miller is somewhat free in its detail, but suggestive nonetheless of the way in which Miller's passage depends on a cinematic focusing on and interplay between foreground and background. Those solitary citizens, the modern Greeks, exemplified for Miller by the superiority of the modern Greek gait, ultimately signify – like the hoplites in *Spartacus* – only once they have been recuperated in the aesthetic depiction on antique vases and, by association, the *polis*, of Greece. Analogically, the modernity of the new Greece is recuperated in the antique, its very restive modernity, is still intelligible in reference to its diachrony. As Miller's attention gradually fades back into the rhythms of Katsimbalis's cadences on the balcony, Miller reads Katsimbalis in a similar way: this man takes on the proportions of a Colossus: 'a figure that had outgrown its human frame, a silhouette whose reverberations rumbled in the depths of the distant mountain sides' (Miller 1958: 40). His archetypal voice, a torrent shot out of his body, for all its inextinguishable and indomitable energy, becomes itself inscribed in the sacred earth.[7]

Miller's reading of Katsimbalis, in fact, exemplifies textual tropes and strategies reminiscent of the Greek modernists. Katsimbalis was their editorial father figure, after all. In the *Colossus*, Seferis is depicted showing Miller a small plot of land on which he would build a bungalow. It seemed a bit shabby and forlorn at first sight, but soon Seferis is 'rhapsodizing' each herb, shrub and cove: 'look at a headland and read into it the history of the Medes, the Persians etc. He could also read into some of the fragments which he would write on his way home' (Miller 1958: 47). Miller was very much 'at home' with this school of reading, he was a Greek modernist of sorts in the way that Seferis, in his turn, became a European modernist. If Katsimbalis was a projection of Miller, Miller too was a projection back of Katsimbalis and his generation. Ultimately, in Miller's exchange of gazes,

Greece's modernity is recuperated into an authorizing cultural agenda that locates Greece's purifying hybridity as Europe's salvation, and Europe's appreciative gaze as a means of articulating Greece.

Cheeky Devils

Like Miller, Storace seems to put her life behind her when she goes to Greece for a year. But Greece does not leave a mark on her in the momentous ways it did for Miller. Greece does not shake her to her core (at least not positively), nor does the country or its inhabitants guide her to her inner self. What is so striking is Storace's passionate insistence on keeping a distance from the experiences and the people around her. She often interprets with insight; she injects irony at every turn often for a distancing effect; but Storace's narrative ends because her year is up, plain and simple. We learn next to nothing about 'the girl whose past has been severed from her' in her travelogue; nor do we sense that she develops in any way. Storace is never quite comfortable in Greece from the outset. Her apartment is located 'at the intersection of a prostitute and a saint' (Storace 1996: 3), between the madonna and the whore, the Ideal and the real. And the two are irreconcilable in any one person or entity. Unlike Miller, who found in Katsimablis the locus for balancing ancient and modern, self and other in a possibly homoerotic and evidently auto-erotic harmony, Storace is defeated time and time again and is unable to reconcile this 'country of the double' (63). The country is figured as Persephone-like, doomed to wander six months in heaven and six in Hades. As one woman tells her 'all our stories come in two versions, and the story that is told in hell will sound different from the same story as they tell it in heaven.' If the book sets out to stage a dinner with Persephone cast as a scene of dialogue, that dialogue is forever interrupted or forestalled by a strange logic: 'And you know that in Greece you never use the past tense when you are speaking of Alexander the Great, although you also know that he is dead. We are telling different stories at the same time' (105). In this land of paralogy, when you see the mad mermaid before you, you must take it as a sign that Alexander lives and you must be heard to shout: 'He lives and reigns.' Storace's packaging of the book as a fairytale and as a text that refers repeatedly to dream books of interpretation would seem to stand her in good stead for such a bridging of worlds, but the book only stages Storace's inability to harmonize these logics.

Her contacts, particularly with Greek men, who are depicted as purveyors of the abstract Nation, constantly affirm only her status outside this polity, forever homeless and a sign of disharmony. In an early scene, Storace goes to the bank to open an account. Symbolically, she seeks integration into the administrative socius. The Greek teller is hardly welcoming: 'You? You have business here? What kind of business can you have here?' he says sneeringly. Storace defiantly takes him to task for his ridicule, but he then proceeds 'to pick up my passport, opens it, and begins kissing my passport picture, making sure I can see that he is using his tongue' (23). Upon reflection, what irks her most is that: 'he is not thinking, he is dogmatizing, sure that he knows all that is essential about me. And this very certainty conceals the powerful drive to make me conform to his sure and certain knowledge of me – he is using it like a policeman's cosh. He is certain he knows how I am arranged as if I were an Orthodox church – he has even, in a secular style, I think with bitter amusement kissed my icons' (23–4).

The dynamics are agonistic. Storace wipes out any trace of Miller's mystical communion. Indeed, the metaphors point to religious tradition only to completely decimate their economy in a way that leaves Storace, literally and figuratively, excluded from this, or any, Greek economy. The relation of Greek and Other is a power game of aggression and possession where communication entails licking, and not kissing, her icon, which, in its religious version, would constitute the aperture through which the worshipper would, normally, attain the divine. But this is not Miller, and there is no unmediated access to the Divine, only a disheartening reaffirmation of a degraded materiality.

Elsewhere, the egocentric hairdresser, O Kyrios Emmanuel, 'believes I am transparent the way an icon is . . . for O Kyrios Emmanuel, I am a looking glass, in which he sees the image of his own honed judgment and the ancient wisdom he has acquired' (112). A wiry Cephalonian further exemplifies the cultivated Greek passion for the icon by chasing her around the room, camera in hand. More than a scene of sexual flight, this is a contestation over the nature of reality: 'He is arguing that I am an image, as he chases me from corner to corner, and that his camera can prove it. I unfortunately, frustratedly, am sure that I am real . . . For [him], I am an image of himself – he sees into the pool of me and sees his own face, thirty or forty years ago' (366). Whereas, in the *Colossus*, Miller looks into Katsimbalis to see himself, Storace sees herself only as the object of this autoscopic regime. To be rendered symbolic, in the process, is demeaning: 'in Greece, the adage that a picture is worth a thousand words is exactly reversed. The light and scenery seem to turn photographs into symbols, not even images, of a kind of general sublime; only words will make experience of being here specific – even glorious photographs seem to take on a curious embalmed quality here, where a word is worth a thousand pictures' (151).

In short, Storace here is resisting the effects of decades of travel literature in Greece. Greece's symbolization was the result of a historical legacy of projecting aesthetic wholeness on her. Greeks had themselves absorbed the consequences of this hegemony and stoked the fires of the myth. Storace, however, rejects its guiding premise: 'No matter where I had traveled in Greece, I have invariably been told that it either is not or is no longer Greece, as if there is an imaginary Greece that exists in perfect intact detail somewhere, much realer than the Greece we live in' (253). The animosity toward Storace and her book in Greece is predicated on two points. First, though the overarching fairytale structure presents the little girl that has left everything behind, it is the very 'Americanness' of the preconceptions she brings with her as well as her unwillingness to understand certain Greek customs or ways of thinking that irks Greek readers. Put differently, though she believes that there should be a renegotiation of the interrelation of the dream/ symbol and the real, that real smacks of American liberal ideas. And, second, her rejection of Greece's imaginary capital, its symbolic capital, strikes a raw nerve. The Greeks themselves are led to realize the redundancy of that symbolic capital in her eyes and this makes for a relationship fraught with anger and frustration. After all, Storace's sojourn takes place in the very year that Greece lost its sentimental bid for the Olympic Games and struggled to convince the West of its historic claim to Macedonia. In other words, though Greeks saw the mad mermaid before them and shouted 'Alexander lives and reigns,' Alexander did not show up.

It is ironic then that Storace sees Greece as the best spokesman of this Symbolic regime and herself as its most notable victim. For years, cultural critics had argued that it was modern Greece that was the victim of the classicizing symbolic economy. Significantly, Storace is driven by the need to elude being held captive by another's gaze: that is, to make sure that others keep their eyes, and hands, off her. The book gives great prominence to patriarchy and homosociality by returning insistently to her contacts with men. For Storace, the historical and much-touted Greek hospitality is a performative display of the absolute power of the male host; men like Katsimbalis who unleash a torrent of words of wisdom are patriarchs who see her as a looking glass. Homosociality run amuck – what Miller reveled in, Storace keeps at arm's length.

Ironically, Storace, the quintessential observer, is forced to come out of her shell and act – actually participates – only in these coercive scenes. On a number of occasions, she is hounded by unwanted male admirers who advertise their assets to her. One old sailor puts his hand on her knee, and Storace responds by inserting herself into a fictional situation in order to find a way out of this very real dilemma: ''Have you ever been with a Greek man?' I run through my menu of options. 'Yes' will mean to him there is no reason to turn him down. 'No' will mean you don't know what you're missing, let me show you. I briefly consider 'I don't remember,' but consider national [pride]; this would probably be grounds for deportation. I settle on 'Why do you ask?'' (240). The sailor then proceeds to explain to her why Greek men are inexhaustible in bed. Time and again Storace, unlike Aphrodite, is glad to escape this and that Adonis (270). She is comfortable only in the company of a ubiquitous male friend, Kostas, who she knew sometime in the past, when he was a student in the United States. Indeed, in the scene with the sailor, it is Kostas who arrives and saves her from the seaman.

But if Kostas is a bosom buddy, we learn little about him, except that he works for the European Union! Nothing is revealed about the nature of their relations. Unlike Katsimbalis, Kostas is hardly larger than life, and certainly not Zorbaesque. He is eminently metacritical: on viewing the Greek movie classic *Stella* with the redoubtable and passionate Melina Mercouri running in the final scene into her lover's dagger, Kostas explicates in detail how the Greek idea of love is melodramatic. No less, one might retort, than the melodramatic scene of dagger consummation in *Romeo and Juliet*. Kostas, like Storace, is an exegete, at one remove from action and lived experience and above the pleasures of melodrama. He is a Greek who has lived abroad and so has the knowledge that comes with being a subject at one remove. Miller had appreciated this in Seferis, but he had roundly ridiculed it in all other Greeks, and especially Greek Americans, who were, in his eyes, at one fatal remove from the source of their own Greek authenticity and one step closer to Western corruption. For Storace, the further from Greece the better – far-flung and Italianate Corfu has 'an orderly sense of past . . . an unusual air of confidence, a respite here from the tension of fragmented identity' (300).

What marks these sexual encounters are questions of an obsessive national identity and nationalism. But whose obsession? These topics bring about an allergic reaction in Storace throughout the book. Her verbal put-downs to men have something of the will to control back. She is doing Greece, and not the other way round. But she is writing, after all, in the early nineties, when war is raging in the Balkans, and Greece is engaged in an international metacritical dispute over the naming and identity of the Former Yugoslav Republic of Macedonia. International public opinion is deaf to exclusive Greek cultural claims on the name of the area. Memorably, Alexander the Great was conscripted to remind one and all of the Greekness of Macedonia. The campaign was barely understood in the west: as one Texan puts it in the book, 'you sure as hell hear a lot about Mr. Great and the Macedonians' (120).

Storace reacts violently to the discourse of nationalism. Though she understands that the ancient labels are often deployed to cover over the deep ambiguity and anxiety that comes with the fear of raising up again the bloody atrocities committed by all parties in the Balkan wars at the turn of the century. The fear of a return of the repressed feeds the national neurosis. Ultimately, this is the double bind that Penelope Delta represents for Storace. She feels for her as a victim of male repression even as she disapproves of her as an idealizer of boys and murderous nationalism. Storace is unmoved by the claims of classicist legitimization on the Macedonia issue, and she shares Kostas's view that Greeks have even less a sense of history than do Americans. They only wield stories of the past against all and sundry. In many scenes, people, chiefly men, harangue her with dogma and slogans, and Storace yokes together such scenes of demonstration and propagandizing with scenes of beating that are figured as a part of civil and private life in Greece. Every time she switches on a television, she sees men beat women; policemen in demonstrations cudgel protestors, especially women. It is no surprise then that the metaphor she uses to describe the banker's attempt to make her conform to his image of her is one of his using 'his knowledge of her as a policeman's cosh.' The sexual nature of the cosh, the repetitiveness of the beatings, make Greece, for Storace, a symbol of sadistic imposition of Self on Other. But it is a violation, as in cases of men beating their girlfriends, which points to a loss of control, when a regime, a relationship, or the Symbolic Law recognizes its redundancy and seeks to cling on by violent self-assertion.

Having lost the Centennial Olympics to Atlanta, Storace focuses on the ceremonies marking the return of the two victorious Greek Olympians after the 1992 Games. The young woman, Voula Patoulidou, who, unexpectedly, won a gold medal in track and field in the 1992 Olympics, allows Storace to comment again on the atmosphere around her: 'When Voula Patoulidou astonished herself and the other competitors, breaking through the tape to win gold, she shouted in a voice strangled for breath, but audible, 'For Greece, for fucking Greece' (63).

Lawrence Durrell, the Bitterest Lemon? Cyps and Brits Loving each other to Death in Cyprus

Lawrence Durrell once told his wife Ghislane that he wore funny hats to draw attention away from his outsized nose.[8] This insight might be applied profitably to fathoming Durrell's emphatic claim – 'this is not a political book' (Durrell 1957: 9) – found at the beginning of the preface to his personal documentary narrative *Bitter Lemons* (1957).[9] For how else might we overlook the politics poking the reader in the eye? To those conversant with the recent traumas of Cypriot history, Durrell's pledge sounds incredible. For his memoir, while it also exhibits marks of a work of fiction,[10] draws from his own stay in Cyprus between 1953 to 1956, just before and right up to the Greek Cypriot insurrection against British colonial rule. Furthermore, he embarks on this apolitical memoir having just held the posts of Director of Her Majesty's Information Service on Cyprus from the summer of 1954 and Director of Public Relations before his departure in 1956. It was at this very time that EOKA, a Greek Cypriot group, with the covert backing of Athens and the support of most of the majority Greek Cypriot population, and at a time of British Commonwealth withdrawal elsewhere, sought to bring about *enosis*, or union, with Greece.

Durrell undertakes to portray the 'unfolding of the Cyprus tragedy' between 1953 and 1956 'in terms of individuals rather than policies' in order 'to keep the book free from the smaller contempts' (Durrell 1957: 9). What these contempts might be, or who was responsible for them, is not made clear immediately; although, on delving into the book, it soon becomes apparent that such contempts emanate more from the excesses of the small and disgruntled band of Cypriot 'extremists' than the effects of over a half-century of British colonial rule. The rhetorical field is clearly laid out. Durrell, the British diplomat, magnanimous and loving, is above the contempts of the situation. Those who would scratch the surface to reveal British machinations, in sharp contrast, are politically motivated and mischievous. A number of illustrious Greek and Greek Cypriot commentators have chosen to challenge Durrell's assumptions over the years. Rodis Roufos, a Greek diplomat stationed in Cyprus at the same time, wrote *Age of Bronze* (1960), a fictional counter-memoir to Durrell's *Bitter Lemons*. A section of this work, which referred to Maurice Fennell's *Sour Grapes*,[11] and which was removed from the final published text for fear of libelous action against it,[12] was scathing in its portrayal of Durrell and of British haughtiness. Seferis, a friend of Durrell's in Greece in the early 1940s, was wary of what he perceived as Durrell's overzealous pro-Brit sentiment in 1953–6;[13] and Cyprus's best known modern poet, Costas Montis (1964), wrote a selection of short reminiscences of the struggle as 'a response to Lawrence Durrell's *Bitter Lemons*'.[14] In contrast, in Britain, the work received critical acclaim and is often considered 'undoubtedly the finest piece of literature to come out of the Cyprus affair' (Bowker 1997: 232). It even won him the Duff Cooper Memorial Award (presented by Queen Elizabeth the Queen Mother) and the offer, albeit rebuffed by Durrell, of a decoration, the Commander of the Order of St. Michael and St. George.[15]

By 1956, when Durrell left Cyprus, the misunderstanding had escalated into a bloody and bitter war with 214 dead that year alone. Eventually, as we saw in Chapter 5, the armed struggle against the British depicted in *Bitter Lemons* would not lead to union with Greece. Instead, it produced a precarious compromise in the form of intercommunal independence in 1960 that itself eventually fell apart in violence when, in 1974, a Turkish invasion led to a *de facto* partition of the island along ethnic lines that remains unrecognized in international fora to this day. Durrell's purpose in 1957 is to plot the 'current misunderstanding' between the British and the Cypriots in the broader context of a longtime Anglo-Cypriot friendship. Since he proposes to render Cyprus through 'the eyes of my hospitable fellow-villagers,' it is important to examine how Durrell goes about seeing through the eyes of others. Second, it is important to examine how the book's politics of representation, Durrell's declared strategy for commenting on the death throes of colonialism in an unpolitical way through a benevolently redirected gaze, speak *for* Cypriots while serving, and speaking for, Her Majesty's interests?[16] In other words, rather than reading after Durrell 'in terms of individuals rather than policies,' I intend to read Durrell's policies and politics through a reading of his individuals to investigate the affinities of such positions to British designs in Cyprus at the time. How does the philhellene Durrell read the Cypriot desire to unite with Greece, with Hellenism, at this sensitive moment for British interests?

The Lay of the Land

The irony of the Cyprus conflict in the 1950s is encapsulated for Durrell in the closing scene of *Bitter Lemons*. A taxi driver who takes the dejected Durrell to the airport, and away from the daily bombings, asserts the fundamental paradox in the situation: 'yes, even Dighenis [George Grivas, the leader of the anti-British fighters], though he fights the British really loves them. But he will go on killing them – with regret, even with affection' (Durrell 1957: 250–1). This dance of death in which Brits and Cyps 'love each other to death' marks Durrell's comprehension of British and Greek interaction in his narrative. And though 'this mythopoeic image of the English which every Greek carried in his heart' may not quite be predicated on a lie, as Pine (1994: 242) has suggested, it is certainly an exaggeration. For the colonial experience in Cyprus, while by no means Fanonian in its repression, nonetheless bore its own forms of subjugation. Few Greek Cypriots would share Durrell's generous assessment of British rule on the island. Though some Greek Cypriots criticize the violent manner in which Greek Cypriots chose, in the mid-1950s, to throw off British rule,[17] there were few who thought this way back in the 1950s, and such retrospective views have been conditioned in large part by knowledge of the later Turkish invasion of the island in 1974.

This 'death embrace' was one that others – Aryans and Semites, Christian and Muslims – had already experienced in the island of love's 'ebb and flow of histories and cultures' (Durrell 1957: 20). His earlier years spent in Greece make Durrell an empathetic interlocutor: this fact he makes evident from his first contact with the vague and spiritless lethargy of the place as embodied by the customs agents he encounters: 'I asked in Greek and was answered in English; I asked again in Greek and was once again answered in English' (Durrell 1957: 22). Durrell 'had a stake in neither culture' (36), British nor Cypriot. Herbrechter (1999: 244) has identified this positioning as part and parcel of Durrell's transcendental homelessness, his search for an imaginary home between childhood in India and an idealized England; or the way he uses the Irish descendance of his mother 'to create an "other" as a counter-balance or counter-stereotype to the predominance of Englishness.' Durrell's wanderings are so perceived, a ceaseless game of escape and self-alienation, wandering to settle a third place. This leads him to 'maintain his colonial difference that engenders the whole desiring process of constructed identities based on this central opposition to being English' (Durrell 1957: 250). He can be more English than the English, or Irish.

To British expats on Cyprus saw one-dimensional Cypriots: 'to the British they were a "bunch of Cyps" – as one might say "Chimps" (136). Durrell's sensitivity here may have been touched by his own recognition, as an Irishman, of the English historical precedent for referring to the Irish as 'Chimps.' Irish otherness differentiates him from these Brits.[18] But, he is equally sensitive to the prejudiced Cypriot views of the British expatriates in Cyprus, for they were 'civil folk who had been brought here, not by any desire to broaden minds cumbered by the problems of indolence and trade, but by a perfectly honourable passion for sunlight and low income tax' (35). In both cases, Durrell disagrees with each group's interpretation of the other, but he is not averse to their mode of critical appraisal. For he retains throughout his work a penchant for characterizing 'national character' in wholesale stereotypes: 'I wished to experience [Cyprus] through its people rather than its landscape, to enjoy the sensation of sharing a common life with the humble villagers of the place; and later to expand my field of investigation to its history – the lamp which illumines national character – in order to offer my live subjects a frame against which to set themselves' (53). Unfortunately, the distinctions drawn here seem to be more complex in practice. Though the first half of *Bitter Lemons* does conform to this model and does focus on Durrell's contact with the villagers of Bellapais, attendant factors of landscape, architecture, and history already color the reader's view of the Cypriots. National character is ascribed not by the individuals themselves so much, but through a privileged interpreter – Durrell himself. Michael Given (1997: 55–65) has shown how Durrell's selective presentation of landscape and architecture in *Bitter Lemons* can be read as a subtle means for the delineation of Cypriot national character.[19] Surveying the book's geographical areas, Given argues that the ascription of identity to particular mountain ranges and monuments imbues the Cypriots themselves with certain cultural traits while repressing others: 'Gothic drama and Gothic contemplation, combined with Anatolian indolence and fatalism, with occasional flashes of Levantine emotion and hot temper. What is most remarkable about this constructed character is what is missing. Nowhere in *Bitter Lemons* is Cyprus allowed to participate in Hellenic or classical civilization' (Given 1997: 58). In Durrell's description, a village can remind one of a 'Cretan hamlet' or Kyrenia exhibit a 'Cycladean allure.' But this is as far as it goes; classical sites and Orthodox monasteries that dot the landscape go unnoticed. Characteristically, as Given notes, Durrell is even oblivious to the neoclassical Ionic style of the Pancyprian Gymnasium, at which he teaches and where, appropriately, he encounters his students' involvement in Greek nationalist activity.[20] The building, based in part on the Erechtheum in Athens,[21] commends itself to him for its 'rococo Doric portals' (Durrell 1957: 126). This repression of Hellenic modes was typical of official British colonial plans. The architect Austen Harrison – to whom *Bitter Lemons* is dedicated – undertook a number of municipal buildings at this time and also followed the architecture of this colonial political project. And it is not quite clear how Durrell's own house in Bellapais is 'in the Turkish Cypriot mode.' Yet, there it sits, with a view of the soft Anatolian plains and the Gothic abbey; while Durrell's daughter, Sappho, sits up in bed to 'gaze out at Turkey' in the distance' (102). This description recalls the closing scene of the best known historical accounts of intercommunal troubles in Cyprus from an unabashedly pro-Turkish Cypriot perspective that ends with its author in the serenity of the Abbey of Peace in Bellapais, among Turkish Cypriots, comforted that he is 'within sight of the Turkish shore' (Oberling 1982: 235).

This negation of Hellenic patrimony in landscape and architecture also carries over to the politics of Durrell's editorship of the British Information Service's house magazine, the *Cyprus Review*, from 1954 to 1956. David Roessel's work has made the case convincingly. Though published since 1948, Durrell revamped the magazine's literary profile by giving prominence to contemporary English writers, in part because he had little success in procuring contributions from mainland Greek writer friends, whom he knew from his sojourn in Greece in the mid-1950s. Living Greek Cypriot writers resident in Cyprus also stayed away: 'few of them would want to appear in a periodical published by the Information Service on Cyprus during the middle fifties' (Roessel 1994b:44). George Seferis's feelings in a letter to Savidis on this matter are a little more explicit:

> But when I see intellectual institutions – quite artfully, I agree – placed in the service of these gentlemen [men who are simply after power, like conquerors of the past], I tend to become suspicious. And when I see intellectuals and friends (e.g. Durrell) become propagandists for these gentlemen and use the friendships they had in Greece in order to infiltrate and enslave consciousness, then I become absolutely suspicious. (quoted in Roessel 1994b: 44)

Some historians and commentators have pointed the finger at the British for resisting *enosis*, or union with Greece, by playing the smaller Turkish Cypriot community against the Greek Cypriots in an exemplary tactic of divide and rule. Indicatively, the magazine *only after* Durrell's editorship began to publish frequent pieces by Turkish Cypriots. By February 1956, it even appeared in a Turkish language edition.[22]

During Durrell's tenure, the impeccable belles-lettrism of the magazine does not admit mention of the armed struggle being waged in Cyprus and the torture chambers of Omorphita, Xeros, or Platres.[23] Aesthetics and politics should not mix. Yet this sentiment translates into a thoroughly readable political pragmatism when juxtaposed to the documentary material of his work in political intelligence (Pine 1994: 253). Durrell's pose was sadly behind-the-times. As Durrell's biographer Ian MacNiven has put it, the wish 'to promote a sense of Cyprus as an independent cultural entity, with Britain as a friendly godparent: this sounded like an unholy alliance between high art and low politics' (MacNiven 1998: 418).

A Character Issue

This demarcation in Durrell's mind, to keep distinct the realms of everyday lived existence and the realm of politics or smaller contempts, structures his stay in Cyprus from the very outset. The early part of Durrell's book is primitivist and Romantic. Durrell arrived in Cyprus after resigning from his previous diplomatic postings in search of the quiet life from which he could write, among the common Cypriots, 'the very sort of characters who rejoice the English heart in a small country town – the rogue, the drunkard, the singer, the incorrigible' (36). Like Henry Miller in Greece before him, Durrell shuns the wearying restraint and poise of the middle class – too like the middle bourgeois of England and France for comfort – for a recognizable authenticity that only emboldens the paternalism and superiority of his affections. Indeed, critics of Durrell, such as Roufos, are categorical in their dislike of Durrell's classist affections. If Keeley (1995) is right to argue that Miller and Durrell are of a generation that ushers in a new philhellenism that discovers the modern Greek over his classical ancestors, it is clear that some Greeks, especially in those turbulent times, did not recognize that Greek's physiognomy. That is, if Roufos's attack on Harry Montague, the Durrell-like figure in his *Age of Bronze*, is anything to go by: '[Montague] disliked most mainland Greeks who did not conform to his conception of what a Greek should be like. He particularly disapproved of the educated; they were too different from his own pets – the picturesque illiterate shepherds and fishermen described in his book about war-time Greece. I knew the symptoms; they were common to most Philhellenes' (Roufos 1994: 60).

When the early vignettes of good cheer in the book are brusquely interrupted by the first glimmerings of resentment toward the British, such eruptions are voiced by a drunken, ox-like peasant named Frangos who proposes to say 'what everyone knows.' In one early scene, Frangos rifles off a 'splendid tirade couched in the wildest argot, against the damned English and those who endured them with such patience' (39). It is endured, in this instance, by Durrell's embarrassed Cypriot co-villagers, with Durrell firmly planted in their circle, happily belonging. This allows him to diffuse the situation by sharing a joke and grafting his family history into *their* cultural heritage. Frangos bellows:

> 'And what do you reply to me, Englishman? What do you think there sitting in shame?'
> 'I think of my brother,' I said coolly.
> 'Your brother?' he said, caught slightly off his guard by this diversion which had just occurred me.
> 'My brother. He died at Thermopylae, fighting beside the Greeks.' (40)

Frangos is oblivious to the classical historical reference and is knocked off his stride by the introduction of a family affiliation just at the very moment when he thought he had spoken for all Cypriots and staked ownership of the higher, moral ground over the foreigner. This, even when as Durrell admits: 'this was a complete lie, of course, for my brother, to the best of my knowledge, was squatting in some African swamp collecting animals for the European zoos' (40). His pose torn down, looking 'like a cornered bull' – or is it a chimp? – Frangos stood wrung out like a wet dish rag, ripe, in this moment of vulnerability, for Durrell to extend his way all the compassion of a superior. Durrell's imperious brotherhood reinstates the right kind of power and intellectual differential: 'I saved him now by calling for more drink and he subsided into a smouldering silence at one end of the room . . . He was obviously turning over something in his mind' (41).

The uncouth Frangos is depicted as one ostracized by his own co-villagers, Durrell included. His brain hurts. He becomes very much the emblem of the Cypriot fighter, dare I say *guerrilla*. And, in later episodes, Durrell and Frangos share the odd uncomfortable but amicable moment, with Durrell always in charge – since, as a rule of thumb, 'a frank and generous statement was the best way of disarming the *enotist* and resurrecting the Cyps' irrational love for the Brits.' This tactic reflects Durrell's more general policy of disarming Greeks by embracing them, by now a recurring metaphor (83). Such exchanges, however defensive in purpose, all lend great credence to Roufos's characterization of Durrell's attitude toward Cypriot grievances in *Sour Grapes*: 'The book is not only very British – which is natural enough – it is Tory British. The way Fennell examines the Revolt reminds one of the half-bewildered, half-patronizing look that an amateur veterinary psychiatrist might cast on a pet animal exhibiting a hitherto unknown form of insanity' (Roufos 1994: 138). Clearly, both Durrell's philhellene condescension, on the one hand, and his hostile belittling of the EOKA rebels, on the other, led his Greek critics to address both these points. To illustrate this reaction, one need only examine the crucial scene, near the end of Roufos's novel, where the protagonist Alexis Balafaras comes face to face with the urbane Colonial Adviser, Terence Fitzgibbon. The episode, titled 'The Inquisitor and Don Giovanni' occurs after Alexis's capture and torture at the hands of the British security forces. In a change of approach, Alexis is brought to Fitzgibbon's office and the two engage in a series of civil conversations, over sherry, on such disparate issues as pseudo-Dionysius, Plotinus, and the nature of political freedom throughout history and across civilizations. Roufos is keen in this scene to stage a meeting of equals that would establish a mutual respect between high British official and Cypriot fighter. The subtext, too, that informs the meeting is also understood by both parties in an unspoken gentlemanly pact – that the British would go to great lengths to secure the collaboration of an educated Greek in exchange for the commutation of Alexis's death sentence. The background music playing from the pick-up, Mozart's opera *Don Giovanni*, allows the two characters to pit their wits against each other in a civilized ambience. For Fitzgibbon, the opera is: 'a unique synthesis of the

European heritage! A Spanish theme, a French play of the grand siècle, an Italian libretto, German music . . . That's what comes of the free intermingling of national cultures. There you have the true humanity, as in Goethe's time. That is what we must restore' (Roufos 1994: 220). Fitzgibbon's appeal to Alexis is pitched through High Art and a common European patrimony – 'Alexis, let us be Europeans. We belong to the same world, you and I.' In so doing, he intimates that Cypriot self-expression, on the other hand, is limited and chauvinist. It is Fitzgibbon's impl-ication that the political freedom now pursued by the Cypriots' small-minded nationalism could in no way aspire to the freedom of the soul embodied by Mozart and achievable only in 'a supra-national commonwealth imbued with respect for the freedom of the individual – even if it disregards collective rights such as self-determination' (Roufos 1994: 213).

By this point, the illusion of an intellectual meeting of equals soon gives way to reveal once more the power imbalance of the situation. Faced by Fitzgibbon's 'father-image,' Alexis the rebellious and idealist Don Giovanni figure, confronts 'the great temptation to surrender to paternal authority', yet opts instead for 'a gesture of freedom and defiance to the father-image of the commander' (221–2). The scene evokes Don Giovanni giving his hand to the statue of the Commend-atore in pledge; seized in an icy cold grip and unrepentant to the end, Don Giovanni is dragged down to the fiery pit. This endgame puts an end to the two men's discussions and leads Fitzgibbon, dolefully, to sign off on Alexis's inexorable fate, but only after Roufos has focused on Fitzgibbon's parting admiration for Alexis's heroic stance: 'and yet, if I'd had a son, I should have wanted him to act in the same way' (222).

Roufos's scene clearly acts to redress the terms of the father–son relationship behind Durrell's depiction of British–Cypriot relations. Durrell hoped to adopt the pose of 'friendly godparent' toward the Cypriots in a way reminiscent of the manner of the British politically (MacNiven 1998: 418). And even if to some, like Roufos, it comes off more like the demeanor of an animal psychiatrist, Durrell was, above all, keen on safeguarding Cypriot innocence and childhood, or even stupidity, from being dragged into the stock market of world affairs. In his mind, it was almost as if British colonialism occupied a space and time before world affairs, before politics. When he first sets foot on Cyprus, Durrell considers Cyprus 'not much of a place' (16). Rimbaud, he notes, had spent some time there: 'What did he think of Cyprus? He does not say. It was simply a place where a few decently paid jobs existed under the British' (19). For a 'heavy and stupefied silence' hangs over Cyprus (22), a detail of the landscape that seems to make its appearance on the typical 'sleepy good-natured eyes of its inhabitants' (28), both Greek and Turk. This is a sleepiness that Durrell conjured up in his description of other colonized spots.[24]

An Englishman's home is his castle, not to say anything about his garden. The house across from the Gothic Bellapaix Abbey that Durrell restores offers him refuge, as does the enduring friendship of a cast of characters from the village. Even in later episodes, at the time of the bombings, 'escaping to Bellapaix was like entering a walled garden'; the nights spent under the village square tree, known as the Tree of Idleness, further portrays the pre-EOKA days as edenic and as somewhat outside history.[25] In the height of the troubles, only the Government House, seat of British rule, is described in comparable terms: 'amidst freshly laundered grass as green as any England can show, outside time' (189). If only the Cypriot had not disturbed the endearing indolence and amiable naivete of his antideluvian state of mind, if he had remained a loafer under the Tree of Idleness rather than a taster of the Tree of Knowledge, Cyprus would have remained, in both literal and metaphorical senses, an English country garden.

Durrell's encounter with a Greek Cypriot who comes closest to meeting him on intellectual terms serves only to reinforce his own positions. The meeting with Panos, a quiet scholar from Kyrenia, takes place on a ramble and picnic to a friend's plot in the country. Panos accompanies Durrell in order to oversee a tree-planting project, and his expertise in this regard is evinced by his horticultural and geographical knowledge (218). Panos's knowledge announces itself in symbolic, Edenic terms. When the first mention of the recent troubles enters their conversation, he is distracted: '[The British] won't take us seriously until the hotheads gain control. Look oleanders. It is too early for snakes is it not? I thought I caught a glimpse of one' (219). Though such imminent biblical portents of doom lurk in the description, we find ourselves, for one last time, in a place sheltered from the mayhem – from a plane that cracked the sound barrier like thunder ahead, the sound of gunshots, or even passing Sabri's allusion to 'bombs.' With Panos's yawning, 'our own silence surrounded us like a cocoon', the characters survey the prospect of the bucolic countryside. From atop a tree, Panos contemplates the return of normalcy. When politics does infiltrate Panos and Durrell's conversation, the good-natured Cypriot is quick to announce himself both as 'reticent to discuss politics' and 'not as patriotic as most people' (223). He is in this not unlike the persona Durrell would have us believe *he* is.[26] Yet, in a mild-mannered tone, Panos also affirms the Greekness of Cyprus on the basis that Cyprus, this earth, is as Greek as the town of Vouni. Though he is put off by the violence that has broken out, Panos believes that *enosis* must come one day (223). In these exchanges, Durrell does not respond to Panos, for he 'promised . . . not to talk politics' (225) and any deliberative exchange is left suspended and not taken up; instead, such talk of politics recedes quietly as the two men become preoccupied, as it were, with their surroundings and the Cypriot earth. Panos's philosophical assessment, that in the sweep of history and time their passage in life is no more than a speck, brings fatalism and not action to the fore. It is a *cri de coeur* for totality before the fall; before the encroachment of nationality, ethnicity, and religion. In short, Durrell has created Panos to speak against the 'smaller contempts.'

For Durrell, the Cypriots involved in the *enosis* struggle are culpable for falling victim to just such contempts. In the process, their fallen state no longer allows them to identify 'abstract guilt . . . abstract justice' (228). They no longer had access to certain timeless verities. When Durrell argues forcefully for the execution of Karaolis, a young man caught and sentenced to death by the British for killing a traitor to the cause, he provokes the ire of Dimitri who is unable to see, like Durrell, that 'crime is crime whatever the motive.' Dimitri is described with all the unmistakeable attributes of Frangos earlier: 'he shook his head from side to side like a bull'; 'his mind refused the jump' (228). He goes on, too, just as with Frangos, to bemoan the modern Greek's incapacity to aspire to 'the exercise of logic which was Socratic' (228). And, with a knowing glance from Panos in Durrell's direction that validates the suggestion that British and Greek Cypriots could no longer speak the same language but only at cross-purposes, Karaolis's eventual death is presented here, as in Roufos's book, as the fateful rap on the door of Anglo-Cypriot friendship's undoing. The eminent sanity of Durrell's interpretation in this scene is assured due to our foreknowledge that the innocent Panos has been shot by his compatriots for consorting with Durrell.[27]

The Politics of Fatherhood

Durrell's positions on the Cyprus issue, as laid out in *Bitter Lemons*, were perfectly in harmony with British positions on the Cyprus issue – a Garden of Eden of a very different variety! Anthony Eden and Harold Macmillan were willing to offer Greek Cypriots a small measure of self-government, but under no circumstances self-determination. The British would, at most, need to placate the Greek Cypriots by arguing for their right to self-determination, but would delay any such action for as long as possible. Like Panos, Durrell believed that *enosis* should (or would) come one day. This was more a diplomat's realization than an earnest hope on Durrell's part. Yet though Panos is willing to accept this pledge so as to ward off violence, he realizes, too, that British intransigence had whipped up the Cypriots and left little room for maneuver. 'Old man, be wise,' Napoleon Zervas once advised Churchill, 'Cyprus promised to Greece is thrice British . . . Note carefully,' he said, '*promised* not *given*' (205).

Durrell also shared with the British authorities the tactical goal of deflecting the issue from one of an anti-colonial struggle to a problem that amounted to an antagonism between Greece and Turkey, and so undermine Greek attempts to internationalize the issue at the United Nations. It was wrong to treat Cyprus as a colonial and not a European problem, Durrell insisted (121). This explains why Roufos's character Fitzgibbon insists to Alexis on a shared European heritage as the foundation of Anglo-Cypriot understanding. When Durrell decries his fellow diplomats' ignorance of the situation: 'they regarded Cyprus as Tobago', this should not be read as merely professional back-stabbing or an allusion to the fact that Cyprus was Britain's one European colony. It was also a calculated démarche in British policy.

Durrell is also sensitive to the British manipulation of the Turkish Cypriots as a bulwark against *enosis* in order to guarantee continued British sovereignty on the island. Durrell's geographical descriptions of Cyprus are telling. Though Durrell is by no means mistaken in his tendency to mark out differences between mainland Greece and Cyprus – and at times he does so quite perceptively – the following descriptions, when added to Given's observation on his landscapes and architectural plans are hardly innocent: 'It's a piece of Asia Minor washed out to sea – not Greece'; 'it's really a piece of Anatolia lopped off'; 'I think you will like Cyprus in spite of it being so un-Greek' (MacNiven 1988: 267, 269, 276).

Durrell marks the irrevocable breaking down of the Anglo-Cypriot friendship over the body of dead young Greek Cypriot man. For both as schoolteacher and colonial adviser for cultural policy, Durrell has overseen the growth of ' a revolution of schoolchildren' (165).[28] As *Bitter Lemons* progresses, Durrell moves beyond parental protection of innocence to the stance of a father who, upon reflection, chides himself for having failed his children. In this way, his own lapsed fatherhood embodies the British Colonial Office's irresponsibility, its inability to think of its subjects until the first bombs started falling. It was in these terms that Durrell encapsulated the problem: 'Surely it was all founded in a childish bad dream from which they would awaken one day and realize that they could enjoy perfect Greek freedom within the Commonwealth – enjoying the best of both worlds? Was it not all due to a lack of education?' (135). It is only when Durrell accepts his diplomatic post that he evaluates the reasons for this lack of education and diagnoses 'our [i.e. the British] failure to project the British ethos by not having earlier built a university, a theatre, a bookshop where one could buy a French newspaper to have made the Cypriot belong' (136). This sentiment, noble enough at first glance, is in harmony with colonialism's 'civilizing mission' and with Foreign Secretary Anthony Eden's desire, in 1955, to promote the idea of a university in Cyprus which, in collaboration with its British counterparts, would push the Cypriots culturally away from Athens (Eden 1960).

Durrell's avowed attempts as Director of Her Majesty's Public Relations Office in Cyprus to ameliorate the situation prove in vain and the worsening situation leads him not to renew his contract. He decides to leave the island, but does not close the chapter on the issue of Anglo-Cypriot friendship. Nor does he abandon the very terms of the colonial relationship that structure it. Karaolis has a foil in *Bitter Lemons* in the figure of Achilles Papadopoulos who is employed in the Colonial Secretary's Office, in the service of the Crown, and who shows Durrell the ropes in his first few days at the job. He strikes Durrell as the quintessential poor-boy-done-well. Durrell finds in him a tribute to the ennobling capacity of the British colonial system.

This sentiment is further brought home in the penultimate scene of the book. The reentry of the jovial co-villager Andreas, last seen in the local tavern bemoaning his son's enlistment in the *enosis* cause, opens a new chapter just as the book draws to a close and Durrell is preparing to turn his back on Cyprus: 'He came panting down the last terrace and gave a tremendous jump into the road, beaming and panting. "Mr. Darling," he cried. "I wanted to tell you that the boy came back! He did not join EOKA because he won a scholarship to London instead" (250). The scene reopens Durrell's relaton with Cypriot youth. As Andreas proceeds to ask Durrell whether his mother would look after the boy in London, Cypriot youth – or is it the emergent postcolonial nationalist elite? – is once again placed in Durrell's charge: "Education is everything," [Andreas] said. "How much we wished for it ourselves. Now perhaps our children can have it." I felt bitterly ashamed of the neglect these people have endured – the Cyps' (250). Durrell's last paternal gesture is the familiar one of the father who has the last word and is, in the end, always right.

It has not been the intention of this section to dismiss Durrell's love for his island of bitter lemons. After all, it is the nature of love often to be misguided and, at times, to be too guided by one of the party's interests. It is selfish and often blind, and reflective assessments of who was at fault for a breakup are rarely instructive. There is something paternal in the gaze from without that seeks to do some good for Hellenism – για την Ελλάδα, ρε γαμώτο. It has been the smaller contempt of this consideration to suggest that Durrell, in one sense, may have quit his post upon his departure from Cyprus but not its mission, as the writing of *Bitter Lemons*, one year later in 1957, seems to bear out. He continued to love Cyprus to death. In this, he was not the only one, as the tragic events of Cypriot history bear out.

It may be that the philhellenic urge, the politics of those from without, encourages the instinct to love those within to death. Loving someone to death may be the appropriate metaphor for many a philhellene encounter as it captures the ambivalence among philhellene and native alike. Once the modern philhellene makes the trip to Greece, he is in a difficult spot. Durrell never returned to Cyprus; nor Miller to Greece (he renewed himself yet again in California). Storace is unlikely to return in a hurry. Ab-sense makes the heart grow fonder, but contact in long-distance relationships will often shatter one's ideals.

Notes

1. 'For Greece, for fuck's sake,' would also be appropriate.
2. The historian Margarita Miliori (2000) has drawn some useful distinctions on this point in her work on nineteenth-century British philhellenism, Hellenism, and Classicism.
3. In the prologue to his *Anthology of Physics* (Φυσικής Απάνθισμα) (1790: στ '), Rhigas affirms that his 'philhellenism' motivates his Enlightenment ideals (όντας φύσει φιλέλλην). The *Ephimeris* of Vienna (discussed in Chapter 2) is 'an offering from philhellenes' to the cause of liberation (προσφορά τοις φιλέλλησι).
4. See the writings of the Greek Committee in London, the *Westminster Review* at the time of the Revolution. Rosen (1992) provides a synthetic account. Roessel (2002) covers the entire modern period.
5. I refer to Victor Davis Hanson and John Heath's *Who Killed Homer? The Demise of Classical Education and the Recovery of Greek Wisdom*. (New York: The Free Press, 1998). For a level-headed critique of this book's alarmism, see Peter Green, *New York Review of Books*, 18 March 1999.
6. Linssen's (1998: 72–100) discussion of principles of Zen is suggestive when placed alongside Miller's *Colossus*.
7. Elsewhere, too, Katsimbalis's speech is flavored with Attic ingredients: 'thyme, sage, tufa, asphodel, honey . . . etc.' (Miller 1958: 31).
8. See photographs of Durrell – the Man who Concealed his Nose with a Hat – in Bowker (1997: 320–1).
9. Durrell did not customarily write prefaces to his travel books (Roessel 2000). Here, Roessel argues that Durrell seeks to 'influence, can we say con, the reader into accepting that Durrell was a thoughtful, unbiased observer who can give a true, disinterested account' (2000: 235).
10. In an interview with Durrell, J. Hawkes describes *Bitter Lemons* as a fiction. 'Lots of people take it as a personal account – I think it's fiction. I think everything you've written is non-fiction and fiction' (Ingersoll 1998: 237). This view sensitizes the reader to the *artifice* of Durrell's narrative.
11. Roufos took this title from a review of *Bitter Lemons* entitled 'Sour Grapes Not Bitter Lemons' by Socrates Evangelides in *The Times of Cyprus* magazine in 1957 (Roessel 1994a: 130).
12. See Roessel (1994a) for more details.
13. In Seferis's diary entry for 1 October 1954, Maurice Cardiff tells Seferis that, since Yugoslavia, Durrell has become a 'right nationalist.' He does not think for himself, but just follows official British policy. Seferis much preferred the pacifist Durrell he knew once in Cairo who used to curse British army officers (Seferis 1986: 147). See also Keeley's (1999: 236) remarks.

14. This quotation appears on the title page of Montis's (1964) book. Unlike Roufos, he makes no mention – veiled or otherwise – of Durrell in the book.

15. Durrell commented on his decision as follows:

> I've been progressively disgusted with our double-facedness in politics. I refused a CMG (Commander of the Order of St. Michael and St. George) on those grounds, though I didn't want to make an issue out of it, and I don't want to – I'm conservative, I'm reactionary, and right wing – so I don't want to embarrass anybody. But the reason I made a political bow-out of the whole thing was that I didn't want to be decorated by people who had bits of the Parthenon lying about in their backyard. (Pine 1994: 393, fn. 41)

16. At this time, Cyprus Radio was also under Durrell's control.

17. Markides holds this position (1989: especially 89).

18. On Durrell's inclination to relate his Irishness to an 'oriental' imagination or to the dynamics of the colonized–colonizer relationship, see Pine (1994: 274); Herbrechter (1999: 245–51).

19. On this, also J. F. Stewart (1998).

20. Originally known as the Greek School, it was founded in 1812 by Archbishop Kyprianos. Inspired by the Greek Revolution against the Ottomans in Greece, Kyprianos tried to instigate revolution in Cyprus and was hanged by the Turks in July 1821

21. In particular, consider the Erechtheum's portico on the east cella and the porch with Ionic columns on the north side.

22. I do not disapprove of the policy *per se*, but the British embrace of it at that very moment is what is suspect.

23. Montis's account – a response to Durrell – makes sure to talk of the torture cells.

24. 'Corfu is Prospero's island in the sense that everyone falls asleep.' Malta also has the same effect on the British, according to Durrell. See the extract taken from 'The Spirit of Place: Lawrence Durrell's Greece' produced for the BBC by Peter Adam in Ingersoll (1998: 163).

25. The title of his collection of poems is taken from the name of the tree which stands outside Bellapaix Abbey in Cyprus, and which confers the gift of idleness on all who sit under it. See the author's note to the collection.

26. 'I dislike writing about politics' (*Bitter Lemons* 121).

27. Anecdotally, this has been shown to be a fiction as the real Panos was still living in Cyprus when David Roessel went to Cyprus in 1994 (Roessel 2000: 244).

28. On the spread of nationalist activity in the schools of Cyprus, by the Church and by EOKA, see Bryant (1998); Demetriades (1994); Maratheftis (1992); Papadopoulos (1987); Persianis (1978). For a discussion of the colonial formation of masculinity in Egypt and Cyprus through literature, see Spanaki (1997).

8

Global Readings

Will the Turk Remain a Turk and the Greek a Greek to the Last?

> . . . and the Turk remained a Turk to the last.
>
> Georgios Vizyenos, 'Moscov-Selim'

It is with this emphatic quote that the late-nineteenth-century writer Georgios Vizyenos's ends his short story 'Moscov-Selim.' Like his five other gem-like tales,[1] the luster of this story derives in part from its complex exposition of identity through an artful problematization of linguistic, gender, and national categories. Many of the seemingly straightforward titles of his stories – 'My Mother's Sin,' 'The Only Journey of his Life' – only draw attention to the very difficulty of fathoming *which* sin and *which* journey he is referring to, if – that is – one has been committed or undertaken in the first place. Consequently, Vizyenos's assertive last sentence cited above should not be taken at face value. Did the war-weary Moscov-Selim, in fact, remain in his heart of hearts a Turk to the last, as the Greek narrator affirms? Who was Moscov-Selim? To read the emphatic last line as a clear indication that he *has* remained 'a simple, strange Turk' is a sign not only of the reader's inclinations to think this, but also the effect of a trusting reader's response to the Greek narrator's resolution in the story's preamble:

> I wish I'd never met you on my path; I wish I'd never known you in my life! You gave my soul enough grief to drink, you simple, strange Turk.
> [. . .] I don't doubt that the fanatics of your race will curse the memory of a 'believer' because he opened the sanctuary of his heart to the unholy eyes of an infidel. I fear that the fanatics of my own race will reproach a Greek author because he did not conceal your virtue, or did not substitute a Christian hero in his account. But don't worry. Nothing will be detracted from your merit because you entrusted the adventures of your life to me; and I shall never be conscience-stricken because, as a simple chronicler, I valued in you, not the inexorable enemy of my nation, but simply the man. So don't worry – I shall write your story. (Vizyenos 1988: 186–7)

But is the story's narrator a trustworthy chronicler? In choosing to focus on the eponymous hero's choice between Moscov and Selim at the story's end, are we, like the Greek narrator, arbitrating between the component parts of his name instead of focusing on the hyphen? For Moscov-Selim's seeming articulation of a position on the matter toward the end of the tale occurs amidst increasingly obtrusive narratorial interventions. In his deathbed delirium, Moscov-Selim's sentences become either 'incoherent' to the narrator or they melt into ellipses (Vizyenos 1988: 228).

The effect of Vizyenos's story rests on the relation between the Greek narrator to his Turkish subject in ways that oblige the careful reader to be skeptical about that narrator's ability or desire to be, as he professes, 'a simple chronicler.' The pregnant moments at the end of all Vizyenos's stories do engender narrative self-reflection on its own recreation.[2] Vizyenos's ending, therefore, may seem to end with a resolution – that 'the Turk remained a Turk to the last' – but it is met with a counter-proposal, which whispers from the white silence of the *hors-texte*. Perhaps it was 'the Greek [who] remained a Greek to the last' (Chryssanthopoulos 1994: 159). 'Moscov-Selim' is narrated by a Greek who, by his strategic and self-conscious thematization of this dynamic, wills other Greeks to read the Turk his way. Overseeing this process is the author Vizyenos and the successive reader of the tale.

Georgios Vizyenos's story was written at a time when large sections of the peoples who considered themselves bearers of Greek consciousness and who still lived in areas of the Ottoman Empire, which were as yet remain 'unredeemed.' They had not been incorporated into the borders of the modern Greek state, as the *Megali Idea* promised. Vizyenos (1849–95) himself hailed from just such a town, Vizyi, in eastern Thrace. The Athens-based litterati labeled him a '*tourkomeritis*,' that is 'one from Turkish parts'; it is clear that his subject position, quite literally, determined his theoretical distance and perspective on the nature of identity. Like Rhigas before him, he was an Ottoman Greek. Like Moscov-Selim's 'sartorially proclaimed ethnic hybridity, a bright red sash [under] an old soldier's topcoat' (190), Vizyenos signifies, and is signified by, a multilayering of identities. This profile elicits in his writing a 'transvestite effect,' 'a mode of articulation, a way of describing a space of possibility [that] puts in question the idea of one: of identity, self-sufficiency, self-knowledge' (Garber 1992: 11; Barbeito 1995).[3]

It is no surprise that Vizyenos's works have of late received much critical consideration and his star has risen high in the literary heavens. The postmodernist turn in fiction, and the concern for the performative fictions of identity construction in Greece as elsewhere in the West at the end of the century, have established him as a challenging precursor and model. This cultural examination of difference at the heart of national identity has coincided with a shift of geopolitical perspective in the eastern Mediterranean. In the 1990s, Greek–Turkish relations in the Aegean, in the Balkans, and especially on Cyprus have been reassessed in concerted attempts at rapprochement. The much-publicized 'earthquake diplomacy' that formalized an intensification of Greek–Turkish contacts at many levels, and not only high-level contacts, have spawned micropolitical joint ventures such as the restructuring and rewriting of reciprocal relations, histories, and realities. A long and treacherous road lies ahead. But it has also been combined by a change in Greece's demography. In a short time, Greece has been transformed from a country of emigrants to a home for immigrants. The change has challenged the prevailing homogeneous images of Greek nationalist self-representation.

The local context is, therefore, influenced by the wider concentric circles of the global networks that intersect with it. It is the purpose of this last chapter to examine the meaning of 'Greek' and 'Turk' – the ultimate antinomy of the region and even of Greek Otherness – at a moment of globalization, in which the migration of people, images, and cultural products dislocates entrenched notions of 'home,' 'self,' and 'other' in confusing and, perhaps, even liberating ways. What do we mean by a 'Greek' and 'Turkish' novel when to talk about roots today, so the adage goes, means also to talk about rootlessness and routes in the post-nation?[4] In Chapter 5, we explored the ways in which three Greek modernists tried to root their versions of Greekness in unGreekness. Nowadays, unGreekness takes root and even prospers in the most traditional of urban neighborhoods and villages.

In this new world of routes, visual media and migration, and their interconnectedness, mark the imagination and subjectivity to a greater degree than those of literature. However, difference is mobilized in many ways, not always cultural, and the symbolic value of authors often holds a lasting cachet. A sleek volume of the late Odysseas Elytis's collected poetry (2002) has sold in unprecedented numbers and has been bought by people who rarely, if ever, read poetry. In Turkey, sales of Orhan Pamuk's novels achieve a similar status. For better or for worse, an archetypal relation is effected between the writer and his or her country. And this 'image' will often complement or resist other prevailing 'images' of that very same culture or people, today when the hyphen of the notion 'nation-state' is being riven apart by the very forces of media, migration, and markets.

In this chapter, I shall be reading a celebrated modern Greek novel alongside a Turkish counterpart. Rhea Galanaki's *The Life of Ismail Ferik Pasha* (trans. 1996), a novel that realizes a new poetics of Greek identity is read alongside the internationally acclaimed Orhan Pamuk's *White Castle* (trans. 1991). I shall consider their remarkable similarities in technique as well as the common modes that they employ to engage issues of otherness and identity. What becomes of 'difference' in postmodern novels in local and global markets (of readership)? What becomes of local difference once it migrates to foreign readerships? What is 'Greek' about a 'Greek' novel? Does a post-national space, shared by Greek and Turkish novelists, provide a place for mutual (self)-understanding wherein neohellenism can reorient itself at the end of the millennium.

'Greek' and 'Turk' in a Global Market: Galanaki's *Pasha* and Pamuk's *White Castle*

Food, like literature, has gone global. The authentic Indian curry, displaced in a world of migration and postcolonial chic, has become part of a transnational restaurant culture which, like film culture, has 'gone global.' Asian restaurateurs, like postcolonial writers, manage the *realpolitik* of metropolitan dominance and so assert an 'authenticity' not normally ascribed to their own culture.[5] Curry served in a bucket, or *balti*, becomes exotic and authentic not because of its remoteness, but as a commodity whose availability and cultural consumption mark it as 'exotic' and 'Indian' in a global sense. In recent years, Greek restaurateurs in Manhattan have risen to this global challenge and offered cross-cultural fusions and regional inflections on Greek cuisine. It may be a sign of the limits of Greek modernity in American eyes that one high-end restaurant was described by one respected magazine as being so chic and stylish a Greek restaurant 'as to be French!'

Readers, like gastronomes, are eager to consume exotically. Writers and their publishers, forever aware of possibilities in transnational markets, and sensitized through their reading of theory to the modes of working through otherness, realize that a novel on the 'periphery' must travel, to Paris, New York, or London, before it returns home as an international success. In so doing, novels from 'peripheral,' and often postcolonial regions, have revitalized contemporary fiction at the center. Of course, the notion of a 'periphery' is a problematic notion, always contextual, and one not to be recommended to those engaging in contrapuntal readings that seek to reinvest local difference with meaning. However, in its very restricted usage here from the perspective of the metropolitan publishing houses with a global reach, their 'stable of writers,' their editors and agents, the term seems relevant.

The Turkish writer Orhan Pamuk has made this trip successfully. His *White Castle* (1979) largely opened the way for him.[6] This should have gladdened the heart of any devotee of Greek literature since the Greek novelist Rhea Galanaki's *The Life of Ismail Ferik Pasha: Spina nel Cuore* (1989), which appeared in Greek at about the time of the English translation of Pamuk's novel, bore a striking resemblance to Pamuk's work.[7] Given the benign push of a decent translation, canny marketing and high-profile critical support, Galanaki's novel had a chance of achieving equal stature. Or so you would think.

Rhea Galanaki has told me that she wrote her book before she had ever read Pamuk's work, let alone met him or even shared a curry with him.[8] The two authors from Europe's margins share remarkable affinities in their textual practices, tropes, and themes. Their subject position would explain this to a degree. This chapter will examine the accessibility of writing strategies, their potential *translatability*, where 'translatability' will mean not the difficulty or ease in rendering an

English translation, but rather it will define their work's susceptibility or access-ibility to forms of (re)cognition, novelistic or otherwise, that will strike a chord with a Western readership. This global economy of meaning that is the inter-national literary canon carries with it a price, a marketing of its own, that impinges on the identity of the literary work itself.[9] The striking similarities and resonances between the two novels merits more exhaustive study.[10] Here, I comment on Pamuk's work only as a stepping-off point to discuss Galanaki. The question of identity will be explored through scenes of return, a theme that has elicited most commentary from critics similarly attuned to postmodern strategies. I follow suit here in order to consider issues stemming from the meeting of postmodernism, global markets, and the Greek and the Turkish novel.

Sp(l)itting Images

The centrality of identity in Western theory and fiction today and the modes for its exposition are not lost on either Pamuk or Galanaki. Updike (1991: 102) asserts that Pamuk 'knows all the tricks western literature has to teach,'[11] including the couplings, splittings, mirrorings, paradoxes, opposites, and the undermining of grand narratives so beloved in the postmodern works of Rushdie, Calvino, and Borges. These do actually exist in the Greek tradition, indeed, most notably, in the work of Georgios Vizyenos.[12] Yet writers today experience what Rushdie has called 'one of the more pleasant freedoms of the literary migrant to choose his parents' (Rushdie 1991: 21).

The White Castle tells of an Italian slave, taken captive at sea by the Ottoman fleet and eventually given to a scholar-inventor named Hoja, the teacher, who is his sp(l)itting image. Traditional stereotypes of East and West are blurred, but an oppositional logic underlies the two characters' profile – the one is a Western slave, a dreamy storyteller and our narrator; the Other is, surprisingly enough, the Eastern master, awed by science and reason, but resistant to writing. At one level, Pamuk enters into a dialogue with Hegel's exposition of dependence and independence of self-consciousness and the distinctions between Self and Other by way of an analysis of lordship and bondage (Hegel 1931: 228–40). Subordination is con-sidered as the condition of development and maintenance of consciousness: 'Self-consciousness exists in itself and for itself, in that, and by the fact that it exists for another self-consciousness; that is to say, it *is* only by being acknowledged or "recognised"' (1931: 229). Pamuk's dispassionate intelligence oversees the exchange and studied conflation of recognizable binaries. Turk and Venetian look long and hard into mirrors, write their past histories as psychotherapy, and delve into various epistemologies – reminiscent of Flaubert's eminently proto-post-structuralist *Bouvard et Pécuchet* – to answer and inscribe 'Why Am I What I Am?'[13]

The commerce of personhood(s) unfold(s) at many points in the novel and it is often driven by a power differential between characters. In one such context, our two protagonists construct a superweapon in the hope that it will assist the Sultan in his next campaign in the West. This campaign ends in disaster when the weapon, the grand size of 'a mosque,' gets stuck in the mud and obliges the Sultan to abandon the siege of the airy white castle of the title, located in Poland. Concurrently, a debate rages over the identity of master and slave peoples; and the game of identity, previously pursued in exchanges between the two protagonists, is transferred to an exchange between Hoja and a series of different peoples. Hoja interrogates unwitting Christian peoples that the Sultan conquers on his path. He seeks to determine their most heinous sins and, by violent means, he hopes to understand 'what kind "they" and, furthermore, "we" were' (133). 'In all this,' as Hegel writes, 'the unessential consciousness is, for the master, the object which embodies the truth of his certainty of himself. But it is evident that this object does not correspond to its notion; for, just where the master has effectively achieved lordship, he really finds that something has come about quite different from an independent consciousness . . . rather a dependent consciousness that he has achieved' (Hegel 1931: 236–7).

As various peoples allied with the Poles are listed, the castle is described as 'purest white and beautiful': 'I didn't know why I thought that one could see such a beautiful and unattainable thing only in a dream' (143). Pamuk evokes such dreaminess as a counterpoint to the scene's historicity, and the castle's cameo appearance in a novel that bears its name serves as a ploy for downplaying its importance in the plot. To this end, in the prologue, Faruk Darvinoglou (son of Darwin), the supposed discoverer and editor of the manuscript before us, contends that he did not 'choose the title of the book, but the publishing house that agreed to print it' (12). Moreover, when he retold the story to friends, Darvinoglou confesses that he would emphasize its symbolic value and relevance to contemporary realities. As a result, 'young people usually more absorbed in issues like politics, activism, East–West relations, or democracy were at first intrigued, but soon forgot my story' (11). As Western readers of a Turkish novel, we are prodded gently to identify with just such readers, we are made conscious of our eagerness or inclination, to grasp a commentary on Turkey and the West which Pamuk offers passive-aggressively by way of Darvinoglou. Simultaneously he disowns the gesture even as he proposes it, with consummate diffidence. Or so he wants us to think, momentarily. It is a gesture similar to one we have encountered early on in *this* book in the deconstructive ploy of placing the 'modern' in 'modern' Greece under erasure. An interpretation is exposed only to be crossed out; however, this crossing out, far from making that reading disappear, makes it that much more unavoidable and worthy of our critical attention. Such diversionary tactics are written to preempt 'sophisticated' readers who might rush gleefully to draw deterministic parallels between the siege of the white castle and the Turks' seventeenth-century defeat in Vienna, and not Poland.[14] Pamuk's narrator obstructs the one-to-one correlation of the white castle with Vienna by mentioning the campaign to Vienna as having taken place *after* the Polish escapade described here and *after* 'Hoja's' return to Istanbul (147). Regardless, the correlation with the Ottoman Turks' failed second siege of Vienna in 1683 remains in the background, under erasure. The Turks' defeat at the second siege of Vienna in 1683 holds enormous importance for Turkish identity. It marks the advance of the Austrians and their allies into Ottoman territory and it leads to a distinct change in their fortunes. They are no longer equal in power to the West and at Carlowitz in 1699, for the first time, they sign a treaty imposed on them by victors (Lewis 1964).

With all this subtle positioning, Pamuk walks the fine line of seeming at pains to keep his novel from being reduced to an allegory of his country – where an 'authentic' cultural identity would run the risk of falling into the totalizing expectations of the metropolitan gaze on the 'periphery' – while courting this very undifferentiated image. In this regard, Pamuk's predicament reminds one of the problem shared by postcolonial writers – in particular Latin American writers – who resist the packaging of their novels as expressions of their whole 'continent.' This is to no avail in Pamuk's case, since even the translator of his last novel admits that he 'deliberately set out to become a world-class writer, [and] has borrowed the attitudes and strategies of Third World authors writing for the consumption of the First World' (Gün 1992: 62).

The campaign for the white castle ends in defeat for the Ottomans and for Hoja. Conqueror has been conquered, and it is at this moment that the Venetian narrator confesses that he and Hoja are able to think the very same things at the same time. The narrator then *seems to suggest* that the two protagonists change clothes and identities, and that Hoja the Turk 'returns' joyfully to Italy as if he were Italian and the Italian narrator 'stays home' in Turkey as if he were Hoja the Turk. By uniting these three levels – at the level of the two protagonists, at the grander level of the European and Turk, and at the metanarrative level of the Turkish novelist writing for translation – Pamuk's notion of exchange is conditioned not by the seeming simplicity of facts provided by either individual or national history but, in fact, by processes of difference that have forever meant the inculcation of Self in Other and vice versa. So much so that it is no longer possible to speak of two distinct entities with any degree of assurance. Master and slave, the role of conqueror and conquered, have been reversed or nullified, at the interpersonal and interethnic level. They are no longer distinguishable.

Galanaki's novel engages the same question of subordination in consciousness and in history. Beaton points to the book's significance as one of the first Greek novels to confront 'the heritage of Greece today [that] includes its history as province of the Ottoman Empire' (Beaton 1994: 292); Lambropoulos (1994) believes that if neohellenists faced up to the Greek Ottoman past as a colonial experience, then the postcolonial prism would offer refreshing new interpretive strategies for analyzing Hellenism. Galanaki may not be as programmatic as Pamuk in her politics, but the exhortations of critics to relocate the study of this novel into repressed 'eastern' or postcolonial contexts, or where the Third World or the 'minor' is read by the center, need to be given further consideration.

The book's title recalls Kazantzakis's *The Life and Times of Alexis Zorba*, which was adapted by film-maker Michalis Cacoyiannis for international release, tellingly retitled *Zorba the Greek* and furnished Western audiences with stereotypes of the quintessential Greek for a couple of decades.[15] In the film, the novel's Greek narrator is transformed into a half-Greek, half-British intellectual who internalizes and internationalizes the clash of civilizations portrayed in the novel's depiction of the Boss and Zorba. Galanaki also offers us a life (a *vios*), the hagiography or *synaxarion* of a Christian-turned-infidel, which evokes a blending of traditions further complicated by a subtitle that reminds us that this saint hailed from the Venetian-ruled Lasithian plateau known as 'a thorn in Venice's heart.'[16] Hagiography carries with it its own typologies, of veneration and secular biography, and the particularities of its encoder's access to a variety of literate/patristic, folkloric, and regional/oral material. If Galanaki is proposing a new prototypical figure, his twin nature or 'origins' rivals that of pagan-turned-Christian saints and another originary Greek figure, Diyenis Akritas the Twyborn, whose epic, for some, marks the beginning of modern Greek literature.[17]

Galanaki's prefatory note to the novel admits to a focus on a sketchily available historical persona, whose personal history and its narration straddles the divide of the public and private sphere. Like Cavafy's poem 'Caesarion,' inadequate sources and the oral tradition provide insufficient 'historical' grounding and so allow the writer greater license. Also, Galanaki's highly poetic style tears overtly and persistently at the novel's underlying claim to historicity. But Galanaki never forsakes this claim to history, and the strong presence of a phenomenal world guards the novel from shifting completely into the realm of the fantastic or the sustained allegory. Conversely, Pamuk's dream-like description of the castle scene keeps history perceptible by signposting the act of its very repression.

The splittings in Galanaki's novel are initiated in a primordial scene, in a cave, when a young boy in hiding from the Ottoman Turks is separated from his mother and is taken captive with his brother.[18] Guilt-ridden by his absence from the village square, alongside the men who fought and were slaughtered in defense of their homes and their identity, the young Emmanuel is sold into slavery in Egypt while his brother, Antonis Kambanis, eventually resides in Athens. If Pamuk focuses the energy of potentiality in the phallic and religiously described superweapon, Galanaki privileges a knife that the boy takes with him from the cave on his travels. The knife is overinvested with symbolic meaning and serves as a reminder to him of the Father's Law. As he leaves the village, Ismail comes across the conquering general Hassan Pasha at the moment that he is thrown from his bolting horse. The young boy moves to help up the fallen rider, but on noticing that 'the conqueror's face resembled his own' (17) and that the Other is also his Double, the boy pushes him away. Master and slave roles are conflated in a proleptic mirroring that prefigures the boy's eventual return to Crete as a conquering Egyptian-cum-Ottoman general. Even the posthumous fate of Hassan Pasha's corpse will echo the young boy's fate later in the novel: 'the Ottomans collected the body of Hassan Pasha, killed by the bolting horse . . . They carried him to Candia secretly, for fear his death would embolden the spirits of the vanquished' (17).

For now, the boy considers himself dead in his first life and now reborn into a second, his Egyptian – 'in the nature of one newly dead and newly born' (19). Emmanuel is Islamicized and assumes the name Ismail, a reversal of the *synax-arion* genre, since a change of identity and name is, conventionally, given to those who convert *to* Christianity and are thus 'reborn.' He is befriended by Ibrahim, the viceroy Muhammed's son, and eventually he climbs up the ranks to become the Minister of War.[19] His 'secret engagement' to Ibrahim and Egypt is described in sexual terms of giving oneself (99), and in terms that conflate Ismail's mother with the one who 'had mothered [his] second life' (134), Ibrahim. Any *cyclical* promise of return, anticipated by the myth of *nostos* is countered by the 'quivering line traced by the course of the Nile' (27).[20] Ismail assumes an Egyptian identity that prevails upon his Greek memories, language, and identity. Only when a cousin brings news to him, in Greek, that his brother lives comfortably in Athens and is one of the benefactors of the Cretan revolutionary struggle against Ottoman rule, does Ismail embark upon *nostos*, return, the circularity that has *always already* been at hand. This course is taken and is reflected in Ismail's correspondence with his brother, Antonis, in Athens, which recalls the psychotherapeutic written exercises between Pamuk's Hoja and his slave lookalike. With a latent homo-eroticism reminiscent of Pamuk's depiction of his own protagonists, Ismail describes his brother's first letter to him as follows: 'touching a woman in the harem had never aroused such desperate passion in him as Antonis's kiss' (59).[21] His reverie in this scene leads him back to images of his mother and father. Later in his last letter, Antonis bids Ismail farewell 'the way I knew you in childhood' (71). Sourbati concludes that Ismail's return to Crete aims to balance the archetypal equation. This return to origins, described as a descent into an embryonic stage dominates the novel's second part. Narrated in the first person by Ismail himself, it traces his nine-month tour of duty, which coincides with his rebirth backwards as a boy, in a reverse process of becoming and belonging with the paternal blood-line and his filial duty.[22] He will become again his father's son and return to relive his mother's last embrace. By spring, Ismail is sent to quell a rebellion in Crete that has been funded by his brother. He returns as potential conqueror to *mirror* and *embody* Hassan Pasha, the conqueror of Lasithi who had fallen off his horse and taken Ismail captive earlier in the novel. He will return to the cave of his innocence where like Jesus-Emmanuel or Zeus, offspring of Rhea, both Galanaki and the goddess from the Lasithian plateau, he will die and be reborn again (Sourbati 1992: 176). Like Pamuk's castle, the narrative and the slippages of identity are ordered by a quest, in this case, a recognition of 'the face of a boy I had been' (*Pasha*, 114–15).

In her analysis, Sourbati (1992: 182) privileges one scene of recognition 'where the *nostos* will end.' Yet there are really a number of central scenes as there are a series of possibilities for all events in the novel.[23] Typical of postmodern historiographic metafiction, analepses, prolepses as well as internal focalizations scramble any notion of linear and homogeneous time and leave us with dissected scenes at different points in the text and from multiple perspectives (Yannakaki 1994). There are multiple staged scenes of return.

One such scene of return occurs on his way to the plateau, in the port of Iraklion, where, years earlier, he had been separated from his brother: 'I told myself that for many centuries the conquerors and the conquered had been setting the scene for the last act of my life in a manner reminiscent of the operatic stage sets I had seen in Europe long ago' (126). The harbor, represented as a European opera set, evokes notions of opera's reliance on script and a stylized excess that proclaims its artifice. By way of opera's 'unnatural' conventions, as in the *favola* or fable of early opera, the drama is set to, and follows, a recognizable tune. Galanaki stresses theatricality throughout as the reader watches Ismail play out or project for himself a number of roles that structure identity along the potential li(n)es of origin, purity, and return. The commerce between author and reader takes center stage in a game of anticipation, thrust and parry. In this first scene of return on Crete, Ismail performs a self-consciousness that comes with realizing oneself to be part of history's grand production. The melancholic image of a piece of driftwood in the harbor left over by the 'craftsmen' of history – the conquerors and conquered of Iraklion – emblematizes his brother's place in the grand narratives of history.[24] His brother had played 'his role well.' Soon the readers become conscious of their role in this grand production and hereafter follow Ismail's ineluctable and choreographed progress in an archetypal unwritten script to the seemingly central scene of *nostos* back to the cave. However, as with Pamuk's centering scene at the castle (set in Poland and not Vienna), a one-to-one correlation of *arche* and *telos* is thwarted – Ismail returns not to the womb-like cave, but to the familial home. A key turns in the house door, and not in the cave as it does in the opening line of the novel and which promised to give life coherence.

Once the *nostos* scene is so unlocked, it brims with allusions to the *Odyssey*'s Nekiya (XI) and Seferis's poetry of returning exiles. Ismail draws blood and summons the spirits of his family. And though he derives some satisfaction from his mother's unconditional acceptance of him and his communion with the house itself, his father, while forgiving, does not acknowledge his right to the family line. His brother appears, 'though his being still among the living should not have permitted it' (149). As in much magical realism, or in folktales, the boundaries of the dead and the living spill over into each other and this in-betweenness manifests itself 'at an imaginary point inside a double-sided mirror that reflects in both directions' (Faris 1995: 172). The fantastic or phantasmic element only heightens Ismail's conscious and willed desire to effect a scene of *anagnorisis*. Ismail perceives his brother in the freezed frame of a photograph, in a theatre's foyer dressed in a linen suit and narrow cravat, which, in its incongruous detail and setting pushes the scene toward comedy. But Antonis's 'framing' and the reference to theatre causes the reader to take a step back from the *récit* into the foyer of the theatre, perhaps, to converse with Antonis about the conventions and artifice of Ismail's staged scene of return. Antonis fixes his gaze off into the distance, through the invisible (to him) Ismail, and away from the mirror that Ismail holds up to him to prove their likeness. There seems to be no contact, visual or physical. Yet Ismail's interpretation of the encounter assures that his brother's obliviousness not obstruct their identification:'He knew that the face of the patriot and national benefactor would reveal its resemblance to the face of the renegade and conqueror. He gazed beyond the scene in an effort to evade acknowledging the resemblance, due not only to kinship, but to a shared solitude . . . I knew that he lived, and would die, utterly alone, like me' (150). Ismail's will to resemblance reflects the implied reader's willed pursuit of a recognition scene, and so subtly foregrounds the conventions and expectations that drive any reading of *nostos*. The detached reflection of the last line of this scene carries an undertow of cruel irony: '[Antonis] was fortunate enough never to set eyes on me again' (150), since Ismail is certainly conscious that Antonis did not set eyes on him on this occasion, in this scene, either.

In his concluding chapter, Pamuk also uses the mirror to play out the paradoxes of sameness and difference. The 'new Hoja' buys a poor devil from the slave market to serve as a supplement for his absent Other – who, due to the previous chapter's ambiguity, is also his Double – and so restages cherished exercises of identity. However, his slave turns away when 'he is brought. . . to face the mirror,' and an exasperated 'Hoja' takes him back to the slave market to sell him back for the artifice of his *supplementary* role-playing hardly rises to the standard of a persuasive reenactment or sustainable illusion.

The third part of Galanaki's novel, the *Epimythio*, follows the 'centering scene,' just as the 'centering' scene of *The White Castle* is followed by the last chapter and the 'new Hoja's' reflection on events. As the title *Epimythio* suggests, this is literally the part 'after the story' (though the Greek translates as 'the moral of the fable'). Predictably, neither its chronology, the moral, nor the difference between life and death is simple. Hard facts are nowhere to be found, only variant accounts of Ismail's death live on in the reconstructed narratives of political and diplomatic interests, gossip, rumor, superstition, and local lore relayed by an omniscient third-person narrator: first, Ismail is poisoned for his treason and crypto-Christianity by Omer Pasha and heard to mutter the name of his mother in Greek and Ibrahim in Arabic; second, his 'murder' is hushed up by the Egyptians so as not to cause diplomatic problems with the Ottomans; third, his fate is disseminated in the imaginings and rumor-mongering of the ship's crew that ferried his body to Egypt. More magical versions follow. In the first, a levitating breeze accompanies Ibrahim's shade or spirit to Ismail's tent and narrates Ismail's encounter with an old woman. From his secret hideout, Ibrahim partially relates what transpires, filtered through a third-person narration, and maintains, often by inference, that the old woman sees a Cross or a mark on Ismail's neck. She speaks in a language Ibrahim can not make out but intimates may be Greek as she exclaims joyfully at this *anagnorisis*. This belated *nostos* is overseen by one of Omer's spies – 'who was able to see what was exactly going on' (163)[25] – and this leads to a poisoning identical or similar to the one given in the first version of Ismail's death above.

In the second version, the Turks of Crete build a cenotaph in Ismail's honor, right next to the tomb of Hassan Pasha, the conqueror of Lasithi, who had fallen off his horse and taken Ismail captive earlier in the novel. Situated by a mosque, where Orthodox and Catholic churches once stood, the cenotaph, now standing on the soil of a Europeanizing modern Greek state, is dismantled in 1930 and a school is built, ironically, against the wishes of those who protest to preserve it out of respect for Ismail's alleged 'crypto-Christianity.' A cenotaph, literally 'an empty tomb,' is signified by successive uniform readings projected onto it. The name of the soldier housed or commemorated in tombs or imagined in cenotaphs is typic-ally unknown, though his nationality is never in question, as Benedict Anderson underscores in his presentation of this figure for nationalism. In Ismail's cenotaph, the soldier's name is well known but his nationality and identity become a source of contestation. This postmodern reversal collapses the distinction between private and public realms that inscribe the narrative of our hero. The act of cenotaphic inscription has always been the fate of the orphan, wiped clean of his origins only to be socioculturally reinscribed – like Mohammad Ali, the once Albanian Omer Pasha, or all the orphans that grew to be janissaires. The cenotaph is a monument to forgetting as part of remembering. And the janissaire serves as the quintessential agent for forgetting. Moreover, when the janissaire would return to conquer his own 'homeland,' he would be the agent of forgetting in others' consciousness.

In the third version, Ismail's soul, reincarnated in the form of a boy, lingers in a school playground nearby and narrates to the schoolchildren a wholly unmagical truth about the *nostos* scene. He confesses to no scene of return, no innocence or purity of soul for, he explains, he had turned the blade of paternal law on himself. This final scene is the most extreme repudiation of all the frustrated returns in the novel and their logic of unity, yet it can not be read as a *telos* and has no privileged status as *the* moral or even *the* ending of the story. Galanaki, however, does stage it as just such an ending. Just as she posited a centering scene, she posits here a realist ending only as an invitation for the rug to be pulled from underneath it. 'However good or bad [realist texts] may be,' Màrquez notes, 'they are books which finish on the last page' (Mendoza and Màrquez 1983: 56). Galanaki's novel fulfils this requirement even as it upstages this convention. As postmodern text, *Pasha* is 'double-coded,' an appealing trait for both popular consumption and 'sophisticated' readership (Eco 1984). The storytelling multiplicity of the novel's last part resists the personal nature of modernist narrative and, instead, endorses the feeling that Ismail's tale also belongs to the reader. The self-reflexivity of its metafiction undermines and denaturalizes the 'truth' in the historical record as it exposes, often by parody, the narrative imperatives of a past order. Echoing Benedict Anderson, Pamuk and Galanaki remind us of the very imaginings that we have forgotten, they remind us how cultural memory is constituted and how it is founded on forgetting. The impulse to deconstruct the very processes of reading that elicit the homogeneities and li(n)es of origin, purity, and return calls forth a regime of reading resistant to deeply ingrained patterns dependent on distinct notions of identity, central scenes of revelation, scenes of *nostos*, and definitive endings. At times these works employ such tropes and typologies, only to pull the rug from under them. They are gestures under erasure, if you will. The 'ending' of Galanaki's novel is a case in point.

The decentering of the centering scenes in both novels also rewrite national myths. Pamuk talks about the Turks' traumatic defeat at the gates of Vienna by displacing this frustrated scene of conquest that marks their exclusion from Europe. He collapses the distinction of inside/outside Europe. The Turkish Self is, and has always been, written and implicated in the European Other, and vice versa, in ways that can not be disentangled. There is (and always has been) an ongoing exchange beyond and between the identity of Hoja and the Italian, the Easterner and Westerner, Turkey and Venice/Europe, slave and master, the other and the self: 'Consciousness finds that it immediately is and is not another consciousness, as also that this other is for itself only when it cancels itself as existing for itself, and has self-existence only in the self-existence of the other . . . They recognize themselves as mutually recognizing one another' (Hegel 1931: 231). For her part, Galanaki focuses on a frustrated *nostos* to critique the logic of history and national identity by deconstructing the modes of narration and reading that generate it. Greek criticism's response to this challenge has been to situate *Pasha* in relation to an indigenous tradition of the Greek historical novel, which it both defies and rewrites.[26] This is a necessary task. But, doing so by seeking its genealogical 'origins' is at odds with the novel's foremost concerns and only exhibits the very discourse of hermetic national philology that the work strives to undermine.

Galanaki has elsewhere stated her indifference to the philosophy and language of the traditional historical novel in Greece, and this reading of 'history' does not do justice to the novel's transnational kinfolk or to its philosophical orientations.[27] For this is a history of the 'conquerors and conquered.' Emmanuel (Ismail) is also Hassan Pasha, victims both of a highly stylized act of self-reading: 'I told myself that for centuries the conquerors and conquered had been setting the scene for the last act of my life in a manner reminiscent of the operatic stage sets I had seen in Europe long ago' (126). Like Pamuk, Galanaki underscores the inner alterity within identity, the inculcation of the Other in the Self, the slave in the master. In other words, the Turk, and the Turkish reader, need not remain a Turk to the last nor the Greek a Greek, to misquote Georgios Vizyenos at the end of his tale 'Moscov-Selim.'

For some, this was too much hyphenation for one identity to bear. Consequently, *Pasha* was nominated to officially represent Greece at an international book festival, but was withdrawn due to stiff opposition in some conservative quarters. And the most prominent review the book received was excoriating. Alev Adil (1996a, 1996b), its reviewer for the *Times Literary Supplement* (5 July 1996), found it 'binarist' and 'chauvinist.' For her, *Pasha* did not even aspire to bad orientalism and its essentialism explored not the 'multiple nature of identity but its fixity and unity.' Adil chastises the book for its intellectual laziness, historical simplifications, and poetic incomprehensibility. This, when in fact, Galanaki's admittedly excessive yet highly poetic style is deployed self-consciously precisely to tear overtly and persistently at the novel's claim to historicity. The phenomenal world lingers amidst this poeticity and so relativizes literature's relation to history, politics, and truth. 'Literature' fights by irregular means against history and politics, exploiting its unstable position in-between realms and genres, culture and politics, as well as in-between Greek and Turk, to pose a threat to those unwilling to read *against* the modes that write them in history as individuals, and as Turks and Greeks to the last.

Thankfully, the review provoked outrage among *TLS* readers (19 July 1996).[28] But it also triggered retaliatory counter-essentialism among its supporters. Friends suggested that Adil's Turkish-Cypriot origin was to blame for her gross misinterpretation of this Greek book.[29] I preferred to pin blame elsewhere by recourse to a different essentialism. Adil had disowned Galanaki's novel not on account of her being too 'Turkish Cypriot,' but too 'Western'! Her imperious call for well-rounded characters bespoke a penchant for European high realism, and not the traditions alluded to by Galanaki's novel. The characters Adil describes as 'ciphers' would not be so viewed were they situated in the relevant traditions of the folktale, the hagiography, local lore, oral family and community history, or even the Balkan postmodern allegory.[30] The novel draws from cultural modes where characters are horizontally dispersed across personas. Adil's review is an example of transnational misreading from a position that purports to defend 'literature': 'I am deeply committed, not to any national identity, but to literature. I would have done my imagined community of readers a great disservice if I had lied to them and praised what I felt to be a bad novel in order to parade my political conscience.' This may be typical of the belles-lettrism's ongoing grudge against post-modernism. But Adil's very likely honest review is not one without a politics. It bears testament to just how deeply ingrained these politics of reading are, and how resistant we are, to reading against our selves.

(Self) Writing, (Self) Reading

As writers, Pamuk and Galanaki themselves play on another stage, on which they perform as self-consciously as does Ismail on the operatic set that is the port of Candia. Such novels position themselves, and are positioned, in a larger global marketplace. Some might reject such notions, rather romantically, in defense of the integrity or 'authenticity' of the writer's craft. I do not mean to denigrate these writers' skills. Nor do I overlook that writers often claim to write with no-one except themselves in mind (if they know who that is). And, sure enough, these works have a very different life in their own countries than they do as works in translation. Very often their local signification may have little resonance and even be unreadable in global contexts. But particularism and universalism also supplement each other as they need each other 'in order to avoid a dialogic encounter which would necessarily jeopardize their reputedly secure and harmonized mono-logic worlds. Universalism and particularism endorse each other's defect in order to conceal their own.'[31] Global readings and nativist/nationalist resistances to them are two sides of the same coin. By preserving such tensions, we assure that cultural difference seeks out new significations beyond the confines of a policed ethnic home.

Clearly, Pamuk and Galanaki's ex-centric narratives share a relation to dominant, global discourses of fiction. My parallel reading of the two novels implies an underlying postmodern archetype that informs their structure and dynamic, that, to a degree, conflicts with their tendency to undermine and deconstruct grand ordering narratives. Does not such a likeness endanger difference in the local setting? Once such a book is translated, how is cultural specificity preserved? In Galanaki's case, the novel's fantastic element recalls certain cultural and communal traditions that are regarded, in a certain sense, as 'Greek.' Splittings, mirrorings and other tropes alluded to in her novel find precursors in the paralogy of the folktale, Vizyenos's subversion of categories and genres, and Cavafy's conception of history. But what if these traits in Galanaki are read by the metropolitan reader as traces of magical realism similar to those found in South American prose? How does such an equation commodify the work's brand of otherness? Does the metropolitan reader who sees only magical realist traces run the risk of colluding in a cultural imperialism of sorts and, by reading difference uniformly around the world, only exoticize or stylize it? How does the equation of this Greek and Turk's work commodify their otherness? Do they collude in a cultural imperialism of sorts and so only contribute to (mis)reading of difference uniformly around the world? The risk here of effacing local difference may be offset by the argument that the reading strategies championed by such novels constitute a cultural community themselves that, in time, will engender new paradigms and visions ready to dismantle such cultural imperialisms. Surely it is perilous to define what, in fact, is the authenticity from which one can claim to know the un-exoticized and un-stylized otherness that stands at the heart of Greek identity. It is perhaps time to acknowledge that there is no local or authentic site or home. There is no site for the 'production of locality' *outside* the networks of globalization or *beyond* its politics.[32] The new homogeneities and heterogeneities of modernity have to be created in full realization of, dialogue with, and resistance against the global systems of meaning that will inform identities and differences on an albeit unequal playing field. We need to speculate on how this master–slave dialectic at the heart of the 'world literature' industry impinges on what it means to be a 'Greek' or 'Turkish' novelist at the local level as well as in a post-national space where meaning is ever translatable and transferable.

There are, surely, other fine postmodern novels in Greece today as there are other able novelists in Turkey.[33] Yet only Pamuk has gained for himself the mantle of the 'Turkish' writer in the West and only he 'is part of . . . the New International Voice – like Isabel Allende . . . who too must not be the only good writer in Chile, although she's the one we buy and read, in translation' (Gün 1992: 59). Pamuk's profile in the *White Castle* coincides with an integrationist geopolitical and cultural vision of Turkey promoted ardently by interests in the West, and especially by the United States. Since *White Castle*, Pamuk's increasing advocacy of minority and human rights in Turkey has further bolstered his image as a figure for Turkish Westernization. But what would it mean if Galanaki aspired to become the 'Greek' novelist in this sense? For starters, it would score a feminist point. However, it is also harder for a Greek author to make an impression abroad as *modern* Greece, a European partner, a member of the First World and the EMU and a claimant of an often slighted 'inner alterity' within Europe, does not, at present, have a pressing claim – classical heritage aside – to the metropolitan imaginary. It is ironic, then, that Galanaki's work projects a 'Greek identity' in the metropolitan imaginary with a book that collapses public and private identity, proposes alternative modes of collectivity, resurrects repressed non-European contexts, and questions the mechanisms of nationalism so unequivocally. Ironically, writers from the margins who wish their complex cultural realities 'translated' for a metropolitan audience may have no recourse other than to see their anti-nationalist work read as a 'national allegory,' even if it is a national allegory about the undoing of the most prevalent national allegories at work in their own countries.[34]

Finally, the designation of a work as a 'national allegory' among Western elite readerships makes it susceptible to another master–slave dialectic. For the work falls under the sway of a multicultural aesthetic that sanctions identity through diversity and vilifies notions of homogeneity. Works must retain just the right amount of national identity, but also steer away from the overdetermined and ideological nationalism inimical to a neoliberal and rational world market of goods and identities. Such local nationalism has no place in a purportedly post-ideological age. Slavoj Žižek (1997: 37) has warned of a postmodern racism that is a symptom of multicultural late capitalism wherein 'liberal 'tolerance' condones the folklorist Other deprived of its substance – like the multitude of 'ethnic cuisines' in a contemporary megalopolis; however, any real Other is instantly denounced for its 'fundamentalism,' since the kernel of Otherness resides in the regulation of its *jouissance*: the real Other is 'patriarchal,' 'violent,' never the Other of ethereal wisdom and charming customs.' From an empty point of universality, there is the danger that the multiculturalist in such a market of identity sanctions forms of the Other's specificity and *jouissance* through the prism of Eurocentric distance and with the power inequalities left intact. Regardless of what the 'real' Other's substance might mean for Žižek, or what it might taste like 'back home,' his conclusions on the current global conjuncture echo some of this study's pre-occupations. 'The relationship between traditional imperialist colonialism and global capitalist self-colonization,' writes Žižek, 'is exactly the same as the relation-ship between Western cultural imperialism and multiculturalism: in the same way that global capitalism involves the paradox of colonization without the colonizing Nation-State metropole, multiculturalism involves patronizing Eurocentrist distance and/or respect for local cultures without roots in one's own particular culture' (Žižek 1997: 44). One need only replace the word 'multiculturalism' with 'ab-sense' in this previous sentence to realize that this current situation is hauntingly reminiscent of the spectral and power relations that have been discussed through-out this study of Greece in and through the eyes of the West.

Notes

1. Vizyenos's six tales have seen a delightful translation into English by William F. Wyatt Jr. (Vizyenos 1988). 'Moscov-Selim' was written two or three years after the publication of his five other short stories (1886) and published in the

journal *Estia*, in installments, from 28 April to 16 May 1895. At the time, Vizyenos was a patient at the Dromokaïtio Asylum, in Athens.

2. Syrimis is more explicit: 'the end of the stories is an opening of the text that penetrates itself in an endless cycle of proceation' (1995: 341).

3. Barbeito (1995) borrows the term from Marjorie Garber, for whom the 'transvestite effect' marks 'the category crisis' and 'entrance into the Lacanian Symbolic' (Garber 1992: 34).

4. See Clifford (1975) and Appadurai (1996).

5. Huggan's (1994) acute consideration of postcolonial chic and how it 'plays' in the Booker Award spurred some of the associations in this section.

6. Panuk's *White Castle* was first published in Turkish with the title *Beyaz Kale* in 1979. Its English translation appeared in 1991 with financial assistance from the Arts Council of Great Britain. His next book, *Kara Kitap* (translated as *Black Book*, 1994), was received with much fanfare.

7. Galanaki's novel will hereafter be referred to as *Pasha*. References to the text are taken from Kay Cicellis's English translation (Galanaki 1996b). That the translation was awarded financial assistance from a UNESCO fund may point to its global 'appeal' and its 'translatability.'

8. The two writers first met in December 1997. Galanaki introduced Pamuk at a bookstore in Patras, western Greece. I introduced Galanaki to Pamuk's work two years earlier in Boston: she had not heard of him. Shortly thereafter, Galanaki published in Greek a reprint of an open letter that she had published to Pamuk in a German journal, in which she considered the bonds that connect them as Greek and Turkish novelists (Galanaki 1996a).

9. For a discussion of such relations, see Gayatri Chakravorty Spivak, 'The Politics of Translation,' in Michèle Barrett and Anne Phillips (eds.), *Destabilizing Theory: Contemporary Feminist Debates* (London: Polity Press, 1982); Edward Said, 'Embargoed Literature,' in Anuradha Dingwaney and Carol Maier (eds.), *Between Languages and Cultures: Translation and Cross-Cultural Texts* (Pittsburgh, PA: University of Pittsburgh Press, 1995). My colleague Jenine Abboushi (1998) has considered transnationalism and the politics of the 'Third World literature translation' in the 'world literature' industry as they apply to Arabic literature in the West. Particularly suggestive is her discussion of novels 'written for translation,' works written in Arabic, the target audience for which is primarily Western.

10. Sourbati (1992) and Thalassis (1991) supply such readings.

11. Reviews by Altinel (1990), Berman (1991), and Innes (1995) discuss just this facet of his work.

12. Beaton (1994) rightly parallels such devices – in particular the exploration of the divided or double self which defies the categories of religion, nationality, and gender – to the short stories of Georgios Vizyenos. 'Two of these stories,'

Beaton adds, 'present a central Turkish character not only in a sympathetic light, but as in some way the counterpart or *alter ego* of a Christian one: Kiamil in "Who was my Brother's Killer?" and Selim the Muscovite, in the story of that name' (Beaton 1994: 292–3, fn. 66). For insightful readings of such issues in Vizyenos, see Chryssanthopoulos (1994: esp. Chapter 7); Barbeito (1995); Syrimis (1995); Alexiou (2002: 275–316).

13. See Donato (1979) for a discussion of the protagonists' epistemic quests; Gourgouris (1995) argues that the work complicates notions of premodern, modern, or 'post-' literary-historical divisions.

14. Berman (1991: 38) picks up on this allusion, but seems to read Darvinoglou's warning in the prologue at face value. As a result, Berman adjudges that Pamuk fails for 'all manner of interpretations leap to mind,' and he quips 'the sly author has only himself to blame.'

15. The first English translation by Carl Wildman in 1953 also chose the same title, *Zorba the Greek*.

16. In her prefatory note, the author explains that her subtitle *Spina nel Cuore* (di Venezia) – 'a thorn in the heart of Venice' – is taken from a Venetian manuscript of the thirteenth century, which describes the rebellious plateau of Lasithi, in Crete. Thalassis (1991: 100) analyses the incongruities of the title in detail.

17. Parts of the epic's action are taken from the oral tradition, from hagiographical texts and the Lives of Theodore Stratelates or even Lazarus, the future stylite of Mount Galesius. See Trapp (1976); Kazhdan (1993). For a discussion on the blending of popular oral tradition and canonical *Lives*, consult Hart (1992: Chapter 7). The predilection for *synaxaria* as genres to base the exposition of a new archetypal figure in Greece has been continued in Thanassis Valtinos's *synaxarion* of émigré protagonist Andreas Kordopatis.

18. In some Asia Minor novels, the fall from a state of Greco-Turkish coexistence to biblical cataclysm begins with separation from the mother. See Elias Venezis's *Number 31328* (1931) or Dido Soteriou's *Farewell Anatolia* (1962).

19. Parallels can be drawn with the historical figure Muhammad Ali (1805–48) since he was a Turk from Kavala who fought with Egyptian forces against the French and soon imposed himself on the Ottoman government as governor. His successors, the khedives, ruled Egypt, by family right under Ottoman suzerainty.

20. Thalassis (1991: 105–10) takes up the complex exposition of circular and linear metaphors, with attendant feminine or phallic connotations. Despite some suggestive commentary, he concedes that the binaries do not support facile distinctions.

21. The fate of his mother does not allow Ismail 'to touch a woman's body without fear' (20). In contrast, Ismail's relationship with his brother is often

portrayed as ever-deferred physical contact (24, 48); their correspondence is described in terms of the fulfillment of a physical need, for Ismail declares: 'Now I know that You have a body – now I can clasp you in my arms' (60); 'I embrace you' (68); 'Yet but if I could but touch you once again before I die' (70) etc.

22. Sourbati considers a parallel between Ismail and Saleem, the protagonist of Rushdie's *Midnight's Children*.

23. E.g. the book's very first paragraph; the multiple versions of the fate of Ismail's mother; and Ismail's later death.

24. Allusions all to 'rotten brine-soaked timbers' of Seferis's *Mythisorema* VIII, which themselves hark back to Calvos's poetry.

25. I prefer here my own translation over Cicellis's version because the 'ακριβώς' (exactly) of the Greek text is crucial. Seeing what *exactly* happens is precisely at issue, and ironic.

26. Diamantis Axiotis's (1999) historical novel focuses on Mohammed Ali, who oversaw Ismail's entry into the military school of Cairo. Mohammed's origins are contested. He is brought up in a Christian family in Kavala, thus echoing dualities of Galanaki's novel.

27. Maronitis (1992: 47) seeks to locate the 'maternal line' for Galanaki's novel in the tradition of the Greek historical novel. Thalassis (without reference to Maronitis's article) rightly questions the appropriateness of such concepts and language for this novel. See comments made by Galanaki and other Greek novelists – Yatromanolakis, Douka, Valtinos – on the relation between history and fiction (*Hetaireia* 1997).

28. Alix MacSweeney's letter attributes Adil's 'radical misunderstanding of the theme' to her inability to conceive that the work is 'remarkable precisely for its rejection of simplistic nationalist stereotypes.'

29. Leontsini (1996) prudently warns against resorting to such nationalist stereotypes.

30. Galanaki's published notes on the work provide some unexpected readings (1997: 13–60). Ismail Kadare's novels are typical of this trait in Balkan postmodernism (e.g. *The Three Arched Bridge*).

31. See Naoki Sakai, 'Moderntiy and its Critique: The Problem of Universalism and Particularism,' in Masao Miyoshi and Harry D. Harootunian (eds.), *Postmodernism and Japan* (Durham, NC: Duke University Press, 1989) and Rey Chow, *Writing Diaspora: The Tactics of Intervention in Contemporary Cultural Studies* (Bloomington and Indianapolis: Indiana University Press, 1993).

32. The discussion around questions of the production of locality can be traced in David Harvey, *The Limits of Capital* (Chicago: University of Chicago Press, 1984); Arjun Appadurai, *Modernity at Large: Cultural Dimensions of*

Globalization (Minneapolis, MN: University of Minnesota Press, 1996); essays by Anderson, Robbins and Cheah in Pheng Cheah and Bruce Robbins (eds.), *Cosmopolitics: Thinking and Feeling Beyond the Nation* (Minneapolis, MN: University of Minnesota Press, 1998); and, more recently, Michael Hardt and Antonio Negri, *Empire* (Cambridge, MA and London: Harvard University Press, 2000).

33. Some time ago now, Jusdanis (1987a, 1991a) argued that Greek modernism neither separated between 'high' and 'low' culture nor affirmed the autonomy of art as in the West until very late. As a result, the postmodern in Greece manifested itself only in some 'personal statements,' since the conditions for the development of a theoretical problematic were absent. Tziovas rightly argued that this opinion was based too heavily on the reading of Greek modernist poetry. For a discussion of the postmodern in Greek fiction, see Tziovas (1993: Chapter 6). Katsan (2002) comments on a set of Greek postmodern novels that engage similar themes to the ones detailed here in this chapter.

34. The postcolonial context provides insight for the Greek case. In a discussion of postcolonial texts, Jameson (1986) maps out a cognitive aesthetics for Third World writers and shows their propensity to expand the individual story into collective terms, as national allegory. Ahmad's (1987) response questions many of Jameson's totalizing and psychographic assumptions as well as his favoring of the concept 'nation' over such alternatives as 'culture,' 'society,' 'collectivity.' Moreover, Ahmad (1987: 15) believes that Jameson understates 'the presence of analogous impulses in US cultural ensembles.' In general, Ahmad complicates many of Jameson's distinctions between First and Third Worlds, and the shifting nature of center and margin in multiple contexts is acknowledged. But a consideration of how states at the margins, or their writers and publishers, envisage or define their relation to a Western center, and how this affects the projection of their self-image, may benefit our understanding of such articulations. Jameson's point came in for more well-deserved criticism in the journal *Public Culture: Society for Transnational Cultural Studies* 6(3), (1993).

Epilogue

No Time for the Past: A 200-Drachma Note, or 10 Euro Cents, Worth of a Conclusion

A poem can not bring about revolution. Nor can a cultural poetics despite the fact that the word 'poetics' is derived from the verb to 'act.' Both can not transform the objective realities of economic, social, and political relations but they have the wherewithal to change the patterns that inform them. For symbolic modes of understanding do have an effect on actual events and realities. In many ways, this book has focused on the difference at the heart of modern Greek identity and culture that has fallen through the interstices of the prevailing metanarratives and symbolic orders. That difference, a repressed modernity, has become emboldened now, at the dawn of a new millennium, at a moment of modernization, stable democracy, and relative prosperity in Greece.

Certainly much has changed in the last decade of the twentieth century. This book began with a commentary on the painful realization that a symbolic order of self-representation had exhausted itself by the early 1990s. By the decade's end, the Macedonian issue, the Athens Olympics of 2004 as well as other perennial (geo) political touchstones of Greek modernity, such as the campaign for the return of the Parthenon (or Elgin) Marbles, were being handled in new ways. It is not clear the degree to which a new mapping of Greece's place in the world is afoot or whether it will constitute a watershed for this phenomenon, or even if events might not slip back into established patterns of defensiveness. But the language of 'rights' and 'ownership' of the early 1990s, discussed in the introduction and rejoined in the discussion of Storace's travelogue in Chapter 7, is being supplanted by a gradualist and strategic language of 'interests.' This does not necessarily signal a backing down from long-held beliefs or the emasculation of resilient formalisms, or deployed essentialisms, as some conservatives fear. But it does suggest the viable currency of a new rhetoric of self-representation, of a self-regard – a poetics of self-reflexive performance – which may unhand Greeks from the double binds of self-colonization. The long-standing dispute over the return of the Parthenon Marbles from the British Museum to a newly built Acropolis Museum is a case in point. During 2002, the Greek side made new initiatives to overcome the impasse. Whereas British Museum officials resort to an imperious irony that only a bygone colonial past would permit – given the museum's mounting deficits – the Greeks have offered to put aside disputes over ownership of the Marbles and have proposed exchanges of collections between Britain and Greece, including the transfer of the Marbles to Athens in time for the 2004 Olympics and even the assignment of a gallery for the Marbles in the new Acropolis Museum. That gallery would be owned by the Biritish Museum. This constructive approach, while not assured of success and coming from the aggrieved in the matter, is neither arrogant nor paranoid.

Cyprus, which has been incorporated in this study of modern Greece, poses as both the key and major stumbling block to the central issue of Greek–Turkish difference(s), Cyprus is the place where the much-touted Greek and Turkish rapprochement is likely to falter or be built. Chapter 5 showed how, for the modernists, Greekness depended on the repression of a Turkish present. Today, the currently discussed solution to the Cyprus problem depends on creating the conditions for a mutually sustainable Cypriot adminstrative and civic identity with European guarantees. This will require the bold negotiation of fluid categories of self-representation. Neither community on Cyprus will relinquish their Greek or Turkish cultural identity. However the cultivation of a Cypriotist lifeworld that depends on the mobilization and control of a difference that both communities will share and that will differentiate them from their respective metropolitan brethren may bring them closer together. This is a daring move that seeks to maximize mutual interest and secure it with external guarantee. And it is a perilous endeavour. But on this depends the future of Greek–Turkish relations, the subsistence of this discourse, and the future of the island.

Greeks are (re)claiming their place in the modern world with a new lease of confidence. It is clear also that in the 2004 Olympics they have a symbolic turning-point. If handled successfully, the Games may mark a new departure psycho-logically as the 1992 Barcelona Olympics did for that city. Here, too, signs of this confidence may be observable in the most inconsequential of details. An arch-itectural competition for the design of ticketing and information booths to be located at the sports venues around Athens during the Olympics has awarded contracts to projects that consciously avoid nostalgia and archaic mannerism or antique-*looking* constructions (αρχαιοπρεπές). Able to be reassembled with ease, temporary and digitally 'clever' kiosks challenge the autochthony of the overall endeavour even as they strive to relate, and eventually, meld their ubiquitous presence with the surrounding urban landscape. So, too, the equally ubiquitous, cheeky mascots, Phoebus and Athena, wear their symbolism lightly and, above all, playfully.

But the change must not remain only on the level of symbolism. It is also a mark of confidence that the decade has seen the (re)negotiation of identity in relation not only to European and global contexts but also to their Balkan and even their Turkish neighbors. The very contexts denied not so long ago, as by the modernists in Chapter 5, reemerge today even as metropolitan European states relate anew to their own onetime colonies and subjects. Doubtless, the ideological drive for this initiative on cultural, diplomatic, and political levels has been influenced by the *internal* sociopolitical and demographic changes that have occurred in Greece: since 1989 a state that had for decades witnessed mass emigration has rapidly absorbed close to 1 million economic immigrants (constituting 1 in 10 members of the state's population). The majority came from the Balkans, as many as half from Albania.

Yiorgos Theotokas in 1929 urged Greeks to turn their backs on Balkan specificities. This attitude became only further entrenched by the Greek Civil War and the Cold War. With the tumultuous events of 1989 in Eastern Europe, Greek society, reasonably well anchored in Europe, set about reacquainting itself with these specificities as well as with the Balkans and its peoples. A host of artists, filmmakers and novelists in particular –Dimitriou, Koumandareas, Yannaris, Goritsas, Angelopoulos, Faïs, Gouroyiannis etc. – have risen with a passion since the early 1990s to engage with the challenge and the energies of this heterogeneity and to write the myths of Greek modernity. Consequently, in the course of this decade, and only after the missteps cited in this book's introduction, Greeks have *begun* to harmonize the conception of themselves as both European and Balkan. Indeed, now they strive to enhance their cherished *European* profile by foregrounding their relation to other *Balkan* societies. They even take the lead in championing the region's interests, in business, diplomacy, and even in matters of culture, to their European allies. The same questions raised in Chapter 1 about Rhigas's cultural hegemony or enlightened regionalism from two hundred years earlier apply once again. But it is also incumbent on Greek citizens and their elected officials to preserve Balkan specificity first *within* Greece. Especially in light of the threats posed by global and multicultural capital in Chapter 8, Greeks have to hold themselves to the standard of understanding the political particularisms that are threatened by globalization. They need also to address the needs of those victimized by it. This entails proper judicial practice in matters of human and minority rights, women's rights, in labor and immigration law, in the combatting of the trafficking in women and children, in the exercise of women's and religious rights. Only then might one have the right to foster such developments among one's neighbors. Balkan (and Greek) social time and praxis must engage constructively with the dictates of an (ideal) European order (which Europeans themselves have not yet realized in praxis).

It is no surprise then that Rhigas Velestinlis has, of late, resurfaced as the poster-boy of this very task. In 1998, the Greek government commemorated the two hundred years since his execution. A spate of conferences and commemorative events were held around the globe and the Parliament of the Hellenic Republic commissioned two works about Rhigas in this year (Kitromilides 1998a, 1998b). The Greek Parliament Building dedicated a special exhibit to Rhigas, alongside one other honorand, Dionysios Solomos, who, in fact, was born in the year of

Rhigas's death. This upsurge in Rhigas's fortunes had begun before 1998. But, with the onset of the troubles in the disintegrating Yugoslavia, Rhigas's federalism and his respect for the peoples in the region caught people's attention. In no time, he became duly memorialized and, while the majority of these events cast him in predictable national terms of the protomartyr and patriot of modern Greece, others went beyond the ethnolyrical strains of his work to consider the *political* dimensions of his ideas for civic society and administration, his policies on asylum, his championing of natural law over the claims of national and religious affiliation, his advocacy of biculturalism and bilingualism, and respect for human rights etc. (Liakos 1998; Noutsos 1999).

At the beginning of the 1990s, the government defiantly minted a 100–drachma coin of Alexander the Great at the height of the Macedonia crisis. In the late 1990s,

Figure E.1 A 200-Drachma note and 10-cent euro coin

it was putting into circulation a 200–drachma note with Rhigas's profile emblazoned on it. The symbolism was telling. By the 1990s, the drachma had became the currency of choice in Albania. A Greek peacekeeping contingent in Kosovo named their military camp 'Rhigas Pherraios' and Greece was both urging the West and itself providing structural funds for the rebuilding of the Balkans after the Kosovo conflict. On 1 January 2001, when Greece joined the European Monetary Union, the euro replaced the drachma and the Greeks, unlike others in Europe, hardly raised a peep for the loss of the drachma, Europe's oldest currency. All over Europe, each euro coin sported a common European motif on one of its sides and a figure chosen by each member state on the other. The Greek government engraved Rhigas on the 10–cents euro coin, a testament to the monumental significance that he has aspired to in the Greek pantheon of modernity (Fig. E.1). The Ottoman Greek Vlach who dreamed of all Balkan peoples, including Muslims, as part of a Greek and Balkan federation, now symbolizes the hope for a Greek and European present and future. *Ideally*, Greek and European modernities will strive in practice to become two sides of the same coin.

References

Abboushi, J. (1998), 'The Perils of Occidentalism: How Arab Novelists are Driven to Write for Western Readers.' *Times Literary Supplement*, 24 April: 8–9.

Abrams, M. H. (1971), *The Mirror and the Lamp: Romantic Theory and the Critical Tradition* [1953]. Oxford: Oxford University Press.

Adil, A. (1996a), 'The Life of Ismail Ferik Pasha.' *Times Literary Supplement*, 5 July.

—— (1996b), 'The Life of Ismail Ferik Pasha.' Letter to the Editor. *Times Literary Supplement*, 19 July.

Agras, T. (1938), 'Ο Καρυωτάκης και οι Σάτιρες.' In G. Sakellariades (ed.), ΄Απαντα -΄Εμμετρα και Πεζά Κ.Γ. Καρυωτάκη. Athens: Govosti.

Ahmad, A. (1987), 'Jameson's Rhetoric of Otherness and the "National Allegory."' *Social Text* 17: 3-25.

Alexandrou, A. (1977),΄Εξω απ ' τα δόντια (1937–75). Athens: Vergos.

—— (1981), Ποιήματα (1941–74), 2nd edition. Athens: Kastaniotis.

Alexiou, M. (1974), *The Ritual Lament in Greek Tradition*. Cambridge: Cambridge University Press.

—— (1982), 'Diglossia in Greece,' in W. Haas (ed.), *Standard Languages, Spoken and Written*. Manchester: Manchester University Press.

—— (1985), 'Folklore: An Obituary?' *Byzantine and Modern Greek Studies* 9:1–28.

—— (1986), 'Modern Greek Studies in the West: Between the Classics and the Orient.' *Journal of Modern Greek Studies* 4(1): 3–16.

—— (1991), 'Literature and Popular Tradition.' In D. Holton (ed.), *Literature and Society in Renaissance Crete*. Cambridge: Cambridge University Press.

—— (1993), 'Writing against Silence: Antithesis and *Ekphrasis* in the Prose Fiction of Georgios Vizyenos.' *Dumbarton Oaks Papers* 47. Washington, DC: Dumbarton Oaks.

—— (2002), *After Antiquity: Greek Language, Myth, and Metaphor*. Ithaca, NY: Cornell University Press.

Alexiou, M. and V. Lambropoulos (eds.) (1985), *The Text and its Margins: Post-Structuralist Approaches to Twentieth Century Greek Literature*. New York: Pella.

Alexiou, S. (1997a), Σολωμικά. Athens: Stigmi.

—— (1997b), Σολωμιστές και Σολωμός. Athens: Stigmi.

References

Altinel, S. (1990), 'Putting a Tangible Shape on Time.' *The Times Literary Supplement*, 12–18 October: 1087–8.

Amantos, K. (1930), Ανέκδοτα Έγγραφα περί Ρήγα Βελεστινλή. Athens: Sideri.

Anagnostakis, M. (1978), Αντιδογματικά · Προβλήματα Πολιτικής και Κουλτούρας - Άρθρα και Σημειώματα 1946–77. Athens: Pleias.

—— (1979), Το Περιθώριο '68–'69. Athens: Pleias.

—— (1980), *The Target: Selected Poems*. Trans. K. Friar. New York: Pella.

—— (1982), 'Μια συνομιλία του Μανώλη Αναγνωστάκη με τον Αντώνη Φωστιέρη και Θανάση Νιάρχο.' *I Lexi* 11: 52–9.

—— (1985), Τα Συμπληρωματικά - Σημειώσεις Κριτικής. Athens: Stigmi.

—— (1989), Τα Ποιήματα 1941–1971 [1971]. Athens: Stigmi

—— (1997), 'Η Σιωπή είναι κι ' αυτή μια πράξη.' *Kyriakatiki Eleftherotypia*, 27 August.

Anderson, B. (1991), *Imagined Communities: Reflections on the Origin and Spread of Nationalism* [1983]. Revised and expanded edition. London: Verso.

Anghelaki-Rooke, K. (1978), Ο Θρίαμβος της σταθερής Απώλειας. Athens: Kedros.

Apostolakis, Y. M. (1958), Η Ποίηση στη ζωή μας [1923], 2nd edition. Athens: Estia.

—— (1967), Τα Τραγούδια Μας. Athens: Bibliopoleion Dim. Papadima.

Appadurai, A. (1996), *Modernity at Large: Cultural Dimensions of Globalization*. Minneapolis, MN: University of Minnesota Press.

Ascherson, N. (1995), *Black Sea*. New York: Hill & Wang.

Athanasopoulos, V. (ed.) (1997), Αυτοβιογραφία. Athens: Okeanida.

Auden, W. H. (1979), *W. H. Auden: Selected Poems – New Edition*. Ed. E. Mendelson. New York: Random House.

Augustinos, G. (1977), 'Consciousness and History: Nationalist Critics of Greek Society 1887–1914.' *East European Quarterly*. Boulder, NY: Columbia University Press.

Averoff-Tossitza, E. (1981), 'Ιστορία χαμένων ευκαιριών - Κυπριακό, 1950–63.' 2 vols. Athens.

Avgheris, M. (1956), 'Θεωρία και Κριτική - Ο Πεσιμισμός στην Ελληνική Ποίηση.' Επιθεώρηση Τέχνης τ. Γ´ 3(13): 4–17.

Axiotis, D. (1999), Το ελάχιστον της ζωής του. Athens: Kedros.

Bakhtin, M. M. (1981), *The Dialogic Imagination: Four Essays*. Ed. Michael Holquist. Trans. C. Emerson and M. Holquist. Austin, TX: University of Texas Press.

Bakić-Hayden, M. and Robert M. Hayden (1992), 'Orientalist Variations on the Theme "Balkans": Symbolic Geography in Recent Yugoslav Cultural Politics.' *Slavic Review* 51(1): 1–15.

Ballard, J. G. (1985), *Crash*. New York: Vintage Books.

References

Baloumes, E. G. (1997), Κώστας Καρυωτάκης - Ο Πεζογράφος. Athens: Ellinika Grammata.

Barbeito, P. F. (1995), 'Altered States: Space, Gender and the (Un)making of Identity in the Short Stories of Georgios M. Vizyenos.' *Journal of Modern Greek Studies* 13: 299–326.

Barbié de Bocage, J. D. (1806), *Maps, Plans, Views ad Coins Illustrative of the Travels of Anacharsis the Younger in Greece during the Middle of the Fourth Century before the Christian Era*, 4th edition. London.

—— (1822), *Atlas des Oeuvres Complètes de J. J. Barthelémy*. Paris: A. Belin.

Barthelémy, A. (1825), *Travels of Anacharsis the Younger in Greece during the Middle of the Fourth Century before the Christian Era*, 6 vols & a seventh in quarto containing maps, places, views, and coins. London: C. Baldwin.

Beaton, R. (1976), 'The Tree of Poetry.' *Journal of Byzantine & Modern Greek Studies* 2: 161–82.

—— (1987), 'The Sea as Metaphorical Space in Modern Greek Literature.' *Journal of Modern Greek Studies* 7(2): 135–52.

—— (ed.) (1991), *The Greek Novel AD 1-1985*. London: Croom Helm.

—— (1994), *An Introduction to Modern Greek Literature*. Oxford: Oxford University Press.

Bekatoros, S. and A. E. Florakis (1971), Η Νέα Γενιά - Ποιητική Ανθολογία, 1965–70. Athens: Kedros.

Benjamin, W. (1997), *Illuminations* [1955]. Trans.H. Zohn. New York: Shocken.

Berman, P. (1991), 'Young Turk.' *The New Republic*, 9 September, 36–9.

Bernadete, S. (1999), *Herodotean Inquiries*. South Bend, IN: St. Augustine's Press.

Bernal, M. (1987), *Black Athena: The Afroasiatic Roots of Classical Civilization*. Vol. 1: *The Fabrication of Ancient Greece, 1785–1985*. New Brunswick, NJ: Rutgers University Press.

Bhabha, H. (ed.) (1990), *Nation and Narration*. London & New York: Routledge.

Bien, P. (1985), 'The Predominance of Poetry in Greek Literature,' *World Literature Today* 59(2): 197–200.

Bohandy, S. (1994), 'Defining the Self through the Body in Four Poems by Katerina Anghelaki-Rooke and Sylvia Plath.' *Journal of Modern Greek Studies* 12(1): 1–36.

Borges, J. L. (1969), *Labyrinths: Selected Stories and Other Writings*. New York: New Directions.

Botzaris, N. (1962), *Visions balkaniques dans la préparation de la Révolution grecque, 1789–1821*. Geneva.

Boumbolides, P. (1965), Ελισάβετ Μουτζά-Μαρτινέγκου. Athens: Philekpaideftike Etaireia.

Bowker, G. (1997), *Through the Dark Labyrinth: A Biography of Lawrence Durrell*. New York: St. Martin's Press.

References

Bowra, C. M. (1978), *Heroic Poetry* [1952]. New York: Macmillan.

Bourdieu, P. (1977), *Outline of a Theory of Practice*. Trans. R. Nice. Cambridge: Cambridge University Press.

Boym, S. (1988), 'Writing in Blood: Death of the Poet and a Theoretical Puzzle.' Unpublished paper given at 'Colloquium on Death' at Center for Literary and Cultural Studies, Harvard University.

—— (1991). *Death in Quotation Marks: Cultural Myths of the Modern Poet.* Harvard Studies in Comparative Literature. Cambridge, MA: Harvard University Press.

Brooks, M. W. (1997), *Subway City.* New Brunswick, NJ: Rutgers University Press.

Browning, R. (1989), *Medieval and Modern Greek.* Cambridge: Cambridge University Press.

Bryant, R. (1998), 'An Education in Honor: Patriotism and the Schools of Cyprus.' In V. Calotychos (ed.) *Cyprus and its People.*

Bürger, P. (1980), *Theory of the Avant-Garde.* Trans. M. Shaw. Minneapolis, MN: University of Minnesota Press.

Burke, J. & S. Gauntlett (eds.) (1992), *Neohellenism.* Humanities Research Center Monograph No. 5. Canberra: Australian National University.

Buzard, J. (1993a), *The Beaten Track: European Tourism, Literature, and the Ways to Culture, 1800-1918.* Oxford: Oxford University Press.

—— (1993b), 'A Continent of Pictures: Reflections on the "Europe" of Nineteenth-Century Tourists.' *PMLA* 108(1): 30–44.

Calotychos, V. (1990), 'The Art of Making Claques: Politics of Tradition in the Critical Essays of Eliot and Seferis.' In M. Layoun (ed.), *Modernism in Greece?*

—— (1992), 'Westernizing the Exotic: Incorporation and a Green Line around a Non-Space.' *Journal of the Hellenic Diaspora* 18(2): 35–67.

—— (1994), 'Bernard Knox, the Oldest Dead White European Males and Other Reflections on the Classics.' *Journal of Modern Greek Studies* 12(2): 277–9.

—— (1997), 'Thorns in the Side of Venice? Galanaki's *Pasha* and Pamuk's *White Castle* in the Global Market.' In D. Tziovas (ed.), *Greek Modernism and Beyond.*

—— (1998a), "Interdisciplinary Perspectives: Difference at the Heart of Cypriot Identity and its Study." In V. Calotychos (ed.), *Cyprus and its People*, 1–32.

—— (ed.) (1998b) *Cyprus and its People.* Boulder, Co: Westview Press.

Camariano, N. (n.d.), *Contributions à la Bibliographie des Oeuvres de Righas Velestinlis.* n.p.

Carson, J. (1983), *49 Scholia on the Poems of Odysseus Elytis.* Athens: Ipsilon.

Cavell, S. (1988), *In Quest of the Ordinary.* Chicago: University of Chicago Press.

Chadzivassiliou, V. (1992), Μίλτος Σαχτούρης : Η Παράκαμψη του Υπερρεαλισμού. Athens: Estia.

References

Chamoudopoulos, D. A. (1964), 'Η Συμβολή των Επτανησίων στη μουσική ζωή της χώρας μας.' *Nea Estia* 76 (899), Christmas.

Chateaubriand, F-R. de (1963), *Itinéraire de Paris à Jerusalem*. Paris: Les Productions de Paris.

Chatziyakoumis, E. K. (1968), Νεοελληνικαί Πηγαί του Σολωμού. Ph.D dissertation, School of Philosophy, University of Athens. Athens: Ethnikon ke Kapodistriakon Panepistimion Athinon.

Chouliaras, Y. (1993), 'Greek Culture in the New Europe.' In H. J. Psomiades and S. B. Thomadakis (eds.), *Greece, the New Europe, and the Changing International Order*. New York: Pella.

Chryssanthopoulos, M. (1994), Γεώργιος Βιζυηνός - Μεταξύ Φαντασίας και Μνήμης. Athens: Estia.

Clifford, J. (1997), *Routes: Travel and Translation in the Late Twentieth Century*. Cambridge, MA: Harvard University Press.

Clogg, R. (1973), *The Struggle for Greek Independence: Essays to Mark the 150th Anniversary of the Greek War of Independence*. Hamden, CN: Archon.

—— (1979), *A Short History of Modern Greece*. Cambridge: Cambridge University Press.

Colocotronis, T. (1986), Ο Κολοκοτρώνης, Απομνημονεύματα του Κολοκοτρώνη (Διήγησις Συμβάντων της Ελληνικής Φυλής, 1770–1836). Athens: Estia.

Colyvas, J. (1980), *Meaning and Form in Karyotakis' Poetry and Prose*. M.Litt. thesis, Faculty of Arts, Birmingham University.

Constantine, D. (1986), *Early Greek Travellers and the Hellenic Ideal*. Cambridge: Cambridge University Press.

Constantinou, M. (1998), 'The Cavafian Poetics of Diasporic Constitutionalism: Toward a Neo-Hellenistic Decentering of the Kyp(riot)ic Experience.' In V. Calotychos (ed.), *Cyprus and its People*.

Constantoulaki-Hantzou, I. (ed.) (1989), Γ. Θεοτοκάς - Νικόλαος Κάλας - Μια αλληλογραφία. Athens: Prosperos.

Constas, K. (1997), Ο Άγιος Κοσμάς ο Αιτωλός. Athens.

Coutelle, L. (1998), 'Ο Διονύσιος Σολωμός και τα Ιταλικά Ποιήματα της ζακυνθινής περιόδου.' *Porphyras* 87 (July–September): 11–22.

Dalkou, G. (1986), Κωνσταντίνος Καρυωτάκης- Δημόσιος Υπάλληλος εξ Αθηνών μεταθείς εις Πρέβεζαν εσχάτως. Athens: Kastaniotis.

Dallas, Y. (1979), Εισαγωγή στην Ποιητική του Μίλτου Σαχτούρη. Athens: Keimena.

—— (1997), 'Ο Σολωμός ανάμεσα σε δύο γλώσσες - Η Αμφίδρομη δοκιμασία της ποιητικής ιδέα' *I Lexi* 142: 688–703.

Danforth, L. (1995). *The Macedonian Conflict: Ethnic Nationalism in a Transnational World*. Princeton, NJ: Princeton University Press.

Dascalakis, A. (1937a), *Les Oeuvres de Rhigas Velestinlis*. Thèse Complementaire pour D. ès Lettres Université de Paris.

References

—— (1937b), *Rhigas Velestinlis: La Révolution française et les préludes de l'indépendance hellénique*. D. ès. Lettres L'Université de Paris.

Davidson, B. (1992), *The Black Man's Burden: Africa and the Curse of the Nation-State*. New York: Times Books.

Deane, S. (1990), 'Introduction.' In *Nationalism, Colonialism and Literature*. Minneapolis, MN: Minnesota University Press.

Decavalles, A. (1994), *Odysseas Elytis: From the Golden to the Silver Poem*. New York: Pella.

de Certeau, M. (1984), *The Practice of Everyday Life*. Trans. S. Rendall. Berkeley, CA: University of California Press

de Man, P. (1979), 'Autobiography as De-facement.' *Modern Language Notes* 94(5): 919–30.

De Marcellus, M-L-J-A-C. (1851), *Chants du peuple en Grèce, par M. de Marcellus*. Tomes I–II. Paris: J. Lecoffre.

Demelis, C. (1990), 'The Suppression of an Imminent Modernism: Y. Ritsos' Responseto K. Karyotakis' Challenge.' In M. Layoun (ed.), *Modernism in Greece?*

Demetrakopoulos, F. (1992), Για τον Σεφέρη και την Κύπρο. Athens: Epikairotita.

Demetriades, F. (ed.) (1994), Αγωγή των Νέων - Το Παράνομο Περιοδικό της ΕΟΚΑ για τους μαθητές των δημοτικών σχολείων. Limassol, Cyprus.

Derrida, J. (1981), *Dissemination* [1972]. Trans. B. Johnson. Chicago: University of Chicago Press.

Dertilis, G. (1985), Κοινωνικός Μετασχηματισμός και Στρατιωτική Επέμβαση, 1880–1909 [1977]. Athens: Exantas.

Diamandouros, N. P. (1984), 'Η εγκαθίδρυση του κοινοβουλευτισμού στην Ελλάδα και η λειτουργία του κατά τον 19ο αιώνα.' In D. G. Tsaoussis (ed.), Όψεις της Ελληνικής Κοινωνίας του 19ου αιώνα. Athens: Estia.

—— (1993), 'Politics and Culture in Greece, 1974–91, an Interpretation.' In R. Clogg (ed.), *Greece 1981–89: The Populist Decade*. New York: St. Martin's Press.

—— (2000), Πολιτισμικός δυϊσμός και πολιτική αλλαγή της μεταπολίτευσης : πλαίσιο ερμηνείας. Trans. D. A. Soteropoulos. Athens: Alexandreia.

Diamandouros, N. P., J. P. Anton, J. A. Petropoulos & P. Topping (eds.) (1976), *Hellenism and the First Greek War of Liberation (1821-1830): Continuity & Change*. Thessaloniki: Institute for Balkan Studies.

Dimadis, C. A. (1991), Δικτατορία - Πόλεμος και Πεζογραφία (1936–1944). Athens: Gnosi.

Dimakis, M. (1964), 'Το αποσπασματικό έργο του Σολωμού.' *Nea Estia* 76(899): 83–90.

Dimaras, K. T. (1978), Ιστορία της νεοελληνικής λογοτεχνίας. Athens: Ikaros.

—— (1985), Ελληνικός Ρωμαντισμός. Νεοελληνικά Μελετήματα 7, Athens: Ermis.

References

Dimiroulis, D. (1985), 'The "Humble Art" and the Exquisite Rhetoric: Tropes in the Manner of George Seferis.' In M. Alexiou & V. Lambropoulos (eds.), *The Text and its Margins*. New York: Pella.

—— (1989), Ο ποιητής ως Έθνος - Αισθητική και ιδεολογία στον Γεώργιο Σεφέρη. Athens: Plethron.

Dimoula, K. (1971), Το λίγο του κόσμου. Athens: Keimena.

Donato, E. (1979), 'The Museum's Furnace: Notes toward a Contextual Reading of "Bouvard et Pécuchet".' In J. Harari (ed.), *Textual Strategies: Perspectives in Post-Structuralist Criticism*. Ithaca, NY: Cornell University Press.

Doulis, T. (1975), *George Theotokas*. Boston, MA: Twayne.

Dounia, C. (2000), K. Γ. Καρυωτάκης - Η Αντοχή μιας αδέσποτης τέχνης. Athens: Kastaniotis.

Dragoumis, I. (1926), Όσοι Ζωντανοί. Athens: Nea Zoe.

Driault, É. and M. Lhéritier (1925–6), *Histoire diplomatique de la Grèce de 1821 à nos jours*. Vol. I: *Driault, l'insurrection et l'indépendance (1821–1830)*. Vol. II: *Driault, Le Règne d'Othon: La grande idée (1830–1862)*. Paris: Didot.

Droullia, L. (1980), 'The View of Modern Greeks through the Mid-sixteenth Century Travellers' Accounts.' *Balkan Studies* 21(2): 275–85.

Du Bois, W. E. B. (1989), *The Souls of Black Folk* [1903]. New York: Bantam.

Durrell, L. (1955), *The Tree of Idleness and Other Poems*. London: Faber & Faber.

—— (1957), *Bitter Lemons*. New York: E. P. Dutton.

Eade, J. C. (ed.) (1983), *Romantic Nationalism in Europe*. Humanities Research Center Monograph No. 2. Canberra. Australian National University.

Eagleton, T. (1989), *Walter Benjamin or towards a Revolutionary Criticism*. London & New York: Verso.

—— (1990), *The Ideology of the Aesthetic*. Oxford: Blackwell

—— (1992), *Walter Benjamin or Toward a Revolutionary Criticism* [1981], 4th edition. London and New York: Verso.

Eco, U. (1984). *Postscript to "The Name of the Rose."* Trans. W. Weaver. New York: Harcourt Brace Jovanovich.

Economides, D. B. (1953), 'Τρία έργα της κριτικής λογοτεχνίας εν Απεράθου Νάξου.' Κρητικά Χρονικά 7, 110–18.

Eden, A. (1960), *Full Circle*. London: Cassell.

Eisner, R. (1991), *Travelers to an Antique Land: The History and Literature of Travel to Greece*. Ann Arbor, MI: University of Michigan Press

Eliot, T. S. (1950), *Selected Essays*, new edition. New York: Harcourt, Brace.

Elytis, O. (1974), Ανοιχτά Χαρτιά. Athens: Asterias.

—— (1976), Άσμα Ηρωικό και Πένθιμο για τον Χαμένο Ανθυπολοχαγό της Αλβανίας [1945]. Athens: Ikaros.

—— (1979), Προσανατολισμοί [1939], 8th edition. Athens: Ikaros.

—— (1980), Άξιον Εστί [1959], 13th edition. Athens: Ikaros.

—— (1981), *Selected Poems.* Chosen and introduced by E. Keeley and P. Sherrard; trans. by E. Keeley et al. New York: Viking Press.

—— (1986), Ιδιωτική Οδός. Athens: Ipsilon.

—— (1995), Ο Κήπος με τις αυταπάτες. Athens: Ipsilon.

—— (1998), *The Collected Poems of Odysseas Elytis.* Trans. by J. Carson and N. Sarris. Baltimore, MD: Johns Hopkins University Press.

—— (1999), *Carte Blanche: Selected Writing.* Trans. D. Connolly. Amsterdam: Harwood Academic.

—— (2002), Ποιήματα. Athens: Ikaros.

Ephtaliotes, A. (1901), Ιστορία της Ρωμιοσύνης. Athens: Estia.

Exarchos, Y. (1998), Ρήγας Βελεστινλής - Ανέκδοτα Έγγραφα, Νέα Στοιχεία. Athens: Kastaniotis.

Faris, W. B. (1995), 'Scheherazade's Children: Magical Realism and Postmodern Fiction.' In L. P. Zamora & W. B. Faris (eds.), *Magical Realism: Theory, History, Community.* Durham, NC & London: Duke University Press.

Faubion, J. D. (1993), *Modern Greek Lessons: A Primer in Historical Constructivism.* Princeton Studies in Culture, Power and History. Princeton, NJ: Princeton University Press.

Fauriel, C. (1824–5), *Chants populaires de la Grèce moderne, recueillis et publié, avec une traduction française, des eclaircissements et des notes, par C. Fauriel.* Paris: F. Didot.

Fermor, P. L. (1966), *Roumeli: Travels in Northern Greece.* New York: Penguin.

Finlay, G. (1876), *A History of Greece from its Conquest by the Romans to the Present Time, 146 BC to AD 1864.* Ed. H. F. Tozer. Vol. VI, Oxford: n.p.

Finnegan, R. (1977), *Oral Poetry: Its Nature, Significance and Social Context.* Cambridge: Cambridge University Press.

Fitzpatrick, T. (1991), 'The Figure of Captivity: The Cultural Work of the Puritan Captivity Narrative.' *American Literary History* 3(1): 1–26.

Fleming, K. E. (2000), '*Orientalism,* the Balkans, and Balkan Historiography.' *American Historical Review,* 104(4): 1218–33.

Fouyas, M. (1972), *Orthodoxy, Roman Catholicism and Anglicanism.* London and New York: Oxford University Press,

Frangopoulos, Th. D. (1978), 'Το ημιτελές στο Σολωμό.' *Nea Estia* 104(1235): 55–9.

Frascari, M. (1984), 'The Tell-the-Tale Detail.' *Via* 7 30–1.

Galanaki, R. (1989), Ο Βίος του Ισμαήλ Φερίκ Πασά -*Spina nel cuore.* Athens: Agra.

—— (1996a), 'Quellwolkengebirge von Unterschieden: Brief an der türkischen Schriftsteller Orhan Pamuk.' *Kultur Austausch* 3: 46–8.

—— (1996b), *The Life of Ismail Ferik Pasha: Spina nel Cuore.* Trans. & foreword by Kay Cicellis. London & Chester Springs, PA: UNESCO Publishing and Peter Owen.

—— (1997), Βασιλεύς ή Στρατιώτης - Σημειώσεις, σκέψεις, σχόλια για τη λογοτεχνία. Athens: Agra.

Gallagher, C. & S. Greenblatt (eds.) (2000), *Practicing New Historicism.* Chicago: University of Chicago Press.

Garber, M. (1992), *Vested Interests: Cross-Dressing and Cultural Anxiety.* New York & London: Routledge.

Gatsos, N. (1987), Αμοργός [1940], 4th edition. Athens: Ikaros.

Gautier, T. (1853), *Constantinople.* Paris: Michel Lévy Frères.

—— (1881), *Loin de Paris.* Paris: Charpentier.

—— (1884), *L'Orient.* Tome Premier. Paris: Charpentier.

Georganta, A. (1992), Αιών Βυρωμανής : ο κόσμος του Βύρωνα και η νεοελληνική ποίηση. Athens: Exantas.

Gilmore, L. (1994), *Autobiographics: A Feminist Theory of Women's Self-Representation.* Ithaca, NY: Cornell University Press.

Given, M. (1997), 'Father of his Landscape: Lawrence Durrell's Creation of Landscape and Character in Cyprus.' *Deus Loci: International Lawrence Durrell Journal* NS5: 55-65.

Gourgouris, S. (1990), 'The Simulations of "Center": Lorenzatos' Neohellenism Against the Modernist Phantom.' In M. Layoun (ed.), *Modernism in Greece?*

—— (1992), 'Nationalism and Oneirocriticism: Of Modern Hellenes in Europe.' *Diaspora* 2(1): 43–72.

—— (1995), 'Research, Essay, Failure (Flaubert's Itinerary).' *New Literary History* 26: 343–57.

—— (1996), *Dream Nation: Enlightenment, Colonization and the Institution of Modern Greece.* Stanford, CA: Stanford University Press.

—— (2000), 'The Ark's Void – Communism and Poetry, circa 2nd Millenium.' In M. Yashin (ed.), *Step-mothertongue: From Nationalism to Mutlticulturalism: Literatures of Cyprus, Greece, and Turkey.* London: Middlesex University Press.

Gumpert, M. (2001), *Grafting Helen.* Madison, WI: Wisconsin University Press.

Gün, G. (1992), 'The Turks are Coming: Deciphering Orhan Pamuk's *Black Book*,' *World Literature Today* 66(1): 59–63.

Harlow, B. (1987), *Resistance Literature.* London: Methuen.

Hart, L. K. (1992), *Time, Religion, and Social Experience in Rural Greece.* Greek Studies: Interdisciplinary Approaches Series. Lanham, MD: Rowman and Littlefield.

Hartog, F. (1987), *The Mirror of Herodotus: The Representation of the Other in the Writing of History.* Berkeley & Los Angeles: University of California Press.

Hatfield, H. C. (1943), *Winckelmann and his German Critics 1755–1781.* Morningside Heights, NY: King's Crown Press.

Hazard, P. (1953), *The European Mind (1680–1715).* [1935]. London: Hollis and Carter.

References

Hegel, G. W. F. (1931), *The Phenomenology of Mind* [1910]. Trans. with notes by J. B. Baillie, 2nd edn. London: George Allen & Unwin; New York: Macmillan.

Herbert, C. (1991), *Culture and Anomie: Ethnographic Imagination in the Nineteenth Century*. Chicago: University of Chicago Press.

Herbrechter, S. (1999), *Lawrence Durrell, Postmodernism and the Ethics of Alterity*. Postmodern Studies 26. Amsterdam & Atlanta, GA: Rodopi.

Herzfeld, M. (1982), 'The Etymology of Excuses: Aspects of Rhetorical Performance in Greece.' *American Ethnologist* 9: 644–63.

—— (1985), *The Poetics of Manhood: Contest and Identity in a Cretan Mountain Village*. Princeton, NJ: Princeton University Press.

—— (1986), *Ours Once More: Folklore, Ideology and the Making of Modern Greece* [1982]. New York: Pella.

—— (1987), *Anthropology through the Looking Glass: Critical Ethnography in the Margins of Europe*. Cambridge: Cambridge University Press.

—— (1990), 'Literacy as Symbolic Strategy in Greece: Methodological Considerations of Topic and Place.' *Byzantine and Modern Greek Studies* 14: 151–72.

—— (1991), *A Place in History: Social and Monumental Time in a Cretan Town*. Princeton Studies in Culture, Power and History. Princeton, NJ: Princeton University Press.

—— (1997), *Cultural Intimacy: Social Poetics in the Nation-State*. New York: Routledge.

Hetaireia Spoudon Neoellenikou Politismou kai Genikes Paideias (Sholi Moraiti), (1997), Ιστορική Πραγματικότητα και Νεοελληνική Πεζογραφία (1945–1995). Athens: Hetaireia Spoudon Neoellenikou Politismou kai Genikes Paideias.

Hirschon, R. (1998), *Heirs of the Greek Catastrophe* [1989]. New York and Oxford: Berghahn.

Hobsbawm, E. J. (1990), *Nations and Nationalism since 1780: Programme, Myth, Reality*. Cambridge: Cambridge University Press

Hokwerda, H. (1990), 'Ελεγεία ή Σάτιρες'. In M. Melissaratos (ed.), Συμπόσιο για τον Κ.Τ. Καρυωτάκη.

Holton, D. (1990), 'Orality in Cretan Narrative Poetry.' *Journal of Byzantine & Modern Greek Studies* 14: 186–98.

—— (1991), *Literature and Society in Renaissance Crete*. Cambridge: Cambridge University Press.

Hroch, M. (1985), *Social Preconditions of National Revival in Europe*. Cambridge: Cambridge University Press.

Huggan, G. (1989), 'Decolonizing the Map: Post-colonialism, Poststructuralism, and the Cartographic Connection.' *Ariel* 20: 115–31.

—— (1994), 'The Postcolonial Critic: Salman Rushdie and the Booker of Bookers.' *Transition* 64: 22–9.

References

Humboldt, W. von (1903-36), *Wilhelm von Humboldts gesammelte Schriften* Vol. 3. Berlin: Leitzmann and Gebhardt.

Hymes, D. (1973), *Breakthrough into Performance. Documents du centre de sémiotique d' Urbino*, 26–7.

Hynes, S. (1972), *The Auden Generation: Literature and Politics in the 1930s.* Princeton, NJ: Princeton University Press

Ilinskaya, S. (1986), Η μοίρα μιας γενιάς - Συμβολή στη μελέτη της μεταπολεμικής πολιτικής ποίησης στην Ελλάδα [1976], 3rd edition. Athens: Kedros.

—— (1990), 'Καβάφης- Βάρναλης - Καρυωτάκης. Τρία περάσματα προς το ρεαλισμό.' In M. Melissaratos (ed.), Συμπόσιο για τον Κ.Γ. Καρυωτάκη.

Iliou, Ph. (1975), 'Σημειώσεις για τα τραβήγματα των Ελληνικών Βιβλίων του 16ου αιώνα.' *Hellenika* 28: 102–41.

Ingersoll, E. G. (ed.) (1998), *Lawrence Durrell: Conversations.* Madison, Teaneck, NJ: Farleigh Dickinson Press; London: Associated University Presses.

Innes, C. (1995), 'Istanbul Expressed.' *The Nation*, 27 March: 425–8.

Isherwood, C. (1938), *Lions and Shadows*. London: Hogarth Press.

Ivask, I. (1975), *Odysseas Elytis.* Norman, OK: Oklahoma University Press.

Jameson, F. (1986), 'Third-World Literature in the Era of Multinational Capitalism.' *Social Text* 15: 65–88.

—— (1990), 'Modernism and Imperialism.' In *Nationalism, Colonialism and Literature*. Minneapolis, MN: Minnesota University Press.

Jelavich, B. (1976), 'The Balkan Nations and the Greek War of Independence.' In N. Diamandouros et al. (eds.), *Hellenism and the First Greek War of Liberation (1821–1830): Continuity and Change.* Thessaloniki: Institute for Balkan Studies.

Jenkins, Romilly (1940), *Dionysios Solomos.* Cambridge: Cambridge University Press.

Jenkyns, Richard (1980), *The Victorians and Ancient Greece.* Cambridge, MA: Harvard University Press.

Johnson, B. (1987), 'My Monster/My Self.' In *A World of Difference.* Baltimore, MD: Johns Hopkins University Press.

Jong, E. (1993), *The Devil at Large: Erica Jong on Henry Miller.* London: Chatto & Windhaus.

Jusdanis, G. (1987a), 'Is Postmodernism Possible Outside the "West"? The Case of Greece.' *Byzantine & Modern Greek Studies* 11: 69–92.

—— (1987b), *The Poetics of Cavafy: Textuality, Eroticism, History.* Princeton, NJ: Princeton University Press.

—— (1991a), *Belated Modernity and Aesthetic Culture: Inventing National Literature.* Minnesota, MN: Minnesota University Press.

—— (1991b), 'Greek Americans and the Diaspora.' *Diaspora* 1(2): 209–24.

References

Just, R. (1995), 'Cultural Certainties and Private Doubts.' In W. James (ed.), *The Pursuit of Certainty: Religious and Cultural Formulations.* London and New York: Routledge.

Kairophyllas, C. (1986), Αυτοί οι ωραίοι τρελλοί. Athens: Ekdoseis Filippoti.

Kakridis, I. T. (1963), 'The Ancient Greeks and the Greeks of the War of Independence.' *Balkan Studies* 4(2): 251–64. Thessaloniki: Institute for Balkan Studies.

Kaldis, W. P. (1963), *John Capodistrias and the Modern Greek State.* Ann Arbor, MI: Edwards Bros.

Kalinderi, M. (1963), Απόσπασμα διδαχής Κοσμά του Αιτωλού. Thessaloniki.

Kalosgouros, G. (1984), Διονύσιου Σολωμού· Τα Ιταλικά Ποιήματα. Athens: Keimena.

Kapsomenos, E. (1979), Η Σχέση Ανθρώπου - Φύσης στο Σολωμό. Chania: n.p.

—— (1983), Λεξικό Σολωμού - Πίνακας Λέξεων του Ελληνόγλωσσου Σολωμικού Εργου. Ioannina: Panepistimion Ioanninon.

—— (1992a), "Καλή ' ναι η μαύρη πέτρα σου" - Ερμηνευτικά Κλειδιά στο Σολωμού. Athens: Estia.

—— (1992b), 'Το σολωμικό κείμενο ως σημαίνουσα ποιητική.' *O Politis* 120 (October–December): 48–52.

Karakasidou, A. (1996), *Fields of Wheat, Hills of Blood: Passages to Nationhood in Greek Macedonia, 1870–1990.* Chicago & London: University of Chicago Press.

Karakassis, S. (1965), Μουσική αποστολή εις Ζάκυνθον από 6.8.1965 έως 4.9. 1965, Αρχείον του Κέντρου Ερεύνης της Ελληνικής Λαογραφίας (Λαογραφικόν Αρχείον Ακαδημίας Αθηνών), αρ, χφ. 2958, σχ. 8ον.

Karalis, V. (1992), 'Η Ποίηση του Νάσου Βαγενά ή το αδίεξοδο της ομορφιάς.' *O Politis* 115: 57–66.

Kargiotis, D. (1999), *Thinking, Seeing: From the Subject to Poetry.* Ph.D dissertation, Department of Comparative Literature, Princeton University.

Karvelis, T. (1976), 'Τίτου Πατρίκιου· Ποιήματα, I (1948–1954). *Diavazo* 3–4 (May–October): 96–7.

Karyotakis, C. (1997), Ποιήματα καί Πεζά. Νέα Ελληνική Βιβλιοθήκη. Athens: Ermis.

Kasdaglis, E. Ch. (1990), Κύπρος - Μνήμη και Αγάπη με το φακό του Γιώργου Σεφέρη. Nicosia: Cultural Centre of the Popular Bank of Cyprus.

Katsan, G. (2002), 'Necessary Fictions: National Identity and Postmodern Critique in Gouroyiannis's Το Ασημόχορτο Ανθίζει.' *Journal of Modern Greek Studies* 20(2): 399–420.

Katsaros, M. (1986), Ανθολογία Ποιημάτων. Athens: Kaktos.

Katsiyianni, A. (1999), Ένας άνισος αγώνας δρόμου - Εκδοτικές πληροφορίες για τα πρώτα ελληνικά μυθιστορήματα. In N. Vayenas (ed.), Από τον Λεάνδρο στον Λουκή Λάρα. Heraklion: Panepistimiakes Ekdoseis Kritis.

References

Kazhdan, A. (1993), *Authors and Texts in Byzantium*. Aldershot, Hants: Variorum.

Keeley, E. (1981), *Odysseus Elytis: Selected Poems*. New York: Viking Press.

—— (1995), 'Byron, Durrell, and Modern Philhellenism.' In J. Raper, M. Enscore and P. Byrum (eds.), *Lawrence Durrell: Comprehending the Whole*. Columbia, MO: University of Missouri Press.

—— (1999), *Inventing Paradise: The Greek Journey (1937-47)*. New York: Farrar, Straus & Giroux.

Kenna, M. E. (1991), 'The Social Organization of Exile: The Everyday Life of Political Exiles in the Cyclades in the 1930s.' *Journal of Modern Greek Studies* 9(1): 63–82.

Kermode, F. (1983), *The Art of Telling: Essays on Fiction*. Cambridge, MA: Harvard University.

Kitromilides, P. M. (1983), 'The Enlightenment and Womanhood: Cultural Change and the Politics of Exclusion.' *Journal of Modern Greek Studies* 1: 39–61.

—— (1992), *The Enlightenment as Social Criticism: Iosipos Moisiodax and Greek Culture in the Eighteenth Century.* Princeton, NJ: Princeton University Press.

—— (1996), 'Balkan Mentality: History, Legend, Imagination.' *Nations & Nationalism* 2(2): 163–91. Septième Congrès International d'Etudes du Sud-Est Européen (Thessaloniki, 29 August–4 September 1994), Rapports.

—— (1998a), Ρήγα Βελεστινλή - Απάνθισμα Κειμένων. Athens: Vouli ton Hellenon.

—— (1998b), Ρήγας Βελεστινλής - Θεωρία και Πράξη. Athens: Vouli ton Hellenon.

Kittay, J. & W. Godzich (1987), *The Emergence of Prose: An Essay in Prosaics*. Minneapolis, MN: Minnesota University Press.

Klironomos, M. (1992), 'George Theotokas's *Free Spirit*: Reconfiguring Greece's Path toward Modernity.' *Journal of the Hellenic Diaspora* 18(1): 79–98.

Kokkolis, X. A. (1978), 'Δεν είναι πια τραγούδι αυτό ' Ο μελοποιημένος Καρυωτάκης. Thessaloniki: University Studio Press.

Kolias, H. D. (ed.) (1989) *My Story: Elisavet Moutzan-Martinengou*. Athens, GA & London: University of Georgia Press.

Konomos, D. (1950), Σολωμού Ανέκδοτα Γράμματα στον Ιωάννην Γαλβάνη. Collection de L'Institut Français d'Athènes 72. Athens: Institut Français d'Athènes.

—— (1958),Ο Νικόλαος Μάντζαρος κι ο Εθνικός μας Ποιητής. Athens: Kambanas.

Kordatos, Y. K. (1924), Η κοινωνική σημασία της Ελληνικής Επανάστασης του 1821. Athens: n.p.

—— (1931), Ο Ρήγας Φεραίος και Η Εποχή του. Athens: Typos Konstantinupoleos

—— (1946), Η Κοινωνική Σημασία της Ελληνικής Επαναστάσεως του 1821. Athens: n.p.

References

Koropoulis, G. (1996), 'Το τεραίν του παραδείσου - Καρυωτάκης και Ειρωνεία.' *Anti* 623: 18–24.

Koumarianou, E. (1971), Ο Τύπος στον Αγώνα. Athens: Ermis.

—— (1991), Η Γέννηση του Ελληνικού Τύπου. *To Vima*, 6 January.

—— (1995), Ο Ελληνικός Προεπαναστατικός Τύπος. Βιέννη - Παρίσι (1784–1821). Athens: Foundation for Hellenic Culture.

Koumas, K. M. (1830–2), Ιστορίαι των ανθρωπίνων πράξεων. Vienna.

Kourkoulas, K. (1978), Η Θεωρία του κηρύγματος κατά τους χρόνους της Τουρκοκρατίας. Ph.D dissertation, University of Thessaloniki.

Kriaras, E. (1969), Διονύσιος Σολωμός, 2nd edition. Athens: Estia.

—— (1986), Διονύσιος Σολωμός - Ο Βίος, Το ´Εργο. Thessaloniki: n.p.

Krikos-Davis, K. (1978), *Kolokes: A Study of George Seferis's Logbook III (1953–55)*. Amsterdam: Adolf M. Hakkert.

Kyriakidou-Nestoros, A. (1975), Λαογραφικά Μελετήματα. Athens: Nea Synora.

Lacan, J. (1978), *The Four Fundamental Concepts of Psychoanalysis*. Trans. Alan Sheridan. New York & London: W. W. Norton.

Laios, G. (1960), Οι Χάρτες του Ρήγα. Δελτίον της Ιστορικής και Εθνολογικής Εταιρείας της Ελλάδος 14: 231–312.

Lamartine, Alphonse de (1875), *Souvenirs, Impressions, Pensées et Paysages pendant un Voyage en Orient 1832–3 ou Notes d'un Voyageur.* Paris: Hachette.

Lambridis, M. (1955), 'Il Gran Rifiuto.' Επιθεώρηση Τέχνης 2(7): 29–42.

Lambropoulos, V. (1987), 'The Aesthetic Ideology of the Greek Quest for Identity.' *Journal of Modern Hellenism* 4: 19–24.

—— (1988), *Literature as National Institution: Studies in the Politics of Modern Greek Criticism*. Princeton, NJ: Princeton University Press

—— (1993), *The Rise of Eurocentrism: Anatomy of Interpretation*. Princeton, NJ: Princeton University Press.

—— (1994), 'Ελληνισμός άνευ έθνους.' *To Vima*, 10 July.

Lambrou, S. (1892), Αποκαλύψεις περί του Μαρτυρίου του Ρήγα. Athens: Estia

Layoun, M. (1988), *Travels in a Genre: The Modern Novel and Ideology*. Princeton, NJ: Princeton University Press.

—— (ed.) (1990), *Modernism in Greece? Essays on the Literary and Cultural Margins of a Movement*. New York: Pella.

—— (2001), *Wedded to the Land? Gender, Boundaries, and Nationalism in Crisis*. Durham, NC: Duke University Press.

Lazaris, V. K. (1996), Οι Ρίζες του Ελληνικού Κομμουνιστικού Κινήματος. Athens: Synchroni Epoche.

Lazos, C. (1986), 'Η Φοιτητική Συντροφιά, 1910-1929 και ο Γιώργος Θεοτοκάς.' *Diavazo* 137, (12 February): 41–4.

Leondaris, V. (1983), Η Ποίηση της ´Ηττας. Athens: Erasmos

—— (1985), Δοκίμια για την Ποίηση. Athens: Erasmos

References

Leontis, A. (1987), '"The Lost Center" and the Promised Land of Greek Criticism.' *Journal of Modern Greek Studies* 5(2): 175–90.

—— (1990), 'Minor Field, Major Territories: Dilemmas in Modernizing Hellenism.' *Journal of Modern Greek Studies* 8(1): 35–64.

—— (1991), '"Byzantium" as a Modern Couterhegemonic Ideal to the West." Oral presentation.

—— (1995), *Topographies of Hellenism: Mapping the Homeland.* Ithaca, NY: Cornell University Press.

—— (1997), 'Ambivalent Greece.' *Journal of Modern Greek Studies* 15(1): 125–36.

Leontsini, M. (1996), 'Η Ιστορία ήταν το πρόσχημα.' *I Avghi*, 27 July.

Leoussi, A. S. (1998), *Nationalism and Classicism: The Classical Body as National Symbol in Nineteenth-Century England and France.* New York: St. Martin's Press.

Lephas, Y. N. (1979), Ο Αλέξανδρος Σούτσος και οι Επιδράσεις του ΄Εργου του στους σύγχρονους τους. Athens.

—— (1991), Παναγιώτης Σούτσος. Athens: University of Athens.

Lewis, B. (1964), *The Middle East and the West.* Bloomington, IN: Indiana University Press.

Liakos, A. (1998), 'Ο δημοκρατικός πατριωτισμός του Ρήγα.' *To Vima*, 28 June.

Liata, E. (1977), 'Ειδήσεις για την κίνηση του ελληνικού βιβλίου στις αρχές του 18ου αιώνα.' *Eranistes* 14: 1–35.

Linssen, R. (1998), *Living Zen.* New York: Grove Press.

Lord, A. B. (1960), *The Singer of Tales*, 1st edition. Cambridge, MA: Harvard University Press.

—— (1991), *Epic Singers and the Oral Tradition.* Ithaca, NY and London: Cornell University Press.

Lorenzatos, Z. (1974), Για το Σολωμό - τη λύρα τη δίκαιη. Athens: Ikaros

—— (1980), '"The Lost Center"' [1961]. In *The Lost Center and Other Essays in Greek Poetry.* Trans. K. Cicellis. Princeton, NJ: Princeton University Press

Lyhnara, L. (1980), Η μεταλογική των πραγμάτων - Οδυσσέας Ελύτης. Athens: Ikaros.

Lykiardopoulos, Y. (1964), 'Η Ποίηση της ΄Ηττας, σύγχρονη αντιστασιακή ποιήση.' Επιθεώρηση Τέχνης 113: 459–60.

—— (1976), Αναφορές. Athens: Erasmos.

McGrew, W. (1976), 'The Land Issue in the Greek War of Independence.' In N. Diamandouros et al. (eds.), *Hellenism and the First Greek War of Liberation (1821–1830).*

Mackridge, P. (1989), *Dionysios Solomos.* Bristol: Bristol Classical Press.

—— (1990), 'Ζητήματα ύψους και ύφους στην ποίηση του Καρυωτάκη.' In M. Melissaratos (ed.), Συμπόσιο για τον Κ.Τ. Καρυωτάκη Πρέβεζα.

—— (1992), 'Dionisio Salamon/Διονύσιος Σολωμός: Poetry as a Dialogue between Languages.' *Dialogos* 1: 59–76.

—— (1997a), 'Ο Καβαφικός Σεφέρης.' In M. Pieris (ed.), Γιώργος Σεφέρης - Φιλολογικές και Ερμηνευτικές Προσεγγίσεις. Δοκίμια εις μνήμην Γεώργιου Σαββίδη. Athens: Patakis, 107–23.

—— (1997b), 'Textual Orientations: Writing the Landscape in Elytis's *The Axion Esti.*' In D. Tziovas (ed.) *Greek Modernism and Beyond.*

MacNiven, I. S. (ed.) (1988), *The Durrell–Miller Letters (1935–1980* [1962]. New York: New Directions.

—— (1998), *Lawrence Durrell.* London: Faber & Faber.

Malanos, T. (1938),´Ενας Ηγησιακός · Συμβολή στη μελέτη του Καρυωτάκη. Alexandria: n.p.

—— (1951), Η Ποίηση του Σεφέρη. Alexandria: n.p.

Mango, C. (1973), 'The Phanariots and the Byzantine Tradition.' In Richard Clogg (ed.), *The Struggle for Greek Independence: Essays to Mark the 150th Anniversary of the Greek War of Independence.* Hamden, CN: Archon.

Manousos, A. (1850), Τραγούδια εθνικά. Corfu: Ermis.

Mantouvala, M. (1983), 'Ρωμαίος, Ρωμιός και Ρωμιοσύνη.' *Mantatoforos* 22: 34–73.

Mantzaros, N. (1963), 'Νικολάου Μάντζαρου· Σκιαγραφία του Σολωμού.' In D. Konomos (ed.), Σολωμικά. Athens.

Maratheftis, M. I. (1992), Το Κυπριακό Εκπαιδευτικό Σύστημα - Σταθμοί και Θέματα. Nicosia.

Marchand, S. L. (1996), *Down from Olympus: Archaeology and Philhellenism in Germany, 1750–1970.* Princeton, NJ: Princeton University Press.

Markides, K. (1989), 'Cyprus and Attempts at Federalism.' In S. Vryonis (ed.), *Cyprus Between East and West: A Political and Moral Dilemma – The Past as Prologue to the Present.* Heraklion: Crete University Press.

Maronitis, D.N. (1975), Δ. Σολωμός· Οι Εποχές του "Κρητικού". Athens: Leshi.

—— (1976), Ποιητική και Πολιτική Ηθική· Πρώτη Μεταπολεμική Γενιά - Αλεξάνδρου - Αναγνωστάκης - Πατρίκιος. Athens: Kedros.

—— (1987a), 'Μύθος και Ιστορία στο Ημερολόγιο Καταστρώματος Γ'. In M. Pieris (ed.),Ο Σεφέρης στην Πύλη της Αμμοχώστου. Athens: MIET.

—— (1987b), Όροι του Λυρισμού στον Οδυσσέα Ελύτη. Athens: Kaktos.

—— (1992), 'Ρέας Γαλανάκη- Ο Βίος του Ισμαήλ Φερίκ Πασά: Reas Galanaki: *Spina nel Cuore* – Σημειώσεις.' *Diavazo* 291: 46–50.

Martinengous, E. (1881), Η Μήτηρ μου - Αυτοβιογραφία της κυρίας Ελισάβετ Μουτζά- Μαρτινέγκου, εκδιδόμενη υπό του υιού αυτής Ελισαβέτιου Μαρτινέγκου μετά διαφόρων αυτών ποιήσεων. Athens: Korinni.

Mayiakos, P. S. (1935), Ρήγας Βελεστινλής ο Θεσσαλός 1757–1798. Athens: Nikos Tilperoglou.

References

Megas, G. A. (1960), 'Παραλλαγή της λαϊκής διασκευής της Ερωφίλης.' In Εις Μνήμη Κ. Αμάντου. Athens: Mina Myrtidi.

Melissaratos, M. (ed.), (1990), Συμπόσιο για τον Κ. Τ. Καρυωτάκη Πρέβεζα, 4–14 Σεπτεμβρίου. Preveza: Dimos Prevezas.

Melissinos, S. (1978), Τα Μνήματα. Corfu: Epy.

Mendoza, P. A. & G. G. Màrquez (1983), The Fragrance of Guava. Trans. A. Wright. London: Verso.

Menounos, I. (1979), Κοσμά του Αιτωλού· Διδαχές, 2nd edition. Athens: Tinos.

Menti, D. (1995), Μεταπολεμική Πολιτική Ποίηση - Ιδεολογία και Ποίηση. Athens: Kedros.

Meraklis, M. G. (1987), Σύγχρονη Ελληνική Λογοτεχνία (1945–1980). Μέρος Πρώτο· Ποίηση. Athens: Patakis.

Meyendorff, J. (1974), Byzantine Theology: Historical Trends and Doctrinal Themes. New York: Fordham University Press.

Michalopoulos, Ph. (1930), Ρήγας ο Βελεστινλής 1757–1798. Athens: P. D. Sakellarios.

—— (1968), Κοσμάς ο Αιτωλός · Ο Εθναπόστολος. Athens: Ekd. Ieras Mitropoleos.

Miliori, M. (2000), 'Αρχαίος Ελληνισμός και Φιλελληνισμός στη Βρετανική Ιστοριογραφία του 19ου αιώνα - Οι πολιτικές και ηθικές διαστάσεις του εθνικού και οι ευρύτερες πολιτισμικές σημασιοδοτήεις της ελληνικής ιστορίας.' Mnemon 22: 69–104.

Miller, H. (1958), The Colossus of Maroussi [1941]. New York: New Directions.

Miller, W. (1978), Greece. Modern World Series. New York: E. Benn.

Minotou, M. (1933–4), 'Τραγούδια από τη Ζάκυνθο,' Ionios Anthologia 7: 145–92; 8: 1–45.

Montis, C. (1964), Κλειστές Πόρτες. Nicosia: National Youth Council of Cyprus Publications.

Morris, S. P. (2001), 'Beyond Continuity: Confronting Neo-Hellenisim in a Classical World.' Journal of the Hellenic Diaspora 27 (1–2): 7–18.

Moskov, K. (1979), Εισαγωγικά στήν Ιστορία του Κινήματος της Εργατικής Τάξης - Η Διαμόρφωση της Εθνικής και Κοινωνικής Συνείδησης στην Ελλάδα. Thessaloniki: n.p.

Moullas, P. (1990), Τρεις Γάλλοι Ρομαντικοί στην Ελλάδα. Μετάφραση Βάσω Μέντζου. Athens: Olkos.

—— (1997), Τρία Κείμενα για τον Μανώλη Αναγνωστάκη. Athens: Stigmi.

Moutzan-Martinengou, E. (1986), My Story. Trans. H. D. Kolias. Athens, GA and London: University of Georgia Press.

Mouzelis, N. (1978), Modern Greece: Facets of Underdevelopment. London: Macmillan.

—— (1992), 'Θεσμοί και πολιτική κουλτούρα', To Vima, 23 August.

References

Nadeau, M. (1989), *The History of Surrealism*. Cambridge, MA: Belknap Press of Harvard University Press.

Nea Estia (1971), Ειδικό Αφιέρωμα στον Κ.Γ. Καρυωτάκη, Vol. 90: 1065. Athens.

Nerval, Gérard de (1964), *Voyage en Orient, Tome I: Europe Centrale Egypte*. Paris: Editions Juilliard.

Nissiotis, V. (1961), 'Οδυσσέας Ελύτης· Η συνείδηση του ελληνικού μύθου.' *Kritike* 13, January–April.

Noutsos, P. (1999), 'Ερωτήματα για τον Ρήγα.' *To Vima*, 21 March.

Oberling, P. (1982), *The Road to Bellapais: The Turkish Cypriot Exodus to Northern Cyprus*. East European Monographs No. CXXV. Social Science Monographs. Boulder, NY: Columbia University Press.

O'Neill, K. (2003), 'The Unfinished Ape: Mediation and Modern Greek Identity in Iakovos Pitsipios's Ο Πίθηκος Ξουθ.' *Journal of Modern Greek Studies* 21:1, May, 67–112.

Ong, W. (1967), *Presence of the Word*. New Haven, CT: Yale University Press.

—— (1977), *Interfaces of the Word: Studies in the Evolution of Consciousness and Culture*. Ithaca, NY: Cornell University Press.

—— (1982), *Orality and Literacy: The Technologizing of the Word*. New Accents Series. London & New York: Methuen.

Orsina, V. (1997), Ο Στόχος και η Σιωπή - Εισαγωγή στην ποίηση του Μ. Αναγνωστάκη. Athens: Nefeli.

Palamas, C. (1925), Γύρω στο Σολωμό. Athens: Stohastis.

Pamuk, O. (1991), *The White Castle*. Trans. V. Holbrook. New York: Brazilier.

Panayiotou, Y. A. (1979), Γενιά του ' 70 - Ποίηση. Athens: Sisyphos.

Panayotopoulos, I. M. (1983), Τα Πρόσωπα και τα Κείμενα Ε΄- Ο Λυρικός Λόγος. Athens: Ekdoseis ton Filon.

Pantazopoulos, N. I. (1964), Ρήγας Βελεστινλής· Η Πολιτική Ιδεολογία του Ελληνισμού - Προάγγελος της Επανάστασης. Thessaloniki: n.p.

—— (n.d.), Μελετήματα για τον Ρήγα Βελεστινλή. Έκδοση Επιστημονικής Εταιρείας Φερών - Βελεστίνου - Ρήγα.

Papadakis, Y. (1998), '*Enosis* and Turkish Expansionism: Real Myths or Mythical Realities?' In V. Calotychos (ed.), *Cyprus and its People*.

Papadopoulos, T. (1969), 'Νέα Παραλλαγή της Βοσκοπούλας. ' Πεπραγμένα του Β΄ Διεθνούς Κρητολογικού Συνεδρίου, 4. Athens, 353–77

Papadopoulos, Y. K. (1987), Κείμενα ενός αγώνα - Παράνομα Έγγραφα του 1955–59. Nicosia.

Papageorgiou, C. G. (1983), 'Οι πρώτοι μεταπολεμικοί ποιητές και ο Καβάφης (Παροικιακός και ιδεολογικός Φυλετισμός).' *Diavazo* 78 (15 October): 122–9.

—— (1989), Γενιά του ' 70· Ιστορία - Ποιητικές διαδρομές. Athens: Kedros.

Papaioannou, M. M. (1955), 'Φαινόμενα ακμής και παρακμής στη νεοελληνική ποίηση. ' Επιθεώρηση Τέχνης. τ. Α΄ 2: 83–92.

References

Papakostas, Y. (1990), Ανάγκη Χρηστότητος· ένα λανθάνον κείμενο κοινωνικής πολιτικής. In M. Melissaratos (ed.), Συμπόσιο για τον Κ.Γ. Καρυωτάκη.

—— (1991), Φιλιλογικά Σαλόνια και καφενεία της Αθήνας. Athens: Estia.

Papakyriakou, S. (1953), Κοσμά του Αιτωλού Διδαχαί, επιστολαί και μαρτύριον. Athens.

Papanastasiou, E. (1921), Τα Βαλκάνια από τον 15ον αιώνα εν σχέσει με το ανατολικό ζήτημα. Αρχείο Οικονομικών και Κοινωνικών Επιστήμων.

Papatsonis, T. (1948), Ο ένδοξος μας Βυζαντινισμός. Nea Estia 43 (499): 462–8, 659–65.

Papayiannidou, M. (1998), 'Η Πηνελόπη και τα Δάνεια του Δείπνου', 4 January.

Papazisis, D. (1976), Βλάχοι. Athens: n.p.

Pappas, C. (1990), Η Ποίηση του Τίτου Πατρίκιου (Στάση Ζωής). Athens: Pelekanos.

Paraschos, K. (1971), 'Νηπενθή', Nea Estia 90: 1065, 1571–85.

Patrikios, T. (1976), Ποιήματα. Athens: n.p.

—— (1978), Μαθητεία Ξανά. Athens: Diatton.

—— (1981), Αντιδικίες. Athens: Ipsilon

—— (1988), Αντικριστοί Καθρέφτες. Athens: Stigmi.

—— (1990), Ποιήματα, I (1948–1954). Athens: Themelio.

Pavlou, S. (2000), Σεφέρης και Κύπρος. Ph.D Dissertation Series no. 2. Nicosia: Cultural Services, Ministry of Education & Culture.

Peckham, R. S. (2001), National Histories, Natural States: Nationalism and the Politics of Place in Greece. London and New York: I. B. Tauris.

Peponis, A. I. (ed.) (1997), Πολιτικά Κείμενα. Athens: Ikaros.

Persianis, P. K. (1978), Church and State in Cyprus Education: The Contribution of the Greek Orthodox Church of Cyprus to Cyprus Education during the British Administration (1878–1960). Nicosia: Volaris.

Petropoulos, J. A. (1968), Politics and Statecraft in the Kingdom of Greece, 1833–1843. Princeton, NJ: Princeton University Press.

Pfeiffer, R. (1976), History of Classical Scholarship (1300-1850). Oxford: Oxford University Press.

Phaltaïts, K. (1986), Ο Άγιος Κοσμάς εις το στόμα του ηπειρωτικού λαού. Athens.

Philokyprou, E. (1992), 'Why the Post-Symbolists Have No Symbols.' Journal of Modern Greek Studies 10 (2): 235–48.

Pieris, M. (1991), Από το μερτικόν της Κύπρου. Athens: Kastaniotis.

—— (ed.) (2000), Γιώργος Σεφέρης- Φιλιλογικές και Ερμηνευτικές Προσεγγίσεις. Δοκίμια εις μνήμην Γεώργιου Σαββίδη. Athens: Patakis.

Pilitsis, G. (1988), 'Five Italian Sonnets by Dionysios Solomos: A Translation and Introduction.' Journal of Modern Hellenism 10: 187–93.

Pine, R. (1994), Lawrence Durrell: The Mindscape. London: Macmillan.

Pitsilides, M. (2000), Οι σκοτεινές πλευρές του Γιώργου Σεφέρη. Athens: Archipelagos.

Pitsipios, I. (1995), Η Ορφανή της Χίου ή ο θρίαμβος της Αρετής. Ο Πίθηκος Ξουθ ή τα ήθη του αιώνος. Ed. D. Tziovas. Athens: Idryma Ouranis.

Politis, A. (1982), 'Το Βιβλίο μέσο παραγωγής της προφορικής γνώσης. Δυσκολίες και προβληματισμοί γύρω από το Θέμα.' Το Βιβλίο στις προβιομηχανικές κοινωνίες. Πρακτικά του Α΄ Διεθνούς Συμποσίου του Κέντρου Νεοελληνικών Ερευνών. Athens, 271–82.

—— (1984), Η Ανακάλυψη των Ελληνικών Δημοτικών Τραγουδιών· Προϋποθέσεις, προσπάθειες και η δημιουργία της πρώτης συλλογής. Athens: Themelio.

Politis, L. (1959), Ο Σολωμός στα γράμματά του. Athens: Estia.

—— (1973), *A History of Modern Greek Literature*. Oxford: Clarendon Press.

—— (1985), Γύρω στον Σολωμό· Μελέτες και ΄Αρθρα. Athens: MIET.

Pollis, A. (1958), *The Megali Idea: A Study of Greek Nationalism*. Ph.D. dissertation, Faculty of Philosophy of Johns Hopkins University.

Polylas, I. (1948), 'Προλεγόμενα.' In D. Solomos, Ποιήματα (1948) τ. 1ος. Ed. L. Politis, 4th edition. Athens: Ikaros.

Porphyres, C. (1992), Αυτοβιογραφία [1956]. Athens: Digenis.

Potts, A. (1994), *Flesh and the Ideal: Winckelmann and the Origins of Art History*. New Haven, CT and London: Yale University Press.

Pratt, M. L. (1992), *Imperial Eyes: Travel Writing and Transculturation*. New York: Routledge.

Prinzinger, M. (1992), 'The Mother–Daughter Plot or toward a Science Fiction of Modern Greek Literary History.' Paper delivered at the Third Wave Conference in Byzantine & Modern Greek Studies, at the Ohio State University.

Psomiades, H. J. (1976), 'The Character of the New Greek State.' In N. Diamandouros et al. (eds.), *Hellenism and the First Greek War of Liberation (1821–1830)*.

Puchner, W. (1983), 'Η Ερωφίλη στη δημώδη παράδοση της Κρήτης.' *Ariadne* I: 173–235.

Raftopoulos, D. (1996),΄Αρης Αλέξανδρου, ο εξόριστος. Athens: Sokoli.

Raizis, M. B. (1972), *Dionysios Solomos*. New York: Twayne.

Redfield, M. (1999), 'Imagi-Nation: The Imagined Community and the Aesthetics of Mourning.' *Diacritics* 29 (4): 58–83.

Ricks, D. (1989), *The Shade of Homer: A Study in Modern Greek Poetry*. Cambridge: Cambridge University Press.

—— (1995–6), '"The Best Wall to Hide our Face Behind": An Introduction to the Poetry of Manolis Anagnostakis.' *Journal of Modern Hellenism* 12–13: 1–26.

—— (1998), 'The Bottom of the Well: Bloodshed, Ballads, and the Poetry of Miltos Sachtouris.' *Journal of Modern Greek Studies* 16 (1): 73–90.

References

Riedesel, J. H. von (1997), *Remarques d'un voyageur moderne au Levant* [1773]. Amsterdam and Stuttgart.

Roessel, D. (1994a), 'Rodis Roufos on *Bitter Lemons*: A Suppressed Section of the Age of Bronze.' *Deus Loci: International Lawrence Durrell Journal* NS3: 129–33.

—— (1994b), '"Something to Stand the Government in Good Stead": Lawrence Durrell and *The Cyprus Review*.' *Deus Loci: International Lawrence Durrell Journal* NS3: 37–50.

—— (1997), '"This is Not a Political Book": *Bitter Lemons* as British Propaganda.' *Byzantine & Modern Greek Studies* 24: 235–45.

—— (2002), *In Byron's Shadow: Modern Greece in the English and American Tradition*. Oxford and New York: Oxford University Press.

Rosen, F. (1992), *Bentham, Byron and Greece: Constitutionalism, Nationalism, and Early Liberal Political Thought*. Oxford: Oxford University Press.

Rotolo, V. (1975), 'The "Heroic and Elegaic Song for the Lost Second Lieutenant of the Albanian Campaign": The Transition from the Early to the Later Elytis.' In I. Ivask (ed.), *Odysseas Elytis*. Norman, OK: Oklahoma University Press.

Roufos, R. (1960), *The Age of Bronze*. London, Melbourne and Toronto: Heineman.

—— (1994), 'Sour Grapes.' *Deus Loci: International Lawrence Durrell Journal* NS3: 134–8.

Rowlandson, M. (1978), *A Narrative of the Captivity and Restoration of Mrs. Mary Rowlandson* [1682]. In R. Slotkin and J. K. Folsom (eds.), *So Dreadfull a Judgment*. Middletown, CT: Wesleyan University Press.

Rozanes, S. (1982), Σπουδές στον Διονύσιο Σολωμό· Το Δαιμονικό Ύψιστο. Athens: ELIA.

—— (1985), Η Αισθητική του Αποσπάσματος· Μια Κριτική Προσέγγιση στον "Λάμπρο" του Σολωμού. Athens: Goulandris-Chorn Foundation.

Rushdie, S. (1991), *Imaginary Homelands: Essays and Criticism, 1981–1991*. London: Granta.

Sachinis, A. (1980), Το Νεοελληνικό Μυθιστόρημα - Ιστορία και Κριτική. Athens: Estia.

Sachtouris, M. (1977), Ποιήματα (1945–1971). Athens: Kedros.

Said, E. (1978), *Orientalism*. New York: Vintage.

—— (1993), *Culture and Imperialism*. New York: Alfred A. Knopf.

Sakellariades, Ch. (1938), Άπαντα· Έμμετρα και Πεζά - Κ.Γ. Καρυωτάκη. Athens: Govosti.

Samouil, A. (1996), "Introduction." In A. Samouil (ed.), Ο Λέανδρος. Athens: Nefeli.

Savidis, G. P. (1961), 'Μια Περιδιάβαση. Σχόλια στο . . . "Κύπρον ου μ ' εθέσπισεν" του Γιώργου Σεφέρη'. In G. P. Savidis (ed.), Για τον Σεφέρη. Τιμητικό αφιέρωμα στα τριάντα χρόνια της Στροφής. Athens: Ikaros.

References

—— (1975), Γιώργος Θεοτοκάς και Γιώργος Σεφέρης - Αλληλογραφία (1930–66). Athens: Ermis.

—— (1981), Μεταμόρφωση του Ελπήνορα · Από τον Πάουντ στον Σινόπουλο. Athens: Ermis.

—— (1989a), 'Το ατελές ποίημα σε ξένους και Έλληνες ρομαντικούς.' *Periplous* 23: 129–50.

—— (1989b), Στα Χνάρια του Καρυωτάκη. Athens: Nefeli.

Schiller, F. (1954), *Über die asthetische Erziehung des Menschen in einer Reihe von Briefen* [1795]. Trans. and introduction by R. Schnell. New Haven, CT: Yale University Press.

Scott, J. W. (1991), 'The Evidence of Experience.' *Critical Inquiry* 17: 773–97.

Searle, C. (1982), 'The Mobilization of Words: Poetry and Resistance in Mozambique.' *Race and Class* 23 (4): 305–20.

Seferis, G. (1967), *On the Greek Style: Selected Essays in Poetry and Hellenism by George Seferis.* Trans. R. Warner and Th. Frangopoulos. London: Bodley Head.

—— (1974), *A Poet's Journal: Days of (1945–1951).* Trans. A. Anagnostopoulos. Cambridge, MA: Belknap Press of Harvard University.

—— (1975), *Days B' (16 February 1925–17 August 1931).* Ed. E. H. Kasdaglis. Athens: Ikaros.

—— (1978), *Collected Poems (1924–1955).* Trans. E. Keeley and P. Sherrard. London: Jonathan Cape.

—— (1979), Γ. Σεφέρης - Κ. Τσάτσος· Διάλογος πάνω στην ποίηση. Ed. L. Koussoulas. Nea Vivliothiki Series. Athens: Ermis.

—— (1979–85), Πολιτικό Ημερολόγιο, vols 1 and 2. Ed. A. Xydis. Athens: Ikaros.

—— (1981), Δοκιμές Α'- Β', 4th edition, 2 vols. Athens: Ikaros.

—— (1986), Μέρες Σ '. [*Days VI*] 20th April 1951–4th August 1956. Athens: Ikaros.

—— (1995), *Collected Poems: Revised Edition.* Trans. E. Keeley and P. Sherrard. Princeton, NJ: Princeton University Press.

Sfyroeras, V., A. Avramea and S. Asdrahas (eds.) (1986), *Maps and Mapmakers of the Aegean.* Athens: Olkos.

Shell, M. (1978), *The Economy of Literature.* Baltimore, MD and London: Johns Hopkins University Press.

Sinopoulos, T. (1957a), Ελένη. Athens: Difros

—— (1957b), Μεταίχμιο Β' *(1949–55).* Athens: Difros.

—— (1979), *Landscape of Death: The Selected Poems of Takis Sinopoulos.* Trans. and introduction by K. Friar. Columbus, OH: Ohio State University Press.

—— (1983), Τέσσερα Μελετήματα για τον Σέφερη. Athens: Kedros.

Skliros, G. (1932), Εμπρός στο Κοινωνικό Πρόβλημα. Athens: Pyrsos.

References

—— (1976), Το Κοινωνικόν μας Ζήτημα [1907]. In L. Axelos (ed.), Έργα. Athens: Keimena.

Skopetea, E. (1988), Το Πρωτότυπο Βασίλειο και Η Μεγάλη Ιδέα - Όψεις του εθνικού προβλήματος (1830–1880). Athens: Polytypo.

Sokolis, S. (1916), Αυτοκρατορία. Athens.

Solomos, D. (1948–69), Άπαντα. Ed. Linos Politis. Athens: Ikaros.

—— (1964a), Αυτόγραφα Έργα. τ. Α΄ Φωτοτυπίες. (Ed.) L. Politis. Thessaloniki: Aristoteleion Panepistimio Thessalonikis.

—— (1964b), Αυτόγραφα Έργα. τ. Β΄. Τυπογραφική Μεταγραφή. (Ed.) L. Politis. Thessaloniki: Aristoteleion Panepistimio Thessalonikis.

—— (1979a), Άπαντα. τ. 1. Ποιήματα [1948]. Ed. L. Politis, 4th edition. Athens: Ikaros.

—— (1979b), Άπαντα. τ. 2 Πεζά και Ιταλικά [1955]. Ed. L. Politis. 4th edition. Athens: Ikaros.

—— (1984), Τα Ιταλικά Ποιήματα. Πρόλογος και μετάφραση Γιώργου Καλοσγούρου. Athens: Keimena.

—— (1994), Ποιήματα και Πεζά. Ed. Stylianos Alexiou. Athens: Stigmi.

—— (1999), 'Αυτόγραφα Έργα,' τ Α΄. (Ed.) L. Politis. Athens: Aristoteleion Panepistimio Thessalonikis; Cultural Foundation of the Bank of Greece; National Book Centre.

Sourbati, A. (1992), *Reading the Subversive in Contemporary Greek Women's Fiction*. Ph.D dissertation, King's College, London.

Soutsos, Panayiotis (1996a), Ο Λέανδρος. Ed. Y. Veloudis. Athens: Ouranis Foundation.

—— (1996b), Ο Λέανδρος. Ed. A. Samuil. Athens: Nefeli.

Spanaki, M. (1990), 'Η "Αποστροφή" του Καρυωτάκη. Γυναικείοι ρόλοι και κοινωνική αμφισβήτηση.' In M. Melissaratos (ed.), Συμπόσιο για τον Κ.Γ. Καρυωτάκη, Πρέβεζα. 385–96.

— (1997), 'Egypt and Cyprus: Representations of Colonialism in Cavafy, Pierides, Roufos, and Durrell.' *Journal of the Hellenic Diaspora* 23 (2): 111–26.

Spatalis, Y. (1929), 'Ο Μαύρος Γάτος,' *Hellenika Grammata* 65 (14 September).

Spiropoulou, A. and D. Tsimpouki (eds.) (2002), Σύγχρονη Ελληνική Πεζογραφία : Διεθνείς Προσανατολισμοί και Διασταυρώσεις. Athens: Alexandria.

Spivak, G. Ch. (1989), 'Who Claims Alterity?' In B. Kruger & P. Mariani (eds.), *Remaking History*. Dia Art Foundation. Seattle, WA: Bay Press.

Stallybrass, P. and A. White (1990), *The Politics and Poetics of Transgression*. Ithaca, NY: Cornell University Press.

Stavridi-Patrikiou, R. (1976), Δημοτικισμός και Κοινωνικό Πρόβλημα. Nea Elliniki Vivliothiki Series. Athens: Ermis.

Stergiopoulos, C. (1990), 'Η μαρτυρία της μορφής στην ποίηση του Καρυωτάκη.' In M. Melissaratos (ed.), Συμπόσιο για τον Κ.Γ. Καρυωτάκη.

References

Stewart, C. (1991), *Demons and the Devil: Moral Imagination in Modern Greek Culture*. Princeton, NJ: Princeton University Press.

Stewart, J. F. (1998), 'Painterly Writing: Durrell's Island Landscapes.' *Deus Loci: International Lawrence Durrell Journal* NS6: 40–61.

Storace, P. (1996), *Dinner with Persephone*. New York: Pantheon.

Stuart, J. (1968), *The Antiquities of Athens* [1762], 3 vols. New York: Blom.

Suleiman, S. R. (1989), *Subversive Intent: Gender, Politics, and the Avant-Garde*. Cambridge, MA: Harvard University Press.

Syrimis, G. (1995), 'Gender, Narrative Modes, and the Procreative Cycle: The Pregnant Word in Vizyenos.' *Journal of Modern Greek Studies* 13 (2): 327–49.

Tangopoulos, D. (1903), 'Η Μοναρχία ενάντια στη δύναμη της διαφθοράς.' *Noumas*, 26 Ιανουαρίου.

Tarkovsky, A. A. (1994), *Time within Time: The Diaries, 1970–86*. Trans. K. Hunter-Blair. London: Faber.

Tennenhouse, L. (1990), 'Simulating History: A Cockfight for our Times.' *Drama Review* 34 (4) (T128): 137–55.

Terzakis, Angelos (1937), 'Ανανέωση Δογμάτων.' *Neoellinika Grammata* 20 (17 April).

Thalassis, Y. (1991), 'Η Μεταμοντέρνα Παράσταση της ευθείας και του κύκλου. Αφ- ορισμός τον στερεοτύπων φύλλου, φυλής, εθνικότητας και θρησκείας στο μυθιστόρημα της Ρέας Γαλανάκη. Ο Βίος του Ισμαήλ Φερίκ Πασά, Spina nel Cuore.' *Speira* 2 (Fall): 99–110.

Theotokas, Y. (1932), Εμπρός στο Κοινωνικό μας Πρόβλημα. Athens: Pirsos.

—— (1938), Νεοελληνικά Γράμματα Β΄, 19 March.

—— (1953), 'Πολίτης της Ευρώπης, *Nea Estia* 54(632): 1505.

—— (1966), Η Εθνική Κρίση. Athens: Themelis.

—— (1971), Ταξίδι στη Μέση Ανατολή και στο Άγιον Όρος, 2nd edition. Athens: Estia.

—— (1975a), Αλληλογραφία, 1930–1966 – Γιώργος Θεοτοκάς και Γιώργος Σεφέρης. Ed. G. Savidis. Athens: Ermis.

—— (1975b), Η Ορθοδοξία στον Καιρό μας – δοκίμια. Athens: Ekdoseis ton Filon.

—— (1976), Πολιτικά Κείμενα. Ed. A. I. Peponis. Athens: Ikaros.

—— (1986), *Free Spirit* [1929] Trans. S. G. Stavrou. *Modern Greek Studies Yearbook* 2: 153–200.

—— (1988), Το Ελεύθερο Πνεύμα [1929]. Ed. K. T. Dimaras, Νέα Ελληνική Βιβλιοθήκη, 22. Athens: Ermis.

—— (1989), Τετράδια Ημερολογίου *(1939–1953)*. Ed. D. Tziovas. Athens: Estia.

Thibaudet, A. (1936), *Histoire de la littérature française de 1789 à nos jours*. Paris: Stock.

Todorova, M. (1995), *Imagining the Balkans*. New York and London: Oxford University Press.

References

Tolias, G. (1998), '"Της ευρυχώρου Ελλάδος". Η Χάρτα της Ελλάδος του Ρήγα και τα Όρια του Ελληνισμού. *Istorika* 27–8: 3–30.

—— (2001), '*Totius Graecia*: Nicolaos Sophianos's Map of Greece an the Transformations of Hellenism.' *Journal of Modern Greek Studies* 19 (1): 1–22.

Tomadakis, N. B. (1935), Εκδόσεις και Χειρόγραφα του Ποιητού Διονύσιου Σολωμού. Athens: Estia

Tommaseo, N. (1841–2), *Canti Populari:Raccolti e illustrati da N. Tommaseo, con opusculo originale del medisimo autore*. Venice: G. Tasso.

Tonnet, H. (1991), 'A propos des premiers romans et nouvelles néo-helléniques.' *Metis: Revue d'anthropologie du monde grec ancien* VI(1–2): 89–114.

—— (1995), 'Sources européenes de "Leandre" de Panayotis Soutsos.' In Ελληνική Εταιρεία Γενικής και Συγκριτικής Γραμματολογίας, Πρακτικά Α΄ Διεθνούς Συνεδρίου Συγκριτικής Γραμματολογίας. Athens: Domos.

Trapp, E. (1976), *Hagiographische Elemente in Digenis-Epos*. Analecta Bollandiana 94.

Tsantsanoglou, E. (1982), Μια Λανθάνουσα Ποιητική Σύνθεση του Σολωμού - Το αυτόγραφο τετράδιο Ζακύνθου, αρ. 11, Εκδοτική Δοκιμή. Athens: Ermis.

Tsaoussis, D. G. (1984), Όψεις της Ελληνικής Κοινωνίας του 19ου αιώνα. Athens: Estia.

Tsatsos, C. (2000), Λογοδοσία μιας ζωής, 2 vols. Athens: Ekdoseis ton Philon.

Tsirkas, S. (1958), Ο Καβάφης και η εποχή του. Athens: Kedros.

Tsoucalas, C. (1969), *The Greek Tragedy*. Baltimore, MD: Penguin.

—— (1981), Κοινωνική Ανάπτυξη και Κράτος· Η Συγκρότηση του Δημοσίου Χώρου στην Ελλάδα. Athens: Themelio.

—— (1991), '"Enlightened" Concepts in the "Dark": Power and Freedom, Politics and Society.' *Journal of Modern Greek Studies* 9 (1): 1–22.

Tziovas, D. (1986a), 'Ο Καρυωτάκης ως Πρόκληση στον Μοντερνισμό.' *Diavazo* 157 (17 December): 100–7.

—— (1986b), *The Nationism of the Demoticists and its Impact on their Literary Theory (1888–1930)*. Amsterdam: Hakkert.

—— (1989a), Οι Μεταμορφώσεις του Εθνισμού και το Ιδεολόγημα της Ελληνικότητας στο Μεσοπόλεμο. Athens: Odysseas.

—— (1989b), 'Residual Orality and Belated Textuality in Greek Literature and Culture.' *Journal of Modern Greek Studies* 7 (2): 321–36.

—— (1993), Το Παλίμψηστο της Ελληνικής Αφήγησης - Από την αφηγηματολογία στη διαλογικότητα. Athens: Odysseas.

—— (ed.) (1995), *Greek Modernism and Beyond*. Lanham, MD: Rowman and Littlefield.

Updike, J. (1991), 'Vagueness on Wheels, Dust on a Skirt.' *The New Yorker*, 2 September: 102–5.

References

Vacalopoulos, A. E. (1970), *Origins of the Greek Nation: The Byzantine Period, 1204–1461*. Revised edition Trans. I. Marks. New Brunswick, NJ: Rutgers University Press.

—— (1976), *The Greek Nation, 1453-1669: The Cultural and Economic Background of Modern Greek Society.* Trans I. Moles and P. Moles. New Brunswick, NJ: Rutgers University Press.

Valaorites, N. (1996), 'Modern Greek Literature after the War.' Personal correspondence with Author.

Valetas, G. (1959), Πολυλά - ΄Απαντα. Τα Λογοτεχνικά και Κριτικά, 2nd edition. Athens: Nikas.

Van Dyck, K. R. (1998), *Kassandra and the Censors: Greek Poetry since 1967.* Ithaca, NY and London: Cornell University Press.

Van Steen, G. (2002), 'Ancient and Modern: To Whom They May (Or May Not) Concern.' *Journal of Modern Greek Studies* 20 (2): 175–90.

Vaporis, Nomikos Michael (1977), *Father Kosmas: The Apostle of the Poor.* Archbishop Iakovos Library of Ecclesiastical Historical Source, no. 4. Brookline, MA: Holy Cross Orthodox Press.

Varikas, V. (1939), Κ.Γ. Καρυωτάκης: Το Δράμα μιας Γενεάς. Athens: Govostis.

Varnalis, C. (1925), Ο Σολωμός χωρίς μεταφυσική. Athens: Stochastis.

—— (1957), Σολωμικά. Athens: Kedros.

Vayenas, N. (1979), Ο Ποιητής και ο Χορευτής· Μια Εξέταση της Ποιητικής και της Ποίησης του Σεφέρη, 4th edition. Athens: Kedros.

—— (1990), 'Ο Καρυωτάκης και τα Ορφανοτροφεία.' In M. Melissaratos (ed.) Συμπόσιο για τον Κ.Γ. Καρυωτάκη, Πρέβεζα.

—— (1994), Η ειρωνική γλώσσα - κριτικές μελέτες για τη νεοελληνική γραμματεία. Athens: Stigmi.

—— (ed.) (1997), Για τον Αναγνωστάκη - Κριτικά κείμενα. Nicosia: Aigaion.

—— (ed.) (1999), Από τον Λέανδρο στον Λουκή Λάρα - Μελέτες για την πεζογραφία της περιόδου 1830–1880. Iraklion: Panepistimiakes Ekdoseis Kritis.

Velestinlis, R. (1994a), Σχολείον των ντελικάτων εραστών. Ed. P. S. Pistas. Athens: Estia.

—— (1994b), Τα Επαναστατικά. Athens: Epistimoniki Etaireia Feron – Velestino-Rhiga.

Veloudis, G. (1982), 'Η Ελληνική Λογοτεχνία στην Αντίσταση.' *Diavazo* 58 (15 December): 29–39.

—— (1983), 'Σολωμός και Σίλλερ.' Αναφορές -΄Εξη Νεοελληνικές Μελέτες. Athens: Filippotis.

—— (1989), Διονύσιος Σολωμός· Ρομαντική Ποίηση και Ποιητική - οι Γερμανικές Πηγές. Athens: Gnosi.

—— (ed.) (1996), "Introduction." Ο Λέανδρος. Athens: Ouranis Foundation.

References

Vergopoulos, K. (1975), Το Αγροτικό Ζήτημα στην Ελλάδα· Η Κοινωνική Ενσωμάτωση της Γεωργίας. Athens: Exantas.

—— (1978), Εθνισμός και οικονομική ανάπτυξη· Η Ελλάδα στο Μεσοπόλεμο. Athens: Exantas.

Vitti, M. (1987), Ιστορία της νεοελληνικής λογοτεχνίας, [1974] revised edition. Athens: Odysseas.

—— (1991), Ιδεολογική λειτουργία της Ελληνικής ηθογραφίας, 3rd edition. Athens: Kedros.

—— (1998), Για τον Οδυσσέα Ελύτη - ομιλίες και άρθρα. Athens: Kastaniotis.

—— (2000), Οδυσσέας Ελύτης - Κριτική Μελέτη. Athens: Ermis.

Vizyenos, G. (1988), *My Mother's Sin and Other Stories by Georgios Vizyenos*. Trans. W. F. Wyatt Jr. Hanover, NH and London: University Press of New England.

Vlachogiannes, Y. (1944), 'Δύο Ποιητές Ανήσυχοι στους τάφους τους.' *Nea Estia* 36: 804–12.

Vlachos, A. S. (1985), Μια φορά κι ' έναν καιρό ένας διπλωμάτης – (50 κυβερνήσεις), 2nd edition. Athens: Estia.

Vogasaris, A. (1968), Ένας άνθρωπος, μια ζωή, ένας θάνατος - Κώστας Καρυωτάκης. Athens: n.p.

Vondung, K. (1983), 'German Nationalism and the Concept of "Bildung."' In J. C. Eade (ed.), *Romantic Nationalism in Europe*. Humanities Research Center Monograph No. 2. Canberra: Australian National University.

Vournas, T. (1955), Φαινόμενα διαλεκτικού εκλεκτισμού. Επιθεώρηση Τέχνης, τ. Β ΄, 8: 120–5.

—— (1956), Ο Πολίτης Ρήγας Βελεστινλής - Μια Βιογραφία γραμμένη σα Μυθιστόρημα. Αφιερωμένη στα Διακόσια Χρόνια από τη Γένεσή του. Athens: Pixida.

—— (1964), 'Η ποίηση της ήττας και η ήττα της κριτικής.' Επιθεώρηση Τέχνης, τ. 109, January, 6–12.

Voutouris, P. (1995), Ως εις καθρέπτην... προτάσεις και υποθέσεις για την ελληνική πεζογραφία του 19ου αιώνα. Athens: Nefeli.

Vranoussis, L. I. (1957a), Ρήγας Βελεστινλής 1758–1798. τ. Α ΄, Athens: Syllogos pros Diadosin Ofelimon Vivlion.

—— (1957b), Τα έργα του Ρήγα τ. Β΄. Athens: Syllogos pros Diadosin Ofelimon Vivlion.

—— (1974), Ρήγας - Βελεστινλής - Φεραίος. Άπαντα των νεοελληνικών κλασσικών. Athens: Etaireia Ellinikon Ekdoseon.

—— (1992), Εφημερίς. Athens: Academy of Athens, Research Centre for Medieval and Modern Hellenism.

Ware, T. (1963), *The Orthodox Church*. London: Penguin.

Warner, R. (1967), *On the Greek Style: Selected Essays in Poetry and Hellenism by George Seferis*. Trans. R. Warner and Th. Frangopoulos. London: Bodley Head.

Winckelmann, J. J. (1873), *The History of Ancient Art*, Vol. 1. Trans. G. Henry Lodge. Boston, MA: J. R. Osgood.

Wolf, F. A. (1869), *Darstellung der Altertumswissenschaft* [1807]. In *Kleine Schriften*. Ed. G. Bernhardy, Vol. 2, Halle.

—— (1985), *Prolegomena to Homer* [1795]. Trans. A. Grafton, G. W. Most, and J. E. G. Zetzel. Princeton, NJ: Princeton University Press.

Wood, R. (1827), *The Ruins of Palmyra and Baalbec*. London: William Pickering.

Woodhouse, C. M. (1976), *The Struggle for Greece (1941-1949)*. London: Hart-Davis, MacGibbon.

—— (1992), 'The Transition from Hellenism to Neohellenism.' In J. Burke and S. Gauntlett (eds.), *Neohellenism*.

—— (1995), *Rhigas Velestinlis: The Protomartyr of the Greek Revolution*. Limni, Evia: Denise Harvey.

Xenopoulos, G. (1901), *Panathinaia* 7: 68.

Yannakaki, E. (1994), 'History as Fiction in Rhea Galanaki's The Life of Ismail Ferik Pasha.' *Kampos: Cambridge Papers in Modern Greek* 2: 121–41.

Yannaras, C. (1991), *Elements of Faith: An Introduction to Orthodox Theology* [1983]. Edinburgh: T. T. Clark.

—— (1986), Ορθοδοξία και Δύση στη Νεότερη Ελλάδα. Athens: Domos.

Yannopoulos, P. (1904), Η Ελληνική Γραμμή, Το Ελληνικό Χρώμα. In ΄Απαντα. Athens: Eleftheri Skepsi.

Yashin, M. (1998–9), Περί κυπριακής λογοτεχνίας και απροσδιορίστων ταυτοτήτων. *SynchronaThemata*, 68-69-70: July 1998–March 1999: 312–21.

Yeoryis, Y. (1989), Ο Σεφέρης περί των κατά την χώραν Κύπρον σκαιών. Athens: Smili.

—— (2000), 'Οι διπλωματικές περιπέτειες του Γεωργίου Στ. Σεφέρη.' *Ta Nea*, 5 February.

Zambelios, S. (1852), ΄Ασματα δημοτικά της Ελλάδος εκδοθέντα μετά μελέτης ιστορικής περί Μεσαιωνικού Ελληνισμού. Corfu: Ermis.

Zamora, L. P. & W. B. Faris (eds.) (1995). *Magical Realism: Theory, History, Community*. Durham, NC & London: Duke University Press.

Ziras, A. (1983), 'Οι διαχρονικές ετυμηγορίες του Κ.Π. Καβάφη.' *Diavazo* 78 (15 October): 130–6.

—— (1987), 'Επιβιώσεις και παρουσία του Καρυωτάκη στην ελληνική μεταπολεμική ποίηση.' Πρακτικά έκτου Συμποσίου Ποίησης, Πανεπιστήμιο Πατρών. Athens: Gnosi.

—— (1989), 'Ποιητές και Ποιήματα μετά το 1980.' *Kathimerini*, 29 January: 18.

References

Žižek, S. (1997), 'Multiculturalism, Or, the Cultural Logic of Multinational Capitalism.' *New Left Review* 225 (September–October): 28–51.

—— (1999), '"You May!" Slavoj Žižek writes about the Post-Modern Superego,' *London Review of Books*, 18 March: 3–6.

Zizioulas, J. D. (1993), *Being as Communion* [1985]. Crestwood, NY: St. Vladimir's Seminary Press.

Zographou, L. (1973), Ο Ηλιοπότης Ελύτης, 2nd edition. Athens: Hermeias.

—— (1981), Κώστας Καρυωτάκης - Μαρία Πολυδούρη και η αρχή της αμφισβήτησης. Athens: Gnosi.

Zoras, G. (1957), 'Το Αποσπασματικόν των Σολωμικών Έργων.' *Nea Estia* τ. ΞΒ΄, τεύχ, 731, 139–48.

Zumthor, P. (1972), 'The Impossible Closure of the Oral Text.' Trans. J. McGarvy. *Yale French Studies* 67: 25–42.

—— (1984), *La Poèsie de la voix dans la civilisation médiévale*. Paris: Presses universitaires de France.

—— (1990), *Oral Poetry: An Introduction.* Trans. K. Murphy-Judy. *Theory & History of Literature*, Vol. 70. Minneapolis, MN: Minnesota University Press.

Index

Index

Index

Dragoumis, N., 151n3
Dragoumis, P., 159
Driault, É. and M. Lhéritier, 89n16
Drosinis, Y., 137
Droullia, L., 56n26
Du Bois, W. E. B., 49–50
Duroselle, B., 19n7
Durrell, L.
  and *Bitter Lemons*, 251–64
    Englishness and expatriates, 253–4
  and modern philhellenism, 239–40
  Prospero's Cell, 241
  see also colonialism

Eade, J. C., 162
Eagleton, T., 209
Eco, U., 277
Economides, D. B., 90n22
Economides, Y., 160
Eden, A., 260
Education Society, 124
Egger, E., 57n31
Egyptians, 43
Eisner, R., 35
Elgin Marbles, *see* Parthenon Marbles
Eliot, T. S., 135, 234n30
Elytis, O., 152n14, 159, 191–2,
    191n20–192n26
  'Aegean,' 168–73
  and the journal *Thiassos,* 174
  Axion Esti, 167, 208, 221–6, 267
  east/west polarity, 166–75
  Heroic & tragic Song for a Second
    Lieutenant in Albania, 199
  Idiotike Odos, 175
  Light-Tree, 175
  Orientations, 168, 173–4
  'Seven Nocturnal Heptastichs,' 235n36
Embiricos, A., 174
Ephtaliotes, A., 50, 124
Epidaurus, 244
essentialism, 3, 126–32, 152n7, 161
Estia, 124, 282n1
Euripides, 43
European Tour, 113
European Union, 1, 2, 7
  and integration, 280
  and Theotokas, 164–6, 191n17

Evangelides, S., 263n11
Exarchos, Y., 44, 54n5, 57n33

Faïs, M., 289
Fallmerayer, Jakob von, 4
Faris, W. B., 275
Farmakides, T., 69
Faubion, J. D., 5, 13, 21n22
Fauriel, C., 91n30
female consciousness
  and contemporary Greek poetry, 228–31
  and (Martinengou's) autobiography, 97–111,
    120n24
Fermor, P. L., 58n42
Finlay, G., 88n9
Finnegan, R., 71, 73
Fitzpatrick, T., 102
Flaubert, G., 269
Fleming, K. E., 49
Florens, J. A., 54n7
formalism, 4, 95–8; 131; 161–2, 287
  see also Mouzelis
Former Yugoslav Republic of Macedonia
    (FYROM), 2
  and minority in Greece, 3
  and national symbols, 3–5; 290
  see also Macedonian Problem
Foscolo, U., 82, 111
Foucault, M., 29; 56n20
Fouyas, M., 226, 235n37
Frangopoulos, Th. D., 76
Frascari, M., 38
French Revolution, 16
Freud, S., 172
Friar, K., 232n13

Galanaki, R. 267–85
Gallagher, C. & S. Greenblatt, 13
Garber, M., 266, 282n3
Gates, H. L., 12
Gatsos, N., 191n19, 200
Gautier, T., 36, 57n29
gaze, 16–17, 38–41, 47, 159–62, 189
  of philhellenism, 38–41, 237–41, 262,
  of a western readership, 277–81
Gazis A., 54n11, 68
gender, 98, 99–110, 171–2, 228–31, 241–50,
  280

Index

Index

modern Greek, 6
  as discipline (relation to Classics), 9–13
modernism, 132–3, 135, 141–7, 157–9, 195–7,
    226–31
  and European modernism, 166–7
  and Greek leftist modernism, 198–220,
    222–3
  see Greekness
modernity, 1–6, 16, 32–4, 47–53, 65–94, 96–9,
    123–6; 157–9; 195–9; 237–41; 265–8; 287–
    93
Mohammad Ali, 276, 283n19
Moisiodax, I., 27, 54n11
Montis, C., 264n14, 264n23
Montesquieu, C., 26
monumentalism 47–53, 63, 150–1
Morris, S. P., 10–11, 20n15
Moskov, K., 125, 151n1
Moullas, P., 36, 203
Mount Athos, 221
Moutzan Martinengou, E., 98–111, 119–21
Mouzelis, N., 18n3, 95–6, 97, 119n2
Musurus, M., 6
mythical method, 166

Nabokov, V., 244
Nadeau, M., 154n33
Nafplion, 111–18
national allegory, 280–1, 285n34
National Language Society, 124
national poet and poetry, 14–5, 72–3, 228
  and Elytis, 228
  and Solomos, 73–87
  and Seferis, 177, 188–9, 195–7
National Schism, 130–1
Nea Estia, 137, 150, 152n16
Nea Grammata, 174, 221
neohellenika, 6
neohellenism, 6–7, 9
  and western hellenism, 51–2, 195–7
neo-Orthodoxy, 224–6
Neruda, P., 198
Nerval, Gérard de, 36
newspapers, 68–9
Nicol, D. N., 19n9
Nietzsche, F., 209
Nikolareizis, A., 233n26
Nissiotis, V., 232n11

Noumas, 125–31
Noutsos, P., 220
novel, 13, 14, 17–18, 96
  and Byronic hero, 113
  and depiction of reality, 97
  and *ethographia*, 97
  and folktales, 97
  and lives of saints, 97
  and the Romantic novel, 111–18
    and *Letters of Ortis* & *Young Werther*, 111,
      121n30
  and western derivativeness, 97

Oberling, P., 255
Olivier, L., 246
Olympics
  and Atlanta, 2
  and Athens 1996 campaign, 4
  and Athens 2004, 249, 251, 287
Omonia Square, 8–9
O'Neill, K., 37
Ong, W., 71–2
orality
  and performatvity in poetry, 80–7
  in revolutionary Greece, 69–73
  Oresteia, 124
Orientalism
  and philhellenism, 50–3, 237–41
  and Nafplion, 114–15
Orsina, V., 198
Orthodox Church 14, 39, 70, 243
orthography 85, 87
Otto 66, 112, 115–18
Ottoman Turks 4, 27
  effects of rule in Greece 61, 64–5, 96, 237

Palamas, Costis, 76, 132, 134, 147
Palamas, Gregory, 225
Pallis, A., 124
Pamuk, O., 267, 269–85
  on master–slave relationships 270–1
Panayiotou, Y. A., 235n38
Panayotopoulos, I. M., 133, 137
Pantazopoulos, N. I., 57n39
Papadakis, Y., 194
Papaditsas, D., 232n7
Papadopoulos, Y. K., 264n28
Papadopoulos, T., 90n22, 264n28

Index

and fragmentariness, 74–7
and German Romanticism, 74–7
and Tomadakis's oral/aural theory, 84–6
and vernacular 73–4
'Free Besieged,' 73, 74, 78
'Hymn to Liberty,' 73, 74, 91n30
'Lambros,' 73
'Ode to Lord Byron,' 73
'Porphyras,' 73, 74
'The Blond Little Girl' [Xanthoula], 83
'The Cretan,' 73, 91n40
'The Poisoned Girl,' 74
Rime Improvissate, 84
Sophocles, 41
Soteriou, D., 189n1, 283n18
Sourbati, A., 274, 282n10, 284n22
Soutsos, P., 57n28, 74, 98, 111–18, 121n31,
151n3
Spanaki, M., 264n28
Spatalis, Y., 133
Spiropoulou, A. & D. Tsimpouki, 13
Stavridi-Patrikiou, R., 152n8, 152n10, 152n11
Stavrou, S., 190n3
Steriadis, V., 231
Stewart, J. F., 264n19
Storace, P., 240–1, 241–3, 261, 287
Dinner with Persephone, 247–51
Strani, L., 82
Stuart, J. & N. Revett, 30
supplement, 32, 34
surrealism
and defamiliarization, 204
and Elytis, 167, 174
and revolution, 154n33
and Theotokas, 164
in France, 145, 172
surveillance 17, 63–8, 95
Syrimis, G., 282n2

Talbott, S., 19n4
Tangopoulos, D., 127
Tarkovsky, A., 14
taxation, 61–3
Tennenhouse, L., 53n1
Tertsetis, G., 88n6, 93n47
Terzakis, A., 191n13, 191n16
Thalassis, Y., 282n10, 283n16, 283n20
Thassitis, P., 232n7, 234n26

Theodorakis, M., 173, 221
Theotokas, Y.
and Balkan identity 158–9, 288–9
and correspondence with Seferis, 133,
160
and Generation of the 1930s, 152n14
on Karyotakis, 132–3, 153n17
Forward with Social Problem, 162–5
Free Spirit, 125, 152n9, 158–66
Hellenism's Contemporary Problems,
159
Idea periodical, 160
Thibaudet, A., 161, 190n9
Thomson, G., 20n17
Thumb, A., 19n9
Thurow, R., 18n4
Todorova, M., 58n49
Tolias, G., 54n11, 55n15
Tomadakis, N. B., 76, 84–6
Tonnet, H., 112, 121n28
Toynbee, A., 20n9
transubstantiation 196, 221, 222, 225–6,
233n19
Trapp, E., 283n17
travel literature 12, 18, 23–4, 47
and maps and geography, 27, 30
and Romantic travelers, 35–8
and Soutsos's *Leandros,* 98
and Storace's *Dinner with Persephone,*
248–9
Trotsky, L., 133
Tsantsanoglou, E., 77–80, 85
Tsarouchis, Y., 173, 221
Tsatsos, C., 188
Tsirimokos, 152n8
Tsirkas, S., 234n27
Tsoucalas, C., 4, 62, 66, 88n4, 119n1, 124
Turkish Cypriots, *see* Cyprus
Typaldos, A., 74
Tziovas, D. P., 21n22, 73, 90n25, 119n6,
155n40, 157, 161, 190n2, 190n5, 204,
285n33

University of Athens, 10
Updike, J., 269

Vacalopoulos, A. E., 65
Valaorites, A., 74